FIELDS OF AUTHORITY

Special Purpose Governance in Ontario, 1815–2015

IPAC
The Institute of
Public Administration of Canada

IAPC
L'Institut d'administration
publique du Canada

The Institute of Public Administration of Canada Series in Public
Management and Governance

Editors:

Peter Aucoin, 2001–2
Donald Savoie, 2003–7
Luc Bernier, 2007–9
Patrice Dutil, 2010–

This series is sponsored by the Institute of Public Administration of
Canada as part of its commitment to encourage research on issues in
Canadian public administration, public sector management, and public policy. It also seeks to foster wider knowledge and understanding
among practitioners, academics, and the general public.

For a list of books published in the series, see page 301.

Fields of Authority

Special Purpose Governance in Ontario, 1815–2015

JACK LUCAS

IPAC
The Institute of
Public Administration of Canada

IAPC
L'Institut d'administration
publique du Canada

UNIVERSITY OF TORONTO PRESS
Toronto Buffalo London

© University of Toronto Press 2016
Toronto Buffalo London
www.utppublishing.com
Printed in the U.S.A.

ISBN 978-1-4875-0018-4

∞ Printed on acid-free, 100% post-consumer recycled paper with vegetable-based inks.

Library and Archives Canada Cataloguing in Publication

Lucas, Jack, 1987–, author
Fields of authority : special purpose governance in Ontario, 1815–2015 /
Jack Lucas.

(Institute of Public Administration of Canada series in public management
and governance)
Includes bibliographical references and index.
ISBN 978-1-4875-0018-4 (cloth)

1. Municipal government – Ontario – History.   2. Local government –
Ontario – History.   3. Public administration – Ontario – History.
4. Administrative agencies – Ontario – History.   5. Urban policy – Ontario –
History.   I. Title.   II. Series: Institute of Public Administration of Canada
series in public management and governance

JS1721.O6L82 2016   320.8'509713   C2016-901511-4

This book has been published with the help of a grant from the Federation
for the Humanities and Social Sciences, through the Awards to Scholarly
Publications Program, using funds provided by the Social Sciences
and Humanities Research Council of Canada.

University of Toronto Press acknowledges the financial assistance to its
publishing program of the Canada Council for the Arts and the Ontario Arts
Council, an agency of the Government of Ontario.

Canada Council   Conseil des Arts
for the Arts   du Canada

ONTARIO ARTS COUNCIL
CONSEIL DES ARTS DE L'ONTARIO
an Ontario government agency
un organisme du gouvernement de l'Ontario

Funded by the   Financé par le
Government   gouvernement
of Canada   du Canada

Canadä

To Daphne

Contents

Foreword

"Plus ça change, plus c'est la même chose." How many times have you read this phrase and rolled your eyes? How often have you used it to get out of a conversation that was going nowhere?

The getaway expression is not some legacy of the dark ages; it is actually a product of the industrial revolution. It was coined by a thoroughly fascinating French intellectual, Jean-Baptiste Alphonse Karr (1808–1890), who deserves to be better known. Karr was born and educated in Paris. He wrote novels but lent his able hand to journalism. He was so good he became the editor of *Le Figaro* by the time he turned thirty-one. It was in his monthly *Les Guêpes* that he first published the line that still seeds words in mouths every day. It was written in 1849, as Europe slowly recovered from the shocks of the revolts and rebellions of the previous year. He had many reasons to jot that line – things were changing, but eerily they seemed to resemble what was past.

Many people consider the saying to be satirical or even cynical. But I don't think it was. Instead, it really captured the dilemma of the emerging sciences of the nineteenth century, that of trying to explain evolution. It won't surprise you that Karr – he was born a year before Charles Darwin – was a keen student of nature and a passionate gardener and lover of flowers. He grew them and tinkered with their genetics, creating a particular dahlia that still bears his name (as does a certain growth of bamboo). He lived by his saying – he was growing a familiar flower, but somehow he had changed it.

Scientists struggle with this problem every day. Things do change but somehow seem to stay the same. The challenge is to uncover the degree to which they change – the degree and the mechanics by which the past yields to the present.

A hundred years after Karr, students of history were comfortable in looking at change over the *longue durée* – a deep spectrum of time. Anglo-American students of government institutions adopted the expression of "path dependency" to illustrate the slow evolution of habits along a particular track that was set during their creation. For them, the challenge was to identify that certain "path" and to document how it resisted change and stubbornly followed a particular destiny. It was useful; it seemed to explain a lot. It showed that things were always brewing on the inside – sometimes the outside too – to keep the institution on an even keel.

Enter Jack Lucas. Focusing his attention on special purpose bodies – agencies, boards, and commissions at the local level – his task is precisely to take up Karr's challenge and illustrate how things really change while appearing to stay the same. He demonstrates how these vital institutions do change over time, and under what circumstances, while maintaining their identity and – more importantly – their legitimacy. The terrain is vast and untilled. Looking at Canada's experience, in light of the particular microcosm of the City of Kitchener, Lucas has created his own dahlia.

In the early 1990s, the Institute of Public Administration of Canada created a study team of scholars from across the country to examine this phenomenon. *Agencies, Boards, and Commissions in Canadian Local Government*, a slim book published in 1994, brushed a rough outline of some of the considerations that had to be taken in order to study this sturdy and enduring feature of governance. The focus of the various contributors to the volume was to justify the ABCs, to speculate on how to measure their effectiveness and how they could evolve in the future.

The volume in your hands (or on your screen), produced more than twenty years later, compels the student of governance to consider the original intentions of the ABCs and to examine how they evolved over the past two hundred years. This is a fascinating study of institutional evolution, one that gives original intentions serious consideration but that shines in its dogged scrutiny of the institutions to show how they adapt in time. Why are they created? When are they abolished? How do they stay the same, while they change? How do they adapt according to political wishes, while staying true to original intentions? In this study, Lucas lifts the skin of politics and touches the vital nerves of governance. He shows how significant changes have been made to the agencies, boards, and commissions that play a vital role in setting the directions of local communities.

These are powerful organizations that have been sadly neglected. I had the privilege of sitting on one of them, the Toronto Preservation Board of the City of Toronto, for three years. This body, composed mostly of experts from the community and a handful of elected officials, was given the mandate to recommend critically important positions to City Council. Collectively, we made decisions on what buildings could be torn down, and which ones could be adapted for modern use. I was impressed by the level of detail our recommendations reached – in one memorable case, we spent a half-hour debating which windows would be appropriate for the repurposed Don Jail. Only very rarely were our decisions reversed by the City of Toronto Council. We made decisions that touched the lives of Torontonians and that routinely involved millions of dollars in private and public money. In all the time I sat on this board, I don't recall any media attention to the crucially important work of these mostly unelected volunteers.

With this book, Jack Lucas shakes us by our intellectual lapels and urges the field to pay close attention to these apparently slow-moving institutions. He compels us to rediscover the roots of these powerful organizations and invites the reader to think hard about how our governance does change over time, even though it often seems to stay the same. Karr would be proud.

Patrice Dutil
Editor, IPAC Series in Public Management and Governance
Ryerson University

Acknowledgments

Among the many trivial theories that I have imposed upon friends and colleagues over the years is this one: the universe of academics can be divided into those who read the acknowledgments section first, skimming the names like a list of celebrity sightings, and those who rarely bother to read them at all. The latter group is surely the more scholarly of the two, but I, being the nosy sort, have always belonged firmly to the former. I have therefore eagerly awaited the day that I could write my own list of thanks. In taking the time to finally write this list, it is clearer to me than ever that I have been fortunate – exceedingly fortunate – in having so long a list of people to acknowledge.

For financial assistance during the writing of this book, my thanks to the University of Toronto, the Government of Ontario, the Social Sciences and Humanities Research Council of Canada, the Institute on Municipal Finance and Governance, the Waterloo Regional Heritage Foundation, the University of Alberta, and the Izaak Walton Killam Memorial Fund. I am also grateful for the generous assistance of archivists across the province of Ontario; thanks especially to Charlotte Woodley, Hilda Sturm, Karen Ball-Pyatt, Susan Mavor, Jane Britton, and Les Bertram. My thanks as well to Daniel Quinlan, at University of Toronto Press, for his guidance and support throughout the publishing process.

I have been blessed, as far back as I can remember, with inspiring teachers. Ian Cotter provided an early spark, as did Ken Reid, who has since become a dear friend. Among the many great teachers I encountered during my years at the University of Waterloo, the University of Toronto, and the University of Alberta, my thanks especially to Robert Williams, Colin Farrelly, Eric Helleiner, Clifford Orwin, Ryan Balot, Ronnie Beiner, Donald Forbes, Rob Vipond, Peter Loewen, Chris

Cochrane, Rod Haddow, and Steve Patten. My dissertation committee – David Siegel, Grace Skogstad, Linda White, and Robert Young – provided careful reading and excellent advice, as did my supervisor, Graham White, whose thoughtful guidance, humour, and encouragement continue to be deeply appreciated. To all of these outstanding teachers, my sincere thanks.

I could not have completed this book without the support of my friends and family. Many thanks to Larissa Atkison, Tom Meredith, Gabriel Eidelman, Zack Taylor, Jill and Fraser Gibson (along with the rest of the enormous Waterloo clan), and especially to my hometown pals – Josh Durston, Geoff Martin, David Emery, Aaron Esseltine, and Rod Martin – for their deep and lasting friendship. I owe a special debt to Francis Bauman and Shane Martin, with whom I have spent countless hours discussing history, politics, and philosophy. Much of what interests me is built on the foundation of those conversations. I have also been blessed with a multigenerational and international chorus of support from my family: Bill and Dorothy Lucas, Jack and Jean Phillips, Craig and Cheryl Phillips, Frank and Janet Hill, and my brothers and sisters-in-law: Tim, Pip, Brenna, Paul, Payge, and Stephanie. My parents, John and Kim Lucas, encouraged me to pursue my interest, stimulated those interests with books and trips and conversations, and supported me through every twist in the road. I could not possibly thank them enough.

I have known Daphne Hill since I was for all practical purposes a child; indeed, according to family lore, we played together in the sandbox as toddlers. The years in which this book took shape are measured out by our experiences together: our wedding, our travels, our jobs, our homes, and most recently, the birth of our daughters, Hannah and Zoe. No corner of my life, and no word of this book, has been untouched by Daphne's friendship and her unyielding support. To Daphne, the foundation, my deepest thanks.

FIELDS OF AUTHORITY

Special Purpose Governance in Ontario, 1815–2015

Introduction

If Canadians remember anything about April 17, 1982, the day that the country's new constitution was signed, they remember the prime minister's smile. The photographs are iconic: Pierre Elliott Trudeau, seated at the end of a small wooden table, smiling like a schoolboy as the Queen signs the new constitution. For those who braved the rain that morning to watch the ceremony – more than thirty thousand spectators, along with hundreds of invited dignitaries – the event was public proof of everything that we know about political institutions: that they are lasting, durable, and *very* hard to change.[1]

In the case of the constitution, at least, all of this is certainly true – but it might only be part of the story. A scan of Canadian newspapers in the days leading up to the signing ceremony suggests that Canadians were busy making changes to many other institutions as well. Just a few days earlier, residents of the Northwest Territories voted in favour of a new territory to the east, a first step on the long road to Nunavut. In Ontario, opposition politicians called for reforms to the Ontario College of Physicians and Surgeons in the midst of physician walkouts across the province. In Quesno, British Columbia, local officials discussed a bylaw that would lead, they hoped, to amalgamation with the nearby community of Red Bluff. And in tiny Georgetown, Ontario, a public panel met to discuss how regional planning institutions might be simplified, reorganized, or even abolished.[2]

The list could go on. Pick any week in Canada's history, and you will find someone, somewhere, working to change the country's political institutions: movements are launched, meetings are called to order, resolutions are proposed, statutes are drafted and passed. Taken individually, political institutions often seem solid as granite, unmoved and unchanging for decades. But when we step back the magnification, so that we can see many institutions at once, we soon realize that Canadian institutions, like all others, float atop a roiling sea of change.

This is a book about that change. It explores how, when, and why political actors make changes to the institutions in which services are delivered, policies are developed, and issues are debated and discussed.[3] It is about the circumstances in which institutions are challenged and the ingredients that are involved in institutional change. And it is about what we can learn from just one *kind* of institution, a humble but fascinating structure that has existed in Canada for centuries: the local special purpose body.

What's So Special about Special Purpose Bodies?

In the autumn of 2007, a team of journalists at the *Hamilton Spectator* published an investigative report on an unlikely subject: special purpose bodies. According to the *Spectator's* investigation, the appointments process for Hamilton's local "ABCs" – agencies, boards, and commissions – raised questions about secrecy and patronage, and suspicions were only heightened when it took months of repeated requests until the city finally released a full list of names. But Hamilton's civic officials had another explanation for the delay: no one had ever asked for the information before. "The volume of trying to collect all this information is unique," explained Kevin Christenson, the city clerk. "The problem ... is just the resources we have in trying to keep up with it."[4]

Local journalists and civic officials are hardly alone in finding local special purpose bodies overwhelming and occasionally bewildering. Academic researchers have often been stymied as well. In his introduction to *Agencies, Boards, and Commissions in Canadian Local Government*, for example, David Siegel admits that he and his co-authors had a difficult time even defining the special purpose body, and the further task of compiling a complete list of local ABCs in Canada proved impossible. "It seems," wrote Siegel, "that an ABC is one of those entities which knowledgeable observers recognize when they see, but find difficult to define."[5]

In the face of such difficulties, one obvious option is to surrender. If local special purpose bodies cause so much confusion, and have so regularly been ignored, perhaps they are simply insignificant. After all, if these agencies, boards, and commissions meant anything to anyone, surely *someone* would have sorted them out by now. Should we move on, then, blissful in our ignorance of these institutions?

Answering "yes" would certainly have made for a shorter book. But the truth is that special purpose bodies *do* matter, every day, for millions of citizens across Canada. The electricity in our homes, the police in our streets, the books in our libraries – all of these are administered by local special purpose bodies. When we send our children to school, roll up our sleeves for a flu shot, or spend a weekend at a local conservation area, we are, often without realizing it, engaging with ABCs. If we care even a little about any of these services, or about the dozens of others that are overseen by special purpose bodies, we need to understand what they are, why they are created, and how they change.

The wide-ranging policies and services that are administered by local ABCs are hardly the only reason we might hope to understand them. They also spend a great deal of money. At times, municipal governments could complain with justification that more than two-thirds of their operating budgets were handed over to local ABCs.[6] Even today, cities like Toronto and Vancouver pass more than a third of their operating budgets to special purpose bodies every year.[7] If we want to understand "how Canada spends," especially at the provincial and local levels, we simply cannot avoid ABCs.

If dozens of policy areas and huge sums of money are not enough, consider a third reason that special purpose bodies might capture our interest: democratic accountability. Public opinion experts often remind us that few Canadians can recall the names of their federal or provincial representatives, and fewer still can remember their local councillors or school board trustees. But what about the members of their board of health, their library board, or their conservation authority? Even the most addicted of political junkies would be flummoxed. In some cases, special purpose bodies are so distant from ordinary accountability structures that they effectively operate as their own level of government, enormously powerful but accountable to no one.[8] Even in less extreme cases, special purpose bodies are often mysterious and opaque, their practices obscure, their personnel invisible, and their functions unclear. If we are interested in democratically accountable government in Canada, local special purpose bodies ought to provoke our curiosity – and also, perhaps, our unease.

However we look at it, special purpose bodies matter. So it is no surprise that Canadian scholars have begun to emphasize the need for research in this area. In one recent assessment of urban political science in Canada, Gabriel Eidelman and Zack Taylor argue that the "politics of special purpose bodies, including school boards, are no less interesting, fierce, or consequential to people's lives" than ordinary municipal politics.[9] Robert Young, another scholar of Canadian local government, has added that "the many agencies, boards, and commissions that are associated with individual municipalities or that operate on a regional basis are largely unmapped."[10]

I believe that the time has come to sharpen our pencils and start mapping. In this book, we begin at the beginning, focusing on the fundamental questions of institutional creation, challenge, and change. Our aim is to answer two questions: how have the basic structures of local special purpose bodies in Canada changed over time? And why have these changes occurred?

The Theoretical Promise of Special Purpose Bodies

The impact of local special purpose bodies on the lives of ordinary Canadians makes their historical development well worth exploring. But special purpose bodies also offer us a valuable *theoretical* opportunity, an opportunity to draw lessons from these institutions that can deepen our understanding of the dynamics of public policy and institutional change. I believe that a study of the development of special purpose governance in Canada offers us a chance to bring together three fascinating theoretical conversations, all of which are active in political science today.

The first of these conversations is about *institutional change*. In the past three decades, as the study of political institutions has returned to the forefront of the research agenda in political science, the question of institutional change has become a source of considerable debate. If institutions provide the deep structural context in which politics happens, many have asked, then how is it that those institutions themselves change?[11] Some have answered this question by arguing that institutions evolve slowly, through processes of "drift," "layering," and "conversion."[12] Others have pointed to the plurality of institutions in the political process, arguing that the "collisions" between those institutions, and the "friction" that their coexistence creates, is what explains institutional change over time.[13] Still others point to external shocks or moments of disequilibrium as crucial sources of change.[14] What is most needed in this debate, I believe, are empirical tests of these competing accounts, built on comparable, long-term inventories of institutional change. This is a conversation to which a study of special purpose bodies – political institutions that have changed hundreds of times through their long and various histories – can clearly contribute.

A second conversation is about *political authority*. Most of us take for granted that policy tasks are assigned to particular political institutions; it makes sense, for example, that hospital policy "belongs" to an institution like the Ministry of Health. But a survey of the history of virtually any policy task reveals that these apparently obvious arrangements were not always obvious to political actors in the past. Hospitals, for example, were once institutions of local charity, assigned mostly to the non-governmental sector and linked tightly to other local charities. Like any policy task, political authority over hospitals has shifted over time as our assumptions about the nature and purpose of hospitals have evolved. The question, then, is *how* policy tasks are bundled together and assigned to political institutions – and how those "bundles" change.[15] The history of special purpose bodies is, at one level, a story of how political decision-makers in diverse contexts have attempted to answer this question. It is an excellent, untapped resource for clarifying our understanding of the long-term development of political authority.[16]

The third conversation concerns *governance*. Few subjects in recent years have grown more explosively, and received more enthusiastic attention, than the study of governance. From researchers who study a single neighbourhood to those who examine policymaking across the globe, attention to governance – the changing patterns of rule in and through which public policies are produced – has been a central theme of contemporary political science.[17] And since 2003, when Liesbet Hooghe and Gary Marks published their now-classic distinction between "Type 1" and "Type 2" multilevel governance, special purpose institutions have been at the centre of these conversations.[18] These institutions are vital to our understanding of institutional fragmentation, efficient service delivery, and the costs and benefits of "functional, overlapping, competing jurisdictions."[19] Yet we know almost nothing about when these institutions are created, how they are justified by living, breathing political actors, and the circumstances in which they are challenged and changed. This, too, is a conversation to which our study of local special purpose bodies can contribute.

Special purpose bodies in Canada have histories that stretch back for hundreds of years; some of them are even older than municipal government itself. They have also existed across dozens of policy domains, from policing to planning to public utilities. This enormous variety allows us to explore how institutions with similar structures, scales, and personnel operate in different policy arenas. We can compare the same ABCs in difference places, or we can compare different ABCs within a single municipality. We can compare a nineteenth-century ABC to one with a similar structure today. The abundance and variety of local special purpose bodies gives us the chance to explore similar kinds of institutional change, and changes to similar kinds of institutions, across diverse geographic scales, policy domains, and historical contexts.

It is these features of special purpose institutions in Canada that will allow us to contribute to the conversations that I have mentioned above. For students of institutional change, this book will present empirical support for a patterned and punctuated view of long-term institutional change. For those who are interested in political authority, we will reveal the processes of "spillover" by which institutions come into conflict with one another, and we will explore how policy tasks can shift from one institution to another as a result of the "authority contests" that these moments of spillover produce.[20] For students of governance, we will demonstrate the enormous historical variation of institutional arrangements even within "type-2" institutions, the reasons for the creation and modification of these institutions, and the basic kinds of changes that these institutions can experience. Above all, however, this book will attempt to integrate these conversations into a coherent whole, demonstrating, in the process, how and why the study of local governance is an excellent place to explore why political institutions are created, how their authority changes over time, and when those institutions are susceptible to challenge and change.

Preview of Coming Attractions

This book is divided into three parts. In the next chapter, I will introduce a synthetic theoretical approach to institutional change, which I call the "policy fields approach," and I will provide a more detailed overview of the kinds of institutions and institutional change that will be our focus for the remainder of the book. We will then turn to empirical analysis. In Part One (chapters 2–4), I offer a political history of special purpose bodies in the city of Kitchener, Ontario. The city of Kitchener was an early aficionado of local special purpose bodies, adopting and even inventing them before many other Canadian municipalities, and our goal in this part will be to examine a diverse range of ABCs through the course of Kitchener's lively and interesting history. This part will help us understand *local* debates and decisions about ABCs.

On its own, however, Kitchener can tell us only part of the story. In Part Two, we move from the local to the provincial scale, studying changes to school boards, boards of health, and hydro-electric commissions across the province of Ontario. While the provincial government will certainly be an actor in our story in Part One, this second part will focus directly on changes to special purpose bodies as an aspect of *provincial* policymaking. Our focus in this second part is restricted to just three special purpose bodies, but the restricted institutional focus comes with the benefit of a wider geographic lens, allowing us to survey changes to these institutions in municipalities across Ontario.

I have relied on four main criteria to choose these three institutions in Part Two: substantive importance, policy scope, duration, and access. The first step was to draw up a list of institutions whose importance for local and provincial politics is widely recognized.[21] I then excluded any options that would produce unnecessary overlap in policy scope – since we have space for just three institutions, it made little sense to study, say, water *and* hydro commissions (since both are in the field of public utilities) or hospital commissions *and* boards of health (since both are in the broad area of health policy).[22] The third step, given our focus on long-term institutional change, was to select institutions with deep histories, whose stories go back to the early twentieth century at the very latest.[23] Finally, after an exploratory plunge into the archives, I selected the institutions for which consistent, reliable, and comparable data were likely to be available.[24] These criteria led me to school boards, boards of health, and hydro commissions in Ontario – institutions of considerable local importance, and embedded within three deeply significant provincial-municipal policy domains.

Explaining Institutional Change

When thirty thousand men and women gathered in Ottawa on the morning of April 17, 1982 to watch the Queen sign Canada's new constitution, they knew that they were witnessing an event of the greatest importance. Most of the changes that we will explore in the coming chapters were greeted with much less fanfare – although, as we will soon discover, even changes to local ABCs can produce enormous public attention and debate. Our basic claim, however, is that all institutional change, from large-scale constitutional transformation to minor structural tinkering, is part of the same fundamental story, a story that must be explained using an approach that combines what we know about institutions with what we know about political authority and governance. Formulating this approach is the task of the next chapter.

Chapter 1

Local Institutional Change
and the Policy Fields Approach

Every successful trawling expedition begins with a good net. Before we begin our empirical analysis, which will require that we search through two centuries of political history, collecting hundreds of instances of institutional change along the way, we need to outline the concepts with which we will sort what is important for our purposes from what is not. In this chapter, we begin with definitions of institutions and institutional change, and then turn to a discussion of central theoretical concepts. These will include, most importantly, the *policy field*, a synthetic concept that is meant to supplement existing approaches to long-term institutional and policy change. The patterns of change that we will discover in the coming chapters can be explained, I will argue, only when viewed in the context of these policy fields.

1.1 Institutions and Institutional Change

Within the great tradition of institutional theory – a tradition that ranges across fields as diverse as sociology, political science, economics, and organization studies – the distinctive contribution of the political science discipline has been a continued focus on the formal institutions of the state.[1] While political scientists have defined institutions in widely varying ways, most institutional research within political science has at least *included* public laws and organizations – constitutions, legislatures, statutes, regulatory agencies, and so on – within its field of study. Even among the "new institutionalists" in political science, the cultural-cognitive institutionalism characteristic of much sociological theory has tended to be explored under the separate rubric of concepts like culture, values, discourse, and ideas.[2]

Our investigation embraces this traditional focus on formal institutions. This is not because institutional "nuts and bolts" are all that we need in order to understand political change – far from it. It instead grows directly out of our theoretical interest in political authority and governance, the processes by which formal institutions gain or lose control over particular public policies. We will have much to say in the coming chapters about ideas, arguments, and beliefs. But we will continue to treat them as separate from, rather than fundamentally related to, the formal institutions that provide our research focus throughout.

For our purposes then, an institution is simply a governmental organization established by public law.[3] A special purpose body is one such institution: a local or regional agency, with a single or limited range of functions, which operates outside the normal municipal-council structure.[4] What is most important about this definition is that it draws a boundary line between special purpose bodies and general purpose governments (such as municipal councils), semi-public agencies (such as local charities), and provincial special purpose bodies. All of the institutions that we will study fit comfortably into this definition.

Our definition of institutional change follows from our definition of the institution itself: it is a formal or informal modification of a governmental organization. More specifically, we aim to understand changes to the *existence*, the *geographic scale*, and the *governing authority* of local ABCs – the means by which, and the scale at which, local policy tasks are administered. When we tease out the elements of this definition, the result is a seven-part typology of change:

Changes to *existence*:
1 Creation: creating a local ABC to perform a policy task that was not previously public. Example: purchasing a private library and entrusting it to a new library board.
2 Elimination: removing a local ABC and the task that it performs from the public domain. Example: dissolving an arena board after the arena is sold to a private club.

Changes to *geographic scale*:
3 Consolidation: merging several ABCs of one type into a larger body of the same type. Example: amalgamating small single-district school boards into larger county boards.
4 Partition: dividing an ABC into smaller bodies of the same type. Example: dissolving township-level school boards and creating smaller single-district boards.

Changes to *governing authority*:

5 Specialization: transfer of authority to a local ABC, partial or complete, depending on distance from council control. Example: creating a council-appointed ABC (partial specialization) or an elected ABC (complete specialization).

6 Generalization: transfer of authority from an ABC to a local or regional council, partial or complete. Example: adding council-appointed members to an ABC (partial generalization), or abolishing an ABC (complete generalization).

7 Provincialization: transfer of authority from an ABC to the provincial government. Example: adding provincial appointees to a board (partial) or transferring responsibility for the task to the provincial government (complete provincialization).

These seven types of change serve as our operational definition of institutional change. We will show in the coming chapters that these changes are both conceptually distinct and exhaustive – all of the changes that we will study can be coded as one or another of these changes.[5] Beneath each of the changes, of course, are important questions about political authority, about the kinds of institutions and actors who should be authorized to make decisions on particular policy tasks. Creation and elimination represent the movement of a policy task from one zone of the political process (the private) to another (the public). Consolidation and partition represent movement up and down geographic scales. Specialization, generalization, and provincialization represent shifts of authority towards or away from general-purpose institutions. By tracking these seven kinds of change, we will be forced to grapple with the deeper question of how, when, and why policy authority shifts from one institution to another.

1.2 Punctuated Equilibrium and the Policy Venue

In the coming chapters, we will discover a common pattern among long-term changes to local special purpose bodies: long periods of stability, in which just one or two kinds of change occur again and again, followed by abrupt shifts to other kinds of change. While change itself is regular and ongoing, the *kind* of change that occurs in a particular policy domain is often stable and consistent for very long stretches of time.

This recurrent empirical finding points us in the direction of a well-known approach to policy change: Frank Baumgartner and Bryan Jones's "punctuated equilibrium."[6] What is crucial about policy change, according to Baumgartner and Jones, is that it is *both* incremental and abrupt, with periods of slow and steady change punctuated by moments of deeper and more significant transformation. To account for the dual nature of long-term policy change, they argue, we need a theory that can explain both.

For Baumgartner and Jones, the key to such a theory is the interaction between *policy images* and *policy venues*. A policy image is the way that a policy is understood and discussed – above all, whether the policy is generally framed in a positive or a negative light.[7] A policy venue is the institutional location in which discussion of the policy takes place. When policy discussion is contained within a particular venue, and the image of that policy is widely shared, incremental change is the result. But when policy images change – and especially when those changes are reinforced by shifts to new policy venues – abrupt and transformational change becomes possible. It is this complex interaction between policy images and policy venues, Baumgartner and Jones argue, that produces patterns of punctuated change.[8]

The patterns that Baumgartner and Jones have found in a range of policy domains, from nuclear energy to public budgets, closely resemble the patterns that we will uncover in the chapters to come. But there is an additional wrinkle in our story: in this study we are focusing not on ordinary policy change but on changes to policy venues themselves. While such changes are clearly, at one level, merely a particular *type* of policy change, they also represent changes to institutional structure.[9] This puts some strain on the vocabulary of the punctuated equilibrium approach, which emphasizes decision-making *within* institutions.[10] To account for policy changes of this sort, I believe that we need to add at least one concept to the punctuated equilibrium approach – and then shift the underlying metaphor of that approach to accommodate the new processes of change that this concept reveals.

1.3 From Venue to Field

For advocates of the punctuated equilibrium approach, the interaction between policy images and policy venues is the key to explaining patterns of change. Policy images suggest particular ideas of a policy task, making some solutions seem more attractive and sensible than others. Policy venues, for their part, mobilize some actors rather than others, thereby reinforcing particular policy images. But when policy images change, and especially when those images shift to a supportive venue from which they can be articulated, rapid change can result. All of this has been demonstrated by Baumgartner, Jones, and their collaborators in a number of studies.[11] Thus far, however, there is an element to the story that these authors have missed.

The missing element, recognized but under-theorized in the punctuated equilibrium approach, is that venues are themselves linked into broader venue-like domains. Political actors operate on the assumption not only that some venues are more favourable to their views than others, but also that there are broad *families* of venues that are more likely to support their preferred policy images than others. There is something beyond the venue itself, in other words, some broader zone of the political process, in which both venues and images operate.

I call this broader "zone" a *policy field*: a network of institutions with authority over a set of public policy tasks, and the policy images within that network.[12] A policy image, in this broader understanding, captures not only the way a policy is understood and discussed, but also the *linkages* among policy tasks, the ways that one task is believed to be like or unlike another. Policy images not only orient actors towards a particular policy issue, but also bring together distinct families of policy tasks, setting them off from other families to which they might plausibly belong. These images are institutionalized within networks of venues, which exist across geography (e.g., similar institutions in adjacent cities) and across scale (e.g., related institutions at the local, regional, and state levels). This network of institutions, with authority over a socially constructed bundle of policy tasks, is, once again, a *policy field*.

Policy fields can be divided into three general types – *unorganized*, *stable*, and *contentious* – depending on the extent to which tasks have been actively bundled together by a policy image and the extent to which those bundles are contested.[13] In some cases, a set of policy tasks are bundled together and assigned to a network of institutions by a clear and uncontested policy image. This is a *stable* policy field.[14] In these fields, the assignment of policy tasks to a particular set of institutions – and the authority of those institutions to administer their assigned tasks – is clearly articulated within the field and largely uncontested outside it.

In other cases, policy tasks are much more loosely related to other tasks in a particular field. Institutions in these *unorganized* fields may have been assigned a policy task largely by default, and actors in the field may lack strong views about whether they should retain the task. Attention to the policy task is low or intermittent, and authority is uncontested only because none have bothered to claim the policy task for themselves. One clue that these unorganized fields exist is that no institutions have been created specifically to address the policy task itself; instead, it is assigned to an institution whose primary responsibility is focused on something else. In the case of public health, for example, we will see in chapter 6 that disease control was assigned first to the provincial executive, and then to municipal governments, but that these assignments were intermittent and pragmatic. The policy tasks that would form the core of a stable public health field were, before the 1870s, unorganized and largely ignored.

At the other end of the spectrum are fields in which authority over policy tasks is claimed by competing institutional networks. In these cases, the "bundle" of policy tasks that is suggested by one policy image is hotly contested by another. Some may see a task as properly belonging to local government, and others to a province or a state. Some may see a task as a matter of, say, defence and national security, others as a matter of environmental regulation. These *contentious* fields, in which political actors actively contest the assignment of policy tasks to particular institutions, are well known in studies of public policy.[15] We will find several examples of such fields in the chapters to come.

1.4 From Earthquakes to Ecosystems: Change in the Political Ecology

The concept of the policy field is meant to supplement and extend the punctuated equilibrium approach, situating the interaction between images and venues within a larger meso-level context. Nevertheless, a focus on the policy field leads us towards a vocabulary that is rather different from the one that has become standard among researchers who rely on punctuated equilibrium theory, a vocabulary that is more carefully attuned to the relational and interactive character of the political process.

In many punctuated equilibrium studies – especially as those studies have come to focus on the complex dynamics of budget policy – the central metaphor is the *earthquake*.[16] Like earthquake magnitudes, changes to public budgets consist of a large number of very small "quakes" and a small number of extremely large ones. And like earthquakes, these patterns of change seem to originate in "stick-slip" dynamics, the "friction" that is created, in the case of budget policy, by the institutions through which all changes are forced to pass.[17] This central metaphor, together with others that also originate in the study of complex systems dynamics – sand piles, avalanches, and so on – has given punctuated equilibrium researchers a useful vocabulary with which to describe their findings.[18] Even so, I believe that a rather different conceptual metaphor is necessary, at least for our purposes, which can capture similar arguments but with a somewhat different emphasis. That alternative metaphor is *ecology*.[19]

Picturing the political process as an ecology of policy fields does not require that we abandon the central concerns of the punctuated equilibrium approach. Ecology is deeply attuned to issues of complexity, to diverse scales of analysis, and to the different temporal frames in which particular changes can and must be viewed.[20] What an ecological approach adds, however, is an emphasis on interaction in a particular environment. An ecological vision of institutional change orients us to the often *interactive* character of such change, and thus to the significance of a process that we will encounter again and again in the chapters to come: *spillover*.

We can define *spillover* as the process by which a policy argument in one field has explicit implications for another field. Spillover occurs frequently in politics, at all possible levels, because policy tasks are inextricably linked to one another in innumerable and complex ways. Consider a simple example:

Non-spillover argument: Our hospital does a great job of *treating* illness, but we don't do enough to *prevent* illness in the first place. We need to hire a public health specialist so that we are better equipped to prevent illness before it occurs.

Spillover argument: Our hospital does a great job of *treating* illness, but we don't do enough to *prevent* illness in the first place. We need to integrate the public health department with the hospital, so that we are better equipped to prevent illness before it occurs.

For a staff member in the local department of public health, the first of these stories would seem little more than an internal debate at the hospital down the street. If the second argument were to gain traction, however, that same staff member would be likely to prick up her ears. Both arguments identify the same basic problem and cause, but only the second suggests a solution that spills over into the terrain of the local public health department.

Spillover processes are a crucial engine of interaction among policy fields. At every level of the political process, from the interaction among colleagues in a single agency to the interaction among enormous fields such as education and health care, spillovers lead again and again to "invasions" of a policy field from the outside. The authority challenges that are produced by these moments of spillover create openings for significant changes to policy fields, and thus to the kinds of institutional and policy change that will occur within them.[21]

These spillover processes occur most frequently in contexts of *geographic adjacency*: contexts in which a number of fields perform distinct policy tasks (such as education, public health, and public utilities) within a shared geographic territory. Because policy tasks in shared geographic jurisdictions are linked in countless ways, it is impossible to fully separate policy fields from one another; arguments in one field therefore inevitably have implications for other fields as well. The spillover that results from these overlaps produces constant interaction among policy fields, ranging from minor interpersonal conflict and "turf battles" all the way to full-scale invasion and institutional restructuring.

Geographic adjacency, then, is one way that policy fields can relate to one another within a wider political ecology. But fields can also be *functionally adjacent* to one another, sharing similar policy responsibilities in different geographic jurisdictions; the public education field in Ontario, for example, might be functionally adjacent to the education fields in Alberta, Quebec, and Nova Scotia.[22] When actors perceive an outside field as functionally adjacent to their own, they often look to those other fields as sources of inspiration, exemplars for action, or cautionary tales. This form of adjacency therefore tends to produce *diffusion* processes, which spread particular policy innovations from one field to another.[23] In some fields – especially when a policy innovation is highly technical – these changes can result in a simple copy-and-paste from one jurisdiction to another. In many cases, however, the real power of diffusion lies in its rhetorical force. Examples of successful innovations in other jurisdictions, when those jurisdictions are seen as examples worth emulating, reduce the perceived risk of a particular change. Innovations of this sort are "theorized" in stories and arguments that translate them into new contexts, emphasize their advantages, and explain how the receiving field is basically similar to the field in which the innovation originated.[24]

Processes of interaction *among* policy fields, then, can be divided into two basic forms: spillover and diffusion. Each tends to occur in the context of a particular form of adjacency, with spillover more common in geographically adjacent fields and diffusion more common in function-ally adjacent fields.[25] Both of these processes, as we will soon discover, are crucial for understanding changes to local special purpose bodies.

These interactive processes *across* policy fields, however, are just one level at which institutional change occurs. Changes *within* fields are also common. Such changes, as Baumgartner and Jones have demonstrated, are likely to be uncontentious, emerging incrementally out of the domi-nant policy image in the field. From the perspective of a policy fields approach, the events that trigger such changes are likely to vary, de-pending upon the kind of field in which they occur. In unorganized fields, in which attention to a policy task is intermittent, changes are likely to be triggered by the arrival of particular problems from the out-side: in the case of an unorganized public health field, for example, this might be the arrival of a contagious disease. In stable and contentious fields, on the other hand, in which attention to a policy task is deep and ongoing, it is *politics*, not problems, that is most likely to trigger a change. Actors in stable and contentious fields are well aware of existing prob-lems, know the available solutions, and push hard to convince political decision-makers that those solutions are attractive. When they are able to do so – often as a result of some shift in perceived political risks and opportunities among decision-makers themselves – only then do we see a change occur. While the tone of the debate in stable and contentious fields will, of course, look very different, the *timing* of individual chang-es within longer patterns of change is likely to be triggered by politics rather than problems in both stable and contentious policy fields.[26]

Thus far, we have identified processes of change that occur either *within* or *between* policy fields. But it is also possible to imagine a third process of change, which takes place not at either of these levels but rather above (or perhaps beneath) every policy field in a given jurisdic-tion (for a summary of each of these processes, see table 1.1). This final category – which we might call *supra-field* processes of change – can be divided into two general types. The first, which straddles the bound-ary between inter-field and supra-field change, is a change to the foun-dational institutional structures of a political jurisdiction – changes to the institutions that determine how and by whom decisions are made across a whole range of policy fields. These include changes to consti-tutions, electoral systems, Cabinet-level decision-making structures, legislative committees, and so on. While it is possible to understand and examine each of these areas as a policy field in itself – determining the structure of a constitution or an electoral system is, after all, itself a policy task – the implications of changes to these institutions are so

Table 1.1. Processes of Change within, across, and above Policy Fields

Intra-field processes	Typically incremental, with timing of change determined by arrival of particular problems (problem-driven change) or shifts in perceived political risk or opportunity (politics-driven change).
Inter-field processes	Change in a field promoted by change in a geographically or functionally adjacent field. Such change can be produced by diffusion and/or spillover.
Supra-field processes	Environmental change leading to shift in actors and/or resources present in a field. Can involve changes to "enveloping" fields and/or changes to long-term processes such as economic, demographic, or ideological change.

far-reaching that they are usually best understood as supplying the essential institutional background features of a whole political ecosystem. Changes to these fields reconfigure membership and decision-making authority throughout a jurisdiction, bringing new actors and images into many policy fields at the same time.

A second category of supra-field processes captures changes that cannot be described as occurring within any particular field. These include demographic and economic shifts, such as urbanization, immigration, economic growth and decline, and so on. We might also include broad ideological trends and political-cultural shifts as similar examples of "ecosystem-level" change. While it is possible to understand political culture as nothing more than the aggregation of policy images that exist within policy fields,[27] it is usually most useful to characterize broad cultural shifts – from, say, broadly "materialist" to "post-materialist" values – as occurring outside any particular field, and having implications for policy arguments within all fields.[28]

The effects of ecosystem-level changes on patterns of institutional change, at least in the local arena that we will be studying, are usually indirect. These changes primarily affect the *resources* of actors within policy fields, which make some actors more or less able to articulate their arguments or navigate challenges to their authority; their impact is therefore best explained in terms of their lower-level effects within and across policy fields. By linking such changes to authority contests within a political ecology, we can more clearly explain how processes of very different temporal lengths, from century-long demographic changes to momentary interpersonal tensions, combine to produce particular changes at particular times.[29]

Table 1.2. Summary of Key Terms

Contentious field	A policy field in which proper bundling of policy tasks is contested by competing policy images
Functionally adjacent field	Fields performing similar policy tasks in different geographic areas, such as education fields in different provinces or regions
Geographically adjacent field	Fields performing distinct policy tasks within a shared geographic area, such as health and education fields within a single province or region
Institution	A government organization established by public law
Institutional change	Modification of the existence, the geographic scale, or the governing personnel of a special purpose body
Policy field	A network of institutions with authority over a socially constructed bundle of policy tasks
Policy image	Ideas about how a policy should be understood, including the institutions to which the policy properly belongs
Special purpose body	A local or regional agency, with a single or limited range of functions, which operates outside of the normal municipal council-committee structure
Stable field	A field in which policy tasks are bundled together and assigned to a network of institutions by a clear, uncontested policy image
Unorganized field	A field in which policy tasks are loosely coupled to existing institutions, often on a pragmatic, ad hoc basis

1.5 Conclusion

The aim of this chapter has been to outline the central conceptual machinery of a policy fields approach to institutional change. I have summarized each of the major concepts in this approach in table 1.2. Viewed in the abstract, outside the context of an empirical investigation, our approach may seem little more than a tangled thicket of concepts. If the proof of the pudding is in the eating, then the proof of the approach is in the explaining. We have now elaborated our concepts, outlined their theoretical foundations, and surveyed the major processes of change that we will try to uncover in our empirical analysis. It is now time, finally, to make the switch from future to present tense: to stop describing what we will do, and to get started on doing it. In the next chapter, the real story begins.

PART ONE

LOCAL ABCs IN KITCHENER, ONTARIO

We begin in Kitchener, Ontario, a city whose early enthusiasm for local special purpose bodies, and whose long and complex experience with special purpose bodies of a great many types, makes it an important and interesting case. Since few readers will be familiar with Kitchener's history, I begin with a brief tour through the city's geography, demographics and culture, local economy, and politics.[1]

Geography and Location

Kitchener, Ontario, is an urban municipality of 137 square kilometres, bordered in a rough diamond shape by the city of Waterloo to the northwest, the Grand River to the northeast, the rural Township of Wilmot to the southwest, and the municipalities of Cambridge (a city) and North Dumfries (a rural and suburban area) to the southeast.

The area that is now Kitchener was originally set aside, in 1784, for Six Nations peoples, as part of a 600,000 acre tract of land provided to those who had fought alongside Britain in the Revolutionary War – and who had lost their traditional homeland to the new United States. Portions of this land were sold, in 1798, to Upper Canadian Loyalists, who themselves sold some of the plot to immigrant Mennonites from Pennsylvania.[2] Originally very hilly – indeed, Sandhills was one of the city's early names – the core of what is now Kitchener was aggressively flattened in the late nineteenth century. While the city is now bordered on one side by the Grand River, the river is quite distant from the city core, serving not as the centre of its early industry, as in many other towns and cities, but instead as an early place of recreation. Nevertheless, as we shall see, the city's proximity to the river, and its position in the heart of the enormous Grand River watershed, would lead Kitchener to play an important role in the development of Canada's first public watershed conservation program.

Demographics and Culture

The first European settlers in what is now Kitchener were Swiss Mennonites, who had migrated from Switzerland to Pennsylvania in the eighteenth century and whose "Pennsylvania-German" culture remains prominent in the rural areas surrounding Kitchener. Between 1825 and 1835, a second group of German-speaking immigrants arrived in the area, tradesmen and artisans from across Germany who were attracted to the area by rumours of its German-speaking residents but whose goals differed markedly from the more agriculturally oriented Mennonites. This combination of immigrants provided the roots, the early "founding ethos," which grew in the nineteenth and twentieth century into a local identity as the urban heart of German-Canadian culture and industry in Canada. In what was known as "Berlin" until early in the twentieth century, Kitchener's social life was for much of its history distinctly German, featuring German choral societies, German gymnastics clubs, and German-language services in the city's churches.

After the Second World War, Kitchener's diversity increased, as Germany's post-war economic boom limited German emigration while many others of Portuguese, Greek, and Polish background moved into the growing city. Today, Kitchener's German heritage is barely noticeable in the demographic statistics – 2 per cent of residents speak German as their mother tongue, compared to 1 per cent in the province as a whole. However, even as the city's demographics become less and less distinguishable from other Ontario cities, Kitchener's German heritage remains etched into the local culture, visible in its street signs, its historic landmarks, and, above all, in its annual Oktoberfest celebration, which attracts nearly one million visitors to the city each year.

Local Economy

Kitchener's early economic growth was made possible by two nineteenth-century developments: the invention of steam power and the arrival of the Grand Trunk Railway in 1856. The former, in a town without easy river access, enabled early manufacturing; the latter allowed Berliners to ship their manufactured goods, as well as their agricultural products, to more distant markets. By the 1870s, the village had become a town, boasting twenty-seven small industrial firms manufacturing products such as buttons, furniture, and leather goods. These industries continued to grow, while a few important new entrants, notably rubber manufacturing and meatpacking, were added to the industrial mix in the early twentieth century. The rubber industry marked the arrival of a new kind of manufacturing in Kitchener; workers at the rubber factories were less skilled and could not aspire to rise through the ranks and into management as had been the case earlier, particularly in the city's furniture industry. Despite these changes, the city's industry remained peaceful and unorganized for much longer than in other Canadian cities. It was not until the 1930s that the city of Kitchener experienced its first major industrial strike.

After the manufacturing boom of the Second World War, the makeup of Kitchener's industrial sector shifted, as traditional industries such as leather goods faded and others, like footwear and meatpacking, came to be dominated by a small number of major players. The city continued to live up to its billing as the "Akron of Canada," providing major goods such as rubber tires, car frames, and other parts to the Great Lakes automotive industry. While the automotive sector industries in Kitchener were largely foreign owned, the city remained below average in comparative measures of foreign ownership, with major industries such as Kaufman footwear, Electrohome appliances, and J.M. Schneider's meats owned not only by Canadians but by residents of the city of Kitchener itself.

As in many other cities, Kitchener's manufacturing industries have struggled in the face of the economic upheavals of the late twentieth century, a struggle symbolized by the empty brick factories in the city's urban core – and especially by the closure of the J.M. Schneider's meatpacking plant, whose Courtland Avenue factory had until recently been Kitchener's largest private-sector employer. Nevertheless, the city has also benefited from its position within the "technology triangle," and the success of the region's post-secondary institutions, including Conestoga College, located in Kitchener, has enabled the city to diversify its local economy. While important challenges remain, observers of Kitchener's local economy also see reason for optimism. The Kaufman footwear factory, once dilapidated and empty, now houses urban professionals in attractive lofts. The once empty Breithaupt Tannery is now renovated and leased for commercial space. Perhaps most symbolic, for advocates of Kitchener's high-tech future, is the striking downtown building whose enormous brick walls still display the name of the original owner, Lang Tannery, in enormous black typeface, a building to which a much more colourful logo has recently been added: Google.

Politics and Government

Kitchener's local political development is in many respects similar to that of other urban municipalities across Ontario: incorporated as a village in 1853, as a town in 1870, and as a city in 1912; governed by a municipal council elected annually until 1962, then biennially (until 1982), triennially (until 2006), and quadrennially since then; governed in addition, since 1973, by an upper-tier regional council, five of whose members are from the city of Kitchener.

We will see, in the coming chapters, that there is a great deal of enormously interesting history beneath this traditional tale of urban growth. There is, however, one additional political detail that readers ought to know from the beginning: until 1916, the city we will be investigating was officially named Berlin. We do not have space to elaborate the dramatic details of the city's name change – those with a sense of Canadian history might well imagine the tensions that existed in a proudly German-Canadian city, with a German name, during the First World War – except to say that the tensions were intense, even violent, within Berlin, and had national implications during the Canadian federal election of 1917. But this is another story for another time.[3] For the moment it is sufficient to know that we will use the city's official name throughout our analysis, referring to Berlin in the period before 1916, and then to Kitchener after that date.

Chapter 2

Berlin, Ontario, in the Age of the ABC[1]

Late on the evening of November 12, 1896, workers at the Hibner Furniture Company in Berlin, Ontario, were cleaning up after a long shift. In the paint shop on the factory's third floor, workers dipped their hands in benzene and began to scrape the evidence of the day's labour from their skin. Gas light illuminated the room. One worker, a boy of fifteen, was irritated by a gas flame near his face, and he reached up absentmindedly to push the flame away.

The boy's hands, still coated in benzene, immediately caught fire. He shook wildly, desperate to extinguish the flames; tiny missiles of burning benzene launched from his hands and streaked across the room. One little fireball landed in a bucket of benzene on the floor, which promptly exploded. The room was now in flames.

Six buckets of water sat near the door, along with a box of sand, prepared for just such a scenario. A large tank and some hose stood ready for use a few steps away. But the boys in the paint shop, frightened by the intensity of the flames, fled from the room, and the fire began to spread.

What followed was a sequence of events so extreme in their accumulated incompetence that it is tempting to picture the scene in the crackling black-and-white of a Buster Keaton slapstick: the town's alarm bell fails to ring; the fire brigade, when it finally arrives, finds its hoses clogged with mud and dirt; after ten minutes' frantic scraping and poking, the unclogged hoses release a stream of water so impotent that it does little more than to splash meaninglessly upon the factory's superheated walls; the fire brigade, overcome by heat and frustration, finally surrenders the building to the flames, training the sad dribble of their hoses on the surrounding structures as the main building burns to the ground.[2]

For a despondent Daniel Hibner, the factory's owner, the fire was the latest in a list of frustrations. "The winter is upon us," Hibner complained in an interview the next day. "Berlin's shipping facilities are not the best and I may decide to go east."[3] Inevitably, the vulturine enticements floated in, from Trenton, Brantford, Paris, and beyond. A town outside Montreal kindly offered Hibner a fully equipped woodworking factory, along with a $15,000 bonus, if he moved his business there.[4] Hibner declared that he would need at least $5,000 to rebuild in Berlin. The town's leaders sprang into action, and rallied to pass a bylaw providing Hibner with his requested funds.[5]

So Hibner remained in Berlin. But what about the wider concerns? What about the faulty alarm system, the incompetent fire brigade? In a letter to the local newspaper, an anonymous writer proposed a solution. "The Fire and Water Committee will always remain the same as long as it is in the hands of men that have to be elected by the people," he wrote. "If you leave it to the Council the town will burn down. What we want – if it can be had – is a Board of Fire Commissioners with power to act."[6] The newspaper's editor agreed: "How to deal with the [fire] problem is the question of the hour. Can the council successfully cope with it? We think not. Experience has taught that what is everybody's business soon becomes nobody's and that such an important department of the public service can be best administered by a board semi-independent of the municipal body."[7]

Berlin's town council quickly took up the cause, asking its solicitor to report on the relevant legislation. The solicitor responded with disappointing news: there was no provision in the provincial statutes for a board of fire commissioners. "When the Legislature again takes down the municipal act for repairs," wrote the editor of the Berlin Daily Record, "it should cover over this opening for improvements with a Fire Commissioners patch."[8]

In the end, then, nothing changed. Daniel Hibner stayed in Berlin. Fire protection remained the preserve of a committee of council. Life moved on. But in the town's immediate reaction to the fire, we have witnessed a peculiar urge, an urge to remove authority from a general-purpose government and place it in the hands of a separate, semi-independent institution. What we have witnessed, in other words, is the urge to create a special purpose body.

Once we are awake to this urge in Berlin, we can see it everywhere. By the time of the Hibner fire in Berlin, responsibility for education, public health, libraries, and parks had already been handed over to special purpose bodies.[9] Ten years later, the town had added the water system, the gas and light system, the street railway, and the police force to the list. By the beginning of the First World War, the situation in Berlin resembled the one described by S.M. Baker, who wrote in *Municipal World* in 1917 that the Ontario municipal council had become "little more than a tax-levying body with little or no control."[10]

Berlin's adoption of special purpose bodies was not unusual. Towns and cities across the province were doing much the same thing in their own municipal spheres. In one respect, however, Berlin's experience *was* unique. Among the fifty largest towns and cities in Ontario, just one municipality consistently ranked among the earliest adopters: Berlin. From library boards to water commissions, planning boards to conservation authorities, Berlin was at the front of the pack, among the first (in some cases *the* first) in the province to adopt.[11]

For an unassuming town in the heart of Ontario, this is a rather peculiar claim to fame, and it makes Berlin, of all the available cases, an excellent place to begin our study of local ABCs. What made Berlin so enthusiastic about special purpose bodies? Why was Berlin so eager to adopt? In this chapter and the next, we will attempt to answer these questions, seeking to discover what Berlin can teach us about the meaning and purpose of special purpose bodies, at the local level, in the age of the ABC.

2.1 Special Purpose Bodies in Berlin: An Overview

The story begins with envy. In 1890, Berlin's nearest neighbour, Waterloo, became the second municipality in Ontario to create a Board of Park Management, and in 1893, Waterloo officially opened its magnificent new park, Westside, to widespread acclaim.[12] Townsfolk in Berlin, irritated by the flocks of Berliners migrating to Westside on weekends and holidays, resolved to build a park of their own; the town needed "something after the style of Westside park, only on a larger scale."[13] A group of leading citizens assembled a petition with 264 signatures asking the town council "for the adoption of the Public Parks Act and to pass a by-law to provide for the purchase of [land for the new park.]"[14]

Technically speaking, to opt into the Public Parks Act meant nothing more than to transfer responsibility for the town's parks from a committee of council to a special purpose board. For Berliners, however, eager to mimic Waterloo's success, it meant something else: a spectacular new park in the heart of town. So when council introduced a bylaw in September 1894 to "adopt" the Public Parks Act, and submitted the bylaw to the people for a vote, the subsequent debate had more to do with plans for the park than with the relative merits of special purpose administration. Of foremost concern was a proposal for a large artificial lake in the park, a proposal that some loved and others derided as a "slimy, odoriferous frog pond."[15]

Still, over the din of the frog pond controversy, *some* discussion of the potential park board could be heard. A few town councillors, led by Dr Levi Clemens, argued that a park board would be too powerful, and that it was foolish to remove so important an issue from the direct administration of council. J.R. Eden, a prominent supporter of the bylaw, disagreed: "Dr Clemens has questioned the advisability of putting such a large undertaking in the hands of commissioners, yet the Free Library Board is a good illustration of the way such public matters are conducted by citizens appointed by the council; the Free Library Board have a right to expend a sum equivalent to half a mill on the total assessment yet probably have never taken half that sum."[16]

Moreover, Eden argued, even a passing acquaintance with the North American scene made the decision an easy one; the park board "has been adopted in every city and town of any importance in Canada and the United States and gives better satisfaction than where parks are managed by a town Council."[17] At the end of September, after a month of debate, the bylaw passed.[18] The first six members of the Berlin Board of Park Management were quickly appointed.

Controversy emerged almost immediately. An important argument in the lead-up to the bylaw vote had been that the new board would get started on the park right away, offering employment to Berlin's workers through the autumn and into the winter.[19] But the new board hesitated, divided between those who wanted to fix up an old park and those who advocated a new park close to the downtown. By the winter of 1894, no contracts had been signed and no progress had been made.[20] Berlin's residents grew impatient, and public debate was widespread; the newspaper reported that "groups of 'fors' and 'against' were to be seen on King Street, discussing the question" of the new park.[21] Before long, however, the advocates of the new park prevailed, and the park board began the business of acquiring parkland.[22]

A few months later, however, tempers flared again. Two Berlin councillors, angry about the park board's purchases, moved to abolish the board entirely. "If the people repealed the Parks Act," they explained, "it would take the expenditure out of the hands of the Commissioners and put it solely into the hand of Council." The motion carried, but by the time a bylaw was drafted and submitted to council a week later, the mood had changed. The Public Parks Act contained no provision for abolition; a private statute from the legislature would be required. Besides, the park board had already signed contracts to purchase the park property, and the legal costs to extricate the town from those contracts would be considerable. Better to wait, the council decided, until the property had changed hands and the provincial government had updated the legislation, and to reconsider the matter then.[23]

The critics' moment soon passed. The new park, once built, quickly became a source of local pride. "We have a park of which every citizen must feel proud," the Berlin Daily Record wrote when the park officially opened in 1897; in the years that followed, panoramic photographs of the park would become a staple in promotional materials for the town. It would be decades before the town would again consider abolishing the board.[24]

By 1897, when the new park finally opened, another issue had moved to centre stage: water. Some years earlier, Berlin's town council had sent a delegation to nearby Guelph to investigate that town's state-of-the-art Holly system, and had asked Berlin voters in 1888 to endorse a bylaw for a municipal water system in Berlin.[25] The bylaw had been rejected, and council had instead signed a contract with a private company for a ten-year franchise. In 1896, the fire at Daniel Hibner's furniture factory had placed the water issue back on the local agenda, and as the end of the ten-year franchise neared, the water question quickly became the issue of the day.[26]

By May 1898, after months of investigation, Berlin's town council had decided that "the Water Works system is a Klondike for its owners," and presented a bylaw for the purchase of the system to Berlin's ratepayers for approval.[27] The town's leading manufacturers, desperate for a reliable water supply, mobilized in support of the bylaw. When anonymous letters questioned whether leading industrialists would pay for their share of the water, the industrialists signed a public letter pledging never to seek exemptions on their rates. The town's mayor, himself a major manufacturer, demonstrated his confidence in the profitability of the water system by pledging to purchase the works if the bylaw was defeated; another group of manufacturers proposed to purchase the works and share half of its profits with the town.[28] These performances were apparently convincing; the bylaw passed.

The question of administration, however, remained open. During the municipalization debate, several civic leaders had recommended commission management. Berlin's mayor had written an open letter to his fellow citizens, outlining his own position on the matter: "The water works plant will not be managed by the Council. The only way it can be managed successfully is by a Board of Water Commissioners, who would receive instructions not to grant free water to anyone. This plant would be managed in the same way as Parks are managed by our Park Commissioners, which plan has worked very successfully."[29]

If the water system was to be managed by a commission, however, the provincial Waterworks Act required that it be approved in another local referendum. Thus, in November 1898, council submitted a water commission bylaw to the voters. In a public meeting in the town's un-insulated market shed, ratepayers shivered while the mayor expanded on his earlier points: "If the [water commission] bylaw is not endorsed, the work will fall upon the Fire and Water Committee of the Town Council, who have already all they can do. The Commission must be composed of fair, economical men, and then the town will be sure to derive a revenue for the works."[30]

S.J. Williams, a leading manufacturer who had emerged as a popular and feisty orator, added rhetorical heat to the frigid environs: "Lay aside all feelings of popularity in favor of business ability ... Let us have the works in charge of a Commission, rather than have them buffetted and kicked around by the Council."[31]

The waterworks system was a paying enterprise, these men argued, and a commission would ensure that it was operated as such. Besides, water commissioners would have a single iron in the fire and could focus their attention on water alone.[32] For the few citizens who turned out to vote, at least, these arguments were convincing. The bylaw passed, and the town's first water commission was elected in January 1899.

The water commission was immediately successful. Despite considerable new investments in the system, including major extensions, the commission recorded large profits from the beginning.[33] Keeping up with demand would eventually become a struggle, but the commission's early years were marked by optimism and success.[34] Each year, Berlin's residents could expect to see a newspaper headline declaring that the water commission had once again enjoyed a profitable year. Indeed, the only significant debate in the commission's earliest years was the question of who would control the commission's abundant profits.[35]

With the early difficulties of the park commission now in the distant past, and the glories of the water commission prominent in the newspapers, municipal ownership under special purpose administration quickly became the order of the day. Local leaders had been calling for municipalization of the gas and light plant for years, and when the private franchise expired in 1903, Berlin's residents voted to purchase the works. When a light commission bylaw was subsequently submitted to voters, its successful passage was unremarkable. The only curiosity, according to the Berlin *Daily Telegraph*, was the number of votes against the proposition. Some voters, the newspaper surmised, simply vote against everything, and "it is not improbable that others voted against it either through failure to comprehend the ballot or ignorance of the effect of the measure."[36] Opposition to special purpose management as such was no longer comprehensible.

So confident were Berliners in the merits of special purpose bodies that the town decided in 1903 to go on the offensive. Berlin's sewer system had begun to encounter major difficulties. The basic problem was simple: unlike many towns, Berlin lacked a body of water into which it could dump its sewage; its industrial effluent, including the stinking waste of the local tanneries, flowed into a local field instead. In earlier years, Berlin had been proud of its ingenious sewage treatment system – a local resident had invented a temporarily effective system of sewage filtration beds – but by 1903, the problem had returned with a vengeance. What was required, of course, was a special purpose commission to improve and then manage the system.[37]

The town soon discovered that there was no statutory provision for sewer commissions. Seven years earlier, when the town had briefly considered a board of fire commissioners, this had been enough to stop the momentum. By 1903, however, commitment and confidence had grown, and a group of local leaders travelled to Toronto to request a private bill (i.e., a statute that would apply only to the town of Berlin). Facing an unexpectedly hostile private bills committee – "there are already too many commissions," one disgruntled member said – Berlin's representatives pressed their case. Perhaps, they asked, the committee would allow sewer commissions at least for those municipalities with complex filtration systems? The committee finally relented, and Berlin's representatives returned to town in triumph.[38]

The town's civic leaders were so confident that the citizens of Berlin would endorse the proposed sewer commission that the vote to create the commission and the vote to elect its first members were held on the same day. "It has been taken for granted," said the newspaper, "that the property-owners will endorse the placing of the sewer farm in the hands of a Commission, and, in order to save time and expense, it has been decided to elect a Commission at the same time."[39] The prediction was correct. The bylaw passed, and the first sewer commission in Canada was elected in Berlin in January 1904.

After 1904, the frantic pace subsided. With education, health, libraries, parks, water, gas, hydro, and sewers under special purpose management, little remained to "commissionize." Of course, when the town purchased the street railway system, it too was placed under ABC management.[40] Only one obvious candidate remained conspicuously uncommissioned: police.

Police commissions had become fairly common in Ontario by the early 1900s, largely because provincial law required them in cities. Towns were free to decide how to administer their police force, and in 1907, Berlin's town council decided to transfer its force from a committee to a commission. The decision was controversial – critics argued that a commission was a needless expense for a medium-sized town.[41] But advocates of a police commission, who argued that "the town should guard against the possibility of interference with its police," ultimately prevailed.[42] In the next few years, the police commission was a source of ongoing debate, and two attempts to abolish the commission, on the grounds that it was expensive, unrepresentative, and unelected, nearly succeeded.[43] By 1910, however, it was clear that Berlin was moving towards cityhood, in which case a police commission would be required, and the controversy surrounding the police commission subsided.

2.2 Why ABCs?

How can we explain this enthusiasm for special purpose bodies in Berlin? The first answer is also the simplest: diffusion. Once the special purpose model had been introduced into Berlin's municipal sphere, it quickly spread: the library board supplied a model for the park board, and the park board a model for the water commission; once the water commission was established, it was easy to imagine a light commission and a sewer commission as well. At each stage in this process, the most recent body provided the basic template. Appointed bodies were therefore seen as ideal as long as the library board or the park board supplied the template, but once the water commission was created – it too was to be appointed, following the model of the park board, until Berlin's civic leaders learned to their disappointment that an elected body was required by law – only then did elected bodies become the new model.[44] The town's police commission, which broke from the general pattern, is the exception that proves the rule; it was precisely because the police commission was so different from the most recent models – it was unelected, it did not require voter endorsement, its members were unfamiliar and distant – that it provoked such controversy.[45] In the town of Berlin, internal diffusion was the engine, and satisficing was the fuel: having discovered an organizational model that worked, Berlin's civic leaders were inclined to use it again and again, and were less and less likely, over time, to make a serious investment in seeking out alternatives.

This simple explanation accords with the available evidence in Berlin. But there is something unsatisfying about it. Like many other stories of organizational diffusion, it leaves an important question unanswered: why did Berlin's leaders learn *these* lessons from their early encounters with special purpose bodies? After all, the town's early experience with ABCs was hardly free of controversy. And Berlin's civic leaders were aware from the beginning of the multitudinous administrative tangles into which their new special purpose bodies inevitably cast them.[46] Why did they advocate special purpose bodies again and again, even in the midst of their frustration with the ones that already existed?

To answer this question requires that we better understand the arguments that Berlin's civic leaders used to defend special purpose bodies, again and again, throughout this period; the argument that emphasized the salient features of special purpose bodies and to see "through the confusing evidence of others' mixed successes."[47] If we are to understand the process of diffusion in Berlin, we need to understand the policy images, and the arguments within those policy images, that helped smooth the process of diffusion from one area of municipal administration to another.

To begin our search for these stories requires that we momentarily step out of Berlin and into the wider literature on special purpose bodies in Canada. Although this literature is lamentably sparse, we can extract two possible "theses" from the available sources. The first candidate, which might be called the Wilsonian thesis, emphasizes the role of special purpose bodies in separating politics from administration. Exhausted by patronage and ward-heeling, the story goes, local leaders (especially middle-class professionals) insisted that important municipal functions ought to be removed from council and transferred to semi-independent agencies, boards, and commissions.[48]

The second candidate, which we might call the "insulation" thesis, puts more emphasis on the self-interest of local elites than on the ideals of administrative reform. On this view, special purpose bodies arrived on the scene just as local elites were losing control of their councils. As low-level merchants, workingmen, and even the occasional socialist gained seats on municipal councils, business elites moved to insulate themselves against a loss of control by carving out, and then taking up positions upon, special purpose bodies.[49]

We begin, then, with two basic theses, one "Wilsonian" and the other "insulationist." Was either of these deployed in Berlin? Let us begin with the Wilsonian thesis. In Berlin's earliest debates about special purpose bodies, we find little more than a smattering of remarks along Wilsonian lines. In 1894, for example, a local citizen argued that a park board would mean that "there can be no cry of favoritism"; in 1898, another prominent citizen claimed that a water committee, as opposed to a water commission, would be "kicked around by council."[50] But it is not until 1907, when town council took up the question of a police commission, that a Wilsonian argument appears with more clarity: a Berlin alderman argued that "the proposed change was in accordance with the civilization of the times, which is governed by the legislative and the administrative. The former bodies, elected by the people, make the laws, and latter, appointed by the government administer and enforce the law. The police belong to the administrative class, and are entitled to protection in the enforcement of their duties."[51]

The Wilsonian image was certainly *available* in Berlin during this period of ABC enthusiasm.[52] But it also faced several challenges. First, while partisan politics did occasionally enter the municipal sphere in Berlin, often in the form of coded endorsements of local candidates by known Conservatives or Liberals, the local field as a whole was already highly depoliticized in partisan terms. Berlin's two newspapers, while viciously critical of one another on provincial and federal issues, consistently agreed on local matters. Editorials in support of local reform in the two newspapers were often interchangeable, and their basic argument, as in many Canadian municipalities before and since, was simple: local government is not an appropriate arena for partisan politics.[53]

Patronage in the municipal sphere was also limited in Berlin. It is true that council controlled a handful of plums in the areas of fire services, policing, public works, and assessment. But the steady centralization of patronage in the era of Premier Oliver Mowat, ably documented by S.J.R. Noel, had transferred the choicest fruits in licensing and several other areas into provincial hands. After Premier Mowat's era, the patronage opportunities available to local politicians in mid-size municipalities like Berlin were highly circumscribed.[54]

In practice, this meant that a Wilsonian argument, built on a critique of patronage and partisanship, had little purchase in Berlin. In larger cities, where intellectual fashions arrived earlier and problems of patronage were more pronounced, the Wilsonian thesis may have been more attractive.[55] But table 2.1, which presents a summary of the public arguments about ABCs in Berlin between 1895 and 1908, suggests that the Wilsonian thesis was rarely deployed in Berlin. Of the sixty-eight arguments for special purpose bodies recorded in Berlin's local newspapers between the years 1895 and 1908, only a few could be called Wilsonian; notice the many blank spaces beside "politics and administration," the Wilsonian category, in the table. There is, of course, one exception: in the case of the Berlin police commission, where patronage and uneven enforcement *were* concerns, the Wilsonian image was more popular, with five recorded arguments.[56] It was largely absent from other debates.

Let us turn, then, to the insulation thesis, our second major candidate. Did Berlin's business elites believe that special purpose bodies would cement their dominance during a period of rapid political change? Unlike the Wilsonian thesis, this is not a question that we can answer by referring directly to the arguments in table 2.1. Even if the insulation thesis did provide the basic justification for special purpose bodies in Berlin, the nature of the argument would lead us to suspect that it was rarely articulated in the public arena. We have little access to the smoky backrooms of Berlin's business elite, so we will have to make our way by seeking more circumstantial clues.

To build a case for the insulation thesis, we would first want to show that Berlin's special purpose bodies were, in fact, dominated in their early years by business elites. If they were not – if business leaders were unable to dominate the new special purpose bodies – the insulation thesis would hardly have remained compelling. Here the evidence is straightforward enough. In the first year of the park board, the water commission, the light commission, and the sewer commission, fully 83 per cent of those appointed or elected also served at some point on the council of the Berlin Board of Trade, the town's most well-known and widely respected organization of local business leaders. If we expand from the first year to the first three years, or even to the first five, the proportion of members with Board of Trade Council experience

Table 2.1. Arguments for Special Purpose Bodies in Berlin, 1895–1908

ABCS are good because …	Park	Fire	Water	Light	Sewer	Police	General	Total
… they run on business principles	2	–	5	3	–	–	–	10
… they separate politics and administration	1	–	1	–	–	5	–	7
… they allow for continuity and specialization	3	2	6	4	7	3	–	25
… they recruit otherwise uninvolved leaders	–	2	–	–	–	–	2	4
… they recruit and empower experts	–	1	–	2	2	3	–	8
… past experience has proved them to be good	3	1	4	–	3	1	–	12
… they're good and that's that!	–	–	2	–	–	–	–	2
Total	9	6	18	9	12	12	2	68

Note: Arguments for special purpose bodies in Berlin newspapers, 1895–1908, coded into seven argument types. The relative prominence of "continuity" and "past experience" arguments suggests the potential importance of capacity and diffusion as explanations for the creation of ABCs in Berlin.
Sources: *Berlin News Record, Berlin Daily Telegraph.*

remains near 80 per cent. In fact, nearly 40 per cent of those appointed or elected to the park, water, light, and sewer boards in their first five years also served on the *executive* of the Berlin Board of Trade, an even more exclusive club.[57] Given that the board of trade council was composed of eight to fifteen members each year, and had an executive of just four, these figures illustrate that the presence of Berlin's business leaders on the town's ABCs was highly disproportionate. Berlin's most prominent businessmen dominated early membership of the town's special purpose bodies.

A second clue in support of the insulation thesis would be a decline in business prominence in other local spheres, including, most importantly, the town council. Here the evidence is less clear. It is certainly true that Berlin's labouring classes became prominent civic actors around the turn of the century, and that candidates endorsed by the Berlin Trades and Labour Council were frequently elected in the early 1900s.[58] It is also true, as Elizabeth Bloomfield has shown, that the dominance of "overlapping elites" in Berlin (i.e., of men who were si-multaneously elite in business, political, and social spheres) faded quickly as the nineteenth century gave way to the twentieth.[59] But the problem with these data is timing. It was in the late nineteenth century, after all, that the board of park management and the water commission were created, and we have argued above that those bodies provided the basic template for Berlin's later ABCs. This early period, according to Bloomfield, was still one of considerable overlapping-elite dominance.[60] The enthusiasm for special purpose bodies therefore appears to have emerged in Berlin before business elites could have felt threatened by the town's labouring class.

Figure 2.1 illustrates the promise and the perils of the evidence in more detail.[61] The black line in the figure marks the percentage of Berlin's town councillors, year by year, who also served on the council of the Berlin Board of Trade – it shows, in other words, a rough approxi-mation of the proportion of town council occupied by prominent busi-nessmen. Notice that the line dips into the mid-twenties before 1898, when the water commission was created; notice the similar dip into the low twenties around 1903, when council decided to create the light and sewer commissions. Have we found the smoking gun?

In short, no. It might be possible to lean hard on these data and to piece together a just-so story about the shape of the line and the creation of special purpose bodies. But to do so would require that we over-interpret the timing of Berlin's ABCs. The principal reason that the wa-ter commission was created in 1898, and the light commission in 1903, has nothing to do with the data in figure 2.1; it is because those were the years that the relevant ten-year franchises expired. What we would see in the figure, if the insulation thesis were correct, is evidence of a con-sistent decline in the dominance of town council by businessmen dur-ing Berlin's period of ABC enthusiasm. The figure's jagged line, more like a mountain range than a gentle downward slope, provides no such evidence. The early years of the twentieth century were the first years that workingmen and other non-elites appeared on Berlin's town coun-cil, and even, in a few cases, in the mayor's chair. Throughout the peri-od, however, the presence of Berlin's business elites in the Berlin council chamber continued to be disproportionately large.

A final point. If the insulation image were active in Berlin, we might expect to find one additional clue in the historical evidence: opposi-tion to ABCs by organized labour. But in fact the opposite is true: Ber-lin's trades and labour council consistently *endorsed* the town's special

Figure 2.1. Percentage of Berlin Council with Board of Trade service, 1884–1930

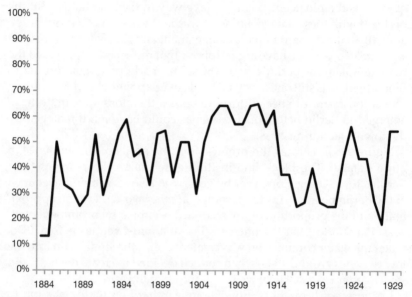

Sources: For councillors, *Berlin News Record, Berlin Daily Telegraph*; for Board of Trade experience, Board of Trade Minute Books, Grace Schmidt Room of Local History, Kitchener Public Library.

purpose bodies. In a referendum on the abolition of the Berlin water commission in 1920 – surely late enough for the town's labour leaders to have grown wise to an insulation effect – the trades and labour council strongly endorsed the commission. Perhaps most important, it was the town council, over which Berlin's elites were ostensibly losing control, that wrote and approved the bylaws to create the town's special purpose bodies.

In the end, then, the circumstantial evidence for the insulation thesis is unpersuasive. Berlin's business leaders appear to have had little reason to find the insulation argument attractive. And Berlin's labour leaders, who were no fools, consistently supported the town's special purpose bodies. Instead, what we see in Berlin during the early ABC period is a council still dominated by business elites and a series of special purpose bodies that mirror and extend that dominance. Table 2.2

Table 2.2. Service on Council and ABCs, with Board of Trade Service, 1880–1930

Service	Individuals*		Years**		ABC Service***	Council Service	Board of Trade****
	N	%	N	%	M	M	%
ABC only	32	17	218	20	3.5	–	19
Council only	120	62	346	32	–	2	18
ABC and Council	42	22	519	48	4.5	4	64

* Number of distinct individuals in each category and percentage of total
** Number of years served by individuals in each category and percentage of total
*** ABCs include park board, water commission, light commission, and sewer commission
**** Percentage of distinct individuals in each category with experience on board of trade council

Note: Comparison of local political actors who served exclusively on an ABC or Council with those who served on both. Those who served on both ABC and council served more years, and were much more likely to have also served on the council of the board of trade.

provides a sketch of the basic terrain. Those who served on council or a special purpose body (not both) served shorter median terms and were much less likely to be prominent business leaders than those who did dual service on council and one or more special purpose bodies. Dual-service politicians comprised just 22 per cent of those who served in Berlin during these years, but filled 48 per cent of the available seats, and many more of them (over 60 per cent) were prominent business-men. If our goal was to vindicate the insulation thesis, this is not the evidence that we would hope to find. Like the Wilsonian thesis, it too must be set aside.

2.3 Berlin's Municipal Field

Our argument thus far has been that successful diffusion relies on a persuasive argument about what is being diffused; in the case of Berlin's special purpose bodies, however, we have suggested that the two most likely candidates, the two candidates most prominent in the literature, ought to be rejected. In making this argument, however, we have re-lied on an important unstated assumption about the evidence that we would need to vindicate a given argument. We must now make that assumption explicit, in the hopes that it will lead us towards more promising explanatory terrain.

Put simply, we have assumed, in keeping with the policy fields approach, that a successful argument would *fit* within prevailing policy images in Berlin's municipal field. An argument will be persuasive only if it is properly adapted to the basic policy image of a given field. From the perspective of the relevant field, the basic empirical claims of the argument must be seen as reasonable – a spade must be a spade. This is not to deny that social actors can and often do redescribe and reframe policy arguments in their field. It is rather to claim, very simply, that they must make their arguments in *relation* to that field, explaining to their listeners how their arguments fit within, or offer a compelling challenge to, the field's dominant policy image. If this argument is correct, then we need to understand the kinds of arguments that might have fit within Berlin's municipal field during this period. Our hope is that by pausing to examine the broader municipal field, we can better understand why the Wilsonian thesis and the insulation thesis fell on infertile ground while another argument could flourish in precisely the same soil.

What, then, was the central policy image in Berlin's municipal field? What was the purpose at which Berlin's political actors aimed? The answer will hardly surprise those who are familiar with North American urban history: in an extremely competitive, largely unregulated, highly decentralized political economy, municipal government was viewed as an instrument for attracting and maintaining local economic growth. Every policy innovation, from tax reform to park construction to water municipalization, was forced to answer a single underlying query: will it attract new industry and reliable workers to our town, without needlessly disrupting the workers and industries who are already here?

This basic agreement in Berlin was supported by two widely accepted foundational premises.[62] First, it was widely believed in Berlin that the town was in constant competition with neighbouring towns, and that a failure to remain attractive would mean their gain and Berlin's loss. This was particularly true in Berlin, it was believed, because of a lack of "natural advantages," such as waterways, in the town. What Berlin lacked in natural advantages, it would have to make up in raw determination, constant innovation, and generous financial inducements.[63] The infantile language of "boosters" and "knockers" would arrive somewhat later, but the basic principle – that excessive criticism of the town would damage its stability and growth – was present from the beginning. The result was predictable. "About the nearest thing to a perpetual motion," wrote a newspaper in nearby Galt, "is the wagging of a Berliner's tongue in laudation of his town."[64] Berlin was not shy about self-promotion.

The second premise, related to the first, was that a successful municipal government must be administered in accordance with "sound business principles." In practice, this meant attentiveness to efficiency and economy, and, more concretely, it meant that successful businessmen must be regularly recruited into civic life.[65] However, even when businessmen were in the minority on council, the town's commitment to business principles remained strong:

> It is sometimes said that a Labour Council is a detriment to a town, but for the past three years the candidates of the Berlin Trades and Labour Council have been in the majority in the Town Council, for one term holding every seat but two, and these years have been among the most prosperous in Berlin's history. Berlin's working-men seem to have thoroughly grasped the necessity of town building; they also seem to take a practical view of their duty towards all classes, and to be ready to combine with the merchant, manufacturer, and professional man for the one purpose of advancing the interests of the town of which they are all so proud.[66]

If a stable and attractive environment for industry was at the core of the municipal policy image in Berlin, if such an environment was the purpose towards which Berlin's political actors were striving, was there anyone who was working to challenge that goal? Perhaps tellingly, it is difficult even to find a serious challenger during this period in Berlin. There is, however, one person who might fit the bill: Allen Huber.

Although "challenger" is an adequate descriptor for Allen Huber, a better term for the man is surely *eccentric*. With his dark, wide-brimmed hat and his wild unkempt beard, Huber bestrode his beloved Berlin pronouncing his hatred of the town's business leaders to all who would listen, liberally suing, harassing, speechifying, and disrupting the town's quiet life with whatever means he could dream up.[67] By a series of exceedingly odd circumstances, Huber was elected mayor of Berlin in 1908 (he had run for the position before – and received fourteen votes), and quickly set about to remake his hometown.[68] Most of Huber's mayoral action can be classified as merely strange – the occasion in which he demanded at a council meeting that the police officer on duty immediately arrest a town councillor may stand as a representative instance

– but Huber did occasionally cut more deeply into the heart of the field. At a meeting of the board of trade, for example (Huber, with no money to his name, was an invited guest, not a member[69]), Huber declared to a stunned audience that he intended to eliminate all tax exemptions for local industries. "The Board of Trade has made Berlin commercially drunk," Huber declared a few weeks later, "and now it has the headache."[70]

What is most telling about Huber, however, is that the result of his many exuberances, beyond the constant irritation of the town's business elites, was essentially nothing. After Huber's bold declaration before the board of trade, the exemptions continued. When Huber demanded the resignation of councillors and commissioners whose private businesses had contracts with the town, they firmly refused. After Huber fired the town clerk, council quickly reinstated him.[71] On one issue – the question of entrance fees at Victoria Park, a sore spot among townsfolk for years – Huber was successful, forcing the park board to restrict its fees to the park's athletic fields.[72] Overall, however, Huber's year in office was little more than an entertaining spectacle, and in his speech to Berlin voters at the end of the year, seeking re-election (very unsuccessfully), Huber's tone illustrated his capitulation to Berlin's central policy image: "In addressing the audience," the newspaper wrote, "the Mayor claimed he tried to run the town on business principles but did not receive the support of the council."[73] After a year in office, even Mayor Huber had some facility in Berlin's native tongue.

2.4 The Municipal Field and Local Capacity

If our argument above is correct – if we can convincingly characterize Berlin during this period as a stable policy field – then we can also begin to understand how the creation of special purpose bodies operated as a *contribution* rather than a *challenge* to that field. Once we understand the stability of the local field, in other words, we can more easily understand why the most attractive argument for special purpose bodies in Berlin did not grow out of Wilsonian reform, or out of elite self-insulation, but was instead an articulation of a determined pursuit of local *capacity*.

To see what we mean by this, we first need to recognize a few basic features of Berlin's municipal government at the turn of the century. Although the complexity of the municipal arena had increased substantially, the basic organizational environment remained the same:

one-year terms for municipal politicians, regular turnover on council committees, limited staffing, and minimal provincial support. Everything, from major policy initiatives to the diameter of the town's water pipes, was decided by politicians. A variety of informal institutions had developed to overcome some of these limitations, such as a customary second term for mayors who had served the town well, but the overall capacity limitations of the municipal sphere were a source of constant complaint.[74]

Within this highly circumscribed environment, an opportunity emerged: special purpose bodies. Unlike councillors, members of special purpose bodies sometimes served terms of three years or more. They were responsible for just one area of service, allowing their members to focus effectively and to develop a specialized competence in a single sphere. Those who were interested in one area of municipal government, but who had little interest in municipal council, could serve the town on special purpose bodies instead. In short, Berlin's leaders argued, special purpose bodies afforded the town the opportunity to achieve two important outcomes that were difficult to obtain on council: continuity and competence.

If we return briefly to table 2.1, and look at the third item in the list (continuity and specialization), we can see the pervasiveness of this basic argument. What was attractive about special purpose bodies, Berlin's leaders consistently argued, was that they allowed their members the time and space they needed to make well-informed decisions about a given policy or service. Local arguments about special purpose bodies were therefore built on a claim about expertise, but the "causal arrow" in that claim ran in an unfamiliar direction: the continuity afforded by special purpose bodies would make their members *into* specialized experts. In an atmosphere of limited capacity and constant turnover, special purpose bodies allowed the town to increase its capacity to carry out the tasks it considered proper to the municipal field.

This emphasis on capacity-building within the municipal field allows us to understand an additional feature of special purpose bodies in this era, a feature that we have thus far neglected: their instability. We noted above that Berlin's town council came close to abolishing the park board in 1895. What we did not mention was that at some point during their early years, council seriously considered the abolition or consolidation of *every one* of the special purpose bodies it had created: the park board in 1895 and 1912, the water commission in 1907 and 1920, the light commission in 1903 and the street railway division of the light commission in 1909, the police commission in 1908 and 1909, and the sewer commission – successfully – in 1911. The very presence of so many special purpose bodies created a tangle of problems: jurisdictional squabbles, accountability issues, policy fragmentation, and so on. In 1911, for example, when a series of events called the competence of the Berlin Sewer Commission into question, council pulled out its heavy weaponry and abolished the commission.[75] In other cases, it threatened to do the same.[76]

We can understand this instability by referring once again to the nature of Berlin's municipal field. When special purpose bodies failed to provide the continuity and competence that they had promised, they came in for hard questioning. The sewer commission, for example, which faced more serious challenges than the other bodies, and experienced higher turnover and more controversy about competence, was ultimately eliminated. And when promising innovations entered the municipal scene, such as the city manager system or the American commission system, Berlin's municipal leaders seriously considered eliminating their special purpose bodies, and to the extent that they were legally permitted to do so, moved to adopt the newer organizational structures.

2.5 Conclusion

Berlin's enthusiasm for special purpose bodies at the turn of the twentieth century was built on a foundation of diffusion. Once the administrative structure of the special purpose body had proven successful in one area, it was enthusiastically applied to others as well. Arguments for special purpose bodies in Berlin made no attempt to challenge the general purposes of municipal government in the town. Instead, they offered an instrumental understanding of special purpose bodies, one that fit comfortably within Berlin's local field. The enthusiasm with which special purpose bodies were embraced in Berlin was therefore a function of the depth to which the basic purposes of the municipal field were accepted by everyone, and of the extent to which special purpose bodies were believed to be capable of providing the means for the town to achieve those goals.

Arguments about special purpose bodies during this period in Berlin remained highly dependent on policy images in the wider municipal field to which they belonged. When special purpose bodies failed to provide continuity and competence, the jurisdictional problems that they created surged to the foreground, and they became vulnerable to demands for abolition and consolidation. For as long as they existed, however, special purpose bodies remained available to political actors, ready to be incorporated into other policy fields and to be defended or criticized on very different lines. As new actors entered Berlin's municipal field, special purpose bodies would be turned to a variety of new purposes. At the turn of the century, however, those newer actors, and the arguments that they carried with them, remained in the unknown future.

Chapter 3

The Special Purpose Routine: ABCs Triumphant

Sometime around 1890, Daniel Detweiler, a salesman for the Jacob Y. Shantz Button Company of Berlin, took a break from his travels to visit the family homestead in Roseville, Ontario. In the comfort of his childhood home, Daniel turned to his brother with a prophecy: the day would come, he said, when hydro-electric power from Niagara Falls would pass through this very village. His brother laughed. Just another of Daniel's fervid enthusiasms.[1]

A decade later, when Detweiler stood before his colleagues at the Berlin Board of Trade to propose that a committee be formed to "secure power from Niagara Falls," the reaction was much the same. The board of trade, too, was accustomed to Daniel's passions; that very evening, he had also proposed full nationalization of the Canadian railway. Perhaps, one member joked, Detweiler might form a "committee of one" to investigate the matter. Detweiler seethed, but he accepted the assignment. The committee of one – a phrase that would one day be etched in bronze upon a monument to Detweiler's name – set to work.[2]

In the ensuing years, Daniel Detweiler worked for the hydro scheme with a zeal so intense that his friends sometimes wondered just what the man did for a living.[3] (They were right to wonder. Years later, after Daniel had died and his widow was living in poverty, it would become clear that he had earned very little, and had spent considerable sums of what he did earn on the hydro movement and other passions.)[4] The committee of one was soon a committee of two – E.W.B. Snider, a former MPP from Waterloo, joined Detweiler in the cause – and then, after a successful gathering in Berlin in June 1902, it became a committee of twenty-one.[5] When Detweiler rose to his feet on October 11, 1910 to propose a toast to the arrival of hydro power in Berlin, it was a committee of thousands – a committee that would soon become, in the form of the Ontario Municipal Electric Association, one of the most powerful interest groups in Canadian political history.[6]

By the time of the switching-on ceremony, Detweiler had moved on to new passions, from deep water canals to town planning and forest conservation.[7] But the success of the hydro movement meant that Detweiler would never again be a committee of one. When Detweiler arranged a gathering in Berlin on the subject of town planning, the local newspaper wrote that Berlin was "once more entitled to be featured as the birthplace of a great movement."[8] When he arranged a similar conference on canals, the newspapers were even more effusive. "Mr. D.B. Detweiler was the hero of the meeting," the newspaper wrote, "frequently and enthusiastically referred to as a man of deep thinking and of great visions."[9] Berlin's pride had fastened upon Detweiler, the "Apostle of Hydro," like a plaque. See here, it declared, that most celebrated of Waterloo County specimens: the energetic entrepreneur.

Daniel Detweiler's white-hot devotion to his causes, combined with his curious tendency to move on to new passions just as they were finding success, makes him a singular figure in Berlin's civic history. But there is also a great deal about Detweiler that is typical of Ontario's politics at the time: the impact of small numbers of devoted activists on local policymaking; the assembly of inter-municipal movements in support of new programs and services; the emergence of new government programs at the local rather than the provincial level. And Detweiler is reflective of the wider history in one other way as well. When the movements that Detweiler helped to establish were successful – in hydro, in planning, in conservation, and beyond – Detweiler stood with his colleagues to recommend that they be entrusted to a specific administrative type: the special purpose body.

The task of this chapter is to understand why this was the case. Unlike the previous chapter, in which special purpose bodies were new and even exotic in Berlin, this chapter explores a period in which their creation had become all but routine. How did this administrative structure come to be cemented into the foundation of Berlin's municipal field?

3.1 Changing Course: Planning and Conservation Movements in Berlin

In a place like Berlin, optimistic and ambitious, the argument was radical: *mistakes have been made*. Yes, the town of Berlin had grown into the city of Berlin – and then, after a name change in the midst of the First World War, had become the city of Kitchener. Yes, the city was the birthplace of the great hydro movement. There was plenty of reason for pride. But the city was also a mess. Roads ended abruptly, or darted off at strange angles. Housing was scarce. Freight cars, shunted off the main tracks, blocked city roads for hours. The city of Berlin had sprouted and spread, willy-nilly, like a crawling perennial. What it needed now was a gardener.

Step outside the city, the same argument went, and the situation was no better. The surrounding countryside had been cleared of trees, and the largest marsh in the watershed had been drained to make more room for agriculture. The forests and bogs that had once absorbed heavy rains and spring thaws were gone, so the rivers, overwhelmed by their new workload, spilled water over their banks instead. The resulting floods destroyed homes, swamped roads and bridges, and wrecked the mill-powered businesses along the riverside.[10]

These arguments about mistakes inside and outside Berlin's borders were daring. Had they been voiced by an outsider, they would hardly have merited a hearing; they smacked too much of the "knocker" to have been digestible from anyone whose loyalty was in doubt. In Berlin, however, the arguments were made by an insider's insider, one whose credentials in the city's establishment were incomparable. That person was William Henry Breithaupt.

William Breithaupt was a man of the railway age. After an education in New York, where he trained as a civil engineer, Breithaupt set off across the continent, designing rail bridges for the Canadian Pacific Railroad, the Santa Fe, and the Mexican Central Railroad. By 1895, Breithaupt had enough experience to set up an engineering firm of his own, in New York City, where his contracts included a request by the United States Senate to design rail bridges to cross the Potomac. Life member of the American Society of Civil Engineers, fellow of the American Geographical Society, member of the British Institute of Civil Engineers – by the end of the nineteenth century, William Breithaupt was firmly established within the fraternity of engineers that was busily spinning webs of steel across North America.[11]

Then tragedy struck. Back in Berlin, on January 26, 1897, William's brother Carl was told that fuel levels were running low at the family-owned gas plant. Carl, the plant's manager, decided to check the levels for himself, and he lit a lantern to inspect the tanks. The bottom was hard to make out, and when Carl leaned in for a closer look, the tank's fumes mingled with the lantern's flame and the remaining fuel in the tank exploded. Carl Breithaupt, just thirty-one years old, was hurled through the air and landed on the roof of a nearby building. Seven hours later, he died.[12]

For the Breithaupt family, and for the wider Berlin community, Carl Breithaupt's death was a heart-rending blow.[13] But it also left a hole in the family's business empire. The family suddenly needed someone else to run the gas plant, the street railway, and other concerns that had been entrusted to Carl. Thus, in 1900, William Breithaupt packed his things in New York City and returned to the town of Berlin.[14]

It did not take long for William to begin to make his arguments. He had spent many days in his youth walking the banks of the Grand River, fishing his favourite holes, and few knew the river more intimately.[15] At first, Breithaupt suggested that the riverbanks be reforested, but he soon realized that the damage was too severe, and the pace of forest growth too languid, for trees to provide a full solution. So Breithaupt began to advocate a new scheme to halt the floods and harness the river: large-scale reservoirs.[16] "One way in which the flow of the spring freshets could be held back," Breithaupt explained in 1909, "would be to reforest the area of the river's source. But that would take an immense amount of money and many years of time. A system of dams and reservoirs is more to be preferred, as it will afford relief much sooner."[17]

Inside the town of Berlin, Breithaupt's principal passion was planning. Breithaupt was well aware of the wider planning movement, then gaining momentum in cities across North America and Europe.[18] That wider movement was diverse; in England, under the leadership of Thomas Adams, it focused on the "garden city" and low-cost housing; in Chicago and New York, it was concerned with the parks and squares of the "city beautiful"; in Toronto, under the leadership of the civic guild, the goal was more attractive buildings and boulevards.[19] In Berlin, however, the vision was firmly corrective. "Town planning," wrote Breithaupt in a professional planning journal, "consists largely in rectifying past mistakes and omissions."[20]

Breithaupt's enthusiasm for planning soon attracted the attention of Daniel Detweiler, who dusted off his hydro playbook and taught Breithaupt the game plan: assemble a committee of devoted local supporters; secure a prominent expert for a public lecture, inviting officials from near and far to attend and discuss the issue; move resolutions at the meeting for provincial and local investigations; finally, call upon the province to pass a statute to authorize real administrative action.

Breithaupt and Detweiler quickly got to work, organizing a local committee (November 1912), arranging an inter-municipal "City Planning and Improvement Congress" in Berlin (December 1912), and hiring a planning expert, Charles Leavitt, to draw up a city plan for Berlin (September 1913).[21] Leavitt's plan arrived in Berlin on March 10, 1914, drawn in colour upon a large, six-foot-by-5-foot poster, which Breithaupt hung in the front office of his Berlin and Northern Railway.[22] It was a beautiful picture, featuring tree-lined boulevards encircling the city and two enormous hub-and-spoke roadways in the less-developed portions of the city.[23] It was also, like many early plans, an impractical work of imagination. Even Leavitt, who had spent little time in Berlin, admitted that it was an "ideal rather than a practical plan for Berlin," intended more as a vision than a blueprint.[24]

The arrival of Leavitt's masterpiece prompted rumblings of dissent in Berlin. Breithaupt and Detweiler, eager to disseminate the plan, asked council for $1000 to print and distribute smaller copies. This seemed a rather generous sum, and the city's finance committee reduced the amount to $300. But even this was too much for some aldermen. "To me," said one alderman, named Hett, "the plan looks like some embroidery outline … it is nothing more than an extraordinary extravagance."[25] In the end, the association got $300 for the printing. But it would be a struggle, in the ensuing years, to squeeze anything more out of the sceptical city council.[26]

It is not our purpose to provide a full history of planning in Berlin; fortunately, much of the terrain has already been covered by Waterloo County's best historian.[27] Still, it is worth pausing for a moment to note how the history of Berlin's planning movement reveals the contours of the city's municipal field in the early part of the twentieth century. When we read Alderman Hett's criticism today, we might suspect him to have been a representative of the city's business elite, for we tend to associate the retrenchment-and-tax-cuts platform that Hett advocated with urban business interests. But Hett was in fact elected as a representative of the town's *working* classes. "This city should not be carried away with these extravagant notions, but should be in the line of retrenchment and not extravagant," said Hett. "I think the rate should be low, so that manufacturers can be attracted to the city. It is in the interest of the workingmen that the tax-rate should not be high."[28] The city's dominant policy image, as we described it in the previous chapter, was alive and well in Berlin, shared among businessmen and labour representatives alike. All were aligned against extravagance. The story of

city planning in the next fifteen years was therefore a story of translation, in which the lofty goals of the movement's most devoted disciples
were adapted to attract the laity.[29]

In 1912, in any case, Charles Leavitt's plan did little more than to add
colour to William Breithaupt's office walls. But when the Ontario Planning and Development Act was passed in April 1917, allowing municipal councils to appoint a six-member planning commission, Kitchener's
council immediately took advantage of the statute. On May 31, 1917,
the city of Kitchener became the first municipality in Canada to appoint
a city planning commission.[30]

The question, of course, is why. Kitchener's council had certainly
done its duty in promoting the new planning bill – it had sent a delegation to Queen's Park in its support, and had also sent a resolution to
encourage its passage – but the principal source of pressure for the law
was the planning and public health officials in the federal Commission
of Conservation.[31] Yet Kitchener was the first municipality to take advantage of the new law. The reasons for this development, at least initially, are hard to come by. Unlike the ABCs of previous decades, which
had prompted wide debate, the Kitchener planning commission received little public attention. Some councillors worried that the new
commission might weaken city council, and most wanted to ensure
that the commission would have sufficient representation from council.
But once these concerns were addressed, the commission was appointed with little fuss.[32]

With a bit of reflection, however, this lack of debate is in fact a revealing clue. For all practical purposes, the new planning commission was
little more than a formal version of what had already existed, for more
than five years, in the form of the Berlin Civic Association. For years,
council had appointed a representative or two to the association, and
had made small grants to cover its expenses, and for years the association had taken it upon itself to make planning recommendations to
council. Council already thought of the civic association as a kind of
advisory committee, and the main members of the association soon
took up positions on the planning commission. Tellingly, we hear nothing more from the association once the planning commission was in
place.[33] From city council's perspective, in other words, the new planning commission was not a radical reform. It was costless tinkering
with the machinery.

By 1917, then, the institutional component of William Breithaupt's
planning vision was in place. Seven years later, after considerable effort,

Kitchener would also become the first municipality in Canada to implement an official city plan and zoning bylaw.[34] The official plan was displayed, in 1924, at the British Empire Exhibition in Wembley, England, where Thomas Adams described Kitchener as "the most advanced in Canada in regard to town planning."[35] For William Breithaupt, the local planning movement was a success.

It would be many years before Breithaupt enjoyed the same feeling of accomplishment in the area of river conservation. In the early 1900s, Breithaupt had employed the same organizational strategies in conservation as in planning. To drum up support, he gave speeches on forests and flooding in Toronto, Galt, Kitchener, and Hamilton.[36] He arranged a conference in March 1909, and then organized deputations to Queen's Park and calls for a provincial commission of inquiry.[37] In 1913, the government agreed to look into the matter, and asked the Ontario Hydro-Electric Power Commission to have an engineer examine the hydro possibilities on the Grand.[38] It seemed that the conservation movement, like hydro and planning, was well on its way.

Then the movement stalled. The Grand River investigation was hardly a government priority and was soon either forgotten or abandoned; by 1917, Breithaupt was once again travelling to Queen's Park to ask the government to write a report on the watershed.[39] Finally, in 1919, the hydro-electric power commission completed the report, but the results were disappointing. According to the engineers, the summer flow levels on the Grand were too low for viable hydro-electric generation.[40] Breithaupt continued to promote the conservation scheme, and a group of Grand Valley business leaders even rekindled the Grand River Improvement Association in 1921, but the effort was in vain.[41] The conservation movement faded into obscurity for almost a decade.

In December 1930, when a coalition of businessmen from the towns and cities of the Grand River Valley organized a conference to create the Grand River Valley Board of Trade, the movement was reborn. Most observers have attributed the rebirth of the movement to an exceptionally destructive flood on the Grand in April 1929, but it is difficult to understand why, if this was the cause, the local actors waited eighteen months before organizing a meeting on the subject.[42] The more immediate motivation seems to have been something closer to the businessmen's hearts: competition. "Our first motive," said F.R. Shantz, a founder of the new board of trade, "must be to bring the claims and attractions of the valley as a whole before those who may be interested, thus combating the strong campaigns made by the large cities."[43] It was only after the new board's flood prevention committee began to have real success, and a Grand River conservation program became an immediate possibility, that the purposes of the board shifted primarily, and then exclusively, to river conservation.[44]

The trajectory of the Grand River conservation movement in the next eight years can be divided into two waves, each of which culminated in an inter-municipal conservation commission on the Grand. The first wave began with the creation of the Grand River Valley Board of Trade, whose flood prevention committee met with William Finlayson, the Ontario minister of lands and forests, about a possible investigation of the watershed. Finlayson was enthusiastic. "Of the many rivers in Ontario, the Grand was only one of many which needed prevention work," Finlayson told the Grand River Valley Board of Trade in June 1931, "therefore he was anxious to see the work go on so that a definite policy of handling this situation might be accomplished which could be used on future occasions in other valleys."[45] The board of trade agreed to pay for the investigation, at a cost of $1500, and the government appointed James Mackintosh, of Ontario Hydro, to serve as the project's resident engineer.[46]

This time, the report was not forgotten. Released on February 11, 1932, the government's report – variously known as the Finlayson report and the Mackintosh report – recommended five reservoirs along the watershed. The report also cited the recent work of the U.S. Army Engineers in the Mississippi Valley as an example of the benefits of a reservoir system.[47]

The report was exactly what the Grand River Valley Board of Trade had hoped for. A committee had already looked into the existing provincial legislation concerning inter-municipal river conservation – conclusion: there was none – and had prepared a resolution "urging the Provincial Government to pass this at the next session of the legislature."[48] The government did not hesitate. At an afternoon meeting at the end of March 1932, William Finlayson met with the board to explain the bill that the government had drafted. "We wanted to set up an organization into which the municipalities of the river valley could come if they wished," Finlayson said. "This legislation provides for a commission, the Grand River Valley Conservation Commission. Every municipality may come in, and if five municipalities are agreed, you may obtain a charter and will then have the power to complete your study."[49]

The key phrase in all of this was "complete your study." The new commission would not have the authority to actually build reservoirs, but would instead carry out a more detailed study based on the findings in the Finlayson report.[50] On April 20, 1934, the Grand River Valley Board of Trade assembled once again, and C.G. Cockshutt, the chairman, laid out the reasons for a commission. "The work of the Boards in connection with the Grand River scheme had now reached a point," Cockshutt said, "when it was necessary that the different municipalities interested should appoint commissioners under the Act and form a commission to take over the work." Brantford, Kitchener, Galt, Fergus, and Caledonia agreed to sign the required petition. At two in the afternoon, on May 30, 1934, Canada's first watershed-based conservation agency sat down for its inaugural meeting.[51]

With the creation of the Grand River Conservation Commission, the second phase began. The commission's initial tasks were first to come to some understanding of the costs of a reservoir system, and then to convince senior governments to support the project. Two developments aided the commission in accomplishing the second task. First, the Great Depression meant that Western governments in general, and the Canadian federal government in particular, were looking for opportunities to provide unemployment relief. Second, the Grand River had herself begun to cooperate. The summer droughts of the 1930s, and especially the drought of 1936, had turned the river into a wretched "open sewer," posing a considerable health threat – not to mention a revolting odour – in towns and cities along the watershed.[52] "It was not hard to focus the attention of the inhabitants, the Councils, and even the Government on the needs of the valley," recalled one participant. "Conservation dams now meant a good unemployment relief measure, a health problem solved, a permanent asset to the municipalities, and an eventual necessity."[53]

Even when everyone could agree that a conservation scheme was desirable, the details were tricky – especially because those involved knew that the Grand River arrangement would serve as a precedent for other river valley projects. In September 1936, a delegation of the Grand River Conservation Commission met with representatives of the Federal Employment Commission in Ottawa, and received a letter two weeks later supporting the proposed conservation scheme.[54] The next step was the province. Members of the commission met with provincial representatives in October 1938, but it was not until June of the following year, in a meeting with the Premier, Mitchell Hepburn, that the government made a clear promise: it would cover 37.5 per cent of the costs of the dam construction project, provided that the Dominion Government provided the same.[55] A few months later, it was back to Ottawa, this time for a meeting with Norman Rogers, minister of labour, and William Euler, minister of trade and commerce. The ministers made no official promises, but they did express support for the plan as a program of unemployment relief.[56] This half-hearted support was enough for the commissioners; in April 1938, a second Grand River Conservation Commission Act was passed, this time with the authority to undertake major public works and to assess the costs against the municipalities that would benefit from the reservoirs.[57] A new Grand River Conservation Commission, with eight member municipalities, was formed in June 1938.[58] Two months later, the commission finally received official word that the dominion government would cover its 37.5 per cent of the construction costs. Armed with statutory authority and explicit funding promises, the new Grand River Conservation Commission set to work.

It took four years for the commission to complete its first reservoir, the Shand Dam, along the Grand River near Belwood, Ontario. At the inauguration ceremony in August 1942, Premier Hepburn stood proudly at the podium and reminded the audience of the government's role in the project. Local dignitaries, including the chairman of the Grand River Conservation Commission, also rose to speak. On the stage behind the speakers, however, was a white-haired man in a dark suit, who sat, smiling, among the assembled dignitaries. It was William Breithaupt. Thirty-four years after his first public speech on the subject of Grand River conservation, Breithaupt watched with pleasure as Canada's first multipurpose water reservoir was officially opened.[59]

It is worth pausing for a moment, before we move on, to reflect on the special purpose bodies that we have examined so far. The planning and conservation stories that we have surveyed suggest two obvious questions. First, why was a special purpose body chosen as the administrative structure for these two new functions? And second, why did it take so much longer for the conservation movement to have success? After all, Breithaupt and his colleagues had drawn from the same playbook in the two movements, and the basic pattern of action – public lectures, inter-municipal meetings, committees of investigation, detailed resolutions, provincial statutes – was all but identical. Why then was the Kitchener planning commission created nearly twenty years before the Grand River Conservation Commission?

On the first question, the answer is simple. Special purpose bodies were chosen by default, with little attention to alternatives, because the local governments involved wanted to make the relevant services public without burdening the local council with responsibility for those services. In both planning and conservation, a devoted organization already existed – the Berlin Civic Association and the Grand River Valley Board of Trade – before the commission was created. And in both cases, these private organizations ceased to exist as soon as the commission was born. The special purpose body was therefore little more than an official version of what already existed in the quasi-public sphere. It was not in any sense a transfer of authority to a new set of actors. Instead, it was a transfer of those *actors* into a more fully public local agency. For the actors involved, the transition was routine.

We will return to the issue of "routine" change below. But we must also consider the question of timing. Why did the conservation movement take so much longer to have success? The answer lies in the contrast between the two movements' basic arguments, and ultimately in the contrast between the two policy areas themselves. In the planning movement, problems were apparent and memorable: every time a freight car was parked in the middle of a street, or a factory set up shop at the end of a residential road, the argument for city planning practically made itself. The conservation movement, on the other hand, struggled to find an argument that was consistently compelling. Initially, the movement depended heavily on the threat of floods for its arguments, but floods, while devastating, proved too intermittent to sustain consistent momentum for change. Breithaupt himself seemed to realize this and began to emphasize the hydro-generation potential of the river conservation scheme, but this argument fizzled after the disappointing conclusions of Ontario Hydro's Grand River report in 1919. It was not until the 1930s, when drought made the Grand River riverbed a putrid sewage dump, and the wider Depression conditions increased public demand for unemployment relief projects, that the conservation movement was finally able to generate the sustained momentum that it needed to bring about an institutional change.

A related problem was political risk. However important the planning movement may have been in the early twentieth century, the planning commission that Kitchener created in 1917 was no more than an advisory body. Council was free to ignore the planning commission's recommendations – and it happily did so, often enough, in the early years.[60] Appointing a planning commission gave cities like Kitchener the prestige of progressivism at little cost. But in conservation, the risks were high. The problem was not confined to a single municipality, which meant that municipalities would have to negotiate with one another on the matter of shared costs. And unlike planning, conservation was expensive. It took years of intergovernmental wrangling before the basic federal-provincial-local agreement was in place, with commitments from federal and provincial governments, and it took several months of inter-municipal squabbling and Ontario Municipal Board appeals before the municipal contributions were also finally decided.[61] Decision-makers at every level had to be convinced that the benefits of the river conservation scheme outweighed the financial and political risks of so large and costly a project.

The central lesson, then, is that some games are harder to play than others. In Kitchener, planning and conservation were advocated by the same people, with the same techniques, during the same period in the city's history. But the nature of the two policy tasks – planning advice on the one hand, expensive and inter-municipal dam construction on the other – meant that the two movements did their work within very different networks of institutions and actors. Because the conservation scheme required funding and approval from multiple municipalities and levels of government, the network in the broader field was both larger and more diverse. This required an argument that would appeal to a wider range of decision-makers. It was not until the Great Depression that a sufficiently robust policy argument, which appealed to all of these actors in their own terms, could finally be articulated.

3.2 Municipal Services: Hospitals, Recreation, Airports

The early histories of planning and conservation in Kitchener reveal the most important features of local special purpose bodies in the first half of the twentieth century. Nearly all of the special purpose bodies that were created during this period emerged out of one (or both) of two general developments: the transfer of a quasi-public service into a more officially public role (planning commissions, recreation commissions); the need to manage a service or policy at an inter-municipal level (suburban roads commissions, area planning boards); or a combination of the two (conservation authorities, airport commissions). All of the special purpose bodies that we will survey in the remainder of this chapter follow one of these three trajectories.

Hospital Commission

The first and most important of the remaining ABCs was the hospital commission. Like most hospitals in Ontario, the Berlin-Waterloo

Hospital was first created, in 1895, as an institution of charity. Its goal was to provide services to those who could not afford private care from physicians in their homes.[62] The hospital was therefore managed by a voluntary board of trustees, who were appointed at the annual meeting of the Berlin-Waterloo Hospital Trust.[63]

This voluntary structure persisted at the hospital for three decades. But by 1920, the hospital's finances were starting to strain. The 1920 annual report showed a deficit, which only grew worse in 1921 and 1922.[64] In 1923, the hospital was able to overcome the deficits with relentless retrenchment, but it was clear to the trustees that no amount of private support would provide a stable long-term foundation.[65] It was time to consider a change. "Whereas the board of trustees at the hospital has realized that substantial repairs and additions be made to the hospital building as well as substantial additions and replacements to the hospital equipment," read a resolution passed at the trust's annual meeting in 1923, "therefore be it resolved ... that the board of trustees approves of the scheme whereby the control and government of the hospital be vested in a board of commission to be composed of representatives of the city of Kitchener, town of Waterloo, and one member to be appointed to represent the members of the hospital trust."[66]

Kitchener's and Waterloo's councils agreed to look into the matter, and formed a joint committee, together with the hospital's trustees, to investigate. A few months later, the committee reported that it too supported the municipalization of the hospital.[67] Council drafted a by-law, and at the municipal election on January 1, 1924, the question was put to a vote – and passed. The necessary private legislation passed in April, and in May, the first Kitchener-Waterloo Hospital Commission was appointed.[68]

On its face, the evolution of the Kitchener-Waterloo Hospital seems to be a straightforward matter of social policy growth: as the charitable responsibilities of the hospital grew, the costs of the service needed to be distributed more widely by transferring the hospital into municipal jurisdiction. But this seemingly sensible explanation is in fact incorrect. The number of "free" (i.e., tax-supported) patients at the hospital fluctuated in the first thirty years, but it did not increase either in absolute terms or as a proportion of the total number of patients served.[69] The hospital's problems were not due to an increase in tax-supported patients. Nor are other obvious possibilities supported by the data: the average per-patient stay at the hospital went *down*, not up, in the first three decades; financial contributions from the province and the municipalities, while somewhat unreliable on a year-to-year basis, steadily increased; and the hospital's revenue from private patients nearly doubled in the first thirty years, as the number of paying patients increased alongside shorter per-patient stays.[70] None of these simple explanations, in other words, helps us account for the municipalization of the hospital in the 1920s.

The real story is a bit more complicated. Between 1900 and 1920, the hospital had become the site not only for emergency care but also for complex medical interventions, such as surgery, which cost a great deal per patient to carry out. The hospital, in turn, refused to charge the full cost of these new and expensive services to patients, who were already complaining about their fees.[71] As the hospital became less an institution of private charity, and more an antiseptic site of complex medicine, local conceptions of the hospital were transformed. This change was embodied, in 1922, in the trustees' decision to fire the hospital's "lady superintendent" and replace her with a male hospital manager; the hospital had shifted, in the view of the trustees, to the domain of complex administration – the domain of men. And if the hospital's new superintendent watched the expense sheets carefully, how much more carefully would he be watched by the municipalities, once he had been given direct charge of the hospitals? "This board will be under the control of the councils," said one local politician, "and therefore they will naturally scrutinize the hospital expenditures more closely than formerly."[72]

The hospital's changed role, combined with the complexity and cost of scientific medicine, explains the pressure from the trustees for the municipalization of the hospital in the early 1920s. But why was the hospital entrusted to a special purpose body? Here the answer is simple. First, the hospital commission seemed to everyone involved to be a natural extension of what already existed – the board of trustees. It was simply a matter of the municipalities taking over the role of the former hospital trust as they took direct financial responsibility for the hospital itself. This would probably have proved sufficient, on its own, to justify the commission structure (as it did in nearby municipalities). In Kitchener, however, the inter-municipal character of the hospital made the decision even clearer. Because the hospital would be managed as a joint Kitchener-Waterloo enterprise, the only conceivable mechanism for its management was the special purpose body. As in the case of conservation, local governments lacked any other machinery for managing inter-municipal services. Thus, in 1924, the Kitchener-Waterloo Hospital was transferred to a local special purpose body, in whose hands it has rested up to the present.

Recreation Commission

If the transition to a special purpose structure had seemed sensible in the case of the Kitchener-Waterloo Hospital, it seemed equally so when council's attention turned to recreation. For decades, Kitchener's recreational programs had been organized by private associations; in the 1890s, for example, when Victoria Park was first created, organizations such as the Berlin Athletic Club operated recreational and sporting events within the city park.[73] Four decades later, the situation was much the same, but the number of associations had multiplied. There were now so many recreational associations – more than three *hundred* – that umbrella committees like the Kitchener Summer Playgrounds Committee had been created to coordinate recreational activities in the city's parks.[74] It gradually became clear to these bodies that a public agency would be advantageous in recreation, and in December 1946, the Kitchener city council, board of park management, school boards, sports association, and recreational council met to appoint an investigative committee to look into the available options.[75] The committee studied the recreational organizations of some twenty Ontario municipalities – in this case, unlike in many others, Kitchener was very much a laggard – and decided that the schemes that had been adopted by the cities of Brantford and Ottawa were most attractive.[76] The system would entail a nine-person recreation commission, with two members appointed by city council, three nominated by the private recreation council, one by each of the school boards, and one by the park board.[77] On June 23, 1947, Kitchener's council passed a bylaw to appoint a nine-person recreation commission.[78] The formation of the Kitchener recreation commission was, in policy process terms, the definition of "normal science" – a committee forms, it carries out research, it considers the options, it adopts the best available alternative. Once again, the special purpose structure was approved with no hesitation.

Airport Commission and Other Special Purpose Bodies

The same was true of the two other special purpose bodies that were created in Kitchener in the years before the Second World War, whose stories are so much like the others that we need not dwell on them for long. The first is the Kitchener-Waterloo Airport Commission, whose task was to oversee the small airfield that had been created by local flying enthusiasts in the early 1930s. So confident was Kitchener's council that the airport would be managed by a commission that it appointed its first airport commissioners before council knew if any legislation existed that would enable the commission to actually *do* anything.[79] The legislation did exist, and by the time the airport officially opened, in 1936, the Kitchener-Waterloo Airport Commission had settled comfortably into its role.[80] Ten years later, when it became clear that a larger regional airport would be desirable, the Kitchener-Waterloo Airport Commission was dissolved and replaced by the new Waterloo-Wellington Airport Commission, with a new airport located a convenient distance from Kitchener, Galt, and Guelph.[81] As in the examples above, the inter-municipal character of the airport, combined with the fact that a private organization was already involved, made a special purpose body the unquestioned choice.

The same was true of the Kitchener Memorial Auditorium. A movement for a large-scale local arena had begun in Kitchener before the Second World War, but a bylaw for the arena had been rejected by voters in 1938. Things changed when the word *Memorial* was attached to the project: now the arena would not only be a venue for hockey games and other attractions, but it would also serve as a "living memorial to those who served from [Kitchener] in the Second World War."[82] A bylaw to approve of the auditorium's costs passed – though still very narrowly – in 1945. Over the next few years, the auditorium's location was a source of considerable political heartburn, but the management of the arena was taken for granted: it would be a commission.[83] The only question was which *kind* of commission to adopt: the seven-person body provided for in the Community Centres Act or the three-person version in the Municipal Act.[84] A few decades earlier, special purpose bodies were unusual enough that Kitchener's municipal leaders occasionally had to adopt less than preferable administrative structures, such as one-year terms for water commissioners. But by the end of the Second World War, ABCs had become so plentiful that selecting a structure for the municipal auditorium commission was akin to choosing an item from the menu at the local diner.

3.3 Explaining Routinized Specialization

In this chapter we have uncovered two pathways to specialization. In the first pathway, a quasi-public organization, such as the Berlin Civic Association or the Kitchener-Waterloo Hospital Trust, is effectively given a special purpose body in which to carry on its work. In the second pathway, municipal governments create an inter-municipal ABC to administer a policy task that crosses municipal boundaries. In some cases, of course, the two pathways combine. Whatever the pathway, however, what we have witnessed in this chapter is *routine* specialization: the creation of special purpose bodies with little hesitation, debate, or even, in some cases, extended discussion. How can we account for this routine?

To answer this question, we first need to step back from the details of individual special purpose bodies and consider how actors in Kitchener's policy field were thinking about ABCs more generally. This thinking can be divided into two phases. In the first phase, between 1910 and the early 1920s, individual ABCs continued to be challenged quite regularly, even while the more general idea of special purpose bodies as such was consistently defended. In 1910, Berlin's council attempted to take direct control of the public transit system, but local residents voted to keep it in the hands of the public utilities commission.[85] In 1912, council made moves to abolish its park board, largely out of frustration with the board's refusal to charge admission at an upcoming civic celebration in the park, but the movement deflated when the controversy was resolved.[86] These were minor skirmishes, prompted in many cases by short-term interpersonal frustrations.

Two events in the early 1920s are a bit more revealing. The first, in 1920, was council's attempt to abolish the Kitchener Water Commission. Councillors had always been frustrated with the commission's unwillingness to keep it informed about basic matters of revenue, finance, and planning, and in 1920, council decided to place the question of the water commission's existence on the annual municipal ballot. But the city's most prominent organizations, including the trades and labour council, recommended that the commission be retained.[87] The resulting vote was surprisingly close – 914 voted to abolish the commission, against 1174 who voted to retain it – but the water commission survived.[88]

The next year, Kitchener's council considered a stranger and more interesting possibility. The provincial Public Utilities Act allowed municipalities to consolidate their water, light, and public transit systems under an elected "public utilities commission."[89] But Kitchener wanted to go further, adding the park board, the sewer committee, the cemetery committee, and the public works department to the new public utilities commission's responsibilities. The result would be an elected commission responsible for virtually all of the city's "hard" services.

The new commission would include two council appointees and a number of directly elected commissioners, and would be able to coordinate "all of the 'working' bodies of the City in one group under men particularly qualified for the tasks assigned them."[90]

It is not easy to see how this arrangement would have worked. Supporters of the super-commission proposal reassured voters that council would retain responsibility for local finance and taxation, and that other areas of administration, like hospitals and libraries, would be untouched.[91] But a public utilities super-commission, with longer terms of office than council, access to water and hydro revenues, and control over a huge range of municipal services, would surely have posed a long-term challenge to the authority and legitimacy of the municipal council. Kitchener's residents were apparently undisturbed by these possibilities. On January 1, 1921, they voted 1532 to 851 in favour of the new commission.[92]

The commission was never created. Even before the municipal plebiscite, Adam Beck and the Hydro-Electric Power Commission of Ontario had made it clear that they would not support Kitchener's proposed private bill. After the January vote, the city's hydro and water commissions – who seem to have assumed, complacently, that Kitchener's voters would reject the proposal – came out strongly against it.[93] By the time the bill reached the legislature's private bills committee, the consensus had crumbled. Two Kitchener residents, including a member of the hydro commission, travelled to Toronto to speak against the bill, and the members of the committee were hesitant to endorse what seemed to them a radical weakening of council.[94] The aldermen who had travelled to Queen's Park to defend the bill were furious – "it is a shame that the will of the people of our city has been deliberately overlooked," one alderman complained – but after the rejection in the private bills committee, the idea was never taken up again.[95]

Ultimately, then, Kitchener's attempt at the public utilities super-commission was a failure. But the super-commission story is revealing in at least two ways. First, it illustrates, as in the previous chapter, that institutional changes at the local level in Kitchener were still fundamentally about *capacity*. What was most attractive about the super-commission was the capacity it would bring to the city: the ability to coordinate hard services, the ability to elect people who could focus their attention on those services, and longer terms of office to ensure continuity and increased expertise. Even at this late date, Wilsonian arguments about politics and administration had little purchase in Kitchener, and supporters of the bylaw went to some lengths to argue that council would *not* be weakened by the reform. The focus, in every sense, was *specialization*: create one commission to focus on the city's "working" policy tasks, leaving council to deal with finance and taxation – and allow voters to choose those most fit to administer the two distinct tasks.

It is possible to demonstrate this ongoing lack of municipal capacity, and the relative organizational strength of the elected special purpose bodies, by tracking the careers of councillors and commissioners in Kitchener over time. Figure 3.1 provides a visual overview of the data. The figure maps the careers of Kitchener's 322 municipal councillors between 1912 and 2010. Each circle (or "node") in the image represents a councillor. The figure can be read roughly chronologically, from the bottom left-hand side of the horseshoe to the bottom right-hand side. The nodes are sized according to the councillors' years of service; councillors with three or more years of shared service are connected by a line. More lines and larger nodes therefore represent a more stable council, with longer years of service and a "core" of councillors with shared service to provide stability and continuity even as other councillors are defeated or retire.

What the graph reveals, very simply, is that the basic structure of Kitchener's council changed little between 1912 and the 1930s. Through the whole of this period, years of service remained low, and links among councillors were weak. These features are particularly stark when we include other municipal bodies within a similar figure, as is done in figure 3.2. Notice, in that figure, how the number of nodes is much lower, the duration of service for many nodes (i.e., their size) is larger, and the links between the nodes are much thicker for members of the light and the water commissions. In the case of the water commission, for example, just ten men occupied more than 86 per cent of the available positions on the commission between 1899 and 1972.[96] It is therefore little surprise that the special purpose body remained an attractive means by which a local government could increase its capacity during this pre-war era.

More broadly, we can understand the routine character of Kitchener's institutional changes during this period by drawing again on the policy fields approach. On our approach, changes at the field level often occur due to the constant ecological interplay among fields, as arguments about political change in one policy field spill over into adjacent fields. We have seen examples of this spillover in Kitchener in this chapter, particularly as private organizations and clubs, with links to a wider

Figure 3.1. Service on Kitchener City Council, 1912–Present: A Network Overview

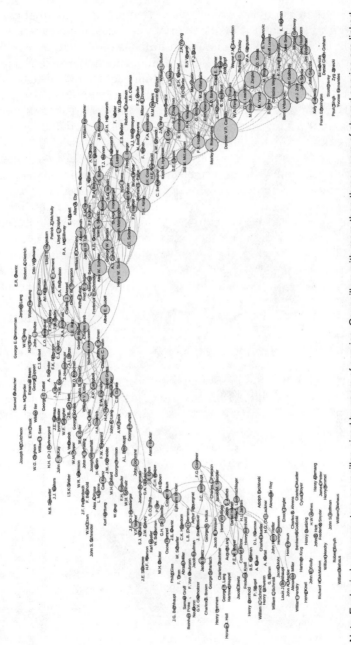

Note: Each circle represents a councillor, sized by years of service. Councillors with more than three years of shared service are linked by a line. The figure can be read roughly chronologically, from left to right, suggesting the increasing stability of city council over time.

Figure 3.2. Service on Council, School Board, and Utilities Commissions, 1912–Present

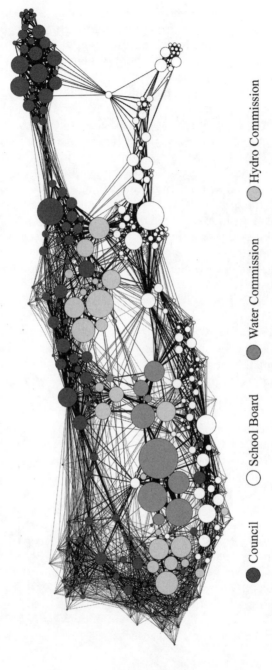

● Council   ◯ School Board   ● Water Commission   ◐ Hydro Commission

Note: Nodes are sized by years of service and shaded by body of principal service (i.e., for those who served on more than one body, the body in which the individual served the highest number of years). Notice the larger circles for the utilities commissions when compared to the council and school boards.

coalition of activists, develop arguments that spill over into the municipal field. William Breithaupt, for example, brought ideas about planning and conservation into Kitchener's municipal field; others did the same in the areas of hospitals, recreation, and airports. But what is crucial about all of these arguments is that the special purpose body was part of the solution, not part of the problem. Again and again, the argument was repeated: Kitchener's municipal government needs to pay more attention, or devote increased funds, to policy task X; it should therefore set up a special purpose body to administer that task.

We can put this point even more simply. Significant deviations from the status quo within a policy field require either that the field is invaded by new actors, with different policy images, or that actors within the field have the interest and capacity to look into significant deviations from the status quo. Few political actors in Kitchener had the capacity or the interest to explore alternative municipal structures in the pre-war era, and those who did have an interest in changing the municipal field – Daniel Detweiler, William Breithaupt, and others – were supporters of special purpose bodies. In the absence of invasions from the outside, then, nobody in Kitchener's municipal field was particularly interested in radical change.

After some twenty pages of historical reconstruction, our basic conclusion – in a stable municipal field, nobody could be bothered to look around for something better – may seem rather dull. But it is important, in any study of institutional change, that we acknowledge the existence of periods like the one we have studied in this chapter: periods in which institutions are stable, the basic need for particular institutions is widely accepted, and changes are made in unchallenging, incremental fashion. Institutional changes can be highly contentious or dully routine – and precisely the same changes, such as specialization or consolidation, will have very different flavours in different fields.

3.4 Conclusions

After 1910, the city of Kitchener accumulated new special purpose bodies in a slow, incremental, uncontentious manner. These new bodies gave Kitchener's municipal government the capacity to handle the increasing number of tasks that it was called upon to perform within the limited nineteenth-century machinery in which council was still required to work. The new tasks often came supplied with experienced policy actors, in the form of third-sector clubs, charities, and non-governmental organizations, and council was quite happy to incorporate those actors into the municipal structure by appointing them to new special purpose bodies. While council was occasionally quite irritated with this or that ABC, its concerns did not grow into a general indictment of ABCs as such. Nor did the city's wider political controversies of this era – the cultural tensions of a German-Canadian town in the First World War, for example – spill over into the institutional arena. The story of institutional change in Kitchener during this period is therefore the story of incremental policymaking in an exceptionally stable policy field.

Chapter 4

Regional Reform and Municipal Restructuring: The Final Chapter?

Dr Stewart Fyfe finally had a plan for his sabbatical. For months, the thirty-nine-year-old professor, member of the Department of Political Studies at Queen's University in Kingston, Ontario, had indulged in the requisite sabbatical-year fantasies: a year in England, perhaps, or in Scotland, or nestled into the hills of New Hampshire.[1] Nothing but a typewriter and time. But the children were in school, and Kingston was a web of social and civic responsibilities.[2] Besides, what was happening in Ontario was rather interesting: after more than a century of somnolence, local governments in the province had finally started to stir. How would Ontario's municipalities adapt to the upheavals of the post-war world? It was a timely question, worthy of exploration. With just the right pitch, it might even merit some research funding from the government.[3]

Provincial officials agreed. "I have read this proposal," wrote the director of Ontario's Municipal Research Branch, S.J. Clasky, in a letter to his deputy minister, "and find it well worth further consideration. Dr Fyfe is asking many of the questions which we are asking ourselves, and has the background experience to give us an informed opinion ... we may be in a position, within the next two or three years, to consider a general review of local government in Ontario in contrast to our present area-oriented local government reviews. When this time comes, a study such as Dr Fyfe's will be valuable."[4]

The problem, from the government's perspective, was that "two or three years" was an eternity away. There were more pressing issues to handle first, not the least of which were the local government reviews that were under development in a number of counties across the province. Finding commissioners to oversee the local reviews was quickly becoming a chore; Kenneth Crawford, Fyfe's senior colleague at Queen's, had already said no to the Waterloo County review. But Fyfe had not yet been asked.

On April 27, 1967, the government's deputy minister of municipal affairs telephoned Stewart Fyfe to dangle the carrot: the government would provide research funds for Fyfe's larger study, he said, if Fyfe would first oversee the Waterloo review.[5] It was too good an offer to refuse. "The Province has pressured me to take on the Waterloo Area Local Government Review," wrote Fyfe to a colleague a few weeks later, "as a price of their giving the grant. Fortunately they agreed that it could be used in many respects as a case study. The duties of commissioner will take some three months over the next year."[6]

In the end, the "case study" swallowed the original project whole. What was supposed to have occupied three months of Fyfe's sabbatical grew to a full year, and then another, and then still another. The Waterloo County area, about which Fyfe knew nothing when he first arrived, would consume all of his research attention for the next three years.[7] By the time Fyfe sat down in February 1970 to write the final pages of his report, his original research plans were a distant memory.[8] All that remained was the Waterloo Area Local Government Review.

Fyfe's final report bore a strong resemblance to the other local reviews that had been completed during the same period. Like the others, Fyfe pointed to problems of urban growth, of annexation, of regional coordination and municipal fragmentation. Like the others, Fyfe recommended that local capacity be improved and local autonomy enhanced. There was one area, however, in which Fyfe's study stood out: its treatment of special purpose bodies. All of the earlier studies had mentioned ABCs, and some had criticized them in some detail – the author of the Niagara Review even wrote a limerick on the subject, which has since become part of the folk wisdom in Ontario's municipal government circles[9] – but Fyfe's report positively *dwelled* on the problem of ABCs. "The Report pays particular attention to the existence of many special purpose boards and commissions in the area," began an internal Ministry of Municipal Affairs summary of the Fyfe report in 1971. "It points out that many local policies are made by bodies substantially removed from the control of municipal councils."[10] When Susan Dolbey, an Ontario civil servant and former student of Fyfe's, was asked to write a report on special purpose bodies for the Ontario government, she too noted that Fyfe's report had "paid particular attention to special purpose bodies."[11] Few other studies had focused so thoroughly on the fragmentation and incoherence that was caused by the local ABCs.

The recommendations of the Fyfe report, had they been implemented as written, might have provided an elegant end to our story, an appropriate closing chapter in this institution's long journey from youthful enthusiasm to comfortable middle age and then finally to institutional death. But the political process is never so tidy. It is true that many of the ABCs that we have explored in the previous chapters – the park board, the recreation commission, the water commission, the planning board – were eliminated in Kitchener in the 1970s. But many other ABCs survived. If regional government was supposed to provide the final chapter on special purpose bodies in Kitchener, then we have been living in the epilogue for four decades.

This chapter seeks to explain this untidy story. We need to understand, first of all, why it was that after seventy years of steady adoption, the tide finally turned against local ABCs in Kitchener. We need to know which ABCs were eliminated, which ABCs survived, and why. In this chapter, we will witness the arrival of what we will call the regionalist policy image in Kitchener, a policy image firmly opposed to special purpose bodies and devoted to local and regional general purpose institutions – and we will see how those new governments created an institutional home for the regionalist image at the local level. Our findings in this chapter will lead us towards the story of *provincial* decision-making on ABCs that we will explore in the second part of this book – and will show us why such an investigation is necessary for an adequate understanding of local special purpose bodies.

4.1 The Road to the Waterloo Area Local Government Review

If there was a single clue, in the post-war years, that things were going to have to change in Waterloo County, that clue was annexation. In 1952, the city of Kitchener annexed some 3,500 acres from Waterloo Township, an enormous parcel designed to give Kitchener space to grow for a generation.[12] As figure 4.1 shows, however, the annexations continued: small bites in 1954, 1955, and 1956, and then another enormous 3,700-acre plot from Waterloo Township in 1958. "The township in its present geographical configuration has often been referred to on the map as a rather laggard looking doughnut," wrote Stewart Fyfe in 1970, "a tasty morsel that has felt the bite of its neighbours on numerous occasions."[13]

Figure 4.1. Kitchener Annexations 1900–1970

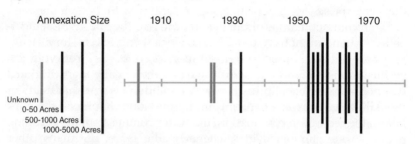

Note: Notice the explosion of annexations in the post-war period.
Source: Farrow, *Waterloo Area Local Government Review*, 6.

These frequent annexations did more than merely annoy Kitchener's rural neighbours. They also put increasing strain on rural finances in Waterloo County. As Kitchener, Waterloo, and Galt repeatedly annexed land from the surrounding townships, the county's assessment declined, making the municipalities that remained responsible for an ever-higher proportion of the county's costs. By 1959, the towns of Preston and Elmira were publicly speculating about withdrawing from the county. From the county's perspective, this was the doomsday scenario. "The county could lose almost 29 per cent of its assessment," wrote the newspaper, "a staggering blow."[14]

The problems of county finance prompted the first stirrings of speculation about the future of local government in the area. One news report in 1959, surveying developments across the province, suggested that two trends were visible. The first was "toward abolition of the county as an outdated and superfluous political relic." The second was to reintegrate urban areas into the county structure, using a "metro status similar to that of metropolitan Toronto."[15] It was the latter option, in the early 1960s, that began to gain momentum. The Ontario Liberal Party included "a metro form of government for Kitchener, Waterloo, Galt, Guelph, and Preston" in its 1962 party manifesto; that same year, Ontario's deputy minister of municipal affairs said publicly that metro government in Waterloo County "will come, perhaps not next year or the year after, but it must develop."[16] Metro government was coming to Waterloo County.

The link between idle speculation and actual change, in Waterloo County, was provided by planners. Local enthusiasm for area planning – that is, for planning that went beyond the borders of a single municipality – had emerged in Waterloo County shortly after the Second World War. In April 1947, Kitchener had collaborated in the creation of the Kitchener-Waterloo and Suburban Planning Board, an advisory board with representatives from Kitchener, Waterloo, and Waterloo Township. Though the board had no real planning powers, it provided an important forum for inter-municipal discussion and enjoyed some significant early successes: an official plan for roads, adopted by all three municipalities in 1959, as well as an official plan for parks, developed in collaboration with the Grand River Conservation Commission, adopted in 1953 and fully implemented by the early 1960s.[17] The early successes led the members of the planning board to think even bigger, towards planning across the county as a whole. In May 1961, the board undertook a growth study for the entire county, a "two-year plan of campaign which, if it is to be successful, will require a degree of co-ordination, co-operation and understanding long needed but rarely seen among councils and officials, boards and commissions throughout the county."[18] With support from Kitchener, Waterloo, and Waterloo Township, the Waterloo County Area Research Committee was struck, and began to churn out studies on everything from county commerce to county soil.[19]

For all of the enthusiasm, however, the committee's early reports did little more than to add weight to the shelves in municipal offices across the county.[20] What was needed was a more concrete and powerful institutional home for area-wide planning. So in 1962, planning enthusiasts in Kitchener organized a meeting of local boards and councils, with hopes for a joint planning board to cover the whole of the county. What they got instead was another committee, the Waterloo County Area Planning Coordinating Committee, which worked for the next two years to raise awareness of area-wide planning problems. In 1963, the committee convinced J.W. Spooner, minister of municipal affairs, to visit the county to see its problems for himself. The carefully stage-managed visit was convincing, and Spooner asked his own community planning branch to write up a report on the area, which concurred with the local planning activists: the four suburban planning boards in the area should be replaced with a single county planning board. The local municipalities supported the report, and on April 14, 1965, the "super-planning board" – officially known as the Waterloo County Area Planning Board – began its work.[21]

The new planning board became entangled with the question of regional government almost immediately. A few weeks before the board's work began, J.W. Spooner had announced that the government would carry out special studies "in nine areas where rapid urbanization has caused growing pains," and that the studies would be the responsibility of the new area planning boards.[22] One member of the Waterloo County board, an alderman from Kitchener, moved that the board make a formal request for a local study, to begin as early as possible in 1965. Others were more hesitant, hoping to assemble a skeleton staff for the board before undertaking the study. "We have been talking as though this is a regional government committee," complained one member of the new board, "rather than a planning committee."[23]

Still, the momentum was hard to resist. Soon after he was hired, the board's new planning director said publicly that the Waterloo County area "comes as near to a logical region as one can get," and endorsed a local government study as soon as possible.[24] By the end of June 1966, the process was in motion. "No one will say anything publicly about progress made toward the [local government] study," wrote the local newspaper, "but most top officials of the county and the cities of Kitchener, Waterloo, and Galt have reached almost complete agreement on the issue."[25] A few days later, Waterloo County officially invited the government to undertake a local government study; other local municipalities soon followed suit.[26]

The Ontario government quickly hired Ron Farrow to serve as research director for the Waterloo area study.[27] Farrow was a veteran of local area reviews, having served in a similar role for the Niagara study, and he knew that the appearance of neutrality, among sensitive and competitive local governments, was paramount.[28] He also had a sense of humour. "The office [for the study] had to be located in the centre of the area to give the utmost impression of impartiality and neutrality," wrote Farrow to a friend. "When we worked out the precise centre of the area in geographical terms we discovered that it was in a washroom in a B/A gas station. More appropriate accommodations have been found, even though they are a little off-centre."[29] The Waterloo Area Local Government Review had begun.

4.2 Local Government and Its Problems

What were the problems that the Waterloo area review was supposed to solve? It is tempting, from the distance of nearly half a century, to simply refer to the Fyfe Report to answer this question, assuming that the problems that Stewart Fyfe discussed were the problems that most concerned local residents. Before we do this, however, it is worth pausing to consider the problems that were most important in Kitchener *before* the Fyfe study began.

The first problem was workload. Beginning in the early 1960s, local newspapers began to run a new kind of story, a story whose premise had not been explored in the local media before: the enormous burden of civic office. "What makes a person spend 200 hours a year – the equivalent of five weeks – doing work for which he is not paid, seldom praised, and often criticized?" asked one newspaper article. "There are 50 such persons in the Twin Cities – all school trustees serving on the five school boards in Kitchener and Waterloo."[30] The same was true of municipal council – a "tedious, demanding" job.[31]

One way to overcome this problem was a two-year term. A longer term of office for municipal councillors would mean that they would spend less time learning the job and more time doing it, making council less frustrating for councillors and more useful for residents. The proposal had been suggested in Kitchener before, but had been rejected by local voters twice.[32] By 1962, however, local residents were convinced that a two-year term would be an improvement, and a plebiscite to endorse the change passed easily.[33]

Another possible change concerned municipal administration. Nearly every year, in the early 1960s, Kitchener's council had struck a committee to consider how its internal operations might be reorganized.[34] In 1965, the committee recommended that the city hire a manager, abolish its standing committees, create an in-house legal department, and – most important for our purposes – reorganize the city's agencies, boards, and commissions: "We feel that over the years council has delegated too much authority to special purpose boards and commissions. This has doubtless occurred because council has been too much involved in administrative matters. Aldermen have therefore been happy to be relieved of part of their work load. With the adoption of a manager system, council should have more time to deal with policy matters and it may be that some of these functions should be brought back under direct council control."[35]

Even before the Fyfe report, then, Kitchener's municipal leaders had begun to entertain the possibility that some of its ABCs might be eliminated. But this report was the exception rather than the rule. When it came to special purpose bodies, the option that Kitchener's elected

officials entertained most frequently in the 1960s was not elimination –
it was consolidation.

The first example was in parks and recreation. For many years, the
park board and the recreation commission had worked together closely, the park board responsible for the parks and the recreation commission responsible for the activities within them.[36] The system worked,
but it was also a bit odd – why not combine the two bodies so that the
necessary coordination could occur regularly, around a single table? In
1963, a Kitchener alderman proposed a joint meeting between the
boards to discuss the question, and the next year, Kitchener's council
created a committee to look into the matter.[37]

Nearly everyone agreed that the change would be a good thing. The
recreation commission, eager to get on with things, voted unanimously,
late in 1964, in favour of amalgamation.[38] The park board was a bit
more reticent, but only because its longest-serving member, A.R. Kaufman, was vehemently opposed, largely on the grounds that the new
commission would include councillors who would not be willing to do
any hard work.[39] Whatever the exact nature of Kaufman's objections –
the man was nearly eighty years old and had become a bit eccentric,
refusing to state his views with reporters in the room – the process
moved along without him.[40] In December, everyone on the board except Kaufman voted to amalgamate with the recreation commission.[41]
The provincial legislature passed the necessary private statute in 1965,
and a new parks and recreation commission, consisting of the mayor,
an alderman, and eight council appointees, soon began its collabora-
tive work.[42]

While the parks and recreation commissions were busy discussing
the terms of their union in Kitchener, a much larger wedding was also
underway along the Grand River. As we know from the previous chapter, the Grand River Conservation Commission had been created in
1934, with eight area municipalities as members. What we did not mention, however, is that a second watershed agency – the Grand Valley
Conservation Authority – was created in 1947 as part of the Ontario
government's post-war conservation authorities program.[43] Some worried, unsurprisingly, that the work of the authority and the commission
would overlap, but supporters of the authority promised that the two
were distinct. "We need the brains and initiative of every section of the
valley," argued one, noting the wider municipal membership of the authority. "There is a world of work to be done without conflicting with
the job anyone else is carrying on."[44]

Thus, for more than twenty years, the Grand River watershed enjoyed not one but two watershed conservation agencies. The jurisdictional squabbles that this situation created are hardly surprising, but they remained mostly minor for the first ten or fifteen years.[45] It was not until the 1960s, when the authority began to make moves towards a full-scale dam construction project of its own, that the continued existence of the two agencies became a matter of more serious concern.

The basic problem was that the authority and the commission were both developing dam construction plans. While the conservation authority was busily planning its new Guelph dam, the commission developed a $15 million plan of its own for dam construction at Ayr and West Montrose, with 25 per cent of the costs to be covered by the commission's eight member municipalities and the remaining 75 per cent by the federal and provincial governments. Everyone balked. The municipal members wondered, understandably, why the costs should not be distributed among a larger set of Grand River municipalities. The province, for its part, saw an opportunity to finally rid the watershed of a superfluous conservation agency. "It might not be fair to say the [minister] delivered an ultimatum," reported the newspaper, "but he politely but firmly stated the commission had to become amalgamated with the authority."[46]

Even after the quasi-ultimatum, the commission resisted, submitting a proposal to the province that would maintain the two agencies with more clearly defined and separate roles. The proposal went nowhere – the provincial government refused to acknowledge that it had even received it.[47] At last the commission relented, and amalgamation negotiations began. The two agencies submitted a proposal to the province in July 1965, and in 1966, the Grand River Conservation Authority – an amalgamation of the two older bodies even in name – was created to manage the Grand River watershed.[48]

By the time Stewart Fyfe arrived in Waterloo County, then, Kitchener and other area municipalities had already begun to tinker with their local institutions. The changes that they had made – longer terms of office, a single super-committee in council, amalgamated special purpose bodies, and so on – were intended to increase the efficiency with which local decisions could be made. But none of the changes had grown into a general indictment of local special purpose bodies. As always, this or that ABC could come in for serious questioning. But when Kitchener's planning director, William Thompson, unleashed a furious assault on local ABCs as such in a report to council in 1965 – the same year that council's own report had more gently noted the need for changes to

ABCs – council immediately disavowed Thompson's suggestions.[49] Criticism of local special purpose bodies was still criticism of particular institutions, at particular times, on particular problems.

A final example helps to illustrate this point. When Kitchener's planning board agreed to support the creation of the Waterloo County Area Planning Board in 1965, it insisted that non-councillors be appointed to the board. Kitchener's council endorsed the idea. "All of the members of the area board should not be politicians," said William Thompson – the same man, ironically, who had lambasted local ABCs a month earlier – "some members should not have to worry about votes. It's going to be a powerful board and its chairman will be Daddy Warbucks, and should also be a layman. It's a prestige position for a politician."[50] The basic dogma that had developed among interested officials at the provincial level – namely, that if a local ABC had to exist at all, it should be composed of councillors – had simply not been absorbed in Kitchener. Everyone recognized that the problems in Kitchener were severe – annexation controversies, overwhelmed aldermen, the pressures of rapid growth. But special purpose bodies were not – yet – the villain.

4.3 The Waterloo Area Local Government Review

By the spring of 1967, Stewart Fyfe had been appointed to undertake the Waterloo review, and Ronald Farrow, the research director, had completed and published his background research in a slim but informative *Data Book*. Farrow and Fyfe sent out a request to local municipalities, special purpose bodies, civic organizations, and interested citizens to submit briefs to the local review on all topics related to local government reorganization. The public stage of the Waterloo area review had finally, officially begun.

Fyfe and Farrow received more than one hundred briefs.[51] The submissions ranged from short interventions by private citizens to the exceptionally detailed multi-volume submission of the Kitchener Planning Board – a submission that seemed intended as much to say "we could have done this without you" as to provide Fyfe with a summary of the board's views.[52] Every municipal government, and many special purpose bodies, submitted a brief to Fyfe.

What is most interesting about the municipal briefs is how thoroughly they confirm the argument that we have made above; namely, the absence of a widespread local indictment of special purpose bodies. Table 4.1 summarizes the recommendations contained in the

Table 4.1. Summary of Recommendations to Fyfe Commission on ABCs

	Kitchener	Waterloo	Galt	Preston	Hespeler	Elmira	Bridgeport	Ayr	Wellesley	Wilmot Twp	Wellesley Twp	Woolwich Twp	Waterloo Twp	Waterloo County
Airport commission	✓			✓									X	
Board of health		X						✓						
Grand River Conservation Authority	✓			✓										
Hospital commissions	✓													
Hydro commissions	✓		✓	✓	✓			✓						
Library boards	✓	✓		✓										
Parks and recreation commissions	X								X				✓	
Planning board: County				X					X				X	
Planning boards: Local	✓	X	✓		✓			✓						
Police commissions	✓				✓	✓								
Water commissions	X		✓											
General statement				X								X	✓	X

✓ Recommend keeping the ABC
X Recommend abolishing the ABC
Note: Blank spaces indicate no recommendation.
Source: Municipal Research Correspondence Files, RG 19-56, Archives of Ontario.

municipal briefs. A black X indicates abolition, and a checkmark indicates preservation. Blank spaces indicate that the municipality made no recommendation one way or the other.[53] As the table suggests, there were certainly some criticisms among the submissions. Whoever wrote the municipal brief for Wellesley Township, for example, had had enough of local ABCs: "The trend to the formation of these special purpose bodies – they number more than 30 in some municipalities – has resulted in a bewildering assortment of boards and commissions and a weakening of local government. It has created confusion for the electors who don't know who to blame when something goes wrong. It has produced frustrations for the elected representatives who must answer to the people for actions over which they have little or no control and who must raise the money for programs they have not initiated. This trend must be halted."[54]

For every criticism, however, there was an equally passionate response; Waterloo Township, for example, acknowledged the force of arguments like those in Wellesley Township's brief but went on to make a full-throated defence of local ABCs.[55] Nor is there a coherent pattern to the recommendations (except insofar as the cities were more inclined to discuss ABCs). Some municipalities thought that water commissions should go, and others that they should stay. Some supported planning boards, and others did not. Even Kitchener, whose council devoted an entire supplementary brief to the subject of ABCs, did not make a consistent argument either way; some ABCs should be preserved, Kitchener's council decided, and others should be eliminated.[56]

If Waterloo County's municipalities were not yet ready to say that special purpose bodies should be abolished, this is not to suggest that we cannot find such a view within the municipal briefs. We can – in the fiery red pencil of Ron Farrow, the research director, who annotated each of the briefs with sometimes incisive, sometimes scathing, and often exasperated remarks.[57] Farrow's red annotations reflect a clear and sustained perspective on local ABCs, a perspective that had already been expressed in provincial reports throughout the 1960s.[58] The argument was simple: except in highly unusual circumstances, municipal policymaking was properly the domain of municipal council. If council was incapable of handling the workload, the solution was to strengthen council, not to preserve the ABCs. "Could councillors not perform the same function?" scribbled Farrow, like an exasperated teacher, when local hydro commissions insisted that they be preserved.[59] Of course, the question was rhetorical. For Farrow, as for most provincial officials who concerned themselves with the question, the answer was an obvious *yes*.

The distance between the consistent regionalism of Farrow and Fyfe and the more pragmatic positions of many local officials became even clearer when Fyfe and Farrow turned from written briefs to oral hearings. When Kitchener's councillors argued, as they had in their briefing, that planning boards be preserved, Stewart Fyfe was deeply sceptical. When local public utilities commissions argued for their own preservation, Fyfe was respectful but uncompromising. Perhaps the clearest articulation of the two positions came in an exchange between Fyfe and a Kitchener alderman on the subject of planning:

FYFE: The number of boards and commissions and their independent powers and organizations is an element in this. Why not go for the Ottawa
Bill for example, [which] says that there be no planning boards. Planning
should be a direct responsibility of Councils. Why keep a part in the authority which is doing minor administrative jobs? Why shouldn't this be
under Council with proper staff?

HONSBERGER (Kitchener): This type of person, and we've got all kinds of
them on boards and commissions that are willing to serve ... We're trying to take advantage of that type of person as much as possible and to
involve them in civic administration which is part of the aim of government. Get citizens involved and maintain their interests. This we feel is
one way of doing it. We don't feel that we should abolish all the boards
and commissions.[60]

This is as close as it is possible to come to a clear statement of the difference between the two positions. This is not to suggest that Honsberger's view fully captures Kitchener's position on ABCs, let alone the
views of the other local municipalities. What it does provide, however,
is a nice example of the difference between Stewart Fyfe's general opposition to ABCs and the more selective acceptance of ABCs at the
local level.

By June 1968, the briefs were submitted and the hearings were complete. All that remained was to write the report. After months of delays
and countless drafts, Darcy McKeough supplied Fyfe with a deadline:
the report, he declared, *would* be printed and bound by the first day of
March 1970.[61] Four weeks before the deadline, with no time left for delay, Fyfe locked himself in a hotel room in Hespeler and spent eight
days pounding out the remaining pages.[62] The *Waterloo Area Local
Government Review* was finally complete.

Fyfe sent his manuscript off to a local printery, which worked around
the clock to produce 3,500 copies of the report in time for the March 1
deadline. The delays had only increased local interest in the report –
amazingly, given the tepid response with which most government reports are greeted today, local officials were concerned enough about
a leak that the printery was monitored regularly by local police.[63] At
8 pm on March 10, 1970, Darcy McKeough stood before an audience of
1,000 at Waterloo Lutheran University and announced that the report
was complete. "Perhaps all of you here are familiar with the history,
some would say the long history, of the Review," said McKeough. "It
will be our job, yours and mine, to study this opinion and to use it as

the basis for coming to some constructive conclusions about the future of this area."[64]

What did the report recommend? On the big question – regional government, yes or no? – Fyfe hedged, offering a one-tier solution called "Scheme A" and a two-tier regional option called "Scheme B." On ABCs, Fyfe was less equivocal. Planning boards, hydro commissions, parks and recreation commissions, and water commissions should be abolished, their tasks folded into the duties of local councils. On boards of health, library boards, and police commissions, Fyfe's recommendations were vague but unsupportive. The general argument was clear: whenever and wherever possible, special purpose bodies should be folded into municipal council. And when this was impossible, their boards should consist of a majority of elected councillors.[65]

No one liked the report. Or rather, *almost* no one. After Darcy McKeough's presentation, as local officials thumbed through the report, the reeve of Woolwich Township ran up to the minister, interrupting an interview with a local reporter (and thereby guaranteeing coverage in the next day's press). "Congratulate Dr Fyfe on an excellent report," said the reeve. "It is almost exactly the same idea that we proposed in our Woolwich brief. I know it will work because we'll make it work."[66]

Few others were interested in making the Fyfe report work. Kitchener's council, having recommended a massive one-tier urban complex, found little to love in either of Fyfe's suggested schemes. The many municipal governments that had recommended a two-tier system could not fathom why "Scheme A," the one-tier option, had even been proposed. Those whose primary concern was planning – whose enthusiasm had prompted the review in the first place – may have been the most disappointed of all. Dr Ralph Krueger, a local professor and dean of the county's planning activists, summarized the reaction plainly. "After great labor," wrote Krueger, referring to the Fyfe report, "the elephant had given birth to a mouse."[67]

At the provincial level, the reaction was no more enthusiastic. Darcy McKeough, perhaps sensitive about steamrolling over a major process of local consultation, was diplomatic, assuring locals that all options were open and that all possibilities would be seriously considered.[68] But Premier Robarts was less inclined to pull his punches. "It doesn't represent government policy," said the premier, repeatedly, when asked about the report. "It is only one man's approach to the subject ... food for some careful thinking."[69] The Fyfe report, in other words, was the beginning, not the end, of local reform discussions in Waterloo County. McKeough asked for responses to the report from local municipalities, ABCs, and other interested parties, and he and his officials began to draft legislation for a reorganized system of local government in Waterloo County.

The local reaction to the Fyfe report, in the days and weeks after its release, revealed some interesting features of the municipal field. The hydro utilities, whose commissioners had unanimously demanded that local hydro structures remain untouched, redoubled their efforts in response to Fyfe's call for their abolition. "We have a fight on our hands," said one hydro commissioner, a fight that will require a "strong front."[70] Hydro-related briefs poured into McKeough's office from local commissions and the Ontario Municipal Electric Association, all of them singing from the same hymn book. Hydro generates revenue and ought to be separate from municipal finance. Hydro commissions were created by local referenda, so referenda are required for their abolition. Hydro is different, special, unique. In short: leave hydro alone.[71]

No other local players were as well organized and active as the hydro officials, but others still did their best to make a mark on McKeough. Local planners re-emphasized the need for strong regional planning and bemoaned the fact that Fyfe's attention had shifted from planning, the most serious problem in the county, to matters of local representation and accountability.[72] The local board of health restated the need for a separate, independent public health agency.[73] Everyone tried to explain to the minister how Fyfe's suggestions had been inadequate, incomplete, or just plain wrong.

By March 1971, the provincial government was finally prepared to present a proposal of its own. By now Darcy McKeough had moved to a new ministerial post, so the new minister, Dalton Bales, travelled to Waterloo on the 16th to announce the details of the plan. Once again, local officials and reporters gathered together en masse, eager to learn of their fate.

The broad contours of Bales's proposal were unsurprising. There would be regional government in Waterloo, along with amalgamated lower-tier municipalities. The urban municipalities in the southern part of the county would be amalgamated into a single large city, the name for which – Cambridge – was chosen in a local referendum the next year.[74] (Among the alternatives proposed by furious locals: Bittersweet Hills, Forgetit, and – my personal favourite – Darcy's Folly.)[75] The city of Waterloo proved once again to be a survivor; there would

be no amalgamation in Bales's proposed scheme, now or in the fore-
seeable future.[76]

Bales also made it clear in his presentation that many local ABCs
would be abolished. Parks and recreation commissions, planning boards,
and water commissions would disappear. Library boards, however,
would survive. Police commissions and boards of health would be regional, but would remain independent of council. And hydro commissions, while stripped of their responsibilities for gas and transit, would
carry on as separate, elected bodies.[77]

Why did *these* ABCs survive? What was it about library boards, police boards, boards of health, and hydro commissions that allowed
them to overcome the ongoing and occasionally scathing criticism to
which they had been subjected in recent years? The answer is probably simplest in the case of the hydro commissions. As we have seen
above, hydro officials in Waterloo County were actively opposed to
generalization and expressed their views plainly to anyone who would
listen. With the support of the Ontario Municipal Electric Association,
the hydro commissions made it clear that they would not fade away
gently. When I asked Stewart Fyfe why the hydro commissions survived, his answer was plain: "Hydro was a power unto itself."[78] Darcy
McKeough seems to have held roughly the same view. At a town hall
meeting in Kitchener in 1970, McKeough's remarks on the future of the
Ontario Water Resources Commission had obvious hydro-related un-
dertones: "[McKeough] talked about Kitchener's water problems and
conceded to Mr Weber that the day might come when the Ontario
Water Resources Commission could have a water grid similar to the
power grid of Ontario Hydro. But he said the province would want to
be careful that the OWRC didn't build too powerful an empire beyond
government control."[79]

This was not the last that Darcy McKeough would say about public
utilities in Ontario; in fact, at the time of this speech, a major study of
hydro structures at the provincial and local levels had already begun.
But any changes to local hydro commissions would require a coordinated, province-wide approach. For the moment, hydro commissions
would be left alone.[80]

Hydro commissions, then, survived the transition to regional government because of the enormous organizational capacity of the local
commissions, Ontario Hydro, and the association (the Ontario Municipal Electric Association) that connected the two. In policing and public
health, the story was somewhat different. Whereas hydro commissions

had blinked brightly on the radar through the entirety of the Waterloo review process, police commissions and boards of health were much less visible. Fyfe did not receive a single brief from a police commission in the Waterloo area, and all of the municipalities that mentioned policing – just three of fourteen – recommended that the boards be retained. Boards of health were even less salient, their structures ignored by all but one of the municipal briefs. Fyfe himself endorsed the continued existence of police boards, rather half-heartedly, in his final report. On public health, Fyfe was somewhat more critical, making the standard regionalist argument that public health services should be integrated into other areas of municipal policymaking, but he did not explicitly recommend that boards of health be abolished.[81] At the local level, the public pressure for generalization of policing and health, before the transition to regional government, was practically non-existent.

Provincially, the story was rather different. Susan Dolbey's definitive 1970 report on local special purpose bodies was consistently, even radically opposed to ABCs. (The true test of regionalist radicalism in Ontario is where one stands on school boards and conservation authorities. Dolbey recommended the abolition of both.) On boards of health, Dolbey took the standard position that they ought to be abolished. On police commissions, however, even Dolbey drew back. Where regional governments existed, she suggested, policing should be regionalized. It would also be good if the majority of the police board was composed of councillors, to limit conflict between councils and their boards. But police boards gave citizens the confidence that the local police system was insulated from politics, Dolbey argued, and "to achieve this end there may be merit in continuing to call this body a board rather than a committee of council."[82]

Police boards, then, also survived, entrenched within a century-old view that policing must be – and must be *seen* to be – removed from the control of municipal councillors. For many years, libraries had shared in a similar logic. Just as local policing ought to be distant from political influence, the argument went, so too should library operations. After all, how would *Slaughterhouse Five* or *Catcher in the Rye* have fared around the council table? And what about less literary titles, like *Fifty Shades of Grey*? Better for all involved to insulate both council and the libraries from such ticklish decisions.[83]

Adding to the pressure for the status quo were the library's budgets. From time to time, when libraries needed new buildings or branches, the library budget could become a source of local discussion and debate.

Most of the time, however, the library went about its business quietly, its budgets stable and its board members reappointed year after year with little fuss. Just three municipalities had even mentioned libraries in their briefs to Stewart Fyfe, and Fyfe himself had vacillated on the question of whether they should be dissolved. It seemed that libraries were as unlikely a candidate for generalization as police commissions.

Beneath the current of quiet politics, however, there was considerable pressure for change. Hollis Beckett's report on the Municipal Act had recommended more direct council control over libraries, and the Ontario Municipal Association had resolved that library boards become committees of council at its 1969 annual meeting.[84] The next year, Susan Dolbey's report on local special purpose bodies recommended that councillors comprise a majority of the members of library boards, fully control library budgets, and make all appointments to the boards.[85] But it would take several years before these possibilities would grow into a wider provincial debate on the composition and existence of the boards.[86]

In the meantime, provincial decision-makers were indecisive. As late as Dalton Bales's regional government announcement in 1971, there are strong hints that the provincial government was seriously considering eliminating the boards. Bales's own remarks on library boards during his speech were equivocal: "For the time being we would leave [libraries] as an area responsibility. Again we would recommend that the responsibility be left with area councils, but that they be instructed to involve some citizens' advisors in the same way as in recreation."[87]

By the time of the bill, however, the equivocation had disappeared: library boards would remain as-is. The dynamics of this provincial decision remain rather obscure and probably merit a study of their own. However, research by Lorne Bruce, Ontario's leading library historian, suggests that libraries were left untouched in part because the province was already considering a province-wide study of library board structures.[88]

In the end, then, when the Region of Waterloo became an official legal entity, in January 1973, many special purpose bodies were eliminated. These included the parks and recreation commission, the water commission, and the planning board, as well as less prominent bodies like the auditorium commission. The basic regionalist thesis on ABCs – special purpose bodies ought to be eliminated and transferred to general purpose governments – was, in all of these abolitions, upheld and confirmed.

Even so, the exceptions are glaring. Beyond the borders of Waterloo Region, two major ABCs remained: the Grand River Conservation Authority and the Waterloo-Guelph Airport Commission. Many municipal ABCs also survived. Hydro commissions were proudly unchanged across the region. The same was true of library boards and boards of health. Police boards had been abolished, only to be recreated at the regional level in a new and even more powerful form.

We have argued in this section that each of these "survival stories" is different. No single factor was shared by the ABCs that survived and absent from those that did not. What is important to notice, however, is that the decision-making process on special purpose bodies during the transition to regional government was not local but provincial. Looking back at table 4.1 above, what is most obvious in retrospect is that it would have been impossible to predict, on the basis of the municipal briefs, which ABCs would survive and which would not. If we had looked instead at the regional government legislation that had already passed in Ontario – legislation that had already established similar regional governments in other parts of the province – our predictions would have been very much on the mark.

This is a new development in our story. In the two previous chapters, it has been possible to tell the story of local institutional change in Kitchener as a *local* political process. The provincial government and provincial officials were actors in that story, to be sure, and provincial law made some local ABCs mandatory, but we have also found a great many local institutions whose creation and development were primarily the result of local political action. It has been possible to tell such a story right up to the point at which the Waterloo Area Local Government Review began. After that point, however, the story of local institutional restructuring in Kitchener, as in every other part of Ontario, has become much more clearly a matter of provincial policy debate.

There was no formal jurisdictional change in the late 1960s that led to this shift. In the 1960s, as in every previous decade, the provincial government retained full legal authority over the final status of local institutions across the province. But *normative* authority had changed. The deep involvement of the Department of Municipal Affairs in Waterloo County's reorganization – in which local actors, however frequently they were asked to express their views, were finally reduced to spectators – represented the first full-scale invasion of the municipal field by the province in Kitchener's history. The transition began gently; when the Waterloo County Area Planning Board was created, for example, one board member recalled that ideas were "being very cleverly suggested by the provincial municipal affairs people, that it would be a good idea to look at this, and it would be a good idea to look at that."[89] A decade later, provincial suggestions had become provincial decisions.

We must be careful not to overstate the difference between provincial and municipal opinion during this period. For all of the complaints that the province received from locals in the transition to regional government, the reaction would surely have been all the more furious if locals had been opposed to the regionalist vision tout court. The policy image we have called "regionalist" had many defenders at the local level. Those who were involved in planning, for instance, commonly made regionalist arguments and were frequently critical of special purpose bodies (with the occasional exception of planning boards, which were their own institutional homes).[90] We have also found traces of the same argument in some of the Fyfe commission's municipal briefs. Overall, however, those who were involved in local politics in Kitchener had a much more pragmatic view of ABCs, a view that was conditioned as much by local capacity and the relationships among local institutions as by any abstract theory of local administration. The limits of generalization in Waterloo Region – that is, the extent to which ABCs could by fully and finally eliminated – were the limits to what was thought possible by provincial, rather than local, decision-makers.

4.4 The Survivors: Special Purpose Bodies in the Regional Years

If we temporarily exclude the ABCs whose boundaries went beyond the borders of Waterloo Region – the conservation authority and the airport commission – four important ABCs survived the transition to regional government: boards of health, the regional police board, the municipal hydro commissions, and the municipal library boards. Each of these four ABCs was to be the source of intermittent discussion in the coming decades.

The first to face the fire was the board of health. By the time of Stewart Fyfe's report, every municipality except Kitchener had abolished its municipal board of health and joined a consolidated "health unit" at the county level. Fyfe criticized the isolation of the public health system from other municipal services, though he did not explicitly recommend that the boards of health be dissolved.[91] But Fyfe's remarks were provocative enough to trigger some defensiveness from local public health officials. "Education and health are both specialized activities," argued the chairman of the Waterloo County Board of Health, "and should remain the responsibility of non-council boards which can give them their full attention and interest."[92]

The regional board of health did not last long. The region's first chairman, Jack Young, was an orthodox regionalist, committed to bringing as much as possible under the direct authority of regional council. In the spring of 1974, Young proposed to the region's health and social services committee that regional council take over the responsibilities of the regional board of health. The committee agreed and passed the matter along to council, which voted unanimously to abolish the board. "The death certificate for the Waterloo Region board of health was filled out Thursday by regional council," wrote the *Kitchener-Waterloo Record*. "All that remains to be done now is for the provincial government to sign it."[93]

In fact, all that remained was an enormous provincial battle, one that pitted the regionalists in the Ministry of Municipal Affairs against public health activists in the Ministry of Health in a war that had been ongoing for a decade. We will discuss the contours of this battle, and the reasons for the regionalists' victory, in chapter 6. As far as Waterloo Region was concerned, the request went into one end of the provincial decision-making machine, and came out the other end, nearly a year later, as a *yes*. With as little fanfare as possible – the decision was announced in a single paragraph of the Ontario budget as a "pilot project" – the provincial government allowed Waterloo Region to abolish its local board.[94] The necessary bill was introduced in June 1975, and by the end of the summer, the board of health was gone.[95]

If Jack Young and his colleagues were committed to abolishing the regional board of health, they were all the more passionate about the police. Policing had been regionalized in 1973 and was now governed by a board of three provincial appointees and two appointees of regional council. Just months after regional government was in place, regional councillors began to argue that the police board, with its majority of provincial appointees, "negates the philosophy of regional government in that appointed people are not directly accountable to the electorate."[96] Claudette Millar, mayor of Cambridge and regional councillor, said that the structure of the police commission was "one part of the legislation creating the Waterloo system that she never agreed with." Most others on regional council shared her view.[97]

What did the regional councillors want? One possibility was to give the regional council control over a majority of the seats on the police board.[98] A more radical option was to abolish the board entirely, making council directly responsible for the administration of police. "It is preposterous indeed," wrote a local editorial, firmly in support of the more radical option, "for Ontario's Tory government, with its own record of political appointments, to object to local political control. That, we suggest, is a prime case of the pot calling the kettle black."[99] The fact that two of the province's appointees were active Conservatives, the newspaper argued, gave the lie to the claim that the current structure was somehow free of political influence.[100]

These criticisms of the police board washed in and out, like the tide, throughout the 1970s, rising when the police budget was a matter of contention and receding when it was not. Local politicians made official requests for reform or abolition of the police board in 1973 and 1977 with no success.[101] It was not until 1979, with William Palmer's report on Waterloo Region, however, that the possibility for thoroughgoing reform first reached high tide.

William Palmer was a former deputy minister of municipal affairs and a veteran of the regional government reforms across the province. He was also a through-and-through regionalist, an ardent defender of regional government, and a persistent critic of special purpose bodies. In 1979, Palmer was asked to write a report on the operation of Waterloo Region, in large part to clarify (and, it was hoped, dispel) the criticism that the region was expensive and overstaffed, and that some municipalities would be better off if they were to secede from the region.[102] Palmer commissioned study after study on regional operations, assembling a data book of inflation-indexed financial data running to more than a thousand pages, and ultimately producing a report that offered a thorough, well-articulated, and empirically compelling defence of regional government in Waterloo.[103]

Palmer's primary task in the report was to survey the region's finance and operations, but he was also asked to comment on local government in the region more generally. As a result, his report was much more than a defence of the first five years of regional government; it was the clearest articulation of the regionalist vision ever to have been written in the Waterloo area, and perhaps the most fully articulated regionalist manifesto to have been written in Ontario more generally. At the centre of Palmer's argument was that great thorn in the regionalist side: the special purpose body. Palmer could think of no ABC whose reasons for existence outweighed the enormous advantages of their elimination. Library boards, hydro commissions, hospital boards

– all of them should go. But Palmer went further. Conservation authorities should be eliminated, their tasks divided between the province and the municipalities. School boards should be eliminated as well. And there was a final ABC for which Palmer reserved his most trenchant criticism of all: the police board.

Palmer's argument was novel. The basic claim that underlay the existence of the police board, he argued, was that police must be separate from politics. On its face, this claim was indisputable; no one wanted a corrupt and politicized police. But policing, like other public services, was inherently political. It was a matter of deciding what was best for the local community, of weighing the cost of increased police service against the cost, say, of public health treatment or better community centres. Even more importantly, Palmer argued, the claim that a police board provided insulation against local politics was simply bunk. What it did instead was to make policing *less* visible to the public. The possibility of corruption, while remote, was higher, not lower, when the police force was governed by a board whose members were unknown and whose personal and business connections to the community were opaque. Elected officials, who lived in the public glare, had more incentive to resist the temptation to put their thumb on the scales. The very premises with which police boards had been defended in Ontario, Palmer argued, pointed instead to their elimination.[104]

This was the clearest argument for the abolition of the police commission ever to have been publicly articulated in Kitchener's history. It accomplished precisely nothing. The Waterloo Region Police Board persisted, after the Palmer report, just as it had done before, carrying on unchanged through the entirety of the 1980s. Provincial governments went on appointing the majority of the board's members, sometimes making choices that pleased local councils, other times making selections that paid back partisan debts. When Bob Rae's NDP government hinted that it might consider changing the boards, local officials once again sprang into action, making all of the old arguments for council control of policing. But nothing became of the issue. It was not until Rae's government was replaced by the Conservative government of Mike Harris, in 1995, that the structure of Ontario's police boards finally changed.

The Harris government made two changes to the structure of the boards. The first was a minor adjustment to the appeal process for budgets, which weighted the process ever-so-slightly in favour of councils rather than police boards.[105] More important was a change to the boards' personnel; the majority of the board members would now be local rather than provincial appointees. In Waterloo Region, for example, the board would now consist of three provincial appointees, two regional councillors, the regional chair, and one regional appointee who was not a member of regional council. The "swing vote" on the board, in other words – assuming for the moment that regional and provincial appointees would vote en bloc – was the non-council regional appointee. This was local control in its most cautious and limited form, but it was local control nonetheless.[106]

The Harris government's amendments in 1997 were not enough to permanently eliminate police-related budget disputes. There have been regular calls at the regional council table – particularly from Doug Craig, the mayor of Cambridge and a long-time critic of regional government – for deeper reforms to police administration in Waterloo.[107] Overall, however, there is little question that, at least in Waterloo Region, the Harris government's changes took the edge off of the arguments for police reform.[108]

In the case of the region's hydro commissions, we have already noted that municipal hydro commissions were left untouched in the transition to regional government in Waterloo, owing largely to pressure from local commissions and the Ontario Municipal Electric Association. This created an exceedingly odd state of affairs, because after 1973, there were hydro commissions for municipalities that no longer existed. The Village of Bridgeport, for instance, had been eliminated in 1973, but Bridgeport Hydro survived. Those parts of what was now Kitchener that had formerly belonged to Waterloo Township were still served directly by Ontario Hydro. Kitchener's residents were therefore paying three different hydro rates, depending on where in the city they lived.[109]

By the mid-1970s, other problems had also begun to appear. The legislation to create Waterloo Region had stipulated that those who were presently serving on the hydro commissions would continue to do so. The expectation was quite clearly that the government would decide what to do about the commissions before the next local hydro election. By 1975, however, no provincial decisions had been made, which meant that three former mayors were qualified to sit on the commission even though they had lost or retired from their mayoral positions. The situation had turned from tragedy to farce. "People should shake the cobwebs out of their head," said Allan Reuter, Conservative MPP for Waterloo South, when he heard of the problems on the hydro commissions.[110] Waterloo Region's chairman agreed: "One thing we don't need," he said, "is three more commissioners."[111]

While Kitchener waited impatiently, much was going on at the provincial level, as the provincial government struggled to find a way to restructure the hydro commissions without provoking the wrath of the Ontario Municipal Electric Association. We will discuss the government's decision-making process in detail in chapter 7. For Kitchener, however, the answer finally arrived in 1978. The hydro commissions of Waterloo Region would be abolished, with three new urban-rural commissions in their place: Kitchener-Wilmot Hydro, Waterloo North Hydro, and Cambridge and North Dumfries Hydro. This was an innovative solution, neither municipal nor regional, and it was never replicated in Ontario. It was seen as the best way to make local control of rural hydro a viable possibility, with each of the region's major urban areas absorbing a portion of its more expensive rural portions.[112] The new structure prompted some grumbling, especially in the city of Waterloo, where officials felt that the region's smallest city had absorbed more than its share of the region's rural townships.[113] In Kitchener, however, the creation of Kitchener-Wilmot Hydro caused little controversy; Kitchener would continue to elect four members to the commission, just as it had done before, and every Kitchener resident would now – finally – pay the same hydro rate.

This urban-rural institutional structure persisted, with no significant changes, into the 1990s, and when the Mike Harris government introduced the Energy Competition Act in 1998, which required that all local hydro utilities be converted into private corporations, the city of Kitchener decided to retain its utility as a municipally owned business.[114] The new hydro corporation has returned handsome profits to Kitchener and Wilmot, and few have publicly questioned the decision to continue with municipal ownership of hydro.[115] While there is ongoing pressure in the wider hydro field for further consolidation of hydro utilities – the three urban-rural utilities in the Waterloo region being prime examples of where such consolidation might occur – it is unlikely that there will be any changes under the present Liberal government, which has expressed little interest in anything other than voluntary, locally initiated restructuring.[116]

Unlike the three other survivors, all of which have come under considerable public criticism during the regional years, the Kitchener Library Board has continued to cruise along below the radar.[117] This was especially true after 1984, when the Ontario government amended the Public Libraries Act to give municipal councils full control over appointments to the library board (previously, public and separate school boards had appointed a minority of the library boards' members).[118] Since that time, the structure of the library board has been the very definition of quiet politics in Kitchener, provoking almost no public discussion at all.[119]

Overall, then, three of the four most important ABCs to have survived the transition to regional government have persisted, in modified form, up to the present in Kitchener. What is equally important about this period, however, and distinguishes Kitchener's post-regional politics from the earlier period, is that few *new* ABCs have been created. Kitchener's council has created a handful of new bodies, such as a board to oversee its cultural centre, the Centre in the Square. At least one important ABC has also been created at the regional level, an economic development agency by the name of Canada's Technology Triangle – but this body would almost certainly be a committee of regional council, were it not for ongoing tensions between Waterloo Region and the city of Cambridge.[120] The general pre-regional pattern, which added new ABCs in Kitchener on a steady basis for decades, has disappeared in the regional era.

4.5 Conclusions

Two empirical observations emerge from this final chapter on Kitchener's experience with special purpose bodies. The first is simply that the presence and power of local ABCs has declined in recent decades. Many of the bodies to which we devoted our attention in the previous chapters, from park boards to water commissions to planning boards, have been eliminated. The ABCs that have survived, such as police commissions and library boards, have been gently restructured to maximize council's control over the membership, if not the final decision-making, of the boards. Councillors at the local and regional level in Waterloo Region today control a much wider range of policy issues than was the case before 1973. In this respect, at least, the regionalist vision has been a success.

During the same period, however, the *initiative* for local restructuring has shifted from the local to the provincial level. This is not to suggest that the interest in local reform has disappeared among locals. On the contrary: local politicians have continued to call for changes to this or that institution quite regularly from the 1970s to the present. But those calls for change have accomplished nothing in recent decades in the absence of a commitment to institutional restructuring by the government of Ontario.

As the provincial government has become ever more involved in local institutional reform, the nature and patterns of local change have shifted. The most common process in recent years has been what we might call *disruption*. The main feature of this process is that changes occur only during periods of significant overall disruption to local structures, the most important examples being the regional reorganization of the 1970s and the Mike Harris restructuring of the late 1990s. The reasons for this change, once again, have more to do with provincial than with local politics. Ontario's post-war governments, taken generally, have either been interested in local restructuring or have avoided it completely – Robarts, Davis, and Harris being examples of the former, and Peterson, Rae, McGuinty, and (probably) Wynne being examples of the latter.[121] Only in the midst of widespread disruptions to local government, in other words, are significant changes to library boards, police commissions, or hydro utilities likely to be considered. Thus, Ontario's local governments are forced to wait – some patiently, others less so – for the next provincially initiated period of disruption.

These developments in Kitchener during the recent past are also relevant to our theoretical concerns. What is perhaps most interesting about the post-regional experience with special purpose bodies, for our purposes, is that the regionalist policy image, which was rather foreign to most local officials in the 1960s, has become deeply entrenched in the municipal field after 1973. This is so for two reasons. First, the introduction of regional government in 1973 gave the regionalist image an institutional home *within* the local field. While all local governments in the region have been critical of ABCs, from time to time, after 1973, the most sustained attack has consistently come from the region of Waterloo. It was the region's initiative that led to the abolition of the board of health in the 1970s. It was the region that pushed hard for the abolition of the police board. And it is the long-time chair of the region, Ken Seiling, who has been the area's most consistent local critic of special purpose bodies in recent decades.[122]

The second reason for the increased presence of the regionalist image at the local level is local *capacity*. Many of the changes to local governments since the 1960s have increased the capacity of municipal councils to develop and implement policy themselves. Terms of office for municipal councillors have increased, from one year to two in 1962, to three in 1982, and finally to four in 2006.[123] Municipal staffs have grown larger and more professionalized. Highly skilled administrative officers are now responsible for the entire administrative apparatus of the municipality. Capacity is still a problem – *the* problem – at the local level in Ontario, but these changes make it less attractive for local councillors to leave important areas of local policymaking to special purpose bodies.

This suggests a final theoretical conclusion. What we have witnessed in the course of this chapter is in some respects the dissolution of Kitchener's municipal field itself. A policy field, recall, consists of a network of political institutions covering a particular bundle of policy tasks, as well as the policy images in that network. On the issue of local institutions, however, it is no longer possible to describe the field in Kitchener as exclusively or even primarily local. The provincial government, while always an important player, has become the *primary* actor in this final chapter, the proper locus for an explanation of how and when local institutional changes occurred in the city of Kitchener after the mid-1960s. On some policy tasks, to be sure, Kitchener's policy field could still be described as fundamentally local. But this is no longer true of decisions about the existence and structure of local political institutions.

It is clearer than ever, therefore, that a study of local institutional change at the municipal level, in the single municipality of Kitchener, Ontario, can take us only part of the way towards a full understanding of local special purpose bodies in Ontario. In the course of the past three chapters, we have encountered important moments – moments of increasing frequency, it would seem – in which decisions simply emerge from the "black box" of provincial policymaking with little local involvement. While the institutions that we are exploring are local, their story is only partly a local one. Thus, the story of municipal ABCs from a very different angle – from the perspective of the province of Ontario as a whole – begins in the next chapter.

PART TWO

LOCAL ABCs IN THREE PROVINCIAL-MUNICIPAL DOMAINS

We now turn from the local to the provincial level, from a focus on a single city to a focus on the evolution of special purpose bodies across the province of Ontario. In this second part, we restrict our attention to just three institutions – public school boards, boards of health, and hydro commissions – but we track the development of those institutions in cities, towns, and rural areas throughout the province as a whole. As in Part One, we will begin with a brief sketch of the political-historical terrain for those who are unfamiliar with Ontario's history. We will then fill in this sketch with relevant detail as we proceed through each of the next three chapters.[1]

Ontario was born, in 1791, as the province of Upper Canada, a sparsely populated British colony stretching from what is now Windsor at its southwestern point through to the border with the somewhat more well-populated colony of Lower Canada to the east. After a series of popular rebellions in 1837 – dispatched quickly in Upper Canada, but more prolonged and bloody in Lower Canada – the two colonies of Upper and Lower Canada were joined to form the United Province of Canada, a colony divided into two administrative units (Canada East and Canada West) but governed by a single united parliament. By the early 1860s, this united legislature, fractured by complex ideological, religious, and regional cleavages, proved repeatedly unable to sustain confidence in a government. The resulting political deadlock, combined with long-standing concerns about economic viability, westward expansion, and continental defence, led to the formation of a new federal state known as the Dominion of Canada, one of whose provinces was Ontario.

Since Confederation, in 1867, Ontario's politics have often been described as staid, even bland, dominated by a tradition of incrementalism and managerial competence that some have traced back to the nineteenth-century administration of Ontario's longest-serving premier, Sir Oliver Mowat. Premier Mowat's careful incrementalism, combined with a shrewd use of patronage, allowed his Liberal Party to dominate provincial politics in the nineteenth century;[2] in the twentieth century, beginning with James Whitney's Conservative victory in 1905, it was the Conservative Party that has dominated.[3] For much of its history, in other words, Ontario's party system has conformed to the Canadian "brokerage" model, a system in which a brokerage party of the centre, whose goal is to minimize rather than emphasize social and ideological cleavages, is able to dominate. In the closing decades of the twentieth century, Ontario's political landscape was more volatile, with Liberals, New Democrats, and Conservatives taking up government in rapid succession. The early decades of the twenty-first century have been dominated by the Liberal Party; whether this represents a return to brokerage politics, or a blip in the more recent story of volatility, remains to be seen.

Beneath the surface of apparently bland incrementalism, Ontario's political history is rich with important political and social change. This is particularly true of two eras in the province's post-Confederation history, the first stretching from Oliver Mowat's election in 1872 through to the end of James Whitney's premiership in 1914, and the second from the election of George Drew's Progressive Conservatives in 1943 to the end of the so-called Tory Dynasty in 1985. These two periods of "province-building" established the foundation for provincial politics as it plays out in Ontario today. In the former period, this meant (under Mowat) establishing the constitutional autonomy of the provinces, and reorienting the Canadian federal system towards profound decentralization; it also meant (under Mowat and Whitney) building up the infrastructural foundations for a provincial economy that would become the country's manufacturing heartland for more than a century.

These early achievements provided the basic context, and the constitutional autonomy, for a powerful Ontario state. But it was not until the end of the Second World War that Ontario's government began to resemble something that might be recognizable to observers today. In the midst of an extraordinary economic and demographic boom, and under the leadership of a string of Progressive Conservative premiers, Ontario's government took on a program of expansion whose ambition and scope was rivalled only by the later state-building of the Quiet Revolution in Quebec. The explosion in provincial spending during this period provided the architecture in which Ontario's citizens continue to live their lives, both literally – hundreds of thousands of Ontarians are born, educated, and employed each day within buildings that were constructed during the early post-war era – and also in the major areas of policy debate that continue to dominate Ontario's political discourse. While Ontario has experienced extraordinary social change in recent decades, the province's politics continue to play out upon a stage that was constructed during these two major periods of provincial development.

What Do School Boards, Hydro Commissions, and Boards of Health Do?

In the chapters to come, we will explore the long-term institutional development of public school boards, local boards of health, and hydro commissions. While the actual policy tasks in which these boards have been engaged have evolved considerably through the years, it may still be useful to begin with a very brief introduction to the basic policy responsibilities of each of the three local institutions.

The responsibilities of Ontario's school boards have changed a great deal since the nineteenth century, as local authority for curriculum development, teacher certification, education finance, and even some aspects of collective bargaining have shifted to provincial and professional bodies. Speaking generally, however, school boards are responsible for operating public education programs within the boundaries of provincial education policy. This includes decisions about local budgets, program offerings, setting and adjusting hiring numbers for teachers and administrative staff, school closures, transportation to and from schools, and a range of other policy tasks related to local education provision. While these decisions are firmly bounded by provincial mandates, local school boards still exercise considerable authority over many aspects of educational provision in Ontario.

Of the three policy domains that we will explore, fiscal issues have been most contentious in education, where school boards' authority, until recently, to determine the amount to be levied from property taxes, combined with the municipalities' responsibility to actually collect those taxes, produced considerable resentment among municipal officials. Within this context, the details of educational finance have varied. Through the nineteenth century, Ontario's public schools were funded almost exclusively from local property taxes. To attempt to equalize educational opportunity across the province, the Ontario government began to provide grants to less wealthy boards in the early twentieth century; through the middle years of the century, the province added to these grants by providing funds for an increasingly lengthy list of "approved expenditures" in local schools. This program was replaced in the 1960s by the Ontario Foundation Tax Plan, which required schools to levy a provincially mandated property tax rate, in addition to which the provincial government would provide funds to bring each board up to a provincially determined "expenditure ceiling." Despite many adjustments, this system remained in place until the 1990s, when the provincial government took control of local property taxes for education and developed a new provincial funding formula for school board finance. While subsequent governments have made adjustments to this formula, the basic principles of the system – a provincially determined property tax rate combined with a provincially determined allocation to each board – remains in place today.[4]

Local health units in Ontario, governed by boards of health, are responsible for health promotion and the prevention of disease – that is, for health issues that address entire populations and particular categories of citizens (new mothers, substance abusers, and so on) rather than individuals. Today, local boards of health set policies and budgets for their local health units within the boundaries of five provincially mandated areas of responsibility: community sanitation, disease control, health promotion, family health, and collection of epidemiological data.[5] The relative importance of each of these policy areas, as well as the local board's authority to determine how they will be provided, has evolved since the birth of public health policymaking in the nineteenth century. Since the 1980s, however, the Ontario government has been much more involved in setting the general mandatory policy areas for which local health units are responsible.

Local boards of health have traditionally had considerable authority to determine their own budgets and simply inform local councils of the amount that they will need. Unlike in the area of schools, however, this authority has not developed into a tradition of serious tension between boards of health and local councils. Not only are public health budgets typically quite small as a proportion of a municipality's overall costs, but as we will see, local councillors have often served on local boards of health, ensuring a more intimate link between public health and local council than in the case of education. As in the case of education, provincial financial support for public health programs has also grown in the post-war years – with the exception of a brief period of fiscal downloading by the Progressive-Conservative government of Mike Harris – so that about three-quarters of public health budgets in Ontario cities today are typically covered by provincial funds.[6]

The task of a municipal hydro utility – whether that task is administered by a municipal council, a hydro commission, or, more recently, a local distribution company – is to deliver electricity to homes and businesses within its geographic boundaries. Local utilities are responsibility for maintaining the electricity system's low-voltage distribution system (as opposed to high-voltage "transmission"), and within the confines of the province's broader regulatory context, the local hydro utility also sets and collects the rates at which final consumers will be charged for usage. Since 2004, local utilities have been required to charge customers according to a set of "regulated price plan" rates determined by the Ontario Energy Board. Any profits made by the municipally owned hydro commission, after setting aside funds for maintenance and reserves, are handed to the municipality.[7]

Chapter 5

Public School Boards

A light-haired boy stands in the foreground of the drawing, hands in pockets, his eyes fixed directly upon us. Behind him, around a dark wooden table, sit a woman and six men, all of them hunched forward, straining to see something on the table, a document perhaps, hidden from our view. In the caption below the drawing, the boy speaks. "Some call me the child of today," he says. "I am also the citizen of tomorrow." The words grow ever more refined, straining our credulity, like homework completed by a parent. "The present discussion over township boards or three-trustee boards by the people is, I believe, to decide which method will enable them to provide the best training for me," the boy says. "I am trusting to school boards, teachers, and the department of education to give me the best chance to prepare myself for the future."[1]

Inside the borders of this single drawing – the cover of the *Canadian School Board Journal* in April 1925 – is all that we need to grasp why school boards in Ontario have been, for more than two centuries, a subject of endless passion and dispute. The weight of parental hope, the perpetuation of civic virtue, the future of the nation: all of this presses down upon the men and women hunched around that table. Nowhere else does so humble an administrative structure bear so great a cultural burden; nowhere else could the eyes of a child be drafted into the service of so seemingly dry a debate. It is this, we will see, that makes the history of the school boards different from that of any other special purpose body in Ontario.

For the moment, however, we are getting ahead of ourselves. Before we can compare school boards to other special purpose bodies, we first need to understand the school boards themselves. This is the task of the present chapter. Our goal is to create an inventory of institutional changes in the field, and then to explain how and why those changes have occurred. As in our study of Kitchener, above, we will soon see that changes to school boards in Ontario are distinctly patterned over time; we will also see that the education field has for much of Ontario's history been divided into distinctly urban and rural components. The changes to public school boards that we will examine in this chapter originate in changes to the structure of these complex, and occasionally contentious, policy fields.

5.1 Local Structural Change in Education in Ontario: An Overview

In the history of education in Ontario, books are measured by the ton and archival materials by the mile. The available sources resemble nothing so much as a documentary tsunami, ready to crush the naive researcher in an instant. Lest this seem an exaggeration, consider just one among many astonishing facts: in the late nineteenth century, Ontario's Department of Education produced more correspondence than the British Colonial Office. More paper, in other words, was generated in administering the Ontario education system than in administering the entire British Empire.[2] While it may be tempting, given this flood of documents, to avoid the subject of education altogether, no treatment of local institutional change in Ontario could be convincing if it was missing a discussion of school boards. So let us build ourselves an ark and proceed.

To make our task manageable, we will restrict our focus in this chapter to *public school boards*. This means that we will focus on changes to those boards with responsibility for public, elementary-level education in the province. This is not so great a restriction as it may seem; not only have the separate school boards generally followed the structure of the public ones, but the story of the secondary school boards has intersected with that of the public schools so frequently and – after 1960 – so completely, that in telling the story of the public school board we will also survey a considerable portion of the secondary-level story as well.

We begin, then, with figure 5.1 and table 5.1, an inventory of structural changes to public school boards in Ontario from the early 1800s to the present. This inventory is not comprehensive – so many boards have existed, across so many municipalities, that we can find minor tweaks and adjustments in nearly every legislative session – but it does capture the most important changes over time. The figure captures the

Figure 5.1. Public School Boards in Ontario: Overview of Change Events

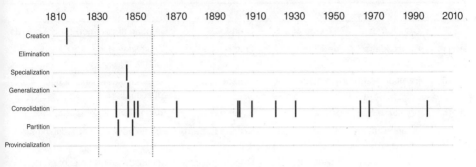

Note: See table 5.1 for a brief description of each event.

seven types of institutional change that we first described in chapter 1: creation and elimination; specialization, generalization, and provincialization; and consolidation and partition.

The figure suggests that we should begin our exploration by focusing on three broad episodes: the first in the early 1800s, when school boards were created; the second from 1840 to 1850, when the field underwent a frenzy of structural change; and the third from 1870 to the present, with a very long string of consolidation. Our goal is to understand this basic clustering, and to show how the shifts from one pattern to another originate in underlying shifts to the policy field.

5.2 Creating School Boards in Ontario, 1807–1816

School boards arrived in Ontario in two types: the district board and the common school board. The former, introduced in 1807, was created to administer the province's eight new grammar schools, which had been created to educate the children of the Upper Canadian elite.[3] Previously, parents had been forced to choose between sending their children to Britain – which few, even among the elite, could afford – or to the closer and less expensive schools in the United States. But an American education would mean an indoctrination into republicanism, the very doctrine that had torn America away from the empire. It was to avoid this terrible fate – a generation of Upper Canadian elites with republican educations – that the Upper Canadian grammar schools were created.[4]

Table 5.1. Event Catalogue: Public School Boards in Ontario

Year	Change type	Statute	Applicability	Description
1816	Creation	47 Geo III, c 6	Ontario	Creation of common school boards
1841	Consolidation	4–5 Vic, c 18	Ontario	Consolidated township school boards
1843	Partition	7 Vic, c 29	Ontario	Reversal of township school board consolidation
1846	Specialization	9 Vic, c20	Ontario	Trustee term lengths extended
1847	Generalization	10–11 Vic, c 19	Ontario (urban)	Appointed school board in cities and towns
1847	Consolidation	10–11 Vic, c 19	Ontario (urban)	Consolidated urban school boards
1849	Partition	12 Vic, c 83	Ontario (urban)	Consolidated urban school boards removed
1850	Consolidation	13–14 Vic, c 48	Ontario (urban)	Urban school boards reinstated
1853	Consolidation	16 Vic, c 186	Ontario	Provision for union board of education
1871	Consolidation	34 Vic., c.33	Ontario (rural)	Limited provision for township school boards
1903	Consolidation	3 Ed VII, c 31	Ontario (urban)	Consolidated boards of education in large cities
1904	Consolidation	4 Ed VII, c 33	Ontario (urban)	Consolidated boards of education (extended)
1909	Consolidation	9 Ed VII, c 94	Ontario (urban)	Consolidated boards of Education (extended)
1921	Consolidation	11 Geo V, c 89	Ontario (rural)	Provision for suburban township school units
1932	Consolidation	22 Geo V, c 42	Ontario (rural)	Provision for Township school boards
1930s	Consolidation	N/A	Ontario (rural)	73 voluntary township school boards created
1940s	Consolidation	N/A	Ontario (rural)	441 voluntary township school boards created
1950s	Consolidation	N/A	Ontario (rural)	38 voluntary township school boards created (to 1957)
1964	Consolidation	12 Eliz II, c 95	Ontario (rural)	Mandatory township school boards
1968	Consolidation	17 Eliz II, c 122	Ontario	Mandatory county school boards
1997	Consolidation	46 Eliz II, c 3	Ontario	School board consolidation

Note: This table provides the basic data for figure 5.1.

Sources: Statutes of Ontario; annual reports of the minister of education.

As early as 1800, the colonial secretary had suggested a general administrative structure for the new grammar schools: the board would consist of the governor, the lieutenant-governor, the bishop of Quebec, the chief justice of Upper Canada, and the speaker of the Assembly, along with three appointees "from among the most respectable of the inhabitants in the province."[5] This structure might well have been used if the original plan for the grammar schools, beginning with just two and expanding with the population, had been implemented. But regional jealousies meant not two but eight grammar schools, and for that reason, it seems, a simplified structure was needed. Each school would be administered by five men appointed by the Upper Canadian executive.[6] These would be institutions created for, and administered by, the Upper Canadian elite.[7]

The new schools were immediately the subject of withering attack in the elected legislative assembly. Critics proposed and passed bills to abolish the grammar schools, only to be blocked or ignored in the appointed legislative council.[8] This ongoing controversy has led some to interpret the 1816 Common Schools Act, which introduced government funding for common schools in Upper Canada, as a mere token, a self-protecting bone thrown out by the elites to appease the raving masses.[9] But a system of common schools had always been in the plans, and even the archest of arch-Tories – men like John Simcoe, John Cartwright, John Strachan – had explicitly endorsed the idea.[10] In fact, it was not the critics, but rather John Strachan himself, who composed the first draft of the 1816 bill.[11]

The structure of the common school boards was more complicated than the district boards. Any group of parents, having collected no fewer than twenty pupils, and having constructed a schoolhouse at their own expense, could elect three trustees to administer the school. The school would then be eligible for a grant to support the teacher's salary. Above the elected three-trustee board would be a district board of five executive-appointed men to oversee all of the common schools in the district.[12] The district board had considerable legal authority over the common school trustees, but the de facto reality was an extremely decentralized common school system with only the most minimal oversight.[13]

Where did this structure come from? Unfortunately, the available sources allow for little more than informed speculation. We do know that the broad structure was already present in Upper Canada in the form of the "subscription school," a school in which a group of residents would agree to support a school and would then elect some trustees to administer it.[14] We also know that the Upper Canadian statute resembles, in some respects, an 1812 school law from New York State, which also provided for elected three-man boards.[15] Contemporary observers noticed the similarities between the Upper Canadian law of 1816 and the New York law of 1812, and it would not be surprising, given New York's broader influence on local structures in Upper Canada, for the school provisions to have crossed the border as well.[16] There are as many differences between the two laws as there are similarities, but it may be that the New York common school structure provided a partial model for Upper Canadians.

Finally, and most speculatively, we can simply note that the three-person board was "in the air," as it were, during this period. Consider, for example, the recollections of a contemporary resident of Lancaster County, Pennsylvania: "Whenever a neighborhood felt in need of a schoolhouse, one was erected at some point convenient to those who contributed towards its erection. The patrons selected trustees, whose duty it was to take charge of the school property and to select a teacher for the school."[17]

Even in Pennsylvania, where state legislation for common schools would not arrive for many years, the same basic model had been used. What we *can* say, then, taking all of this together, is that the Upper Canadian model for the common school boards, consisting of a locally elected board of trustees to oversee a single schoolhouse, would have struck few as unfamiliar when it was introduced in Upper Canada in 1816.

By 1816, then, two laws existed, each of which created a distinctive form of local administration in Upper Canadian education. The first type, the district or grammar school board, was centrally appointed and would remain so until the 1850s. The second type, the common school board, consisted of local trustees who were elected at annual meetings. The first was designed to administer a decentralized but provincial system of elite grammar schools, and the second to aid a system of local, voluntary common schools. While the grammar schools were reviled by Reformers in Upper Canada, who would have preferred to eliminate them completely, the birth of the common schools was in no sense a defeat for the upper classes; from the beginning, most Upper Canadian elites believed that a system of grant-aided common schools was necessary, and desirable, for the province.

5.3 Challenge and Reform, 1831–1850

By the 1830s, both Tories and Reformers agreed that the Upper Canadian school system could use an update.[18] Proposals for change were plentiful already in the 1830s, and a few bills passed through the legislative assembly only to be rejected in the appointed legislative council. It was not until the creation of the United Province in 1841, and the election of a Reform coalition in that same year, that a significant school reform bill was finally passed into law.

When reform arrived, however, it arrived with force. The provisions of the new Common School Act of 1841 were radical: a new superintendent of schools, separate schools for religious minorities, new reporting requirements, and much more. For our purposes, however, the most important change was the total abolition of the three-person school board, replaced across the province by five-person boards for each of the province's rural municipalities, called townships. More than a century before Premier Bill Davis had dreamed of "township boards," they were already the reality in Ontario.[19]

The 1841 law represented the culmination of myriad reports and proposals, nearly all of which had advocated some form of township administration for the common schools.[20] The accepted wisdom was simple: township administration had worked elsewhere, and it would be effective in Upper Canada as well. But the new boards were an immediate disaster. In some townships, the school commissioners became "petty tyrants"; in others, the commissioners were so overwhelmed by their work that they simply closed all of their township's schools.[21] The legislation itself was very vague, and the appointment of a superintendent to administer the system was delayed. The result was "government-imposed chaos," a system that one critic described as "complex, mystical, overbearing, tyrannical, and unprecedented in Legislation."[22] After a year's trial, the township boards, which would become the subject of endless controversy in future decades, were consigned to the dustbin for the moment. In 1843, the government passed a statute returning the system to the former three-man boards.[23] Other alternatives appear not to have been considered; after the 1841 fiasco, no one was in the mood for experimentation.[24]

The 1843 statute was an improvement, but it still had a serious flaw. The government's intention was for the bill to pass alongside Robert Baldwin's 1843 municipal bill, but the Baldwin bill stalled in the legislature. This meant that some provisions of the school act, referring as they did to non-existent townships and counties, were rather confusing.[25] When the Reform bloc of 1841 was replaced by a Tory coalition in 1844, the new superintendent of schools for Upper Canada was asked to tidy up the legislation in a new draft bill.

That new superintendent was Egerton Ryerson. Ryerson had been involved in Upper Canadian educational debates for more than a decade, and had spent his first year as superintendent on a fact-finding mission of intercontinental proportions, travelling through Europe and the United States in search of models for Upper Canada to follow. Ryerson knew an opportunity when he saw one, and the draft bills that he submitted in 1846 and 1847, both of which passed, did much more than tinker around the edges. The new legislation made three major changes. First, the term of office for school trustees was extended from one year to three. Second, and more radically, three-person district boards were abolished in all incorporated municipalities, replaced by a single municipal board. Third, and still *more* radically, the new municipal boards were no longer elected, but would instead be appointed by municipal councils.[26]

Ryerson had a clear rationale for the changes. In cities and towns, he argued, "there should be a gradation, and therefore a system of Schools ... but such a system of Schools in a City or Town, involves one general system of management, and therefore, one authority."[27] And since those who make decisions about taxes and spending should be responsible to the people for those decisions, school trustees ought to be integrated into the municipal system itself. In theory, at least, it all made sense: if council was doing the taxing, it should also control the membership of the local school board.[28]

In practice, however, Ryerson's legislation was met with a torrent of rage. Vilified as a Prussian despot, a wolf in Methodist clothing, Ryerson was forced from offence to defence, explaining and defending his legislation in countless letters to politicians, newspapers, and concerned citizens.[29] By 1848, the administrative machinery had itself begun to strain. In Toronto, the city's municipally appointed school board requested an enormous sum from city council, an amount so large that it would require a quadrupling of local assessment. Council balked. How could it be, they complained, that a board that *we* appointed can now dictate to *us* about taxes? It was "an anomaly at once repugnant to British freedom and common sense."[30] The council sought the opinion of the attorney-general, who informed the council that it was required

by law to comply with the school board's request. Furious, council opted for an alternative solution: it closed the schools. For six months, the
doors to the common schools in the largest municipality in Upper
Canada were locked shut.[31]

The Toronto crisis gave the Reformers another opportunity to ham-
mer Ryerson as the "Prussian saddlebag centralizer" they suspected
him to be.[32] Ryerson had allies of his own, including some locals who
felt that the new legislation was an improvement,[33] but in a legislature
dominated by Reformers, Ryerson's position was precarious. In the
midst of the controversy, a Reformer named Malcolm Cameron submitted a bill eliminating Ryerson's municipal boards and radically weakening the position of the superintendent. Ryerson interpreted the bill as
a direct attack and threatened to resign. Robert Baldwin, worried about
what would certainly be a very public resignation, tiptoed away from
the Cameron statute and asked Ryerson to draw up a revised bill.[34]

Thus, in 1850, Ryerson drafted yet another bill. He preserved the basic
structure of his earlier system – three-person boards in rural areas, municipal boards in incorporated municipalities – but made all of the trustees elected again. Ryerson then summoned up his rhetorical strength
and went to work, declaring that the period of legislative experimentation in Upper Canada was complete. "After successive years of somewhat indefinite legislation in school affairs," wrote Ryerson, "we have at
length reached that calm and settled period in our educational history
when the fruits of our united toil and labour will be permitted to ma-
ture and ripen to an abundant and glorious harvest."[35] This time, even
the critics agreed. After a decade of constant change, the foundation
had finally set, and would remain in place for nearly a century.

Is it possible to neatly summarize this remarkable decade of change?
The honest answer, probably, is no: this was a period of extraordinary
complexity, perhaps the most interesting and important decade in
Canadian history, a period to be explained in chapters and books, not
paragraphs. We can make a beginning, however, if we notice that the
policy images relating to education in this period were both deeply
held and weakly resourced. For both Tories and Reformers, the school
board debates in this period were linked to arguments about local autonomy, religious liberty, and representative taxation, arguments that
drilled to the very core of Tory and Reform self-understandings. But the
institutional context of the same period was so unpredictable, with frequent shifts in the legislature, unstable executive-legislative relations,
and an extremely circumscribed civil service, that neither the Tories nor

the Reformers could cement their preferred structures in place. It was a period of "bureaucratic pluralism" – weak state structures, a multiplicity of policy actors, and no clear institutional "home" for a policy task like education.[36] It was not until 1850, when responsible government had been established, the party system had begun to stabilize, and Ryerson had established a clear bureaucratic home for education policy, that the endless reforms of the 1840s finally began to subside.

5.4 Consolidation Attempts, 1865–1873

By the late 1860s, Ryerson was nearing retirement.[37] The school system he had overseen for more than two decades was not quite the one he had imagined in the 1840s, but on the most important battlefront, Ryerson's victory was complete: by 1870, fully 97 per cent of Ontario's public schools were tax supported, or "free."[38] But there was work to do before Ryerson could retire happily, and that work included two important structural reforms.[39] First, Ryerson hoped to consolidate rural school districts at the township level, thereby completing in rural Ontario what he had accomplished in towns and cities back in 1847. Second, in urban areas, Ryerson hoped to combine common school boards and grammar school boards into unified boards of education.

To explain these proposals, Ryerson set out across the province in the winter of 1866, and again in the winter of 1869, holding conventions in nearly every county in Ontario.[40] It is all too easy, in our age of multi-lane highways and online communication, to underestimate the importance of these conventions. Not only were they exceptionally well-attended – an audience of 100, even in the midst of a terrific blizzard, was considered an embarrassment[41] – they also went for hours, sometimes lasting through the afternoon and well into the evening. Nor should we forget the hardships of the county tours for Ryerson himself, who was then in his sixties. "I had a hard and cold drive, yesterday forenoon, from Brantford to Simcoe," wrote Ryerson, in one of many instances of discomfort, "through the furious snowstorm in an open buggy; but I had a grand rest last night, and am all right to-day."[42] A grand rest indeed; one suspects that such a ride today would put most of us to sleep forever.

Whatever the hardships, Ryerson travelled from county to county, delivering a lengthy stump speech at each stop (running to two or three hours) and defending his proposals against critics. In 1866, the focus was township boards. Ryerson's first idea was that the rural schools be turned over to township councils – he still believed that it was best to give the schools directly to those with the authority to tax – but it was immediately clear that this proposal was a non-starter, hated by trustees and councillors alike.[43] Ryerson compromised, suggesting an elected township board instead, and pointed to examples in places like Massachusetts and Ohio to demonstrate the advantages of larger rural boards.

What were those advantages? For Ryerson, who never gave one reason where ten would do, the list was long: a simplified system, an end to disputes about district boundaries, graded schools in rural Ontario, more stable employment for teachers, a more egalitarian tax system, and so on.[44] At the county conventions, Ryerson focused his attention on the advantages of the new boards for parents and trustees. In private, however, Ryerson admitted some doubts about the township boards, even while he was defending them during his tour: "The doings in the very states where the Township Boards obtain are so very far behind what I had expected and what we are doing in this Country, and so many of them reduce compliance with the conditions to the lowest minimum, that my anticipations as to the results of the Township System are hardly as sanguine as they were, especially where a majority of the townships are non-progressive. But still I am satisfied that the Township Board is a remedy for many evils, and an important step in advance, and that we can make it work much better than they do in the United States."[45]

Ryerson's loyal deputy in Toronto responded with encouragement, writing that Ontarians would "be able to work Township Boards vastly better than they do in the United States." Despite his doubts, Ryerson agreed.[46] A township system would help to do away with rural trustees who were regularly derided as illiterate, stingy, and uncomprehending of the world, trustees who, in the words of one man in Stratford, were "chosen simply to be obstructives – for the purpose of having no school – to prevent a school being built."[47]

Ryerson persuaded twenty-five county conventions in 1866 to pass resolutions in support of his township board proposal. Eleven voted against.[48] Ryerson was encouraged by this result, but he also realized that it was not decisive enough to justify a mandatory provision. So when he returned to the road in 1869, Ryerson offered his audiences a voluntary township system in place of the mandatory version; having made this change, the provision was widely endorsed.[49]

The major structural issue in 1869, however, was not the township board but the urban board of education. The basic problem that Ryerson hoped to solve had been brewing for decades. Under the existing system, in place since the 1850s, grammar school trustees could meet together with common school trustees, combining their funds (local tax revenue from the common schools and the provincial grammar school fund) to provide a "union school" for local pupils. According to the provincial inspectors, however, the result was to make the grammar schools into nothing more than glorified common schools. When Ryerson learned what had been done in New York, Boston, and elsewhere to solve this problem – the wholesale union of grammar and common schools under a single elected board – he believed he had found the solution. An urban board of education would unlink the urban schools from the county councils, would allow urban communities to develop an integrated system of education, and would provide grammar schools with the local tax revenue that they so desperately needed.[50]

During the 1869 county tour, this proposal provoked little controversy. But the reason for the quiet reception was largely structural: the conventions began with the common schools and *then* discussed the grammar schools. Discussion of the common schools went on for hours, and by the time the grammar schools came up, audiences were exhausted. There *were* a few common objections to the change, the most important of which was that an elected grammar school board would exclude the best trustees, such as clergymen, who would have no interest in the worldly grime of a local election campaign. In general, however, Ryerson's grammar school provisions were endorsed by the exhausted few who remained at the county conventions until the very end.[51]

Thus, when Ryerson presented his school board proposals to his political superiors in the early 1870s, he could claim with only a little exaggeration that they had been endorsed by interested local citizens from one end of the province to the other.[52] But Ryerson's lengthy efforts proved to be in vain. Although the school legislation that passed in 1871 was historic in other respects – it made tax-supported "free" schools mandatory – on the matter of school board structure, little changed. A tepid provision for voluntary township boards was included in the legislation, permitting consolidation only after a majority vote in two-thirds of the township's school sections. On the matter of urban municipal boards, even less had changed, with common (now "public") boards and grammar (now "high school") boards remaining strictly separate. Despite months of travel, gallons of ink, and hours of speeches, Ryerson's structural program was incomplete when he finally retired in 1876.

The reason for Ryerson's failure was partly personal. The late 1860s and early 1870s marked Ryerson's most fraught relationship with his political superiors since the volatile 1840s. While he travelled across the province in 1869, Ryerson was involved in an ongoing and increasingly serious dispute with two Cabinet ministers, the provincial treasurer and the provincial secretary, the stress of which drove his loyal deputies in Toronto nearly to the brink of collapse.[53] And if Ryerson's relationship with the Conservatives was tense, his relationship with Edward Blake, leader of the Liberals, was downright venomous.[54] Ryerson had few defenders in the legislature by the early 1870s, and the debates on the reform bills that he proposed were remarkable in their personal hostility towards Ryerson himself.[55]

Beyond the breakdown in personal trust, legislators on both sides of the aisle in Ontario had serious doubts about Ryerson's proposals. On the township boards, the primary concern was fairness. If one district had recently built or renovated a school, and was then forced to enter a township board, would it not be unfair to ask the residents of that district to pay for renovations in school sections that had not been so progressive?[56] As for the urban municipal boards, many Ontario legislators insisted that the cure was worse than the disease: grammar school funding under the new system would be funnelled even more completely into the common schools as grammar school trustees, among the most well-respected men in the county, were replaced by illiterate elected demagogues.[57] Ryerson attempted to meet this concern, suggesting that a portion of the new board of education might still be appointed, but his efforts failed.[58] By the time the legislation passed, all that remained was a weak provision for township boards, and no provision of any kind for boards of education.

5.5 Urban Consolidation, 1900–1910

Those who were old enough to remember Ryerson's county visits in the late 1860s might have experienced a feeling of déjà-vu when they opened their newspapers in 1903. The municipal board of education was back. Four decades after Ryerson had first proposed it, Richard Harcourt, Ontario's enthusiastic and progressive minister of education, stood in the legislature to announce that the sixty-five trustees who were currently administering Toronto's public schools, high schools, and technical schools would be merged into a single, elected, twelve-person board.[59] Citing New York, Chicago, Philadelphia, and England as examples, Harcourt argued that the bill was "a very important one in an educational sense, and that if successful in Toronto would doubtless be extended to other cities" in Ontario as well.[60]

The other cities proved impatient. One year after he had introduced the Toronto legislation, Harcourt was back in the legislature with another bill, explaining that "since the establishment of the Board of Education in Toronto petitions have been received by the Government from a number of municipalities, asking that the act be extended."[61] And so it was: first in 1904 to cities, towns, and villages that were not part of a high school district, and then in 1909 to any municipality in which the high school district was coterminous with the municipality.[62]

We need not dwell on this episode for long. The legislation was entirely uncontroversial and received only limited coverage in Ontario newspapers; even the province's specialized education journals seemed to think the changes too obvious for extended comment. Because the law was permissive, rather than mandatory, it was wholly uncontroversial at the local level as well. Those who wanted the change could have it, and those who did not could simply ignore the new statute.

By the early twentieth century, then, the undemocratic arguments of the 1870s had lost their force in the face of the desperate need for consolidation. The new statute had bipartisan support, and the program that began under the Liberals in 1904 was continued by the Conservatives after 1905. The law *was* restricted slightly in 1911, when a requirement for a local referendum was added to the bill – but the general trend towards consolidated urban boards continued.[63] In urban Ontario, wholesale consolidation had begun. But it would be fifty years before elementary and secondary boards would finally unite across the province as a whole.

5.6 Township School Boards, 1925–1932

Ryerson's proposal for urban boards of education had been enacted at the turn of the twentieth century, but it was another twenty years before his other structural proposal – township school boards – returned to the top of the agenda. Although the possibility of rural consolidation had been discussed, here and there, for many years, it was not until Howard Ferguson became premier in 1923 that real reform became a possibility again.

For Ferguson and his Department of Education staff – Ferguson retained the position of minister of education while serving as premier

– the problems were tragically clear. Since the late nineteenth century, rural Ontario had been emptying out, as the children of Ontario farmers joined thousands of new immigrants in urban centres to pursue urban employment and the comforts of modern life.[64] This rural depopulation had culminated, in the aftermath of the conscription debates of the First World War, in the one-term triumph of the United Farmers of Ontario.[65] In the field of education, an internal departmental memo addressed to Ferguson explained that the demographic changes in rural Ontario created "at least three serious conditions in the rural school situation which should be remedied."[66] First, attendance was inefficiently low; schools that were once "filled with forty children now shiver with a beggarly half-dozen."[67] The department's own statistics bore this out. In 1922, for example, six schools had an average daily attendance of two or fewer; in nearly a quarter of the province's schools, fewer than ten students attended class each day.[68]

The second problem was that "the cost of maintaining the schools in any township is not fairly spread among the ratepayers." This was particularly true in the freshly settled parts of the province, where, according to one writer in the *Canadian School Board Journal*, the "Trustee levy varies in Ontario from 3 or 4 mills on the dollar in some sections to 60 and even 70 mills on the dollar in others."[69]

Lastly, the memo explained, "the opportunities for High School education are inadequate and unequally distributed" in Ontario. While urban students could access a high school within walking distance of their home, secondary schooling was miles away from many rural pupils.[70] "These conditions can be remedied," the author of the memo concluded, "only by securing adequate cooperation among the trustees in the rural municipalities. The purpose of the proposed Bill for Township Boards was to provide means for securing such cooperation."

Howard Ferguson agreed. Ferguson was genuinely concerned about equality for rural pupils and was distressed by the differences between the opportunities of rural and urban pupils: "Why should rural communities not have advantages in their elementary schools similar to those enjoyed by urban municipalities? Why should a high school education not be accessible to every rural child? Why should he not have the same opportunity as the urban child to choose a course that meets his needs? ... I am convinced that there is no good reason why all these facilities should not be at his disposal, and we should not be satisfied with the educational situation in this Province till these advantages are brought to the door of every rural child."[71]

The township school board, which would equalize taxation across the township and provide for more coherent overall planning, would go some way towards resolving this inequality. Thus, on April 1, 1925, Ferguson stood in the House and introduced a bill requiring the mandatory consolidation of all school district boards into five-person township boards of trustees.

Ferguson did not intend to pass the bill. Instead, his plan was to introduce it, discuss it in the legislature, and then withdraw it for consideration at the upcoming meeting of the Ontario Educational Association.[72] The goal was gradual persuasion: each year, he would introduce the bill and push it a step further – now through first reading, now second, now into committee – before once again withdrawing the bill for further review.[73] Perhaps, after two or three years, the bill could slide all the way through to the lieutenant-governor's desk without rancour.[74]

Unfortunately for Ferguson, the story of the township boards bill was less a Whig tale of progress than a Nietzchean story of the eternal return of the same. Every year, Ferguson introduced the bill, and every year, trustees at the annual Ontario Educational Association meeting "jumped to their feet hilariously to yell and wave their approval of a resolution" to reject the township boards.[75] Ferguson often discovered, having made the evening trek from Queen's Park to the University of Toronto's Convocation Hall to check in on the OEA proceedings, that his bill had been rejected before he had even been given a chance to defend it.[76] It was a frustrating process, and in one letter, A.H.U. Colquhoun, Ferguson's deputy minister, joked darkly about a solution. "Have the Criminal Code modified by this Legislature," Colquhoun suggested. "I would respectfully request you to revise the clause respecting murder so that I could dispose of the whole Trustee Association after due notice to their families."[77]

Ferguson wisely decided not to murder the trustee association, nor did he choose, despite some threats, to simply ram the bill through the legislature. Ferguson might have resolved the deadlock had he been willing to soften the legislation, making township boards voluntary.[78] Unlike Ryerson, however, Ferguson was resistant to a permissive provision, believing that the result would be an administrative crazy-quilt, one more complication in an already overcomplicated system.[79] Ferguson's successor, George Stewart Henry, did not share this reticence, and in 1932, the Henry government passed a statute allowing township councils to voluntarily reorganize their school sections into township boards. Figure 5.2 illustrates the results. In the next twenty

Figure 5.2: Township School Board Adoption in Ontario, 1937–1957

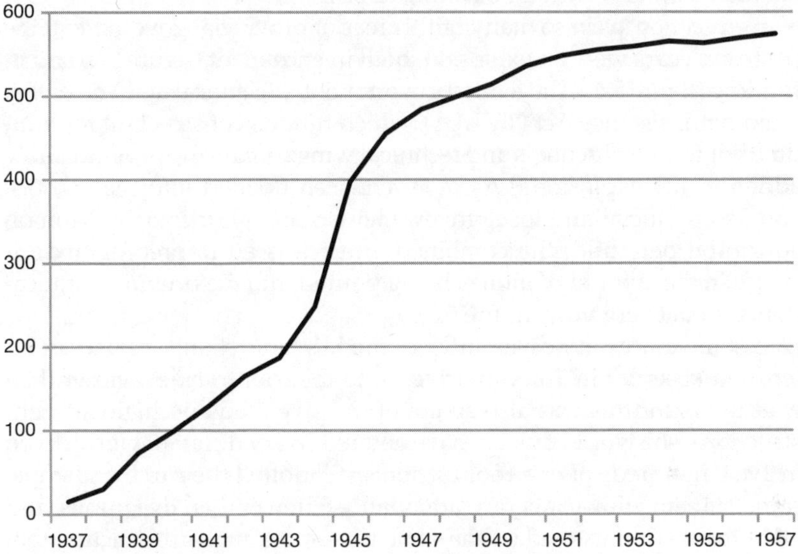

Source: Annual reports of the minister of education, Ontario.

years, especially after 1938, when the Department of Education decided to promote the township board with financial incentives, more than half of the school district boards in Ontario were reorganized into township sections.[80]

5.7 School Board Consolidation, 1964–1969

By the time William Davis became minister of education, under Premier John Robarts, in 1962, Howard Ferguson's worries about permissive boards had proved prescient. The province was indeed a patchwork. Union boards, boards of education, township boards, separate school boards: all of these and more dotted the landscape, making the administrative map of Ontario's education structures look like a painting by Mondrian.[81] Moreover, as figure 5.2 suggests, the rate of adoption of voluntary boards had slowed to a crawl. While this may not have meant that the voluntary process had reached its natural endpoint – we will have more to say about this below – it certainly led those involved in education in the 1950s to believe that further adoption of township boards in Ontario would be halting at best.[82]

In education, as in so many other areas of provincial government, the post-war years were an explosion, both in enrolment (figure 5.3) and in funding (figure 5.4). The federal government's Technical and Vocational Training Assistance Act (TVTAA), which funded construction for hundreds of technical schools and technical wings across the province, only added to the explosion.[83] As more children flooded into the schools, and as provincial and local governments spent an increasing sum on education per child, the combined effect was an unprecedented increase in the amount of money being poured into the provincial education system every year (figure 5.5).

In some places, however, little seemed to have changed. Had an interested observer in Toronto driven into the countryside – easier than ever to do, for this was also an era of massive road and highway construction – she would quickly have entered a very different world. Even in 1964, hundreds of one-room schools still dotted the rural landscape, some of them with an average attendance of fewer than five pupils, and all of them administered by the same three-person board structure that had been in place in Ontario for nearly 150 years.[84]

Like Ferguson, Davis and Robarts were deeply committed to equality of opportunity for Ontario pupils. The Ontario Foundation Tax Plan (OFTP), which had been developed by Robarts and his staff in the early 1960s, had been a first attempt to equalize education funding across Ontario; on Robarts's instruction, however, the plan was developed to accommodate very small school boards.[85] But no amount of formula tweaking could hide the fact that the three-person board, overseeing the one-room school, was a barrier to full equality; the larger schools were able to offer broader and more specialized curricula and programming simply for reasons of scale.[86] Eventually, after brief resistance, Robarts and Davis bowed to the overwhelming consensus within the Department of Education.[87] On February 27, 1964, William Davis rose in the legislature to introduce a bill that would permanently abolish the school-district board. "I think … Honourable Members will agree," said Davis, "that these amendments mark something of a milestone in the administration of the school boards in this province."[88] On January 1, 1965, for the first time since 1841, the township board became the smallest local unit of administration for education in the Province of Ontario. The government's decision to abolish the school district board provoked complaints among rural trustees, and Robert

Figure 5.3. School Enrolment in Ontario, 1930–1960

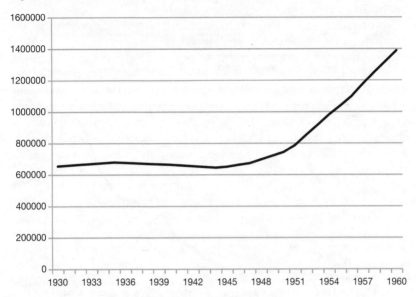

Source: Annual reports of the minister of education, Ontario.

Nixon, a member of the Ontario Liberals, took the opportunity to squeeze in a sound bite of nostalgic lament for the death of the "little red schoolhouse." But the Liberals ultimately supported the bill, which passed into law with little fuss.[89]

Davis and his ambitious staff had no intention of stopping at township boards. The 1964 legislation contained a requirement for a "County Consultative Committee," whose task was to consider the feasibility of even larger units of administration. In the years that followed, Davis made no secret of the fact that larger units would be advantageous for education. Teaching and administrative staff had become professional and knowledgeable, Davis argued, and it no longer made sense for the Department of Education to be making decisions that could safely be left to the boards themselves. Moreover, the administrative division between primary and secondary schooling at the local level had become an anachronism, particularly after the department had restructured its own internal operations to dissolve the division between primary and secondary education. What was needed was a board of education large

Figure 5.4. Provincial and Local Sources of School Board Revenue in Ontario, 1900–2011

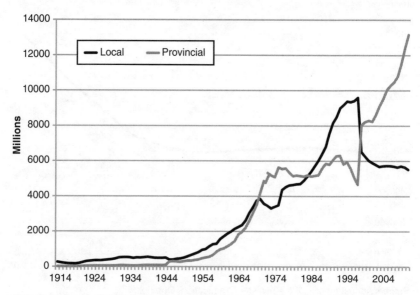

Note: Sources of school board revenue in Ontario, adjusted to constant 2002 dollars.
Source: CANSIM table 4780010.

enough to handle both primary and secondary schooling, well-funded enough to provide a necessary supply of administrative experts, special education consultants, and supervisory personnel, and democratic enough to guarantee ongoing local legitimacy.[90]

A number of alternatives were considered, but in an attempt to maintain some semblance of order in the local taxation system, and with a nod to tradition, the government decided that the optimal unit for the larger boards, for the moment at least, was the county.[91] On November 14, 1967, in Galt, Ontario, Premier Robarts announced the plan. A short while later, Davis stood again in the legislature to announce the county boards, "the most significant development in the organizational structure for education," he said, "in the history of this province."[92] He was hardly exaggerating: with the 1968 legislation, the educational structure of the province had been transformed from one that would still have been recognizable to Egerton Ryerson to one that was radically new.

Figure 5.5. Provincial and Local Education Revenue, Proportions, 1914–2011

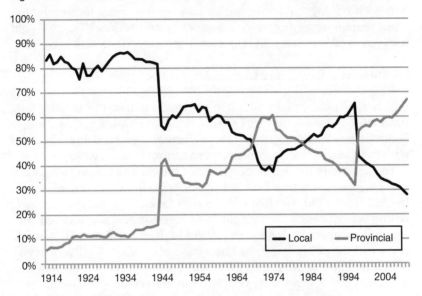

Source: CANSIM table 4780010.

It did not take long before county school boards came to be taken for granted. Initially, however, they sparked considerable controversy. In the legislature, Nixon and others questioned the wisdom of the county as the administrative unit, a weak argument made weaker by the fact that the Liberal party had proposed county boards in its own election manifesto.[93] Teachers' and trustees' associations complained about a lack of consultation, though Davis and his officials insisted that no one could have been surprised by the government's decision.[94] A few local newspapers wrote scathing editorials, arguing that county boards were the sharp edge of a centralizing axe. "Local autonomy," predicted the editor of the *Simcoe Reformer,* "will become a relic of the past both in educational matters and in the whole range of civic administration."[95] Overall, however, while the criticism provoked considerable heat in the legislature and a certain amount of concern within the Conservative caucus, the criticisms of the bill were largely procedural.[96] Most accepted both the major premise, educational equality, and the minor one, the need for larger units.[97] The bill passed into law, and in 1969, the county boards were born. The new boards quickly became the complex and professionally staffed organizations for which Davis and his colleagues had been hoping.[98] But could they take on their new responsibilities while remaining legitimate local democratic institutions? This, it would turn out, would become an important question in the years to come.[99]

5.8 Interlude: Explaining Consolidation

We are now finally in a position to pause to evaluate this century-long process of consolidation in Ontario. Why did Davis succeed where Ferguson and Ryerson had not? What changes allowed Davis to proceed with the changes that had once been so controversial even to propose?

The answer to these changes involves the conjunction of two crucial changes, each of which affected the distribution of resources within the education field. The first was support for educational restructuring within the education policy field itself. Egerton Ryerson enjoyed considerable support from his staff and could draw on his county tours to claim that the public supported his proposals as well. But Ryerson was not elected and could not count on support from the provincial Cabinet, a fact that became increasingly clear, to Ryerson's irritation, in the 1860s and 1870s.[100] The arguments that Ryerson had once used to establish his independence from the political chaos of the 1840s had now come back to haunt him, and Ryerson ultimately came to see the advantages of having a seat at the Cabinet table from which to defend his proposals.[101]

The situation was different with Ferguson and Davis. Unlike Ryerson, both of these men were ministers of education and were strong voices at the Cabinet table. Ferguson, of course, was also the premier, which meant that the minister-to-premier conversation took place within his own brain. Davis's relationship with the premier was not *quite* that close, but Davis was nevertheless serving under a man, John Robarts, who respected Davis and who had spent two years in the Ministry of Education himself.[102] In contrast to the Ryerson years, support for local structural change in the 1920s and the 1960s went all the way up to the top of the pyramid.

Cabinet-level support, then, was the first important change. The second was *rural opposition*. To understand Davis's success requires that we recognize a central aspect of the consolidation debate from 1860 to 1960: it was, from the beginning, a *rural* issue. The exact administrative equivalent of the township board had been installed in urban areas in 1847 and had never been seriously questioned after 1850. In urban areas, consolidation was a non-issue; it was in rural Ontario that the battle over school consolidation would be won or lost.

An event in the 1920s makes this especially clear. At precisely the same time that Ferguson was proposing and then withdrawing his township board bill, his government passed a statute permitting consolidated boards in townships that bordered on urban areas.[103] The statute was designed to accommodate early suburbanization, especially in the areas surrounding Toronto, and was adopted for the first time in North York in 1928 – just as Ferguson's township bill was generating such hostility from local trustees.[104] The problem, once again, was rural. And to understand how it developed, we need to briefly return to each of the three major episodes in this story – Ryerson in the 1860s, Ferguson in the 1920s, and Davis in the 1960s – in a bit more detail.

What is odd, at first glance, is that support for township boards appears to have *decreased* between the Ryerson and the Ferguson years. In 1866, Ryerson was able to convince more than three-fifths of the county conventions to pass resolutions endorsing mandatory township boards, and when he made the boards voluntary in 1869, all but four of the conventions endorsed his scheme.[105] By 1920, however, Ferguson's proposal, virtually identical to Ryerson's 1866 draft, was firmly rejected by trustees. Two changes help to account for this difference.

The first is organization. Ryerson's basic strategy was to travel from county to county, discussing his proposals with all who attended the county conventions. Naturally, the meetings were held in urban centres, and attracted a great mix of people, some from the city and others from the countryside. These meetings put Ryerson at an advantage. Because much of his audience – those from urban areas – had lived under consolidated boards for decades, Ryerson could assume that some of his listeners would be receptive to the notion that what was working in the cities ought to be extended to the townships as well.[106] Moreover, Ryerson was always the best-informed person in the room, always equipped with examples and evidence, always ready to explain how his proposals had been tried with success elsewhere in the world.[107] The attendees were not pushovers, of course, and they sometimes resisted Ryerson quite strenuously. But the structure of the conventions gave Ryerson a very real opportunity to persuade his listeners of the value of his suggestions. In a non-trivial number of cases, people arrived at the conventions prepared to reject Ryerson's proposals, only to be persuaded during the meeting that there was nothing to be feared in adopting them.[108]

In the Ferguson era, the organizational picture was very different. Ferguson was no less interested than Ryerson in seeking the endorsement of local representatives before passing his legislation. But the process by which Ferguson sought that endorsement had changed. Rather than travel from county to county, defending his legislation in a favourable (if not always friendly) environment, Ferguson defended his legislation before the provincial education association, which was then dominated by its vocal and active trustees section.[109] The trustees were barely interested in Ferguson's arguments; indeed, as we noted above, they sometimes rejected the township board proposal before Ferguson had even arrived at the meeting to speak. Whereas Ryerson entered the county conventions from a position of strength, Ferguson walked onstage at the OEA annual meetings in a position of considerable weakness.

This organizational difference tilted the scales against Ferguson. But a second factor was even more important: a difference in the two periods about the purpose of the township board. The crucial difference was the consolidated school, a multi-room building that organizes students into graded classes, the kind of school that is now standard in public education in Ontario. The consolidated school had become popular in Ontario as part of the "new education" movement around the turn of the twentieth century, and a number of rural reformers saw the consolidated school as an important component in any attempt to stem the tide of rural depopulation.[110] In Ryerson's era, however, which predated the new education movement by several decades, the rural consolidated school was not a viable option. Ryerson occasionally expressed the hope that a larger township board might mean that schools could occasionally be combined or divided on the basis of local population fluctuations, and he was also interested in promoting the graded school.[111] But no one who knew the pitiful condition of Ontario's roads as intimately as Ryerson did could possibly have imagined a system of centralized, consolidated schools in the 1860s. Instead, when Ryerson defended the township boards, he focused on their benefits for parents, who could send their children to the nearest school (rather than the school that happened to be in their district) and for teachers, who could be moved to a different school whenever they were getting "stale."[112]

Some of Ryerson's arguments remained attractive to Ferguson and others in the 1920s.[113] But the real motivation for township boards under Ferguson, the problem that prompted Ferguson to advocate the township system so passionately, was attendance. Between 1860 and 1920, the one-two punch of rural depopulation and urbanization meant that rural schools faced perversely low attendance rates at the same time that enrolment in urban schools was exploding.[114] The obvious solution was a consolidated rural school: instead of a system of underpopulated one-room schools, one or more larger schools could be built in central locations throughout the township. The new schools would allow for multiple teachers, graded classes, and more flexibility in the face of demographic change. Ferguson's advisers had little doubt that township school trustees, who would be responsible for students across the township as a whole, would come to the same conclusion.[115] In the absence of some form of school consolidation, it is impossible to make sense of Ferguson's most common arguments for township school boards.[116]

There was just one problem: many rural trustees, or at least the most vocal among them, were stridently opposed to consolidated schools. Critics argued that central schools would negatively influence their children, drawing them away from the farm and towards the urban professions and the vices of urban life.[117] There were also more quotidian concerns: the roads were still terrible, and transportation technology was in its infancy. Of the 116 vehicles transporting students to consolidated schools in 1935, fewer than half were motorized; the remainder were pulled by horse.[118] One woman in Norval, Ontario, summarized the problem plainly: "Health is emphasized in capital letters in the new curriculum, and yet this plan is advocated of having little children wait in snow or rain or the bitter cold of our Ontario winters for a van that may be stuck for hours in a snow-bank while they freeze. Many roads are blocked for weeks for motor traffic and no regular schooling could be obtained if we were dependent on a motor van, and the hazards of icy roads."[119]

Taken together, then, an organizational context that put Ferguson on the defensive, combined with deep rural opposition to consolidated schools, meant that Ferguson had to abandon his most powerful argument for the township system, insisting again and again that there was no necessary relationship between township boards and consolidated schools.[120] This was true enough – a township board did not *necessitate* a consolidated school – but any thinking person could see the obvious connection. Thus the rural trustees came to be the guardians of the "little red schoolhouse," the defenders of rural tradition against centralizing tyrants like Ferguson.[121]

When we turn from the 1920s to the 1960s, the differences are glaring. In the first place, William Davis rejected the notion that the support of

Ontario's rural trustees was necessary before proceeding with structural change.[122] The principal reason for this was funding. As figure 5.5 shows, the overwhelming source of educational spending (nearly 90 per cent) during the Ferguson years was local taxation, and for that reason, the system was still widely viewed as a matter best left to locals. "I have always felt," wrote Ferguson, "that since the ratepayers pay for and must actually operate the school system, the Department should not arbitrarily impose new conditions ... if the local trustee board chooses to continue unnecessary expenditure, and the ratepayers approve of it, I suppose they have that right."[123] By the 1960s, however, nearly 40 per cent of school board revenues were now coming from the province, producing a change in basic attitudes on the necessity of local consultation.

The situation in rural Ontario had also changed enormously. The "little red schoolhouse" still had some appeal in the 1960s, but references to such schools took on an increasing note of nostalgia, a grudging acceptance that the one-room schoolhouse belonged to a world that was now fading away.[124] The great rural dispute between the resisters and the adopters – between those who wanted to build walls between rural and urban society and those who wanted to promote rural life by extending modern comforts into the countryside – had been won by the adopters.[125] In many places, the countryside had come to resemble the cities, as townships around major cities absorbed new suburban population growth.[126] And whereas 52 per cent of primary school students had gone on to high school in the early 1920s, the number had reached 94 per cent by 1959, which meant that parents had grown accustomed to more distant schools and to the yellow school buses, driving atop much-improved roads, that were quickly becoming a new staple of the rural landscape.[127] Thus, while the township board proposal continued to involve considerable political risk, Davis was by the 1960s free at least to state the obvious: township school boards meant consolidated schools, and the end of the one-room schoolhouse.[128]

In some ways, the rural education field in the 1960s still resembled the field from a century earlier. It was still contentious, with considerable disagreement about purposes and jurisdiction between provincial officials on the one hand and rural trustees on the other.[129] By the 1960s, however, the strength of those who defended these two positions in the field had shifted decisively. In an earlier era, rural Ontario enjoyed widespread cultural authority (even in urban areas), it was articulate and well-organized, and education was funded almost entirely at the local level.[130] By the 1960s, all of this had changed. No longer was education exclusively, or even primarily, funded by local taxation. No longer was rural Ontario the cultural heart of the province. No longer was rural opposition grounded in a critique of urban squalor, a critique that had come to seem old-fashioned. The result, after more than a century of debate, was rural school board consolidation.

5.9 Consolidation and Reorganization, 1995–1998

By June 1995, when Mike Harris's Progressive Conservative Party won a surprising majority victory in Ontario, school boards had become exactly what Bill Davis had hoped: large and sophisticated bureaucracies with the capacity to provide specialized services like psychological assessment, special education for disabled and gifted students, and advanced technical support and training. More than half of the province's school boards had more than 10,000 students enrolled, and thirteen boards had more than 40,000 students attending school within their boundaries.[131] But two problems had emerged. First, while education spending had increased since the Davis years, provincial education spending had not, meaning that school boards were increasingly dependent on local tax revenue (see figure 5.4 above). This trend, combined with the provincial government's decision to permit school boards to spend beyond their provincially defined "expenditure ceilings," meant that the educational spending gap between assessment-rich and assessment-poor parts of the province was widening. In report after report, a broader equalization of educational spending – either through pooling of local tax revenue, increased provincial spending, or both – had been recommended, to little avail.[132]

The second challenge was legitimacy. Since the Davis years, the new school boards had been subjected to ongoing and increasingly scathing attack, accused of providing education of declining quality at increasing expense, and of wasting funds on administrative costs rather than – in what would soon become a 50,000-volt term – on "classroom spending."[133] Under governments of all persuasions, a consensus had emerged that *something* had to be done about the problem of education finance and school board administration. The NDP's minister of education, Dave Cooke, argued that the school system was top-heavy with board-level administration, and suggested that further consolidation was in order; the authors of his government's Royal Commission on Learning, released just months before the NDP government's defeat, explicitly disagreed.[134] In early 1995, it remained to be seen how Mike Harris, a former school board chair, and John Snobelen, a business owner and self-appointed change management guru, would attack the problem.

The first manoeuvre was no surprise: $400 million in spending cuts to education, part of a wider program of retrenchment in the government's economic statement of November 1995.[135] To soften the blow, 78 per cent of the province's school boards immediately raised property taxes.[136] Harris was furious, interpreting the move as the boards' refusal to take their medicine like the others. "Old spending habits didn't just die hard," wrote John Ibbitson, "they didn't die at all. From that moment on, the days of the boards were numbered."[137]

John Snobelen, the minister of education, had already begun to explore his options. Soon after he had been appointed, Snobelen met with John Sweeney, a former Liberal Cabinet minister who had served as director of education for a Catholic school board and who done research for the Bob Rae government on school board consolidation. Like many others, Sweeney believed that the quality of students' education should not depend on their geographic location – and thus that the education system ought to be reformed to equalize fiscal capacity across the province. But Sweeney also believed that much too much money was being spent on board-level administration. John Snobelen agreed with both arguments, but it was the latter claim, which Sweeney defended in a 1996 report, that excited him the most.[138] Snobelen expected that Sweeney's report "was going to give him extra ammunition," and when the report did indeed claim that too much money was being spent at the board level, Snobelen quickly added it to his rhetorical arsenal.[139] "We must design the entire educational system as a service organization," said Snobelen, "and we must ask ourselves if we could be giving our customers better value for their tax dollar."[140] Snobelen had decided to grapple with the education system, including the structure of the local boards. What remained was to decide just what, exactly, was to be done.

The first option was the most radical: abolish the boards.[141] To preserve a bit of local control and autonomy, a few minor powers could be decentralized to the parents' councils that had been created under the Rae government in every school in the province.[142] Infrastructure and transportation could be handled by the municipalities, which were already experts in hard services. Everything else – curriculum, finance, administration – could be uploaded to the province. In a single sweep, the government would eliminate a major administrative irritant, gain full control of education spending, and simplify the administrative structure of the province.[143]

The seriousness with which the Harris government entertained this proposal remains a matter of some dispute. It appears that an alternative arrangement – a system of mega-boards, perhaps as few as four or five across the province – was also on the menu at the same time.[144] But the proposal was at least being seriously considered. In September 1996, Snobelen emerged from a Cabinet retreat in Vineland, Ontario, and spoke about school board abolition with excitement, as did Al Leach, the minister of municipal affairs. "There's a lot of people, particularly at the municipal level, that would eliminate school boards all together, that say there is no need for trustees," said Leach. In the midst of the excitement, one reporter asked Leach what would become of the vacant school board offices. "Leach smirked and said: 'Turn them into social housing.'"[145] For the first time in Ontario history, it seemed, the province was on a real path to school board abolition.

Two problems quickly emerged to stop the abolition as quickly as it had started. First, local school boards demonstrated that they still had some fight in them, especially in the assessment-rich parts of the province that would suffer in any province-wide equalization scheme.[146] In Snobelen's own riding, the local board of education delivered a quarter of a million leaflets to local homes, warning of higher taxes, decreased local control, and the redistribution of local funds to areas outside the region.[147] Second, and more importantly, Ontario Catholics reacted to the proposal with an immediate promise to "resist with all of [their] political and legal energy." If Harris chose to proceed, the Catholic coalition would unleash a campaign of total war, including a well-funded (and almost certainly successful) constitutional challenge.[148] Harris, already at war on several fronts, decided that the battle would not be worth the casualties. "The government would very much like to do it," said an informed source at Queen's Park, "but they can't for constitutional and political reasons."[149]

If the school boards could not be abolished, they could at least be enfeebled. So in January 1997, as part of its extraordinary "Megaweek" legislative package, Snobelen introduced Bill 104, the Fewer School Boards Act, which reduced the number of school boards in the province from 129 to 66, reduced the total number of trustees from nearly 2,000 to about 700, and capped trustee salaries at $5,000. Every part of the province would now be covered by four basic school board types: public English, public French, separate English, and separate French. From a peak of administrative complexity at mid-century, when school board types could be measured by the dozen and school boards themselves by the hundreds, the Ontario educational system had been reduced to fewer than 100 mega-regional boards, and just four general types, by the end of the twentieth century.[150]

While the basic structure of Ontario's school boards created by the Harris government's reforms remains in place today, debates about education governance in Ontario since the Harris years have been anything but quiet. A protest by three of the province's largest school boards in the early 2000s resulted in a total provincial government takeover of those boards; the boards were returned to the control of local trustees only after the election of the Liberal McGuinty government in 2003.[151] The tensions among a provincial funding scheme, board-level collective bargaining, and provincial mandates in areas ranging from class sizes to teacher preparation time has repeatedly strained relations with teachers and has resulted in ongoing collective action. To reduce these tensions may require institutional reforms that would be more deeply contentious than the tensions themselves. In the meantime, policy debates in Ontario's educational field continue to play out within institutional structures whose basic shape was determined by the Harris government's transformative reforms of the late 1990s.

5.10 Conclusions

The story of local education structures in Ontario is one of exceptional complexity. Not only have school boards been the subject of ongoing discussion and debate within the provincial bureaucracy, they have also linked up with powerful wider debates: debates about decentralization and democracy in the 1840s, about rural and urban life in the 1920s, and about Catholic constitutional rights in the 1990s. So many processes seem to have been in play through this history, so many different structures and arguments, that simple generalization seems impossible. Is there anything that we can say, speaking generally, about the structural history of Ontario's public school boards?

What we can say, to begin, is that the very complexity that we have uncovered serves to justify our basic theoretical approach. All of the major institutional changes in education in the past two centuries have resulted from interaction among long-term trends, field-level changes, and ordinary political happenings, an interplay of processes that vary widely in power, duration, and scale. We cannot explain the mandatory consolidation of the 1960s, for example, by pointing exclusively to the weakening of the rural voice, the birth of the provincial service state, the explosion of rural enrolment, or the arrival of Robarts and Davis at the top of the hierarchy. It is all of these things and more. What we can do, however, and what we have attempted to do in our discussion above, is to explain how all of these processes affected the policy images and political strength of those within the education field: to show, for example, how the increase in provincial funding for education between 1920 and 1960 gave Bill Davis more room to ignore the complaints from parts of rural Ontario about mandatory consolidation.

Beyond this basic argument, however, whatever else we can say about the school boards rests on an important feature of the history of education structures in Ontario: for much of its history, we are not dealing with one policy task, but with several: urban primary structures, urban secondary structures, rural structures, and Catholic school structures. These tasks are deeply interrelated, and arguments in one area had important effects in the others, but each task can also be said to have an internal organization – a policy field – of its own. If we narrow our focus to one or another of these fields, the overall picture begins to clarify.

Consider, for example, the distinction between the urban and rural primary school fields. In urban areas, the question of structure was all but resolved by 1850; it was not until more than a century later that we find serious debate in urban areas on the question of education structures. Even the move to united primary and secondary boards at the turn of the twentieth century was uncontroversial, endorsed voluntarily by most towns and cities across the province. By the mid-nineteenth century, the central policy image in this field had been established, the purpose of which was to provide a tax-supported system of graded schools to urban pupils, and it remained firmly in place for a century.

In the rural field, the story was very different. Whereas the transition from single-district school boards in urban areas took about three years to firmly establish (1847 to 1850), the same move in rural areas was introduced by Ryerson in 1866 and was not fully implemented until almost a century later. The rural field was more contentious than its urban cousin, largely because a coalition of rural trustees consistently defended the single-district board as a central and valued feature of rural life, a feature that (they claimed) the elitist centralizers at the Department of Education were bent on destroying. It was not until the rural coalition was weakened by demographic change, by suburbanization, and by changing views among rural dwellers themselves, that mandatory consolidation was finally possible.

This history of local education structures confirms, at the provincial level, what we have been claiming at the municipal level in the chapters above: while institutional structures and political culture *do* serve to empower and disempower particular arguments within policy debates, those structures and cultures must be understood in a disaggregated, ecological context. Examining institutional changes at the level of the field allows us to understand how these broad structures and cultures filter through the institutional structures and operational cultures of the field itself. It helps us see how broader developments – such as the reduced cultural status of rural Ontario and the construction of much better roads across the province – can combine, in the context of individual fields, to shift resources towards or away from particular actors and coalitions. Above all, this particular case teaches us how shifting field-level resources allow broadly similar policy ideas – such as arguments about township school board consolidation between 1860 and 1960 – to have widely varying power and success.

Table 5.2. Newspaper Sources for Ryerson County Conventions

Convention Date	Location	Newspaper	Newspaper Date
January 16, 1866	St Catharines	St Catharines Constitutional	January 18, 1866
January 17, 1866	Cayuga	Chatham Weekly Planet	February 1, 1888
January 19, 1866	Brantford	Brantford Expositor	January 26, 1866
January 22, 1866	Newmarket	Newmarket Era	January 26, 1866
January 23, 1866	Barrie	Barrie Northern Advocate	January 31, 1866
January 27, 1866	Goderich	Goderich Semi-Weekly Signal	January 30, 1866
January 29, 1866	Stratford	Stratford Beacon	February 2, 1866
January 30, 1866	Sarnia	Sarnia Observer	February 2, 1866
February 1, 1866	Chatham	Chatham Weekly Planet	February 8, 1866
February 3, 1866	St Thomas	St Thomas Weekly Dispatch	February 8, 1866
February 9, 1866	Milton	Canadian Champion	February 15, 1866
February 23, 1866	Brockville	Brockville Reporter	March 1, 1866
March 3, 1866	Ottawa	Ottawa Citizen	March 5, 1866
February 9, 1869	Barrie	Barrie Northern Advance	February 18 1869
February 13, 1869	Sarnia	Sarnia Observer	February 19, 1869
February 17, 1869	Chatham	Chatham Weekly Planet	February 25, 1869
February 18, 1869	London	London Advertiser	February 18–19, 1869
February 19, 1869	St Thomas	St Thomas Weekly Dispatch	February 25, 1869
February 22, 1869	Brampton	Brampton Times	February 22, 1869
February 23, 1869	Milton	Canadian Champion	February 23, 1869
February 24, 1869	Guelph	Guelph Evening Mercury	February 26, 1869
February 29, 1869	Hamilton	Hamilton Spectator	February 23, 1869
March 4, 1869	Cobourg	Cobourg World	March 12, 1869
March 5, 1869	Belleville	Intelligencer	March 12, 1869
March 10, 1869	Brockville	Brockville Recorder	March 18, 1869
March 18, 1869	Ottawa	Ottawa Citizen	March 26, 1869

Note: All newspapers accessed at the Archives of Ontario.
Source: Department of Education annual reports.

Chapter 6

Local Boards of Health

We now turn from education to public health. This may seem anticlimactic at first; after all, few special purpose bodies can compete with school boards for historical depth and political significance. But local boards of health, like school boards, have historical roots that run deeper than municipal government in Ontario, and like school boards, local boards of health have been at the centre of some of Ontario's most dramatic moments of crisis and change. We will find, I hope, that our investigation in this chapter will prove to be no less interesting, and no less useful for our project, than our discussion of education above. As we shall soon see, the distinctly patterned character of changes to public health institutions – and the abruptness with which those patterns change – will provide us with our clearest example yet of the explanatory value of the policy fields approach.

6.1 Overview of Structural Changes

We begin with the big picture. Each of the thirty-five lines in figure 6.1 marks a change event in the structural history of local boards of health in Ontario. The seven rows in the figure represent our seven basic types of change: creation, elimination, consolidation, partition, provincialization, generalization, and specialization.

A few general patterns are clear in the figure. Between 1830 and 1875, we see nothing but creation and generalization, followed by a string of specialization and consolidation from 1875 to 1970. A long stretch of generalization then brings us up to the present. This suggests a clustering into three periods: the first from 1830 to 1875, the second from 1875 to 1970, and the third from 1970 to the present.

Figure 6.1. Local Boards of Health in Ontario: Overview of Change Events

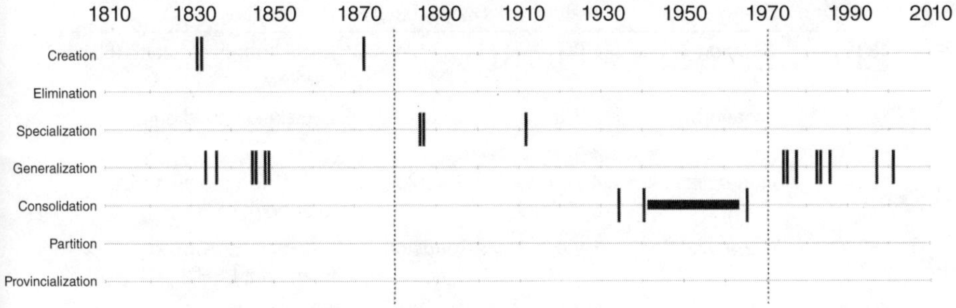

Note: See table 6.1 for a brief description of each event.

6.2 Creating Local Boards of Health, 1830–1875

On April 26, 1832, Sir John Colborne, lieutenant-governor of Upper Canada, issued a royal proclamation to the people of his province. The proclamation might have addressed a great many issues, from Reform agitation to provincial education policy. In April 1832, however, Colborne was concerned with something more immediate and terrifying: cholera.

Vibrio cholerae is a swift and savage killer. A day or two after ingesting the bacterium, the victim begins to notice the signs: cramps, vomiting, diarrhoea. A few hours later, the victim will already have purged a quarter of his bodily fluids; after a day, fully twenty litres will have been lost. Within days, the disease will have drawn nearly all of the fluid, and finally the life, from the victim's blue and shrivelled body. As he is laid to rest, the fluid that the victim expelled, containing as many as ten million cholera bacteria in every millilitre, will already have begun to find its way into the bodies of tens, hundreds, even thousands of new victims.[1]

At the time of John Colborne's proclamation, however, all of this, aside from the horrific consequences, was unknown.[2] In the face of an incomprehensible terror, Colborne did what many have done: he appealed to God. The province of Upper Canada, he proclaimed, would devote a full day to "fasting, humiliation, and prayer, against the dangers threatened by the progress of a very grievous disease."[3] But Colborne's appeal arrived too late. Just two days after the proclamation was issued, the dreaded disease arrived on Canadian soil.[4]

Table 6.1. Event Catalogue: Changes to Local Boards of Health in Ontario

Year	Change type	Statute	Applicability	Description
1832	Creation	N/A	Ontario	Local boards of health (LBH) created
1833	Creation	3 Wm IV, c 47	Ontario	Legislation creating LBHs
1834	Generalization	4 Wm IV, c 23	Toronto	City of Toronto authorized to appoint LBH
1837	Generalization	1 Vic, c 27	Kingston	Kingston authorized to appoint LBH
1847	Generalization	N/A	Ontario	LBH appointments temporarily handed to municipalities
1847	Generalization	10–11 Vic, c 49	Brantford	Brantford authorized to appoint LBH
1849	Generalization	12 Vic, c 81	Ontario	All municipalities authorized to appoint LBHs
1849	Creation	12 Vic, c 8	Ontario	Municipalities required to appoint LBHs during emergencies
1873	Creation	36 Vic, c 43	Ontario	Post-Confederation re-enactment of Public Health Act
1884	Specialization	47 Vic, c 38	Ontario	LBH mandatory for all municipalities
1895	Specialization	58 Vic, c 49	Ontario	LBH term lengths increased
1912	Specialization	2 Geo V, c 58	Ontario	Significant amendments to Public Health Act
1934	Consolidation	24 Geo V, c 47	Ontario	Permissive provision for consolidated health units
1940	Consolidation	N/A	Ontario	First consolidated health unit officially created
1945–9	Consolidation	N/A	Ontario	23 health units created in Ontario
1950–4	Consolidation	N/A	Ontario	2 health units created in Ontario
1955–9	Consolidation	N/A	Ontario	6 health units created in Ontario

Table 6.1. Event Catalogue: Changes to Local Boards of Health in Ontario (*cont.*)

Year	Change type	Statute	Applicability	Description
1960–4	Consolidation	N/A	Ontario	4 health units created in Ontario
1965–76	Consolidation	N/A	Ontario	3 health units created in Ontario
1967	Consolidation	N/A	Ontario	Permissive provision and grants for district health units
1974	Generalization	23–4 Eliz II, c 46	Ontario (urban)	MHO no longer a member of LBH in large places
1975	Generalization	24 Eliz II, c 46	Waterloo Region	Waterloo Region Board of Health dissolved
1978	Generalization	26–7 Eliz II, c 33	Ontario (regions)	Regional boards of health dissolved in York and Halton
1983	Generalization	31–2 Eliz II, c 72	Ontario (regions)	RBH dissolved in Durham, Haldimand, Hamilton, Niagara, Peel
1983	Generalization	31–2 Eliz II, c 10	Toronto	LBH dissolved in Toronto, Etobicoke, North York, Scarborough
1986	Generalization	34–5 Eliz II, c 46	Ottawa Region	Ottawa-Carleton LBH dissolved
1997	Generalization	46 Eliz II, c 30	Ontario	Dissolution of LBH moved to regulation
1997	Generalization	46 Eliz II, c 26	Toronto	City of Toronto authorized to appoint LBH
1999	Generalization	48 Eliz II, c14	Ontario (urban)	Hamilton, Ottawa, Haldimand, Norfolk can appoint LBH
2001	Generalization	50 Eliz II, c 25	Oxford	Oxford authorized to appoint LBH

Note: This table provides the basic data for figure 6.1.
Sources: Statutes of Ontario, Ontario Department of Health annual reports.

More earthly preparations for the arrival of cholera had been ongoing for more than a year. The British Colonial Office had sent instructions to the colonies in the spring of 1831, and in September, a group
of physicians met in Quebec City, delegating one of their members to
travel to New York and report on the sanitary measures there.[5] By
February 1832, the physicians had drafted a bill providing for a board
of health for Quebec City, consisting of fifteen executive-appointed
members as well as any clergymen who were willing to help. The bill
was quickly passed.[6]

In Upper Canada, preparations were more sluggish. Colborne had received the same communications as his Lower Canadian compatriots,
and the regulations of the London Central Board of Health had been
circulating in Upper Canadian newspapers for months.[7] Aside from
his royal proclamation and some tentative correspondence, however,
Colborne and his officials had done little to prepare for the disease.

By June 1832, anxious Upper Canadians had grown impatient. In
Kingston, magistrates organized a public meeting to discuss the epidemic, and residents voted to appoint a medical board and a board of
health to oversee the town's preparations.[8] The legality of these decisions was questionable, but the editor of Kingston's *Upper Canada
Herald* was unworried. "When a pestilence is at the door," he wrote, "it
is foolish to stand about every little punctilio in law."[9] Other Ontario
towns proved equally willing to overlook the little punctilios: in Belleville, Port Hope, and Prince Edward County, townsfolk soon met to
appoint their own boards of health and to cobble together funds for
temporary hospitals and treatment centres.[10]

Later that week, Colborne finally took action. In a circular to his district magistrates, Colborne authorized local boards of health and promised £500 to each district to assist with costs. The structure that Colborne
had in mind for the boards was vague; he merely asked that his magistrates "convene ... a Board of Health" along with an optional "Medical
Board" in each district.[11] In all but one of the province's districts, a public health structure of some kind was quickly assembled. Table 6.2 summarizes the arrangements; the most common was a two-tier structure,
with a board of health at the district level and a local board in each of
the major towns. In fact, however, structural variation was considerable. In some districts, local boards were independent of the district
board, while in others, the district board retained control. Some districts appointed large boards of health that included physicians, while
others appointed small lay boards along with advisory medical boards.

Table 6.2. Regional and Local Structure of 1832 Boards of Health

Name	District Level	Local Level
Bathurst	None	None
Eastern	General board and medical board	None; Members of district board take local areas
Gore	General board	Boards of health
Home	De jure general board	General board is focused exclusively on York
Johnstown	General board	Boards of health at Prescott and Brockville
London	General board and medical board	Branch medical board in Norfolk County
Midland	General board	Boards of health and medical boards
Newcastle	Expenditure committee	Four boards of health and one medical board
Niagara	General board	Four boards of health
Ottawa	General board	None
Western	General board	Two boards of health

Source: Aitchison, "Development of Local Government in Canada," 665–7.

The broad template may have been shared, in other words, but the local structures were idiosyncratic, suggesting that the overall structure of the boards was largely improvised by locals.[12]

By the time the Upper Canadian legislature met in the autumn of 1832 for its regular session, the worst of the cholera outbreak had passed. Still, everyone agreed that a public health statute would clarify the system that had emerged during the crisis. With little fanfare, the assembly passed a public health bill. In "each and every town in the Province, and in such other places as may be deemed necessary," the new act declared, a three-man board of health would be appointed by the provincial executive.[13] For the first time, the Upper Canadian statute books contained a provision for local boards of health.

Unlike the 1832 health system, the centre of gravity in the 1833 act was the local rather than the district level. Colborne's 1832 circular had authorized boards of health at the district level alone, but as we have seen, most districts also created branch boards in their major towns. The authors of the Public Health Act appear to have grasped this local reality; it would be a century before the province's boards of health would again be anything but local.

A year later, the shift towards local control continued. When the Town of York was incorporated in 1834 as the City of Toronto, the new city council was given the authority to appoint a committee from among its members to serve as a board of health.[14] Three years later, the Town of Kingston was given the same authority,[15] and gradually this provision spread outward. When the Town of Brantford was incorporated in 1847, it too was granted authority to appoint its board of health, and when the province was threatened that same year by a typhus outbreak, the government simply declared that all incorporated places should appoint their own local boards of health.[16] Two years later, this temporary provision became permanent. Municipal councils in townships, villages, towns, and cities were given authority to delegate their powers as health officers to a board of health, consisting of whomever the council deemed best for the job.[17]

What explains this twenty-year period of generalization? One obvious possibility is the ascendance of the Upper Canadian Reformers; perhaps public health, like local government more generally, was considered by the Reformers to be a matter of local autonomy. In fact, however, this cannot be the answer. Not only is the timing all wrong – many generalization events in public health occurred during periods of Tory control – but there is also no evidence that local health administration had been politicized along Tory-Reform lines.[18] Instead, the generalization arose from more mundane considerations: it was simply a de jure recognition of what had for many years been the de facto reality. While the authority to make appointments had officially been the preserve of the provincial executive until 1849, the reality was that those appointments were little more than rubber-stamp approvals of locally generated lists. Service on local boards of health in this era was first-come, first-appointed; the first list to arrive in Toronto was the one that the lieutenant-governor approved.[19] As the communities that were in fact appointing their local boards became actual legal entities, the authority to make the appointments was gradually transferred from provincial to municipal hands.[20]

Beneath the generalization process in this early episode was a basic and widely shared assumption that public health was fundamentally a matter of local concern. At the provincial level, the model was "fire-alarm oversight" – intermittent attention provoked only by pressing emergencies.[21] Local boards of health were shelters in which to huddle while the angel of death passed overhead, and when the danger was gone, the shelters were packed away until they were needed again. At the provincial and local levels, the actors involved in public health policy were transient and temporary, and they rarely questioned the status quo. The result was fifty years of pragmatic tinkering and the slow, steady drift of generalization.

6.3 The Rise of the Sanitarians, 1870–1900

In the summer of 1873, cholera threatened yet again. The Public Health Act of 1849, which had been the basis of Ontario's health system for two decades, was no longer on the statute books, a victim of Confederation in 1867. Faced with the first major outbreak since Confederation, the Ontario Legislature quickly enacted a statute similar to the 1849 Health Act. In the field of public health, it seemed, little had changed.[22]

Just a few years later, however, *everything* had changed. A new provincial board of health now coordinated health policy across the province. Permanent boards of health were now mandatory in every municipality in Ontario. A small and devoted group of activists were travelling through the province, preaching the gospel of public health and lobbying the government for radical structural reforms. How had this occurred?

Simply put, the *sanitarians* had arrived. In the 1870s, a group of urban physicians in Ontario began to take a serious interest in what was previously an unorganized field, advocating a wholesale transformation of provincial health structures with passionate, missionary zeal.[23] At the heart of the movement was a new policy image, the central purpose of which was to establish in every municipality a public health system equal to those in the largest and most advanced cities of the Anglo-American world.

This structural goal was supported by a classic example of what Deborah Stone has called a "causal story" – a policy argument grounded in a narrative of problems, the causes of those problems, and potential solutions.[24] To generate their central problem, the sanitarians made a classic move: they transformed the acts of the gods into the foolishness of humankind. "The amount of preventable disease – of disease the causes of which may be readily removed by sanitary administration," wrote the *Sanitary Journal*, the flagship periodical of the Canadian sanitary movement, "is as needless as it is appalling. Providence is often charged with the infliction of calamities which are entirely the result of our own folly. The majority of diseases are the products of our own imprudence or ignorance."[25] Under the sanitarians' new causal story, there would be no more days of fasting, humiliation, and prayer.

If preventable disease was the problem, the villain was *ignorance*. Politicians and the laity simply knew too little about disease, and for that reason, they chose to think about the matter only when death was already at the door. From ignorance arose fire-alarm oversight, and from fire-alarm oversight came hundreds, perhaps thousands, of needless deaths. Public health is typically ignored, wrote the *Canada Lancet*, "until the approach of cholera or some other fearful epidemic arouses us from our slumbers, and then frantic efforts are put forth ... when it is, in all probability, too late. If on the other hand such measures were regularly and systematically attended to ... neither the much dreaded cholera nor any other form of epidemic could obtain a foothold among us."[26]

The ignorance that the sanitarians decried had two sides. The first was *informational*; neither the federal nor the provincial government had actually gathered reliable public health information, and as a result, their decisions were uninformed. But the problem was also *institutional*. Those who were in a position to make decisions about public health often knew nothing about the subject. More often than not, the sanitarians complained, public health decisions were left to "four or five burly agriculturalists whose whole knowledge of disease may be limited to a case or two of cucumber cramps."[27]

To complete their causal story, the sanitarians proposed two solutions. To solve the informational problem, federal and provincial sanitary authorities were needed who would collect and distribute reliable public health data.[28] As for the institutional problem, the solution was expert authority. Again and again, sanitary advocates emphasized the need for trained physicians at every level of the system. "We might better put a blacksmith in charge of a milliner's shop," wrote the *Sanitary Journal*, "than to choose as our health officer one who does not understand the nature of those vital actions which human bodies undergo in health, and of those processes which are coincident with disease."[29] Only with physicians in positions of institutional leadership would Canada begin to see a reduction in epidemic illness and death.[30]

This new sanitary movement – a near-perfect example of what Peter Haas has called an "epistemic community"[31] – came equipped with a powerful new policy image. But the mere *presence* of the new sanitarian ideas, however compelling, cannot generate structural change. Together with their new ideas, the Canadian sanitarians learned in the 1870s to lobby effectively, and by the early 1880s, they had established themselves in crucial positions of institutional leadership.[32] From those positions, the sanitarians were able to set the agenda in the public health field for decades to come.

Our focus, of course, is local structural change, and we must be careful not to drift unnecessarily into the broader history of Canadian public health. To understand the local changes in the coming decades, however, we do need to say something, however briefly, about the conception and birth of Ontario's 1882 provincial board of health.

The nutshell version of the story runs as follows. The sanitarians' first strategy was to "shop" for venues, calling for changes at all levels and supporting whatever proposals happened to pop up.[33] This approach was unsuccessful, and over time, the sanitary movement came to focus on the provinces, and especially Ontario, as a strategic first move in the larger battle. The sanitarians demanded a provincial board of health, empowered to gather statistics and reports, to study "best practices" in other jurisdictions, and generally to coax and cajole local actors into improving their local health services.[34]

The structure that the sanitarians proposed was primarily American in origin, but the means by which they sought to bring it about were initially inspired by the British.[35] In England, sanitarians had demanded a report on public health in the early 1870s, and the results of that report led eventually to a strengthened Public Health Act in 1875.[36] The sanitarians in Ontario pushed for a similar report, with hopes for a similarly potent act.[37]

Success came in 1878, when Premier Oliver Mowat announced a Select Committee on Public Health to investigate the public health system and to make recommendations for improvements. Mowat admitted that "the importance of adopting sanitary measures which were not yet in use had not excited a great deal of public attention," but said that the issue of public health "had been impressed on his attention by a number of medical gentlemen of the highest standing in Toronto and elsewhere." These gentleman were of course the sanitarians, whose basic talking points Mowat proceeded to rehearse.[38] The select committee quickly got to work, circulating surveys to physicians and municipal governments and collecting a diverse array of materials from the United States, Ireland, Scotland, and England.[39]

Fortunately, the select committee's survey returns have survived, providing us with a rare glimpse into the state of Ontario's medical opinion at the time. Table 6.3 provides a summary: on the left-hand side are the ten most frequent structural suggestions, along with the percentage of respondents who mentioned them; on the right side of the table

Table 6.3. Responses to Select Committee Physician
Survey on Public Health Governance

Occurrences	N	%	Combinations	N	%
Local board of health	75	37.1	Local board of health	30	14.9
Municipal council	65	32.2	Municipal council	18	8.9
Physicians	59	29.2	Physicians	15	7.4
Appointed inspector	57	28.2	Ontario government	13	6.4
Ontario government	36	17.8	Local board of health + physicians	12	5.9
Medical health officer	25	12.4	Local board of health + council	12	5.9
County board of health	9	4.5	Municipal council + physicians	11	5.5
Provincial board of health	8	4.0	Appointed inspector	6	3.0
Education department	5	2.5	Municipal council + Ontario government	5	2.5
Police	3	1.5	Medical health officer + Ontario government	5	2.5
Other	1	0.5	Provincial inspector	5	2.5

Note: Table records responses to open-ended question about who should be responsible
for public health. List on the left are the most frequent suggestions, and list on the right
are the most frequent whole suggestions including combinations. For instance, if a
respondent wrote "doctors and local board of health," this would count towards local
board of health and physicians on the left-hand side, and towards "local board of health
+ physicians" on the right-hand side.
Source: Original survey returns, RG 49-92, Archives of Ontario.

are the most frequent actual suggestions mentioned in the survey returns.[40] (If a physician wrote "local board of health and qualified doctors," for example, this would count towards both "local boards of
health" and "physicians" on the left-hand side, but only towards "local boards + physicians" on the right-hand side.) For the sanitarians,
the results must have been disappointing, filled with heresy on the one
hand (9 per cent would put public health exclusively in the hands of
municipal councils) and unrealistic radicalism on the other (another 8
per cent would prefer to transfer the entire system to the province).

Almost none of those surveyed mentioned the sanitarians' own treasured goal – a provincial board of health – and no single option stood out as strongly preferred to any others.

This variety of opinion did not prevent the sanitarians from trying to tease a mandate out of the surveys. Edward Playter, the most enthusiastic sanitarian in the country, combed through the surveys on the committee's behalf, underlining useful passages and scribbling exasperated responses to heretical opinions in the margins.[41] But even the most meticulous cherry-picking could not save the committee's final report, whose critiques were compelling but whose suggestions were equivocal and abstract.[42]

For Oliver Mowat, the select committee's report may have been the best of both worlds: its existence could demonstrate Mowat's progressive bona fides,[43] while the inconclusiveness of the report allowed Mowat to avoid actually doing anything about the matter. The sanitarians, of course, had other ideas. In 1879, they began a new campaign of persuasion, aimed straight at the top of the pyramid. They would lobby Mowat himself, and they would do so until the answer was yes.[44]

And so they did. On New Year's Eve of 1879, the sanitarians handed Mowat a draft bill for reform of the Ontario public health system, and Mowat stated in no uncertain terms that the proposed reforms were too expensive to be considered.[45] The sanitarians left empty-handed, as they did again, after a similar meeting, the following year. But they continued to press, making resolutions in every conceivable venue, calling for petitions and letters in the professional journals, organizing speeches, questions, and calls for reform in the legislature itself.[46] Finally, in 1882, the effort bore fruit. A draft bill for a provincial board of health, drawn up by the Ontario Medical Association, was presented in the legislature, debated, amended, and passed.[47] After a decade of prospecting, the sanitarians had at last struck gold.

The 1882 Public Health Act had no immediate effect on the structure of Ontario's local boards of health. We have taken the time to describe its history, however, because the strategies that the sanitarians employed in 1882 remained in their arsenal as they turned their attention from the provincial to the local level. Even more important, the provincial board of health provided the sanitary movement with a crucial institutional home inside the provincial government, a home from which they were able to develop and advocate further reforms to the health system. Before long, the provincial board of health (PBH) became the central node in an increasingly vocal public health network.

The secretary of the PBH, Peter Bryce, was a dedicated organizer, arranging sanitary conventions and public meetings across the province, and helping to organize the Association of Executive Health Officers of Ontario in 1886.[48] The PBH also quickly became a problem-and-policy production machine. Although the PBH had little power to actually *do* anything in Ontario, it did have the capacity to survey the provincial health system and to use its institutional position and annual reports to lend weight to criticisms and proposals that were formerly confined to specialist journals and sympathetic newspapers.[49]

For Bryce and his PBH colleagues, the problems in public health in the 1880s were considerable. Much of the province was doing precisely nothing to improve public health, and even where fledgling boards of health did exist, they were often composed of local politicians who lacked even the most elementary understanding of human disease.[50] Because the PBH depended upon local sources for its statistics, it would remain ineffective until proper local boards of health were in place. For better or worse, the local boards were "the fighting arm of the service," and in most parts of the province, the army was non-existent.[51]

To solve this problem, Bryce and his colleagues proposed a variety of solutions. The most obvious step was to make local boards mandatory. Not only would this improve the PBH's own statistical information, it was also important for its own sake.[52] "If a [local] Board were appointed," wrote the PBH *Annual Report*, "whose special work it would be to deal with matters of health, these important concerns would not be simply allowed to continue unheeded, as in most cases they do at present."[53] But even if mandatory local boards *were* established, most sanitarians agreed that further provisions would be needed to insulate the boards from stingy municipal councils. Here the sanitarians had two general proposals. First, term lengths for local boards might be extended from one year to three, following some American examples, making the board a less convenient locus for patronage and promoting more long-term thinking.[54] Alternatively, members of the local board of health might be elected directly. Inspired by the education system, sanitarians argued that elected boards of health would give the local health system the legitimacy it needed to make real public health improvements.[55]

A final cluster of proposals concerned local health officers. For the sanitarians, the health officer – the only sure expert in the local health field – was the cornerstone of the local health system. A first step in strengthening his position, they thought, might be to make the health officer mandatory in every municipality. In addition, the medical health officer might be made the executive officer of the local board of health, to oversee the activities of the board directly.[56] Initially, neither of these suggestions related directly to the structure of the local boards of health, but as we shall see, the sanitarians' commitment to empowered health officers would ultimately have a profound effect on their proposals for local structural reform.

Almost immediately after the PBH was created, then, a mass of proposed reforms began to fill the pages of the provincial board's annual reports. These reforms elicited mixed opinions among members of the field at the time, though committed sanitarians could generally be counted on to support the PBH's suggestions. Despite the increased status of the sanitarians, however, changes to local health structures still required changes in legislation, which meant that the ambitious proposals presented at the sanitary conventions, the association meetings, and in the pages of the PBH's annual reports would have to be filtered through the cautious pragmatism of Oliver Mowat and his Liberal colleagues.

For this reason, the first step was modest: mandatory local boards of health. The reform would require that every municipality appoint a local board, but the membership of the board would be left entirely to municipal council. Even this proposal, however, was deemed too risky for the government's final session in 1883; Mowat, bombarded by accusations of centralization, was likely reticent to add fuel to the rhetorical fire.[57] After the 1883 election, however, in the relative safety of a first session, Mowat introduced the amendment for mandatory boards of health, and despite some criticism at Queen's Park, the bill became law without provoking any noteworthy public ire.[58]

The sanitarians continued to press for reform, growing more organized and vocal by the year, but it would be more than a decade until they would pass a legislative amendment of similar importance. In 1895, after years of advocacy, the secretary of the provincial board of health, Peter Bryce, finally persuaded the Liberal government to introduce a term-length amendment to the Public Health Act, extending the term of service on local boards of health from one-year to rotating three-year terms. The amendment appears to have passed almost completely below the public radar.[59] Thus, by the turn of the twentieth century, the overwhelming majority of Ontario municipalities had local boards of health,[60] the members of which enjoyed greater continuity than did the councillors who appointed them.

We are now in a position to briefly summarize this early period of sanitary activism. In the early 1870s, a group of committed activists began to organize in Ontario, inspired by similar movements in Great Britain and the United States. These "sanitarians" carried a new causal story into the public health field, one that successfully disrupted the fire-alarm pattern of local health policy before the 1870s. For the sanitarians, contagious disease was not only manageable but *preventable*, as long as competent physicians had the information that they needed and were empowered to address the problem directly.

The sanitarians' invasion of the public health field was institutionalized in the 1882 provincial board of health, which served as the sanitarians' centre of organization, problem-generation, and policy proposals in the coming years. The reforms that the PBH advocated in the early 1880s were intended to distance local boards of health from the influence of municipal council and to strengthen the position of the local health officer within the local health system.

Figure 6.2 provides some useful final evidence for the argument that I have been making thus far. The figure plots three trends. First, the black line plots public attention to contagious disease, measured by the frequency with which the words *cholera, typhus,* and *smallpox* appear in newspapers across Ontario. The black circles plot disease outbreaks and disease scares in Ontario. The black diamonds plot major provincewide changes to local public health structures between 1825 and 1900.[61]

Two observations emerge from the figure. First, in the years before 1875 or so, we can see a tight connection among public attention, disease outbreaks or scares, and legislative change. Legislative changes during this period are always associated with disease outbreaks or scares, though the provincial government was evidently satisfied with the performance of the 1849 Public Health Act during the 1854 and 1866 outbreaks. After 1875, however, legislative changes are less clearly linked to outbreaks and public attention. All of this supports our basic claim above: after 1875, it was not the fire-alarm response to disease outbreaks, but rather the constant pressure of the new sanitary movement, that produced legislative change.

The second observation that we can draw from the figure concerns the black "attention" index. Before 1875, the peaks and valleys are sharp and steep, but after 1875, the line never again returns to zero, suggesting that disease had become a more permanent consideration in the minds of Ontario's newspaper editors – and perhaps the public at large. This may reflect a more international focus in Ontario newspapers – the spike in the 1890s, for example, reflects coverage of a horrific cholera epidemic in Russia – but it is also, I believe, a marker of the sanitary movement's success. The changes in newspaper coverage in the second half of the figure suggest that the intermittent attention that

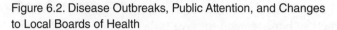

Figure 6.2. Disease Outbreaks, Public Attention, and Changes
to Local Boards of Health

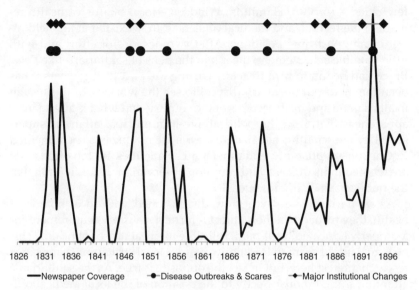

Note: Black line graph plots frequency with which *cholera, typhus*, and *smallpox* appear
in newspapers across Ontario. The line plots a frequency count divided by the number
of available newspapers for the year. Black circles plot major outbreaks of disease
and disease scares in Ontario. Black diamonds plot major province-wide changes
to structure of local boards of health in Ontario.
Source: OurOntario.ca.

was characteristic of the earlier period had been transformed into one
of more constant, if still highly variable, public attention to disease.

6.4 The Turn to Consolidation, 1900–1967

The sanitarians' goal had always been to establish a public health system in every municipality at a standard previously reserved for very
large cities. To accomplish this, the sanitarians first attempted to make
local boards of health more independent of municipal councils, and as
we have seen, they had some early success in achieving this goal. But

their broader hopes went unrealized. The structural changes for which they had worked so hard seemed to have little effect. In all but a very few cities – Toronto, Hamilton, Windsor – local boards of health remained ineffectual, and medical officers, if they existed at all, held insignificant, part-time positions. After two decades of effort and with little tangible achievement, the ink in the pens of sanitarians like Peter Bryce had begun to turn to acid: "During the past twenty years it has been the lot of our Secretary [Bryce] to see the working of the system in all its parts and in all sections of the country, and what is abundantly apparent is that until the political age in municipal affairs is superseded by the scientific age manifest evils are not likely to be remedied … Cheapness, pliability, and other similar qualities are too often what are wanted in its officers, and common observation makes it plain that the public pays dearly for such."[62]

As sanitarians like Bryce grew disillusioned with local boards of health, they turned to a more direct reform: a statutory requirement for a properly educated, well-paid, full-time medical officer of health. This new goal might seem to lead us away from local structural change, our research interest here, but in fact the opposite is true. As the sanitarians' attention shifted more directly to the position of the local medical officer, their causal stories also began to shift, generating a new set of structural proposals for local boards of health.

The basic problem, as far as the sanitarians were concerned, was twofold. First, municipal council had the authority to hire and fire the medical officer of health. In many municipalities, this meant that the position was something of an honorary title, passed around among local physicians by the annually elected council.[63] It also meant that a medical officer who pushed too hard for reform could simply be replaced by a more pliant officer. Thus, no matter how independent the local board of health became, the council's power to appoint and dismiss the medical officer of health prevented the local system from becoming effective.[64]

The second problem was more personal. In most municipalities the medical officer's position was part-time, filled by physicians whose primary occupation was private practice. This raised a conundrum. Suppose, for example, the medical officer visited one of his private patients and discovered that the patient had smallpox. His duty as a medical officer was clear: report, isolate, quarantine. If the patient refused to be isolated, however, what then? What if the patient threatened to take his business elsewhere if the physician held to his medical-officer duties too firmly? For the sanitarians, the answer was clear: in all but a few heroic cases, the physician's primary loyalty was to the work that put bread on the table: private practice. Thus, medical officers chose to make public health their priority only in the most serious situations.[65]

The solution to these problems was a well-paid, full-time medical officer of health, the kind of officer who was already making progress in places like Toronto and Hamilton.[66] But it was immediately clear that many municipalities were unwilling, and often unable, to raise the funds required to pay for a full-time local health officer. This brought the sanitarians back around to the question of local structure, and as they pondered the problem, two general solutions began to emerge.[67]

The first was provincialization: abolish the local health system and replace it with provincially appointed and provincially funded medical officers. This option had always had a following among some Ontario physicians, and it had the advantage of solving the funding problem and the local independence problem in a single stroke.[68] But it would also mean a considerable increase in provincial expenditure and would expose the provincial government to cries of centralization and autocracy. At the political level, therefore, it would prove to be a difficult sell.

The second option was consolidation. If municipalities joined with their neighbours to form a larger board of health, perhaps at the county level, the public health system would be removed from the day-to-day surveillance of parsimonious municipal politicians. And by enlarging the tax base from which to draw funds for public health, consolidation would make a full-time medical officer a more realistic proposition.[69] Peter Bryce and his colleagues had in fact been advocating consolidation for years, and in 1891, Bryce had been able to add a permissive provision for county medical officers to the Public Health Act.[70] But the provision was never implemented, or even seriously discussed, serving only as a harbinger of future change.

Thus, after the turn of the century, the sanitarians started again from scratch. They proposed a research questionnaire on the subject of county boards of health, to be distributed to physicians and local politicians. But when they had drawn up the survey and passed it to the provincial secretary (who was responsible for the PBH at the time), the secretary had second thoughts. An election was looming; how might the county boards be perceived by the voting public? "Under the existing circumstances," the provincial secretary wrote to the PBH, "nothing further had better be done."[71] The survey idea was dropped.

But the sanitarians continued to press for change. In 1906, when Premier James Whitney replaced all but one of the PBH's members, the remaining member wrote to his new colleagues to explain the work of the previous board. "I submit for your consideration the draft of a new Health Act as drawn up and approved by your predecessors in office at considerable trouble," he wrote, explaining the limitations of the current local structures in detail. What was needed was a "central county or district health authority with a qualified M.H.O. who will devote all his time to the work." The new PBH, still bursting with sanitarians, needed little convincing and quickly took up the cause with an enthusiasm that rivalled those they had replaced.[72]

By the early 1910s, William Hanna, the provincial secretary, had been persuaded that the public health system needed fixing. Hanna was an important member of James Whitney's more progressive and urban-oriented Conservative government of 1905, and he was willing to entertain proposals for changes to the public health system. But he was equally convinced that consolidation was a non-starter; local governments would not surrender control without a fight, and county governments would be ungrateful recipients of the new (and costly) responsibilities. Instead, Hanna drew up a compromise bill, one that might satisfy the sanitarians without requiring any radical structural change. He (or rather Premier Whitney) also chose once again to replace the PBH in its entirety, perhaps in the hope that a new PBH would be less dogmatic on the question of county boards of health.[73] Whatever the motivation, the new PBH *was* more receptive to Hanna's alternative proposals, and on March 14, 1912, Hanna introduced the new public health bill – popularly called the "Hanna Act" – in the Ontario Legislature.[74]

The Hanna Act may not have included a provision for county boards of health, but it did make a number of important changes to the local health system.[75] First, the local health officer, now called the "medical health officer" or MHO, could be dismissed only with the consent of the provincial board of health. Once he was hired, in other words, the MHO could do his work without fearing that an excess of enthusiasm would earn him an immediate dismissal.[76] Second, in a nod to the sanitarians' call for consolidation, the Hanna Act added provincially appointed district health officers to supervise, inspect, and report on the public health in districts across the province. This change, modelled after a similar provision in Quebec, did not originate with the sanitarians; it appears, rather, to have originated with Hanna himself.[77]

The third and most important change concerned the position of the medical health officer. In the Hanna Act, the MHO became the executive officer of the local board of health, and was also required to be a *member* of the local board.[78] The MHO was thus responsible for the day-to-day administration of the local public health system, and his position on the local board gave him a key role in local health policy-making as well. Because the MHO would serve on the board of health for years, even decades, his accumulated expertise would make the de facto policy leader on the local board.[79] "It may be concluded from the new Act," wrote envious sanitarians in London, England, "that the Canadian Legislature does not share the traditional English objection to giving administrative authority to the expert."[80]

To the sanitarians, the Hanna Act was certainly an improvement over the former system. But a crucial problem remained: despite all the changes, the MHO was still, in most places, a part-time position. The problem that the sanitarians had bemoaned for decades – the disincentives created by the MHO's financial dependence on his private practice – remained stubbornly in place. Thus, the sanitarians once again returned to the solution that they had now been proposing for two decades: consolidation.[81]

Success did not come quickly. Year after year, sanitarians travelled the province, extolling the virtues of a consolidated health system, citing successful examples from elsewhere, publishing speeches and articles in journals and local newspapers.[82] But resistance proved stronger than anticipated. Local officials, especially in rural areas, resented the Hanna reforms and declared that they were "no longer going to submit to the tyrannical centralizing policy of the late and preceding governments."[83] The government's typical response was therefore to interfere in local services only when absolutely necessary.[84]

For much of the 1920s, the sanitarians must have felt that they were shouting into the void. Their devoted missionary work seemed to yield few converts.[85] As the 1930s approached, however, public opinion seemed to begin to shift. Local newspapers began to comment favourably on the idea of local consolidation. Women's clubs and other local groups held well-attended public debates on the subject.[86] And when Dr Forbes Godfrey was replaced as minister of health by Dr J.M. Robb, a man who was enthusiastic about consolidation, an opportunity for action finally appeared.[87] In March 1931, Dr Robb stood before the House and introduced a health consolidation bill.[88]

The bill was rather odd. It contained not one but two basic models for public health administration. The first model, as expected, was a permissive provision for county-level consolidation. But the second model was a provision for *provincialization* of the local health system. Under this second model, local governments could choose to upload their public health responsibilities to the province, with public health thereafter administered by a provincial employee, called a district health officer, rather than the traditional local structure.[89]

None of these provisions was new, but their combination in a single bill made for a perplexing jumble. The bill may have been poorly received by the Conservative caucus; it was certainly received with trepidation by locals who worried about the added expense of a county-level health system and about the loss of local control that either of the two new options would entail.[90] A little while later, Dr Robb stood once again in the legislature and announced that he was withdrawing the bill. "The people of the Province are not quite ready for it," said Dr Robb, nor were the federal or provincial governments prepared to contribute funds to the new health units.[91] Local consolidation would have to wait.

The sanitarians kept up the pressure. Having failed to achieve a general provision for county-level consolidation, they pushed instead for a demonstration unit, a consolidated local health system in a single county to serve as a test (or, for the sanitarians, as proof) of the effectiveness of public health consolidation. In 1934, the sanitarians finally succeeded, and the counties of Stormont, Glengarry, Prescott, and Russell agreed to form a demonstration health unit with funding from the Rockefeller Foundation.[92] To permit the experiment, the legislature passed a provision for consolidated health units, one very similar to the county health provisions in Dr Robb's 1930 bill.[93] This time, however, perhaps because the amendment was thought to be relevant to the demonstration unit alone (nothing in the legislation itself suggested this), it provoked almost no discussion or debate.[94] In their decades-long campaign for consolidation, the sanitarians had finally gained a toehold.

The demonstration unit was a success, and in 1940, after considerable discussion, the United Counties of Stormont, Glengarry, and Dundas agreed to continue the consolidated health unit on a permanent basis.[95] The provincial government, for its part, agreed in January 1940 to cover half the costs of the health unit for the first year.[96] For the first time, the province of Ontario had established a consolidated public health structure at a super-municipal scale. And in keeping with the 1934 statute – which moved the exact membership of the board of health to regulation – the province also, for the first time in nearly a century, appointed a representative of its own to sit on the local board of health.[97]

Armed with new legislation and a financial incentive (50 per cent provincial funding for health units), the sanitarians once again set out across the province to preach the gospel of consolidation. They were delayed, at first, by the Second World War, which caused serious staff shortages among doctors and nurses in Ontario.[98] After 1945, however, the number of health units exploded. By 1949, some twenty-three units had already been created; eight more would be added in the following decade. By 1966, fully 93 per cent of the province was covered by full-time public health services, either in health units or in municipal health departments.[99]

Some had even begun to think that the *county* was too small an area to provide the advanced services demanded in a progressive post-war society. Stephen Lewis, an NDP MPP and member of the legislature's Standing Committee on Health, took up the cause with enthusiasm, criticizing geographic inequalities in the public health funding system and advocating regional health units, provincially appointed medical officers, and statutory standards for public health services across the province.[100] The Conservative government responded quickly, appointing a Local Health Services Task Force and introducing, on April 7, 1967, a series of amendments to the Public Health Act. Under the amended statute, the province would encourage the formation of twenty-nine district health units in Ontario, providing 75 per cent funding as an incentive to make the change.[101] The legislation also required that all local health systems, whatever their structure, provide full-time health services to their population. The new district system was not adopted with uniform enthusiasm across the province; in the more heavily populated southwest, adoption rates were much lower, suggesting that local governments surrendered local control over public health only when financial incentives were irresistible. Even so, an observer of the public health field at the end of the 1960s would have concluded that the sanitary movement had finally achieved victory: after nearly a century of advocacy, every square inch of the province was finally covered by mandatory, full-time public health services.[102]

For almost a century, then, the public health field in Ontario was remarkably stable, dominated by a coalition of actors whose persistence and organization were totally unmatched by opponents. After setbacks and disappointments, such as the 1912 Hanna Act or the 1930 county health bill, the sanitarians simply kept pressing. This persistence was aided first by significant institutional power – the provincial board of health, and its reports and proposals, was totally dominated by sanitarian perspectives – and then also by significant organizational power as well. In the Hanna Act of 1912, for instance, municipal health officers

were required *by law* to travel at municipal expense to an annual conference to meet with their municipal and provincial colleagues. The act
also required that medical health officers be officially qualified, meaning that Ontario medical health officers also typically shared the same
educational experience – a public health diploma at the University of
Toronto – as their colleagues.[103] All of this provided a foundation for
continuity, persistence, and domination in the public health field.[104]

Because the sanitarians so effectively dominated the public health
field during these years, problems and policies tended to remain consistent from year to year; indeed, many of Peter Bryce's proposals from
the 1890s were still being advocated forty or even fifty years later. It was
therefore in the political arena that the pace and timing of the structural changes was determined. Two factors were particularly important. The first was ministerial support; when supportive ministers such
as William Hanna or J.M. Robb were at the helm, real change became an
immediate possibility; when less receptive ministers were in charge, on
the other hand, the sanitarians were forced to bide their time. A second
important factor was the proximity of an election. When provincial
politicians saw an election on the near horizon, they were more hesitant
to make changes that might be interpreted as centralizing or radical. It
was therefore in the first legislative session after an election that the
sanitarians enjoyed their most significant successes, including the move
to mandatory local boards in 1884, the term-length increases in 1895,
and the Hanna Act in 1912. The final important risk factor, then as now,
was spending. When the sanitarians could show that their suggestions
would not raise problems of taxation and spending – as in 1934, when
the health unit experiment was covered by a Rockefeller grant – provincial objections to the changes tended to dissolve.

6.5 A Second Invasion, 1965–2010

The post-war years were a time of triumph for the sanitarians. Much of
what they had worked for decades to accomplish had finally been realized within a few short years. But – to briefly adopt the Hollywood
cliché – *all was not as it seemed*. While the sanitarians were celebrating,
new forces had emerged that would soon seriously threaten what they
had created.

The danger had been developing since the Second World War, but
became increasingly clear in the early 1960s. "There is a missing link in
our Canadian political structure," wrote Eric Beecroft in 1962. "The real

enemy of effective local self-rule today is the fragmentation of our communities into governing entities which are unable, singly, to attack the major items of our increasingly urgent regional agenda." The solution to this problem, Beecroft argued, was *regional government*.[105]

Beecroft's article testified to a small but growing policy field, one born from the new study of economic development, planning, and provincial-municipal structures. For members of this new field, the central argument ran as follows. In the advanced post-war economy of the 1960s, municipal governments were no longer effective, efficient, or competitive. This was in part because they were too small, with each municipality covering just a fraction of the genuine economic region of which they were a part. But it was also because they were fragmented, with policy-making power divided among a perplexing array of special purpose bodies. For these new critics – let us call them the *regionalists*, as we did in chapter 4 above – significant local reform was required, involving larger geographic scales and the widespread elimination of local ABCs.[106]

For the regionalists, then, the problem was local incapacity and fragmentation, the villain was inadequate size and a plethora of local ABCs, and the solution was general-purpose regional government. Throughout the 1960s, report after report made similar arguments along these lines.[107] In time, these arguments began to capture the imagination of the most powerful members of the provincial Cabinet. Bill Davis, for example, who was busy making similar arguments in the education field, was receptive to the regionalist story, particularly in the early years.[108] John Robarts, the premier, was also enthusiastic.[109] And Darcy McKeough, who would ultimately serve as the tip of the government's regionalist spear, had embraced the regionalist vision with the passion of a convert.[110] As for the loyal opposition, the only criticism on the regional file was that the government was not proceeding quickly enough.[111]

Something had begun to shift. A new policy field, oriented around local fiscal policy and local administrative structure, had begun to coalesce, with Ontario's increasingly powerful Department of Municipal Affairs as its institutional home. Within this field was a fledgling coalition of "regionalists," which came to include some of the most powerful voices around the Cabinet table, with a policy argument that consistently advocated general-purpose regional government. Most importantly, the regionalists also developed a new line of defence on what might have been thought to be their major point of weakness: local autonomy. Against those who might claim that regional government would weaken local autonomy, the regionalists argued that local autonomy meant the capacity to act, the ability to actually *do* something, and that municipalities in their present form had lost this capacity in any meaningful sense. True defenders of local autonomy, they argued, should therefore embrace a larger and more powerful local government at the regional level. This argument was not always persuasive, of course, but it did create the *possibility* that defenders of local autonomy might plausibly endorse regional restructuring without abandoning their localist principles. Like the arguments for school board consolidation earlier in the decade, the regionalist argument in favour of local autonomy had a certain persuasive brilliance.[112]

The regionalist vision quickly became official policy. The government's intention was stated in *Design for Development, Phase Two*, which suggested about seventy regional governments across the province and also recommended the widespread abolition of local special purpose bodies.[113] "This is an historic time for local government in Ontario," declared a triumphant Darcy McKeough in the legislature in 1968. "The province is embarking on a programme which will recast and reform our entire municipal system in a way more fundamental than any ever attempted since the present system was organized. I think, Mr Speaker, that observers will look back and say that local government in Ontario was established in 1849 and re-established in 1968."[114]

How does this regionalist story relate to public health? The answer is simple: from the beginning, local boards of health were a prime regionalist target. Public health was a clear example for the regionalists of a function that could easily be handled by a general-purpose regional council, thereby eliminating the fragmentation caused by special-purpose bodies.[115] If the regionalist vision was to become a reality, local boards of health were exactly the kinds of structures that would have to disappear.

Thus, by the late 1960s, the public health field, which had been dominated by the sanitarians for nearly a century, was being invaded, and regionalist ideas spilled over ever more explicitly into what was formerly the sanitarians' terrain. At first, the minister of health, Dr M.B. Dymond, had been able to resist and delay successfully.[116] But when the new regional government in Waterloo wrote to the government, on May 15, 1974, requesting an amendment to allow a committee of regional council to replace the regional board of health, the battle could be delayed no longer.[117]

The sanitarians fought hard, and they tried to portray the outcome of the Waterloo Region conflict as a successful compromise. But the truth is that the sanitarians lost. In 1975, Waterloo Region's request was granted, and the regional board of health was eliminated, its responsibilities transferred to regional council. Just two years later, the same change occurred in York Region, and then in Halton Region.[118] The sanitarians continued to resist, insisting that no further abolitions should be permitted. But the regionalist invasion had become too strong to withstand. In 1980, the Ministry of Health commissioned a study, together with the Ministry of Intergovernmental Affairs, in the hopes of demonstrating that public health suffered under the new committee structure. But the study concluded that few changes were apparent.[119] This was the sanitarians' final move, and they were forced at last to concede. The transfer to general-purpose bodies would now proceed unopposed, and by the end of the 1980s, all of the province's regional governments, from Ottawa-Carleton to Niagara, had dissolved their boards of health and transferred responsibility to regional council.[120] In public health, at least, the regionalists had triumphed.

Why did the sanitarians prove so unable to resist these changes? After all, the sanitary coalition had dominated the field for nearly a century and had demonstrated again and again that its members had the patience and determination to see their structural vision realized. Whatever defeats the sanitarians had experienced in the preceding decades had been temporary, followed eventually by victories. What had changed?

To answer this question requires that we recognize once again that the success of a policy field invasion is not merely a matter of the invaders' strength. It also depends on the capacity of the members to resist. And in the case of public health, two general processes had occurred in the post-war years, both of which had decisively weakened the sanitarians' ability to resist the regionalists' new vision.

The first process was in fact a prior invasion. In 1972, as part of a massive restructuring that transformed Ontario's "departments" into "ministries," the Ontario government created the Ministry of Health, incorporating the Ontario Hospital Services Commission and the Ontario Health Insurance Registration Board directly into the ministry. As a result of this restructuring, the public health system became a tiny sliver in a much larger pie.[121] Although this process had begun many decades earlier, with the addition of the hospital program to the Department of Health, the hospitals branch and the public health branch were previously kept so separate from one another as to be de facto separate departments, even issuing their own separate annual reports. By the early

1970s, however, successive reorganizations had made public health a small part of a much larger whole, and while the sanitarians remained the leading voices within the public health field, that field grew increasingly marginalized, gaining little attention in the now enormous health-care field.[122] In the mammoth Ministry of Health, the sanitarian voice was now just one among many.

The sanitarians were further weakened by a second key process: the transition from a "departmentalized" to an "institutionalized" Cabinet structure.[123] In a departmentalized structure, long-serving ministers make decisions for their departments in consultation with the premier, and Cabinet typically defers to those decisions.[124] In the institutionalized Cabinet, on the other hand, major decisions are made by general-purpose Cabinet committees, consisting of an inner core of Cabinet ministers who set and monitor the government's overall goals, and to which individual ministers are often required to defer. Like the move to regional government at the local level, the shift to an institutionalized Cabinet was an attempt to overcome fragmentation and incapacity by means of strengthened general-purpose structures of some kind.[125]

One result of the institutionalized Cabinet was a much-reduced term length for Cabinet ministers. Cabinet shuffles became more frequent, and expertise at the ministerial level was de-emphasized, even discouraged, being thought to lead to that fearful bugaboo, *portfolio loyalty*. A stream of non-specialist and decidedly non-sanitarian ministers began to trickle in and out of the health system; whereas before 1970, five of the province's eight ministers of health had been trained as physicians, just one of the twenty-one individuals who have served as minister of health since 1970 has been a physician.[126] The commitment of these ministers to the status-quo public health system was limited; one of the ministers, Dr Richard Potter, began his time in office by publicly speculating about the total abolition of the local public health system; his predecessor, for his part, had initially been quite enthusiastic about provincializing the position of the medical health officer.[127] The sanitarians fought back as best they could and were often successful in moderating the reformist enthusiasms of their new ministers. But they could no longer count on a sanitarian ally at the top of the pyramid.

Thus, while the strength of the regionalists was growing, that of the sanitarians had been shrinking. The sanitarians' institutional resources had largely disappeared, and they could no longer count on the automatic acceptance of their policy assumptions by others in the Ontario Ministry of Health. While the sanitarians were never permanently defeated, their position in the field would never again return to the position of dominance that they had once enjoyed.

By 1980, then, the Ontario government's policy on regional boards of health had been decided in favour of generalization: those who were happy with their local boards could keep them, but any requests by regional governments for abolition of the local boards would quickly be granted. This basic policy persisted in the coming years, and even a major new version of the Public Health Act, the 1983 Health Protection and Promotion Act, did little to change the basic trajectory of structural developments in the public health field. For a time, structural debates in the public health field subsided.

A decade later, however, when Mike Harris and his fellow common-sense revolutionaries decided to embark on a campaign of massive municipal restructuring, public health structures once again moved into the crosshairs. In the last chapter, we described the background to the Harris government's municipal disentanglement plans, noting that the process began in an attempt to upload the costs of education while maintaining the provincial-municipal expenditure balance. We need not repeat that story here, except to discuss how changes to the public health system took place within this larger context.

Two related changes during the Harris era are particularly important. First, in 1997, the Harris government moved the dissolution of local boards of health from the Health Protection and Promotion Act to regulation. To abolish a local board of health, in other words, a legislative amendment was no longer needed; local governments like county councils simply needed to make a request to the provincial government.[128] The second, related change took up the process of generalization that had stalled in the 1980s; in the new municipalities of Toronto, Chatham-Kent, Ottawa, Hamilton, Haldimand, and Norfolk, responsibility for public health was given to municipal councils directly or, in Toronto, to a council-controlled board of health.[129] In some cases, such as Hamilton, this was an extension of the previous regional policy, while in others it meant the abolition of a local board of health. In every case, however, it meant that the pattern of generalization in Ontario continued.[130]

Thus, despite the Harris government's many changes in public health – the most notable being the total (and temporary) download of public health costs to the municipalities[131] – the structural changes in the field during the Harris era were consistent with the process of generalization that had begun in the 1970s. The basic argument of the regionalists in the earlier period was simply applied more widely in the

1990s: municipal governments should have the freedom to weigh local policies and priorities against one another, and the abolition of local ABCs such as boards of health allowed them to do just that. The result, at the turn of the millennium, was that a considerable proportion of local public health structures were under the direct or indirect control of general-purpose local governments.

These structural changes in the 1990s are certainly important, but at the time, they were the definition of "inside baseball." Even in the legislature, public health was an afterthought, swallowed up in changes to municipal funding, education financing, housing and welfare downloading, and municipal amalgamation.[132] It took two unexpected events early in the new millennium to bring public health back into the public eye.

These events, of course, were the Walkerton water crisis of 2000 and the SARS outbreak of 2003. Unfortunately, we cannot dwell on the dramatic details of these events – the heroes and villains, the tragic deaths and the joyous rock concerts, the praise for some and the public crucifixion of others – except to outline their impact on proposals for structural change. In Walkerton, it may be recalled, it was the public health system, in the person of a medical officer named Dr Murray McQuigge, that emerged as the public hero of the tale, which meant that the recommendations and criticisms of Justice Dennis O'Connor's Walkerton Inquiry were largely focused elsewhere.[133] Justice O'Connor's report *did* find worrying incapacity and inattention in the public health field, but these problems were the fault of local and municipal governments, rather than public health actors, and could be overcome with increased attention to public health and a strengthened role for the medical health officer.[134]

If Walkerton brought public health back to a simmer in the public consciousness, it was the 2003 SARS outbreak that brought it to a boil. In the aftermath of the outbreak, numerous investigations and commissions were launched, and unlike the Walkerton Inquiry, this time the public health system was squarely in the crosshairs.[135] In the final report of Ontario's SARS Commission, Justice Archie Campbell, the commissioner, pulled no punches. During the outbreak, he wrote, the "public health system was broken, neglected, inadequate and dysfunctional. It was unprepared, fragmented, uncoordinated. It lacked adequate resources, was professionally impoverished and was generally incapable of fulfilling its mandate."[136] On the matter of local health structures,

Campbell suggested that a majority of the positions on local boards of health be provincial rather than municipal appointments.[137] And even *with* this change, Campbell argued, local boards should be put on probation: if the system was not significantly improved by the end of a six-month trial, it should be completely provincialized. "Ontario cannot go back and forth like a squirrel on the road," wrote Campbell, "vacillating between the desire for some measure of local control and the need for uniformly high standards of infectious disease protection throughout the entire province."[138]

Neither of these recommendations was implemented. Instead, the Ministry of Health initiated a new round of investigations, researching the optimal size for local health units and working towards a performance measurement system for local boards of health.[139] Even so, the Campbell Commission's reports give us an interesting glimpse into the policy images in the field in the most recent past.

In some respects, the positions that we find articulated in the Campbell commission reports are similar to those we have encountered above. What is most needed, many argue, is expert authority: medical health officers and other officials must be made more independent of local municipal politicians.[140] This is a familiar argument, a central commitment of the sanitarians for more than a century. What is remarkable, however, is the extent to which local boards of health and municipal councils have become almost totally assimilated in the minds of many health officers. Whereas local boards of health were once the *solution* to the problem – and municipal councils the villains – those boards are now often seen as indistinguishable from municipal councils themselves.[141] This is a result of three decades of generalization. For twenty-first-century sanitarians, it is perfectly appropriate to assimilate local boards of health to municipal councils; in many cases, they are governed by the same people.[142]

What is clear from these recent reports is that the central actors in the public health policy field have never abandoned their commitment to specialization. But a significant proportion of local medical officers now believe that the only effective form of specialization – the only form of specialization that will truly remove the public health system from the influence of municipal governments – is provincialization.[143] This view, too, has been around for more than a century, and was clearly articulated by physicians already in 1878.[144] In the past, however, it was the officers and officials who spent their day-to-day lives in the local health system who resisted the move to provincialization. If the Campbell Commission is to be believed, this resistance appears to be fading.

In 2011, the provincial government passed a statute allowing the chief medical officer of health to issue directives to local boards of health during periods of emergency, a modest step towards provincialization.[145] This statute may prove to be the beginning of a new episode of provincialization, or it may be nothing more than a blip, a minor correction in the face of global epidemic threat. But there the pressure for provincialization, both from other public health fields in Canada and within the Ontario system itself, lingers in the public health field today.

6.6 Conclusions

Our investigation of public health in Ontario has uncovered three major episodes in the history of local health structures: the first from 1832 to 1875, during which the field was *unorganized*; the second from 1875 to 1970, during which the field was *stable*; and the third, from 1970 to the present, during which the field was *contentious*. Our first priority, therefore, has been to explain two major shifts in the field, the first in the 1870s and the second in the 1960s. In the first case, a tightly knit coalition that we have called the sanitarians entered the public health field, bringing with them a policy image built on disease prevention and expert authority; within a decade, the sanitarians' views were institutionalized in the field, and the sanitarians were able to dominate structural policy in the field for nearly a century. By 1970, however, the sanitarians' position had weakened, and when a regionalist argument opposed to local special purpose bodies spilled over into public health, the sanitarians proved unable to resist the changes that the regionalists demanded. Taken broadly, then, we have explained changes at the episode level – the broad patterns of institutional change across time – by pointing to shifts in the field's broad policy images, and we have explained changes in the images themselves by pointing to successful invasions from proximate policy fields.

These episode-level explanations cannot account for the pace and timing of the structural changes *within* our three major episodes. For this we need to rely on the character of the policy fields themselves. The character of the changes within each of the episodes follows from our general expectations about these fields. In the first episode, structural changes emerge from immediate and pressing problems, such as disease outbreaks (e.g., 1832, 1847, 1849, 1873) or changes to municipal structures (e.g., 1834, 1849). Policies during this period, in which the field is unorganized, are incremental and pragmatic, and the decision-making process is almost totally non-politicized.

In the second episode, particularly after the sanitarians had established themselves in the provincial board of health, problems and policies became steady and stable, repeated year after year in reports, meetings, and editorials. The sanitarians pressed constantly for change, and their patience and commitment enabled them to wait for opportunities to make the changes they desired. Generally, this meant that changes were made during periods of low political risk, such as a government's first session after an election. It is no coincidence that the most significant early changes in the field – the move to mandatory boards of health in 1884, the extension of term lengths in 1895, and the new Public Health Act in 1912 – were all passed in the first session of a legislature, when political risk was low. A second important factor was the sanitarians' level of Cabinet support. Some early ministers were more enthusiastic about reform than others, and the sanitarians were forced to wait, sometimes for years, until a hesitant Cabinet minister was replaced by a more sympathetic one. Overall, however, it was the constant labour of the sanitarians in a stable field, combined with periodic political opportunities, that best explains the timing of changes during the second episode.

As we move into the more contentious environment of the third and most recent episode, political opportunities become even more central. The sanitarians and the regionalists differed both on problems and on policies; the battle for which approach would dominate was often fought out politically, as each coalition mobilized supporters among local voters, local and provincial politicians, and important players in the provincial Cabinet. It seemed at first that the sanitarians might have the strength to resist the regionalist critique – their minister was deeply committed to local boards of health, and the regionalist challenge seemed at first to be little more than a "pet project" of Darcy McKeough – but it quickly became apparent that the sanitarian policy image was not as powerful as it had initially seemed to be. It became increasingly difficult for the sanitarians to make their voices heard at the political level, which the regionalists came to dominate. They have faced this same challenge to the present day.

The status of the policy field, therefore – whether unorganized, stable, or contentious – has an important structuring effect on problems, policies, and politics within the public health field. But events within the fields can and do strengthen or weaken a particular policy image. The SARS outbreak of 2003, for example, had a destabilizing effect on the old regionalist image of public health as general (controlled by councils) and local/regional (as opposed to provincial). Major reports in the aftermath of SARS called for consolidation, specialization, and even provincialization in Ontario's public health system. We cannot yet say whether these events will prove to be the beginning of a new episode, but they illustrate how events *within* episodes can affect the policy images by which those episodes are typically structured.

Chapter 7

Hydro-Electric Commissions

If ever we are tempted to forget about "the Hydro," the monuments are there to remind us. In Toronto, a statue of Sir Adam Beck, the first chairman of the Hydro-Electric Power Commission of Ontario, looms over motorists on University Avenue, his bronze eyes fixed on Queen's Park to the north. In Niagara Falls, a generating station is now a national historic site, its ornate stonework and neoclassical columns still solid after decades of disuse. In tiny Roseville, Ontario, a man once known as the Apostle of Hydro is commemorated with a six-foot cairn, permanently lit, according to legend, with free hydro power.[1] For many in the twentieth-century church of Hydro, the voice of "the Hydro" was the voice of progress, of collective solidarity against private monopoly. And the core of that church, its parish priests, were the hydro commissioners, the men who served, sometimes for decades, on hydro commissions in towns and cities across the province. It is to these commissions that we now turn.

7.1 Overview of Structural Changes

Figure 7.1 provides an overview of structural change events in hydro from 1810 to the present, capturing the same seven types of change that we have surveyed in the previous chapters. A few patterns are clear in the figure: a long string of creation and generalization from 1850 to 1890; then a second period in the early twentieth century composed of specialization and provincialization; a third period of generalization and consolidation in the 1970s and 1980s; and a small cluster of consolidation and elimination in the recent past. As in the previous chapters, our goal is to investigate these four episodes and to explain the background, timing, and pace of changes between and within them.

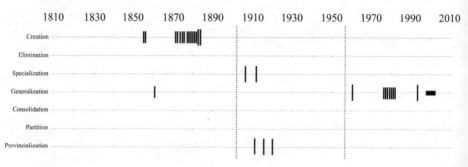

Figure 7.1. Hydro Commissions in Ontario: Overview of Change Events

Note: See table 7.1 for a brief description of each event.

7.2 Water, Gas, and Light Commissions, 1850–1883

The story of hydro-electric commissions in Ontario begins, appropriately enough, in the water. But it does not begin in the water that pours over Niagara Falls each day; that story would come some years later. Instead, the story begins in calmer water, in pipes, flowing beneath the growing towns and cities of southwestern Ontario. It begins with municipal waterworks.

In the summer of 1854, a group of doctors and dignitaries in Hamilton, Ontario, began to agitate for a clean water supply. Their demand, in itself, was nothing new: calls for a municipal water system in Hamilton stretched back more than two decades.[2] In 1854, however, cholera was raging, and Hamilton's doctors had begun to blame the water, particularly the putrid wells in the city's Corktown district. The municipal council responded by sponsoring a design competition for a local water system.[3] And when the council then invited T.C. Keefer, Canada's most prominent water engineer, to judge the competition, it began to seem that a municipal waterworks system might be more than a distant dream.[4]

The details of the system itself – the source of the water, the structure of the pipes and reservoirs, the extraordinary costs – need not detain us here. For our purposes, what matters is that the city entrusted the design and construction of the system to a special purpose board. The structure of the board was simple. Five men would be elected to serve, one from each of the city's five wards. The term length would be five years, with rotating replacement; one man would stand for re-election

Table 7.1. Event Catalogue: Changes to Hydro Commissions in Ontario

Year	Change type	Statute	Applicability	Description
1856	Creation	19 Vic., c.54	Hamilton	Creation of Hamilton Water Commission
1857	Creation	20 Vic, c 56	St Catharines	Creation of St Catharines Water Commission
1861	Generalization	24 Vic, c 56	Hamilton	Abolition of Hamilton Water Commission
1872	Creation	35 Vic, c 79	Toronto	Creation of Hamilton Water Commission
1872	Creation	35 Vic, c 80	Ottawa	Creation of Ottawa Water Commission
1873	Creation	36 Vic, c 102	London	Creation of London Water Commission
1874	Creation	37 Vic, c 78	Peterborough	Creation of Peterborough Water Commission
1874	Creation	37 Vic, c 79	Windsor	Creation of Windsor Water Commission
1876	Creation	39 Vic, c 47	St Catharines	Creation of St Catharines Water Commission
1878	Creation	41 Vic, c 26	Brampton	Creation of Brampton Water Commission
1878	Creation	41 Vic, c 28	Owen Sound	Creation of Owen Sound Water Commission
1878	Generalization	41 Vic, c 27	London	Abolition of London Water Commission
1878	Generalization	41 Vic, c 41	Toronto	Abolition of Toronto Water Commission
1879	Creation	42 Vic, c 77	Guelph	Abolition of Guelph Water Commission
1879	Generalization	42 Vic, c 78	Ottawa	Abolition of Ottawa Water Commission
1881	Creation	44 Vic, c 41	London East	Creation of London East Water Commission
1881	Creation	44 Vic, c 44	Parkdale	Creation of Parkdale Water Commission
1882	Creation	45 Vic, c 25	Ontario	Provision for creation of water commissions
1883	Creation	46 Vic, c 21	Ontario	Provision for creation of gas and light commissions

Table 7.1. Event Catalogue: Changes to Hydro Commissions in Ontario (*cont.*)

Year	Change type	Statute	Applicability	Description
1906	Specialization	6 Edw VII, c 40	Ontario	Extended term length for hydro commissioners
1911	Provincialization	Geo V, c 119	Toronto	Toronto Hydro-Electric Commission
1913	Specialization	3 Geo V, c 41	Ontario	Public Utilities Act
1916	Provincialization	6 Geo V, c 18	Central Ontario	HEPC takes control of Central Ontario System
1920	Provincialization	10–11 Geo V, c 18	Ontario (rural)	Rural power districts
1961	Generalization	10–11 Eliz II, c 106	Ontario (large cities)	Large cities may opt for appointed hydro commissions
1977	Generalization	25–6 Eliz II, c 28	Waterloo Region	Hydro commissions reorganized
1977	Consolidation	25–6 Eliz II, c 28	Waterloo Region	Hydro commissions consolidated
1978	Generalization	26–7 Eliz II, c 31	York Region	Hydro commissions reorganized
1979	Generalization	27–8 Eliz II, c 70	Halton Region	Hydro commissions reorganized
1979	Generalization	28–9 Eliz II, c 33	Niagara Region	Hydro commissions reorganized
1980	Generalization	28–9 Eliz II, c 59	Hamilton-Wentworth	Hydro commissions reorganized
1980	Generalization	28–9 Eliz II, c 40	Ottawa-Carleton	Hydro commissions reorganized
1980	Generalization	28–9 Eliz II, c 59	Sudbury	Hydro commissions reorganized
1994	Consolidation	43 Eliz II, c 31	Ontario	Consolidation made easier
1998	Consolidation	47 Eliz II, c 15	Ontario	Energy Competition Act prompts widespread consolidation

Note: This table provides the basic data for figure 7.1.
Source: Statutes of Ontario.

each year. The structure was approved in the Canadian legislature in June 1856, and four years later, to the delight of Hamilton's residents, the new waterworks was inaugurated by His Royal Highness himself, the future King, Edward Prince of Wales.[5]

Why did Hamilton choose a special purpose structure in 1856? Unfortunately, the available evidence on this question is incomplete. We *do* know that when New York City decided to build a water system in the early 1830s, responding, like Hamilton, to an outbreak of cholera, it entrusted the design and construction of the works to a commission – and we know that Hamilton's water commissioners knew of the developments in New York and were admirers of its commission.[6] As in Hamilton, the New York commission was a five-man board, but in New York, commissioners served one-year terms and were appointed by the state governor.[7]

Closer to home, the Montreal waterworks predated Hamilton's system by several years, and there were numerous points of contact between the two cities, including T.C. Keefer, the water engineer. But there is no evidence that the Montreal system was administered by anything other than a municipal committee in its early years, and it was not until 1920 that Montreal entrusted its water supply to a special purpose body.[8]

Thus, the exact source of inspiration for the structure of Hamilton's water commission remains unclear. It may have been partially inspired by the New York system, or it may have been the product of local improvisation; it was probably a little of both. On the question of *why* Hamilton opted for a special purpose body, however, our evidence is more satisfying, for much to our good fortune, Hamilton's water commissioners took it upon themselves to write a short treatise on the subject in 1860.[9]

The treatise was prompted by the threat of elimination. As the construction of the water system was nearing completion, Hamilton's council began to think that the day-to-day operation of the works could safely be left to a council committee. The water commissioners took a different view. "The Commissioners are unanimously and decidedly of the opinion," they wrote, "that the water works should be managed by persons specially elected for that purpose."[10] To support their position, the commissioners presented four interrelated arguments: first, the one-year term for municipal councillors did not provide the continuity that was necessary to manage the waterworks; second, councillors spend the first six months of their term finding their feet and the second

six months preparing themselves for election, leaving no time for difficult (and sometimes unpopular) decisions; third, while voters elect
councillors, they have no control over committees, and they would thus
have little say over who should oversee the waterworks system; fourth,
most major council decisions are made by council, not by committees,
and the media presence at council meetings makes for pontification
and grandstanding rather than sober reflection.[11] Taken together, the
argument was simple: council lacks the continuity, the capacity, and the
expertise to competently manage the waterworks.

By 1856, then, a model for a municipal water commission was on the
statute books in Canada, and arguments in support of that model had
begun to circulate. But when Toronto's city council asked for its own
waterworks legislation the following year, it decided to change the model slightly. Toronto, too, had been discussing water for decades, and it
too had held a design competition for a new system in the 1850s.[12] By
1857, Toronto council was confident enough in its plans for a municipal
waterworks that it asked the legislature for an enabling statute. The bill
itself proved briefly controversial – some aldermen knew nothing about
the bill until they heard that it was before the Private Bills Committee –
but it was also, according to its authors, "as nearly as possible a tran-
script of the bill authorizing the city of Hamilton to construct water
works."[13] The only departure, Toronto's solicitor explained, was the
commission structure, which "would be placed in the hands of the
Council, instead of being elected by the people."[14] The board would consist of three men, rather than five, and would be appointed rather than
elected.[15] The reason for the change was pragmatic: a ward-based system
in Toronto would simply make for too large a commission.[16] In the end,
the details mattered little: as the economic boom of 1857 gave way to
bust in 1858, the prospect for a municipal water system in Toronto faded,
and the enabling legislation sat idly on the statute books, unused.[17]

The issue returned to the agenda in Toronto in the early 1870s. In
1872, an enabling bill was once again introduced in the legislature, and
the bill contained a provision for a waterworks commission. This time,
the commission would consist of five members: four men elected at
large for two-year terms, and the mayor.[18] In 1872, after decades of discussion and debate, a Toronto Waterworks Commission was elected
and asked to design an upgraded system for the city of Toronto.[19]

By the early 1870s, then, two basic models for waterworks administration were in the statute books. The first, originating in Hamilton,
was a ward-based model with lengthy rotating terms. The second,

originating in Toronto, consisted of the mayor and four at-large commissioners elected for two-year terms. What happened next is summarized in table 7.2. St Catharines and Ottawa, both of which had drafted their waterworks legislation before the Toronto model became law, followed the earlier Hamilton system.[20] After 1872, however, the Toronto model became the basic template for all future water commissions in Ontario. In some cases, the process by which one bill influenced the next was literally a matter of cut-and-paste, with portions of earlier bills glued into the draft versions of later ones.[21]

Over time, of course, the Toronto model was adjusted. In smaller places, a 2 + 1 system (two commissioners and the mayor) seemed more appropriate than Toronto's larger 4 + 1 system. Eventually, the legislature simply permitted both options, leaving the matter to locals to decide. The term length for commissioners also varied at first, but stabilized at one year by the end of the 1870s. After London requested permission to abolish its commission in 1878, permission to do so was built into all later bills.[22] Thus, between 1870 and 1880, what we see is steady tinkering: first the Toronto model replaces the Hamilton model, and then the Toronto model is itself refined as it spreads across the province.

By the early 1880s, the municipal water movement had picked up steam. Nearly every year, the provincial government could expect to receive one or two requests from municipalities for enabling legislation. The Mowat government's preference, however, was for general legislation rather than private bills, so in the 1882 session, Mowat decided to introduce a general provision for municipal waterworks.[23] The bill passed through the legislature with little comment, hardly acknowledged at all except as one of the session's "measures which will tend to obviate the necessity of seeking to obtain by private Acts powers which may, with equal safety and greater expedition, be granted under general Acts."[24] Appropriately, however, these few words were spoken by Lieutenant-Governor John Beverley Robinson – a man who had served alongside a fresh-faced councillor by the name of Oliver Mowat on a committee sent to advocate for Toronto's waterworks legislation twenty-six years earlier.[25]

The content of the new waterworks legislation was wholly unsurprising. Municipalities could choose between a 2 + 1 or a 4 + 1 structure. A provision for abolition was included. Term lengths were one year. In an early draft of the legislation, the bill began with a long list of private waterworks statutes in Ontario; like a biblical chronicle, the legislation was simply the final name in a great and noble string of *begats*.[26]

Table 7.2. Water Commission Structures in Ontario, 1856–1882*

City	Year	Legislation	Number	Elected	Term	Abolish**
Hamilton	1856	19 Vic, c 64	1/ward	Elected	5	N
St Catharines	1857	20 Vic, c 91	1/ward	Elected	3	N
Toronto	1872	35 Vic, c 79	Mayor + 4	Elected	2	N
Ottawa	1872	35 Vic, c 80	1/ward	Elected	1	N
London	1873	36 Vic, c 102	Mayor + 2	Elected	1	N
Peterborough	1874	37 Vic, c 78	Mayor + 2	Elected	1	N
Windsor	1874	37 Vic, c 79	Mayor + 2	Elected	2	N
St Catharines	1876	39 Vic, c 47	1/ward	Elected	2	N
Brampton	1878	41 Vic, c 26	Mayor + 2	Elected/ appointed	1	Y
Owen Sound	1878	41 Vic, c 28	Mayor + 2 or 4	Elected	1	Y
Guelph	1879	42 Vic, c 77	Mayor + 2 or 4	Elected	1	Y
London East	1881	44 Vic, c 41	Mayor + 2	Elected	1	Y
Parkdale	1881	44 Vic, c 44	Mayor + 2	Elected	1	Y
Waterworks Act	1882	45 Vic, c 25	Mayor + 2 or 4	Elected	1	Y

* Statutory provisions for local water commissions in Ontario from the first statute in 1856 to the passage of the general Waterworks Act in 1882.
** "Abolish" indicates whether the statute gives council the authority to abolish the commission.

The next year, however, the provincial Waterworks Act begat a child of its own. The new statute, passed in 1883 as the Municipal Light and Heat Act, provided for municipal gas and light plants in Ontario, and included a provision for municipal commissions to manage the systems. The structure for the new hydro-electric commissions (what were then called gas and light commissions) was not merely inspired by the 1882 waterworks law: it swallowed the earlier structure whole. "The sections numbered from thirty-eight to forty-five, both inclusive, of the *Municipal Water-works Act, 1882*," read the new Light and Heat Act, referring to the water commission provisions, "are also hereby incorporated with this Act as if the same were repeated herein."[27] In one sentence, the endpoint in the long evolution of water commissions in Ontario became the starting point for an entirely new story. This story was little more than an afterthought in 1883, but it would soon become one of the most pressing political issues in the province.[28]

This era in the history (or pre-history) of hydro-electric commissions in Ontario is one of gradual and incremental change. The basic structure developed in Hamilton was first adapted to suit the Toronto context, and was then tweaked and adjusted as it spread elsewhere. The story is an almost perfect example of path dependence: once a basic structure was in place, future changes were limited to incremental tinkering within that larger structure.[29] But the process that lay beneath the path dependence was not "positive feedback," for it was of no wider consequence to anyone whether Peterborough or Windsor had three or six or twelve water commissioners.[30] Instead, the underlying process was satisficing: no one saw any reason to reach back farther than the most recent legislation when writing up a new bill.[31] Whether to *have* a water commission was a matter of frequent and sometimes heated controversy, and commissions were often abolished as quickly as they had been created.[32] But the structure of the commissions, which passed from the realm of water to the realm of gas and light in 1883 with barely a comment, was a matter of intermittent and minor political interest.

7.3 The Birth and Expansion of the HEPC, 1906–1920

Early in the twentieth century, a new player entered the hydro-electricity field: the Hydro-Electric Power Commission of Ontario (HEPC). The story of the HEPC's birth is dramatic and eventful, but we have space for little more than the nutshell version of the tale. It runs as follows.[33] A coal strike in Pennsylvania in 1902 alerted Ontario manufacturers to the need for alternative sources of energy, and new technologies had begun to make long-distance transmission of electrical power more feasible.[34] In 1902, a group of manufacturers and municipal leaders met in Berlin, Ontario, to discuss the issue, and four years later, after dozens of meetings, two provincial commissions, ongoing lobbying efforts, and a change of government, the Hydro-Electric Power Commission of Ontario was born.[35] In its early years, the HEPC was focused almost exclusively on planning and building a distribution network from Niagara Falls to participating municipalities, and local structures were therefore left largely unchanged.[36] Gradually, however, broader changes began to creep in.

The first site of local change was in Toronto. To prepare for its connection to the Niagara distribution line in May 1911, Toronto's city council drafted a bill for a new hydro-electric commission in the city.[37] The commission would have three members: the mayor, a council appointee, and an HEPC appointee.[38] Prior to 1911, electricity policy in Toronto had only ever been managed by a council committee, and the new bill was widely interpreted as an attack on municipal autonomy.[39] "By some means that would probably not stand investigation," wrote a scathing editorial in the *Globe*, "a bare majority of [council] were stampeded into giving their approval to a proposition that should not have been entertained for a moment ... such subordination of themselves to an outside body was utterly unworthy of men elected by the people."[40] It was not immediately clear who benefited from the new legislation, though the Hydro-Electric Power Commission of Ontario was certainly viewed with suspicion. The controversy gradually subsided, but the new legislation was an early indication that the HEPC would soon be intimately involved in local affairs.[41]

The second major development was what came to be known as the Central Ontario System. For years, the HEPC had been interested in acquiring power-generation facilities in central Ontario in order to expand its network eastward. By 1915, most of the electrical infrastructure in the region was owned by the Electrical Development Company,[42] which Adam Beck, the HEPC chairman, had been trying to purchase for years. When the purchase offer fell through, Beck had then appealed, unsuccessfully, to the federal minister of railways and canals for a water lease along the Trent to compete with the Electrical Development Company.[43] As Beck's frustration mounted, his relationship with the EDC's president became strained, and the controversy began to escalate.

What happened next merits an essay of its own, and we can cover only the barest details here.[44] On the morning of March 4, 1916, the Ontario government met with the EDC's president and made an offer to the company subject to Adam Beck's approval. Then, in the afternoon, the EDC president departed and Adam Beck arrived – at this point, apparently, the two could no longer even be in the same room together – and Beck agreed to the deal.[45] In the process of negotiation, however, the price for the various properties had gone up, and no one had asked the municipal governments in the region if they would be willing to purchase the utilities at the increased price. The result – in what is surely one of the stranger moments of Ontario's political history – was that the HEPC became directly responsible for managing many of the Electrical Development Company's former businesses, including such operations as the gas plants in Oshawa and Napanee, the waterworks in Cobourg, the street railway in Peterborough, and – most peculiar of all – the Campbellford pulp mill![46] The municipalities in central Ontario, having made no commitment to purchase the utilities, were in an enviable bargaining position, and refused to make a purchase on anything but the most attractive terms. "The government has purchased it," said the chairman of Peterborough's Utilities Commission of the town's rickety street railway system. "Let them go ahead and operate it."[47]

In Central Ontario, then, the HEPC was forced not only to distribute electricity *to* the municipalities, but also, in some cases, to actually operate the municipal electrical systems as well. Some have interpreted this as a conscious move towards provincial control of local utilities, and there can be little doubt that Adam Beck's fierce determination to purchase the central Ontario infrastructure contributed to the haste with which the Government of Ontario made a deal.[48] But a careful look at the evidence suggests that neither Beck nor anyone else intended for the government to invade the municipal sphere; everyone believed that the municipalities would purchase the new assets after the deal had gone through. The unintended outcome, however, was the first significant instance in Ontario of the direct provincial operation of local utilities.

In 1920, the HEPC added a second zone of direct administration – called rural power districts – to its list of local responsibilities. This time, the move was entirely intentional. Rural Ontarians had been demanding electrical power since the early years of the hydro-electricity movement, and rural newspapers like the *Farmer's Sun* had often criticized Adam Beck for focusing too heavily on urban manufacturers in Ontario.[49] Beck, for his part, had long advocated rural hydro, sending his famous "hydro circus" through the countryside to demonstrate the glories of the electrified life at agricultural meetings and township fairs.[50] Before 1920, however, rural electrification had proceeded slowly, and in 1919, Beck asked his committee on rural rates to suggest revisions to the rural system. The committee reported that for hydro-electric purposes, township boundaries should be ignored, and that the HEPC should instead establish "rural power districts" of about one hundred square miles across rural Ontario.[51]

Ernest Drury's UFO government, deeply concerned with rural Ontario, quickly passed the legislation. Each rural power district would be operated directly by Ontario Hydro, though each district would be managed separately and would keep separate books. The boundaries of the "RPD" would be purely technical, drawn up on the basis of population density, existing infrastructure, and consumer demand.[52] In the years that followed, the RPDs did provoke occasional controversy, particularly due to relatively high rates (compared with nearby urban centres) and a much-hated requirement that customers sign twenty-year contracts. But the structure itself, which marked a major provincialization of the electricity system in Ontario, prompted almost no discussion in the legislature and little complaint in the years that followed.

By 1920, then, much had changed in Ontario's hydro-electricity field. In most urban areas, municipal governments retained responsibility for their electrical systems, which were administered by elected hydro-electric commissions. The structure of the commissions had changed very little, though the 1913 Public Utilities Act, which consolidated the earlier Waterworks and Light and Heat statutes, allowed for combined "public utilities commissions" to oversee both water and electricity. In Toronto, however, a new structure was in place, one that looked very different from the traditional hydro-electric commission in Ontario, and in large parts of the province, the HEPC had moved directly into what had once been an exclusively municipal domain. In individual municipalities, like London or St Catharines or Waterloo, little might have seemed to have changed. But in the wider picture, viewed across the province as a whole, the administrative map looked very different from twenty years before.

How can we explain these twentieth-century changes? After all, this was a period of deep commitment to municipal autonomy in Ontario, and we might have expected a great deal of controversy as a result of the hydro commission's early provincializing moves. But two important factors prevented any major controversy from emerging. The first was the extraordinary *demand* for hydro-electric power in municipalities across the province. The expansion of the system fit neatly into the standard municipal policy image that we have surveyed in Part One: the need for competitive advantages to sustain and grow the manufacturing economy; the need for cheap power to overcome a lack of "natural advantages" in coal supply; the need to capture the wealth of Niagara Falls before it was monopolized by manufacturers on the American side of the river.[53] Even in rural Ontario, hydro-electricity was often seen as a saviour, bringing urban comforts to rural homes and thereby stemming the tide of rural migration to the cities.[54] When hydro *did* arrive in towns and cities across the province, the local celebrations were enormous, often spectacular. Ontario wanted electricity, and if that meant Central Ontario systems and rural power districts, so be it.

But this is only half the story. There was also a second factor, one that can be summarized in a single name: Adam Beck. Beck had been involved in the hydro-electric movement since the early 1900s, and when James Whitney's Conservatives won the Ontario election in 1905, the balance of power in the burgeoning movement shifted towards Beck, a Conservative.[55] The political gods could hardly have selected a better man for the job. Ferociously competitive, explosive and charismatic, and committed to hydro with a zeal that would put tent-revivalists to shame, Beck stands as a single-handed rebuttal to any who deny the significance of individuals in history.[56]

In his own day, Beck was both loved and loathed. No one denied that Beck was fanatically devoted to "the Hydro," a man of character untainted by indecency or corruption. But he was also reviled for his authoritarian tendencies, his total disregard for the legislature, and his paranoid contempt for Hydro's critics. Premier Ernest Drury called Beck a man with the "instincts of an eighteenth-century aristocrat and the character of a tyrant." But Drury admitted that he was also – in a brilliant example of the ambivalence that Beck inspired – something of a friend. "In spite of our many differences, and some things that were hard to forgive," wrote Drury, "I liked Sir Adam and I think he liked me."[57]

However one felt about Adam Beck, nobody denied his power. Everyone, from the premier on down, saw Beck as a colossus, a man with whom one grappled only when all other options were exhausted.[58] Beck's power had two sources. First, the ambiguous organizational character of the HEPC – a provincial agency on the one hand, a municipal cooperative on the other – allowed Beck all the power of the provincial state when he needed to bring a municipality into compliance, and all the legitimacy of the municipalities when he needed the provincial government to back down.[59] Beck strengthened and cultivated this ambiguity by assembling a coalition of local actors to support his policies, a coalition formalized in 1912 with the creation of the Ontario Municipal Electric Association. In the early years, Beck's HEPC and the OMEA were practically indistinguishable, and Beck's control of the OMEA was "dictatorial": he inspired the association's resolutions, provided the link between the association and supportive newspapers, and even quietly funded the association.[60] Whenever pressure was needed, Beck was ready with deputations of dozens, sometimes hundreds, of municipal representatives, who streamed into Toronto at Beck's call to express their displeasure with the government and to voice their support for the great Sir Adam Beck.[61]

"Safely installed between the provincial and municipal jurisdictions and independent of both, and with a popular mandate and bureaucratic dynamics behind him," writes H.V. Nelles, the dean of Hydro historians, "Adam Beck built his empire."[62] Even contemporary observers were wise to Beck's strategy. W.D. Gregory, who had been commissioned by Premier Drury to study the HEPC's opaque operations, described Beck's tactics brilliantly:

> [Beck] is an expert in the art of creating and organizing public opinion ... before or after the announcement of a project or policy is made by the Chairman, meetings are held, resolutions endorsing the scheme are passed and deputations arranged for. Soon the Hydro Press (so-called) is heard from in its support for the proposed undertaking. When the matter is taken up with the Government, it has to deal with that project which the Commission has already launched and for which a vigorous propaganda is already in full blast. The Government cannot disapprove of the project without running counter to a large body of opinion that has been created in advance.[63]

At the heart of the changes we have uncovered, then, is the "social skill" of Sir Adam Beck, his ability to serve as the voice of the municipalities against the provincial government while simultaneously deploying the resources of the provincial government to consolidate and expand the provincial hydro-electric network.[64] This would not have been possible were it not for the ambiguity of the HEPC itself, though that ambiguity was carefully cultivated by the rhetorical savvy of Hydro defenders like Beck. The two major structural changes in this period – the Central Ontario System and rural power districts – were uncontroversial in part because they did not threaten any existing hydro-electric commissions or local authorities. But they were also uncontroversial because of the extraordinary depth of support enjoyed by Adam Beck and the HEPC in towns and cities across the province. Though Beck would depart in 1925, the policy image, the organization, and the rhetoric that he had created would survive, in Ontario, for decades.[65]

7.4 The Regionalist Challenge, 1960–1980

Much had changed in Ontario's electricity system between 1920 and 1960. The inter-municipal electric railway system into which Beck and others had poured enormous energies had collapsed and disappeared.

Rural Ontario was almost fully electrified. A nuclear test facility was under construction in Rolphton, Ontario, and would go critical in a matter of months.[66] What had not changed, however, were the local structures by which all of this was administered. The same basic structures – elected commissions in urban areas, rural power districts in rural areas, appointed commissions in a few very large cities – still existed across the province, almost totally unchanged after four decades.[67] But the quiet continuity was about to come to an end.

We are already familiar, from the previous chapter, with the "regionalist" challenge in Ontario: the commitment to larger and more powerful units of local government, which grew out of a concern for successful economic development and improved regional planning. For the regionalists, local governments could not be coherent public actors if they were unable to make priorities and decisions *across* policy spheres, which meant that local special purpose bodies – which prevented such decisions – would need to be folded into general purpose local and regional governments if the new, reformed structures were to succeed.

As a result of this argument, hydro-electric commissions were a key regionalist target. In the first major regionalist statement in Ontario – the Beckett Select Committee on the Municipal Act – Beckett and his colleagues were uncompromising, suggesting that the Public Utilities Act be repealed and that public utilities commissions become a committee of municipal council.[68] And Beckett was only the beginning: over the next ten years, as table 7.3 reveals, report after report recommended generalization, consolidation, or both. In many cases, the recommendation was straightforward abolition.[69] In other cases the recommendations were slightly less radical (appointed rather than elected commissions, for example), or electricity was simply ignored.[70] Of all the reports, however, including repeated waves of local government reviews across Ontario, just one – a Hamilton-Wentworth review in 1969 – recommended that elected lower-tier hydro commissions be preserved.[71]

The local government reviews in Ontario were soon supplemented by another cluster of studies, this time focused exclusively on the subject of electricity. The first and most important was Task Force Hydro (TFH), a subcommittee of John Robarts's ambitious Committee on Government Productivity.[72] The TFH final report contained a wide range of recommendations, including a controversial new structural model for Ontario Hydro itself, but what was most important for our purposes was its recommendation on the structure of the *local* system.[73] Unlike most of the local area reviews, TFH did not recommend that

Table 7.3. Hydro Governance Recommendations in Government Reports, 1960–1980

Year	Geographical Area	Description
1965	Province-wide	Beckett Committee: recommends abolition of HCs
1965	Ottawa area	Ottawa-Carleton-Eastview report recommends abolition of HCs
1965	Toronto	Royal Commission on Metro Toronto: no discussion of hydro commissions
1966	Niagara area	Niagara area report recommends abolition of HCs
1966	Peel-Halton area	Peel-Halton review recommends appointed HCs
1967	Province-wide	Ontario Committee on Taxation: no recommendations on HCs
1968	Lakehead area	Lakehead local review makes no recommendations on hydro
1968	Province-wide	Select Committee on Ontario Committee on Taxation: no discussion of HCs
1969	Hamilton area	Hamilton-Wentworth report recommends larger lower-tier HCs
1969	Muskoka	Muskoka area report leaves hydro structure to hydro experts
1970	Province-wide	Dolbey ABCs Report recommends abolition of HCs
1970	Waterloo area	Waterloo area report recommends abolition of HCs
1970	Sudbury	Sudbury area report makes no specific recommendations on hydro
1972	Province-wide	Task Force Hydro report recommends regional consolidation of HCs
1972	GTA East	Report on Area East of Metro: wait for Task Force Hydro report
1974	Province-wide	Hogg report recommends regional HCs where viable
1976	Ottawa area	Ottawa-Carleton Review recommends abolition of HCs
1977	Niagara area	Niagara Region review recommends regionalization, abolition of HCs
1977	Toronto	Royal Commission on Metro Toronto recommends appointed HCs
1978	Hamilton area	Hamilton-Wentworth review: hydro is under study elsewhere
1979	Waterloo area	Waterloo Region review commission recommends abolition of HCs

hydro utilities be abolished. But it did recommend that they be *regionalized*. The problem was not the *existence* of hydro commissions, the TFH report argued, but their *number* – more than 350 across the province at that time.[74] As regional governments were created across the province, the TFH report argued, electrical utilities ought to be consolidated at the regional level. Because the election of hydro commissioners might prove difficult at the regional level, the task force also recommended that the commissioners be appointed rather than elected – but that councillors themselves be banned from service on the commission.[75]

The Task Force Hydro report prompted a more detailed follow-up study, under the leadership of William Hogg, focused on the subject of local hydro structures alone.[76] Like the task force, Hogg concluded that regional hydro commissions ought to be the goal. As for the structure of the commission, Hogg recommended that the most important decision be left to the municipalities: while hydro commissions should stay, council should be free to decide whether those commissions will be appointed or elected.[77]

For more than a decade, then, report after report rolled off the presses at Queen's Park, hundreds, thousands of pages of recommendations, all of them nearly unanimous in the direction, if not the extent of the required changes. But the immediate result of these many reports, this constant pressure for consolidation, generalization, even abolition of hydro commissions, was precisely nothing. Regional government arrived in Niagara, Hamilton, Waterloo, and elsewhere, and hydro commissions continued unchanged.[78] Ontario Hydro was radically restructured, transformed into a provincial corporation, and local hydro commissions were untouched. It was not until 1977, more than a decade after the first reports had been printed, that structural changes finally began.

Even then, the changes were minor. Instead of moving to regional commissions, as TFH and Hogg had recommended, local hydro commissions were simply restructured to match the boundaries of the new lower-tier municipalities that were created in the transition to regional government. In Peel, for example, new hydro commissions were established for Brampton, Mississauga, and Caledon, the three new lower-tier municipalities.[79] The main problem with making more radical moves, in Peel and elsewhere, was distributional: rural customers were served by Ontario Hydro, and if those customers were folded into a regional system with equalized rates, the price of electricity in the region's urban areas would have to go up. Thus, while regional commissions might have remained the long-term goal, lower-tier utilities continued to be the present norm.[80] The structure of the commissions was the familiar 4 + 1 or 2 + 1 model, with larger boards for the larger municipalities and smaller boards for the smaller ones. Only in Waterloo Region, for reasons we have surveyed in chapter 4, were the boundaries of the new hydro commissions different from those of the new lower-tier municipalities.[81] In every other region, the structure of the new commissions would have been entirely familiar to a time-travelling visitor from the late nineteenth century.[82]

There was, however, one important change. Following the advice of the Hogg report on hydro structures, the new legislation allowed the municipal councils to choose whether the commissions should be elected or appointed.[83] After a two-year transition, during which the new commission would be managed by members of the previous commissions (the first commissioners in Mississauga, for example, would be members of the erstwhile Streetsville and Port Credit commissions), municipal councils could pass a bylaw making future commissioners appointed rather than elected. The default, if no bylaw was passed, was an elected commission. Thus, while hydro commissions would survive, municipal councils would now have the opportunity, if they chose to take it, to control the membership of the commission directly.

Compared to the radical recommendations of the reports that we have surveyed above, this is a strikingly modest set of reforms. Much of the province was left entirely as-is; any places untouched by regional restructuring were also untouched by the changes in hydro-electricity. And even where regional government had been implemented, lower-tier commissions were still required by law. There would be no abolition, no consolidation, no generalization. There would merely be the option, in a few regional municipalities, of an appointed hydro commission.

One of the reasons for the rather underwhelming nature of these reforms was simply timing. In some cases, local area reviews and other reports hesitated to make recommendations on the subject of hydro-electricity because the matter was under study elsewhere – by Task Force Hydro, the Hogg Committee, or narrower regional reviews.[84] This meant that regional government arrived without any corresponding changes in hydro, and once the regional transition had passed, the urgency for reform faded. Thus, while much of the local scene was being radically transformed, hydro floated along in an endless stream of reports.[85]

A second reason for the limited reforms is the truncated history of regional government itself. Many of the reports that addressed hydro restructuring from the provincial viewpoint operated on the assumption that the entirety of the province would eventually be covered by regional government.[86] But when the early regional governments proved more controversial than expected, the William Davis government tiptoed gingerly away from its earlier ambitions.[87] Many of the restructuring recommendations for hydro, which depended for their coherence on regional government, were thereby rendered obsolete.

These two factors, timing and truncation, help to explain why, after such effort and emphasis, the hydro reforms proved so modest. But they are hardly satisfying on their own. After all, the changes were minor, and slow in arriving, even in places like Waterloo and Niagara, where the local reports had been quite explicit about the need for abolition. And the truncated history of regional government cannot explain why the changes were so limited even where regional governments *were* installed. In those places, the timing was right and the opportunity was there. So what are we still missing?

The answer is simple: the Ontario Municipal Electric Association. Through the entirety of this twenty-year episode, the OMEA was active, organized, and strenuously resistant to change.[88] When the Ontario Committee on Taxation was asked to investigate local and provincial institutions in the province, the OMEA was there, ready with a submission.[89] When Darcy McKeough announced the new regional policy for the province in *Design for Development*, the OMEA had its counter-reports prepared.[90] When local review commissions asked for input or opened their doors for hearings, the OMEA representatives were first in line to make their case.[91] Their argument was always the same: leave well enough alone. "We urge most strongly," wrote the OMEA in one early submission, "that no action of any kind be taken to destroy the substantial and undeniable benefits which have come from over 60 years of experience with the operations of municipal hydro commissions."[92] There were moments when the association was willing to bend, granting that appointed commissions might occasionally be necessary during transition periods, and granting that upper-tier rather than lower-tier commissions might sometimes be appropriate.[93] But the core argument – the absolute necessity of elected local hydro commissions – was solid as granite.[94]

It must be said, if only to remind ourselves that successful arguments are not always the best arguments, that the OMEA's three central arguments during this period were, frankly, rather unpersuasive. The first was a classic: since hydro commissions had no taxing power, taking their funds exclusively from hydro-electric revenue, their operations must be kept separate from other municipal departments.[95] This argument sat awkwardly alongside the fact that water utilities had been absorbed into regional and municipal governments without any catastrophic consequences.[96] The second argument, that hydro-electric distribution was a highly technical enterprise requiring a commission of specialists, was also easily defeated. "Municipal councils handle responsibilities which are at least as complex and technical as hydro-electric distribution, much more time consuming than hydro-electric distribution, and much larger in terms of payroll and capital projects," wrote one provincial official in 1979. "No harm has come to those services such as transit or water supply which were transferred to municipal councils [in Waterloo Region] in 1973."[97] The final argument, of a somewhat more recent vintage, concerned competitiveness: because the local commissions were competing against gas and other energy suppliers, the OMEA argued, it was crucial that they remain nimble and adaptable in the energy marketplace.[98] But this was simply nonsense. If hydro commissions had ever been nimble competitors, those days had long since passed; by the 1960s, electricity rates, along with most other competitive policies, were determined provincially, by Ontario Hydro.[99] There may have been good arguments for local, elected hydro commissions in Ontario in the 1960s, but if there were, the OMEA had not discovered them.

Still, weak arguments notwithstanding, everyone all seemed to pull punches when it came to local hydro. One provincial report on local special purpose bodies, which had boldly called for radical changes to conservation authorities and school boards, admitted that "any departure from the [separate commission for hydro] is thought to be politically unacceptable at present. Individual commissions, the OMEA and Ontario Hydro have made it clear that they strongly support the elected commission system."[100] A decade later, the author of the Waterloo Region Review Commission report, William Palmer, expressed similar exasperation.[101] Indeed, not even the premier himself was immune; in 1973, after the Task Force Hydro report had been released, William Davis hurried to the OMEA's annual meeting to clarify that he had no plans to eliminate local hydro commissions.[102]

The source of the OMEA's remarkable power during this period came from both above and below. At the provincial level, the association enjoyed sustained support from Ontario Hydro. The available archival evidence suggests, again and again, that the OMEA and Ontario

Hydro carefully coordinated their strategies, with Ontario Hydro regularly insisting that it needed to maintain a close and unmediated connection to "its" municipal authorities.[103] Thus, while Ontario Hydro was willing to endorse a regionalized hydro system, it was resistant to any reforms that might weaken the direct connection between it and local hydro-electric utilities. This provided the OMEA with an important source of provincial support.

The OMEA's strength also came from below. It is easy to forget today that the OMEA was once an association of *elected* representatives, of hundreds of men (and, presumably, a few women) elected to serve on hydro commissions in municipalities across the province. Voter turnout in the hydro commission elections was often abysmally low, but even so, hydro commissioners had ongoing contact with voters and were willing to draw on this resource when threatened. In 1973, for example, when the Task Force Hydro report was released, the issue was vigorously discussed at the association's annual meeting, and the OMEA quickly drafted a provocative leaflet for local commissions to include in their monthly billing statements. The OMEA made it all very easy: all that the local commissions had to do was to order a few thousand copies and add them to the billing statements that it sent out to customers in the mail.[104] The effect of the propaganda, in an era when these billing supplements were rare, was powerful and immediate.[105]

By the end of the 1970s, then, provincial and local hydro-electric utilities may not have enjoyed the same mythical grandeur as in the first half of the twentieth century, but the network of local commissioners, organized and coordinated by the Ontario Municipal Electric Association, was still powerful enough to apply serious pressure, locally and provincially, when they felt threatened.[106] From the perspective of the OMEA, the motto of this third era in the history of local hydro structures was probably *it could have been worse*. In an atmosphere of steady attack, with a new report advocating the abolition of hydro commissions practically every year, hydro commissions were able to emerge from the challenge largely unscathed. In many parts of the province, the system stood exactly as it had in 1960, and even where changes *had* been made, lower-tier hydro commissions were still firmly in place. Yes, in a few places, the commissions were now appointed rather than elected. But in the face of what might have been, had the more radical proposals been enthusiastically embraced, this minor defeat represented a broader, and deeper, success.

7.5 Consolidation and Elimination, 1994–2010

After the modest reforms of the late 1970s were complete, local hydro-electric structures were left alone for another fifteen years. But the structural stability was deceptive. Beneath the unchanging surface, new forces for change had begun to emerge in the field, and in just a few years, the local hydro system would undergo the most significant structural changes in its century-long history.

The problems began at the provincial level. Ontario Hydro, which had once enjoyed a near-mythical status in the province, had begun to waver in the face of planning mistakes and extraordinary costs, particularly in its nuclear division. The man who was chosen to lead Ontario Hydro in 1992 pronounced it a "corporation in crisis"; five years later, after a scathing report had called the province's nuclear plants "minimally acceptable" – the hydro-consultant equivalent of a D-minus – the *Economist* joked that Homer Simpson, the riotously lax nuclear safety inspector in *The Simpsons*, "might be more at home in Canada." "A steady drip of revelations," the *Economist* explained, "has eroded the public's once-solid, even affectionate support."[107]

Unsurprisingly, given the *Economist*'s ideological predilections in the 1990s, the magazine predicted that the result of Ontario Hydro's very public failures would be deregulation. For the magazine's global readership, this may have seemed a bold prediction, but for hydro insiders in Ontario, the changes were already written on the wall. Maurice Strong, the Hydro chairman, had been pushing for privatization since the early 1990s, and Bob Rae, the NDP premier, had seriously considered it before deciding that his government already had more than enough on its agenda.[108] When Rae lost to Mike Harris, however, in the spring election of 1995, the level of urgency among Hydro insiders grew considerably, and the Harris government began to make clear steps towards the disassembly, deregulation, and perhaps even the privatization of Ontario's electricity distribution system.[109]

This provincial-level drama was matched by a somewhat quieter dissatisfaction at the local level. As in the Task Force Hydro report two decades earlier, reports on Ontario's hydro distribution system in the 1990s emphasized the problems created by an overabundance of local utilities in the province. More than three hundred local utilities still existed in Ontario in the mid-1990s, including such behemoths as Finch Hydro (population 458) and Chatsworth Hydro (population 522), and everyone, even the OMEA, agreed that *some* degree of consolidation would probably improve the efficiency of the provincial distribution system.[110]

The question, of course, was *how*. In the first major report on the issue, William Farlinger's *Ontario Hydro and the Electric Power Industry*, the answer was simply to shoot for the moon.[111] The entire distribution system, the report declared, should be merged into a single mega-system and then broken into no more than ten regional distribution utilities.[112] Many hydro insiders, in their dictator-for-a-day fantasies, might have shared this vision for structural change, but even for the Harris government, not shy about rapid and radical reform, the prospect of a hydro mega-merger was daunting. The challenge was to find a policy that might push the local distribution system towards the end that the Farlinger report envisioned without requiring a wholesale takeover of the system.

Gradually, a less invasive solution emerged, built on two assumptions about the future of the local system. First, the end goal for the local system was retail competition, and municipal utilities would therefore need to be prepared to compete within a private retail market. This meant, second, that municipal utilities would need to get bigger. "No longer will the MEU [municipal electric utility] be able to look comfortably to 'Mother Hydro' for supply," wrote the Macdonald Commission's *Framework for Competition* report in 1996. "In the end, we believe that market forces will propel consolidation in the distribution business."[113] This new argument – that market competition would *itself* engender consolidation, rendering Farlinger's mega-merger unnecessary – quickly became the accepted wisdom in the field. But the Macdonald Commission still envisioned a regional system as the end goal of the process, one that would absorb the distribution business of Ontario Hydro. When the time came to explain how this might be accomplished, the commission demurred, writing only that "local participation would probably result in greater acceptance of the outcome."[114]

The next year, a government white paper on hydro restructuring took another important step down the ladder from dreams to reality. "Report after report has said that change is needed," the white paper began, later adding that "industry analysts believe that within ten years, monopoly franchises will have been replaced by competitive supply."[115] In the white paper, however, the idea that Ontario Hydro might be absorbed into the new regional utilities had disappeared. "The Government agrees with the *Advisory Committee* on the need for efficiency improvements and consolidation in electricity distribution," wrote the paper. "It has concluded that geographic rationalization in the distribution sector should proceed on a commercial and voluntary basis."[116] If the hydro-electric system were opened up to competition, in other words, the consolidation and rationalization problem would take care of itself.

Thus, on June 9, 1998, after years of discussion and debate, Jim Wilson, Ontario's minister of energy, stood in the legislature to introduce the Energy Competition Act.[117] By the year 2000 (the deadline was later extended), local electrical utilities in Ontario would be converted into business corporations. The legislation also divided Ontario Hydro into several separate entities, including a commercial generation company (Ontario Power Generation), a commercial distribution company (Hydro One), and a market regulator (then called the Independent Electricity Market Operator). The evolution of this provincial-level system in the ensuing years merits a book of its own: a failed attempt to sell Hydro One, initiated by the Mike Harris government and undone by Premier Ernie Eves; the introduction of the Ontario Power Authority, along with a slate of green-energy incentives programs, under the Dalton McGuinty Liberals; and most recently, the announcement by Premier Kathleen Wynne that the government would once again attempt to privatize Hydro One.[118] At the local level, however, the story was somewhat simpler: the commission structure that had begun in Hamilton in 1856 would, after almost 150 years, finally be retired.

The Energy Competition Act was widely viewed as the most important piece of legislation in the government's new session.[119] Publicly, however, the industry's most prominent lobby group, the OMEA (now simply the Municipal Electric Association), was remarkably quiet. Behind the scenes, the association was pushing hard for additions and amendments to the bill and for clarity on what the MEA felt were inevitable electricity rate increases.[120] But the MEA also seemed to recognize that the greater battle had been lost. Not only was their provincial ally, Ontario Hydro, enthusiastic about the new changes, but there were also cracks in the local system, with some local utilities calling excitedly for greater competitive freedom in the hydro market. "Perhaps a market economy, like democracy, is filled with problems, but it's better than the alternatives," wrote a resigned Bob Lake, the MEA president, at the end of 1998. "So, let's get on with it."[121]

And so they did. The result of the ECA, as everyone expected, was consolidation. In just a few years, the 307 utility providers that had populated the landscape in Ontario in the 1990s had been reduced to fewer than one hundred; by 2010, the number was under 90. More than 80 utilities had been swallowed up by Ontario Hydro (now Hydro One), which had gone on an enthusiastic buying spree after the passage of the ECA. Dozens more were folded into larger, consolidated utilities.[122] Reviewing these changes today, two factors help to explain who sold, who amalgamated, and who retained control: *size* and *municipal amalgamation*. The first factor, size, is especially clear; smaller municipalities were much more likely to sell or amalgamate than larger municipalities. Of the eighty-nine municipal utilities acquired by Hydro One, for example, more than half had populations below 2000, and more than three-quarters had populations below 5000. The median population of the municipalities that sold to Hydro One was 2,135; the median of those that retained their utilities, by contrast, was 27,846.[123] The reason for this divergence was cost. To make the transition from commission to corporation, millions of dollars had to be paid to consultants, lawyers, and technology specialists – the city of Peterborough spent $2.5 million on a new computer system alone[124] – which meant that the only realistic option for tiny places like Chatsworth (population 522) or Flesherton (population 625) was divestment.

The second important factor was municipal amalgamation. During the period that municipal governments were deciding whether or not to hold on to their utilities, the Harris government was also carrying out a massive program of municipal amalgamation, one that ultimately reduced the number of municipal governments in Ontario from 815 in 1996 to 447 in 2001. Many of these amalgamated municipalities also merged their hydro utilities: even if we count only the five largest examples (Chatham-Kent, Hamilton, Ottawa, Brant County, and Haldimand-Norfolk), some twenty-three electrical utilities disappeared simply as a result of amalgamation. Part of the hydro consolidation story, then, is simply a carry-over from the process of *municipal* consolidation that was occurring at the same time.[125]

Municipal amalgamations also contributed to hydro consolidation in a slightly less obvious way. By disrupting the longstanding institutions and traditions of many Ontario municipalities, municipal amalgamations created opportunities for change that might not have been available in the absence of the municipal restructuring. Neil Freeman, who served at the tip of the spear in Hydro One's acquisition program, remembers consulting a map of municipal restructuring across the province and targeting the municipalities that were undergoing amalgamation. In an ideal scenario, Freeman says, the amalgamating municipalities would contain a large rural population (meaning that many customers were already served by Hydro One) and the local decision-makers would be councils rather than commissions. Mapleton Township, in Wellington County, is a good example. Not only did the pre-amalgamation Township of Maryborough considerably outnumber the Village of Drayton, but hydro was also controlled in both municipalities either by town council or by Ontario Hydro.[126] With more customers in the new township *already* served by Hydro One, and with little institutional commitment to local control of the hydro system, the result, for Hydro One representatives like Neil Freeman, was a much easier sell.[127]

By the early 2000s, then, the structure of Ontario's local hydro system had been transformed. More than two hundred utilities had disappeared, some acquired by Hydro One, others merged into large regional utilities, still others swallowed up in the contemporaneous municipal restructuring. In many places, the prediction that utilities would choose the safety of consolidation over the risks of competition had proved prescient. Like many voluntary consolidation processes, however, the success was only partial. As of 2014, twenty-one utilities still serve a customer base of fewer than 10,000, and fourteen employ fewer than ten full-time employees; Toronto Hydro, by comparison, employs more than 1500 full-time staff and serves nearly 750,000 customers. Despite the considerable changes, in other words, the basic problem of the 1990s – an orders-of-magnitude difference between the smallest and the largest utilities – has persisted.

The result is that pressure for further consolidation remains. Among the many recommendations of Don Drummond's 2012 report on Ontario public services, for example, is a call for local hydro consolidation.[128] And a 2012 study of Ontario's hydro distribution sector, under the chairmanship of Murray Elston, a former Liberal energy minister, deplored the current state of the distribution sector and recommended a set of reforms that bear striking resemblance to William Farlinger's recommendations fifteen years earlier: namely, the elimination of both municipal and provincial distribution systems and the creation of six to ten regional distribution systems in their place.[129]

It is hard to know what will become of these recommendations. The Elston Panel report was met with considerable fury in municipalities that have held on to their utilities, and was also sharply criticized by the Electricity Distributors Association (formerly the OMEA).[130] But the Elston report is also filled, like the field more generally, with lamentation about the weight of history in the hydro-electric system, a sense that the system has been labouring too long under the weight of accumulated tradition: "If Ontario was to set out to establish a new electricity distribution system from scratch, it is highly doubtful that it would choose to replicate the current structure ... The current distribution system is mainly a product of history. There is real danger that the heavy hand of history will hold the sector back from contributing to the future economic well-being of the province."[131]

For the moment, the provincial government has chosen to ignore these concerns; worried, perhaps, about the anger that the Elston Panel report provoked in important provincial constituencies, Ontario's minister of energy recently announced that voluntary consolidation would continue.[132] After the initial burst of consolidation, this process has proved very slow-moving, even during "transfer tax exemption periods" designed by the government to provide an incentive for local electricity restructuring.[133] Nevertheless, the pressure for change is real, and local utilities are now more distant than ever from ordinary citizens, their status as "local" more ambiguous than ever before. If a government were determined to act, it may prove easier to overcome the opposition of the local utilities than was the case throughout much of the twentieth century in Ontario.

7.6 Conclusions

The history of local structural change in Ontario's hydro-electric field has been punctuated by three important transitions: the first at the turn of the twentieth century, the second in the 1960s, and the third in the early 1990s. In the first two cases, the shifts were generated by an invasion of the field by new policy actors. In the early 1900s, this invasion resulted in the creation of the Hydro-Electric Power Commission of Ontario, which then served as the institutional basis for expansion and structural change in the hydro field. In the 1960s, the field's dominant policy image was challenged by the "regionalists," who argued that hydro commissions ought to be regionalized, generalized, and in some cases, even abolished. In the early 1990s, on the other hand, a new policy image that focused on deregulation and market competition arrived in the field without the simultaneous arrival of a new coalition of policy players determined to promote the new image. Instead, during this period, the supporters of the traditional policy image in the field – the view that hydro commissions ought to be autonomous, elected bodies

– gradually lost legitimacy, as stories of mismanagement and overbuilding began to bedevil the field as a whole. Major provincial actors began to abandon their commitment to the autonomous local hydro commissions, and when the time came to defend themselves, local hydro commissioners and their supporters found that they suddenly lacked the strength than they had once enjoyed.

As in education and public health, these major shifts in the status of the hydro-electric field – from unorganized to stable in the early 1900s, and from stable to contentious in the 1960s – can be explained in terms of the *availability* and the *resources* of particular policy images in the field. It was the arrival of the hydro-electric coalition's policy image in the early 1900s that marked the beginning of a stable field in the province, and the introduction of a competing regionalist image in the 1960s that marked the shift from stability to contention in the 1960s. The OMEA's success in resisting the regionalist challenge in the 1960s, and its failure to resist a similar challenge in the 1990s, can be explained, once again, in terms of resources: in the intervening years, the institutional support that the OMEA's policy image had once enjoyed, including the full-throated support of Ontario Hydro, had dissolved.

Within each of the four eras in hydro's structural history, our typology of policy fields is again helpful in explaining the timing and pace of structural change. In the first episode, when the field was unorganized, changes were triggered by problems: when a local problem appeared (a fire or an outbreak of disease), it created pressure for a new waterworks system, permission for which was granted by the provincial legislature with little fuss. As the field became more stable around the turn of the century, however, with manufacturers and municipal politicians coordinating to create the HEPC and then the OMEA, policy and politics became more important. In the case of the Central Ontario System, for example, both the problems (lack of control of hydro-electric resources in central Ontario) and policies (purchasing the private systems) had been identified in the field for some time, but it was not until senior political actors were willing to get involved, in 1916, that the proposed changes became a reality. In 1920, by contrast, it was the arrival of a new policy that was decisive: the problem of rural distribution was well known, and politicians of the period were eager to support rural electrification, but it was not until a rates committee proposed rural power districts that an opportunity for change appeared. In both cases, it was the arrival of an opportunity, and the presence of coalitions who were able to take advantage of the opportunity, that triggered the structural changes.

As we move into the third episode, the hydro-electric field becomes more contentious, and the policy-generating capacity of the regionalists – their ability to churn out report after report, particularly in the local government review program – meant that the OMEA could do little to control the emergence of competing problems and policies in the field. What they could do, however, was make constant policy proposals of their own, and draw upon their local and provincial resources to sow fear and doubt in the minds of provincial politicians. By repeating – and occasionally demonstrating – the political risks involved in structural change, the OMEA and their allies were therefore able to prevent the emergence of an opportunity for structural change.

Politics is also important in the final episode. While problems and policies had already clearly begun to develop under Bob Rae, the arrival of the Mike Harris government meant a new openness, at the political level, to fast-paced and wide-ranging structural reform. Even under Harris, the pace of change was reduced by political considerations, as the early recommendations for revolutionary changes evolved into more voluntary and market-driven reforms. This basic attitude has persisted in the field up to the present.

Chapter 8

Conclusion

We began this book with two goals: first, to provide a comparative political history of local special purpose bodies in Ontario; and second, to draw from that history some lessons about the nature of institutional and policy change. In this concluding chapter, we abstract from the detailed investigations above to highlight our major empirical and theoretical findings. Our central argument, as in each of the preceding chapters, is simple: the policy fields approach has enabled us to recognize and explain long-term patterns of institutional change, patterns that are important for our understanding of special purpose bodies themselves and also valuable for our understanding of institutional change more broadly.

8.1 A Summary of Empirical Findings

We have now surveyed nearly two hundred instances of institutional change, across numerous special purpose bodies, in dozens of municipalities, and through more than two centuries of political history. While some of this ground has been covered before – I owe enormous debts to the historians and social scientists on whose work I have relied – this book nevertheless constitutes the first systematic investigation of the long-term dynamics of local ABCs in Canada. We are therefore in a position to make a few general remarks about the development of special purpose bodies and the details of their political histories.

Special Purpose Bodies: Towards a Natural History?

Because our first goal has been to understand the development of local special purpose bodies through time and geographic space, we might be inclined to summarize that development with an approach that has come to be called *natural history*. The basic principle of natural history, as it has been employed in the social sciences, is to understand the common sequences or stages through which particular institutions travel, and to identify the contextual elements, both temporal and spatial, that divert some of those institutions from their "natural" path.

What would a natural history of local ABCs look like? Reflecting on the empirical findings in the preceding chapters, it does appear to be true that one developmental sequence has been more common than others. Creation has come first, of course, but after creation, many areas of local governance have proceeded through a period of specialization, then consolidation, and finally generalization. Recall, for example, the development of the institutions that we have surveyed in Part Two, the timelines of which are summarized in figure 8.1. Each of these institutions has moved through a specialization phase, then a consolidation phase, and then, in the case of boards of health and hydro commissions, a generalization phase. We might even say that the school boards, which have not generalized, are the exception that proves the rule; after all, the Mike Harris government attempted to generalize the school boards, but was prevented from doing so by the political and constitutional realities of the education field.

At the local level, in our study of the city of Kitchener, we can glimpse the same pattern. The story in Kitchener also begins with creation and specialization, proceeds through a period in which local actors emphasize consolidation – think of parks and recreation, for example – and then concludes with a long period of generalization. Here too, the specialization-consolidation-generalization sequence seems to capture the basic natural history of the local ABC in Ontario.

It is crucial to remember, however, how much we have abstracted from the particulars of each case in order to observe this general sequence. Readers will recall the ongoing debates about the very existence of ABCs in Kitchener during what we have just characterized as the specialization period – as well as the lack of a strong local movement, in the early 1970s, in support of any widespread move towards generalization. Similarly, while there are some resemblances among the three institutional sequences in Part Two, what is most striking about the timelines that are summarized in figure 8.1 is how *different* they are from one another. This is all the more true when we remember from the chapters in Part Two how the timelines in the figure hide even greater differences in the detailed histories of each institution. We might grant, for example, that there was indeed a period of consolidation in education, public

Figure 8.1. Change Events: School Boards, Public Health,
and Hydro Commissions

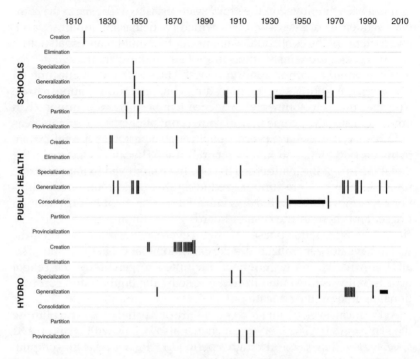

Sources: Compiled version of figures 5.1, 6.1, and 7.1 showing all changes to special
purpose bodies in the public schools, public health, and hydro fields.

health, and hydro, but the nature of that consolidation process varied
profoundly across the three cases. The same could be said for the apparent periods of specialization and generalization as well.

Put bluntly, then, the case for a compelling natural history of local
ABCs is thin. While it is useful to ask about the sequences through
which these institutions have moved, the natural history approach suggests a level of teleology, of inevitability, that simply cannot be found in
our cases. Moreover, as Andrew Abbott has observed, the natural history approach is in fact the most *decontextualizing* of the available contextual approaches; of the explanatory approaches that take spatial and
temporal context seriously, in other words, natural history emphasizes
those contexts the least.[1] A natural history of local special purpose bodies

views the contexts that we have explored in such detail in previous chapters as little more than boulders on the tracks, derailing an institution's development from the natural path that it was meant to travel.

What a natural history of ABCs provides, then, is an important hint: a hint that all of the institutions that we have studied have been subject, at various times and in various ways, to similar dynamics, and that those dynamics have shaped the development of the institutions in ways that give their long-term histories an interesting family resemblance. If this is indeed the case, then the more promising approach is not to identify the "natural" sequence of development of special purpose bodies, but instead to isolate the dynamics that have driven change in the various cases. We can then try to understand the kinds of institutional change that each of these dynamic processes tends to produce.

The Dynamics of Special Purpose Bodies and Patterns of Institutional Change

In the Canadian literature on special purpose bodies, many scholars have argued (or simply assumed) that ABCs are created for one of two reasons. The first is based on what we have called the Wilsonian thesis: the view that politics must be separated from administration and that special purpose bodies can serve as an institutional mechanism by which non-political services such as water, policing, or libraries can be removed from the cut and thrust of local politics. The second argument, which emerged from a more critical historiographic tradition, is what we have called the *insulationist* thesis: the claim that special purpose bodies represent the triumph of local elite interests, offering an opportunity for business actors to continue to control local policy, even as council itself becomes more representative of the wider community.[2]

Both of these arguments have indeed been important in the history of local ABCs. Police commissions, library boards, and public utilities commissions have certainly been defended, at times, using Wilsonian arguments. And historians like John Weaver have demonstrated convincingly that specialized institutions such as ABCs can empower those with particular interests or technical expertise in a certain policy area.[3] Nevertheless, our broader argument – explicit in chapter 2, and then implicit throughout the remainder of our study – has been that these arguments have obscured as much as they have revealed about the development of Canadian special purpose bodies. In contrast to the standard approaches, we have instead focused our attention on three local policy challenges in Canada, each of which has important implications for the dynamics of institutional change. These challenges are *capacity*, *authority*, and *scale*.

First, capacity. It has always been clear to those who are active in municipal politics – and it has become a matter of increasing attention among scholars of local government – that the principal challenge of municipal policymaking is capacity.[4] Even today, when all municipal governments employ skilled professionals, operate sophisticated technical systems for budgeting and planning, and elect political leaders for four-year terms, the capacity challenges are very real. They were even more pronounced in the past, when municipal staffs were microscopic, policy and administration were handled by committees of council, and local politicians were elected annually. In these conditions, the challenge is to find a way to accomplish the tasks that are required of municipal government, and demanded by local residents, within an institutional context of severely constrained administrative, political, and legal capacity.[5]

This capacity challenge has crucial implications for local special purpose bodies. As we have seen in Part One, Kitchener's motivation for creating special purpose bodies, and for transferring existing tasks into the control of ABCs, originated in many cases precisely in concerns about capacity. Again and again, advocates of special purpose bodies argued that municipal leaders lacked the time or knowledge to be able to manage a new policy task, but that a special purpose body would enable an existing group of local experts to competently manage the task – or, alternatively, would enable those who were elected or appointed to such bodies to *become* competent experts.

Stated generally, then, the challenge of local capacity has tended to point local actors in the direction of creation and specialization. When new policy tasks are required or demanded, and when local actors believe that municipal governments cannot handle those tasks, special purpose bodies have an obvious appeal. There are moments, however, when this appeal fades in the face of other local policy challenges. This leads us to a second local dynamic: *authority*.

The challenge of local authority has two components: first, whether it should be local governments, as opposed to provincial governments, who are responsible for a particular policy task; and second, how those tasks should be arranged within local institutions. In the case of public utilities, for example, the first question would be whether services such as water distribution ought to be administered locally or provincially, and the second would be whether they should be entrusted to an ABC, municipal council, or some combination of the two.[6]

Arguments about political authority, as they relate to local ABCs, tend to fall into two clusters. On the one hand, those who believe in powerful local governments, who support the view that local government is "closest to the people" and should therefore have wide policy-making authority, are typically critics of special purpose bodies. These critics argue that ABCs prevent real politics from happening at the local level by making it impossible for local elected representatives to do what politics requires: weighing the value of one good, such as policing, against another good, such as public health. In the contemporary language of multilevel governance, these "generalists" support *type 1* multilevel institutions: layers of nested general-purpose governments, modelled on federalism, in which each level of government is responsible for a diverse basket of policy tasks.[7]

There are some, however, who lean the other way. While few would deny that municipal council has *some* value, many people are interested in local policy not because they adhere to a Tocquevillean ideal of municipal council as the school of democracy, but because they are concerned with a particular policy field. These "specialists" are passionate about libraries, or education, or energy policy, or conservation, and have little interest in local government more generally. What is important for the specialists is that it is possible for policymakers in a particular area, like conservation, to make sensible decisions. The best way to ensure this, they often argue, is to create special purpose bodies to administer those tasks. In the language of multilevel governance, once again, advocates of this second approach prefer *type 2* institutions, divided not into nested geographic orders but into functional bodies, one responsible for libraries, another for education, a third for planning, and so on.

This basic authority dispute emerges quite clearly in our own empirical findings. Again and again, those with interests in a particular policy area, such as health or hydro, passionately defend special purpose bodies in that area. And those who are situated within general purpose structures, and who seek to serve as local generalist policymakers, persistently criticize local ABCs. This characteristic of the local political environment explains a feature of the ongoing debate about ABCs that might otherwise seem puzzling: while there are plenty of critics of local ABCs in general, few are willing to mount a general defence of local ABCs. Those who advocate ABCs tend to support this or that institution, having little concern for special purpose bodies in general. Those who attack ABCs, on the other hand, tend to think that most, even all, of the existing special purpose bodies should be abolished. This difference emerges out of the deeper difference between the "generalists" and the "specialists."[8]

There is a second aspect to this authority dynamic, one that has been noted by previous observers but must be strongly emphasized again: there is, simply put, no "provincial–municipal" relationship. There are instead provincial–municipal relationships, plural, across a wide range of policy fields: the hydro field, the public health field, and so on. Actors in these specialized fields tend to defend local ABCs, preferring a direct relationship between, say, the Ministry of Health and the local boards of health, or Ontario Hydro and the local utilities. Provincial actors in fields outside municipal affairs, in other words, are likely to defend "their" local special purpose bodies.[9] This means that the authority dynamic that I have described plays out in a similar way at both the local and the provincial levels, and has been an important source of change in all of the cases we have studied.

The third and final dynamic is *scale*. If one important question when adding a new policy task at the local level is the question of authority – by whom will the task be administered? – then an equally important question is about the proper geographic boundaries of the task. In recent years, debates about scale have often been dominated by arguments about financial costs, based on the claim that larger units will be able to capture economies of scale. The empirical evidence on this question is contentious and mixed – while no one denies that inefficiencies can be attached to very small units, the debate concerns just how big an institution needs to be to capture the relevant savings – but in the broad sweep of political history, these arguments are only part of the story.[10] The more common argument about scale, when viewed across the long-term history of local government in Canada, concerns something else: *equality*.

In all of the provincial-municipal cases that we have studied, as well as a number of instances in Kitchener, policy actors have tried to justify consolidation in the name of equal service provision. In education, it was equality that motivated Howard Ferguson to pursue consolidation early in the twentieth century, and it was equality that motivated William Davis and John Robarts to pursue the same changes after the Second World War. It was equality that motivated the sanitarians to pursue health units. And it was equality, once again, that prompted the development of power districts and provincialized rural hydro provision.

These debates about equality imply deep assumptions about redistribution, assumptions about some members of the community paying higher than necessary rates to support service provision in more costly areas elsewhere. These questions quickly become debates about appropriate geographic boundaries. The question of scale, so often reduced in the contemporary literature to a debate about economy, is in fact one of the deepest questions of politics, fundamental to the very notion of local government. What are the proper boundaries for a public service? To what extent do people within those boundaries think of themselves as a community, a community to which they are willing to contribute more, if necessary, to support the ability of other community members to enjoy the same service levels? These questions, and the debates about scale that grow out of them, have woven themselves through much of the history of local special purpose bodies that we have studied above.[11]

To capture the sequences of institutional change that we have uncovered, therefore, I believe that we need to attend to three important dynamics: the dynamics of local capacity, authority, and scale. These dynamics are deeply interrelated, of course, as are the arguments that emerge from them. By focusing on these dynamics, we can understand the consistent patterns that we have found across the cases, including the movement from specialization to consolidation to generalization, while also understanding the exceptions. The reason that school boards have not moved to generalization, for example, is not because the school boards are fundamentally different from the other institutions, but because of the peculiar authority dynamics of the education field. By tracking the arguments in each field about capacity, authority, and scale, and the processes of change that these arguments engender, we can begin to make sense of the patterns of change that our empirical investigation has uncovered.

8.2 Theoretical Findings and the Policy Fields Approach

What lessons can we draw from this study for our theories of institutional and policy change? As it stands, the literature on such change is roughly divided into two basic camps. Some scholars, building on concepts of path dependence and punctuated equilibrium, insist that institutional changes are sudden convulsions, abrupt breaks from institutional stability, after which the new institutions usually lock into place until the next convulsion comes along.[12] Others, such as Kathleen

Thelen, grant that sudden change is possible but argue that an emphasis on punctuation has tended to obscure a number of equally important but slow-moving and evolutionary processes of change.[13]

One of the peculiar features of this debate, from the perspective of those of us who are interested in institutional *and* policy change, is that the best arguments on each side have tended to ignore one another. When Kathleen Thelen attacks theories of "punctuated equilibrium," her focus is on institutionalist versions of that theory, grounded in concepts like path dependence and "lock-in."[14] Not once in these critiques does she mention the work of Frank Baumgartner and Bryan Jones.[15] Similarly, when Baumgartner and Jones attack incrementalist theories of policy change, their focus is not on institutional theorists such as Kathleen Thelen but rather on Charles Lindblom and other classic policy scholars.[16] There is nothing especially surprising or censurable in this; these scholars are simply working within different traditions and orienting themselves towards different points of reference. But at a time when the theoretical distinction between institutions and public policies has become increasingly hazy,[17] we need to better integrate theoretical arguments on both sides of this increasingly artificial debate.

I have argued in the chapters above that changes to special purpose bodies have a durably patterned character, with one or two kinds of change occurring repeatedly for long stretches of time. While change itself is ongoing, the *kinds* of change that we see in each field are stable for very long periods of time. Shifts from one kind of change to another occur abruptly and infrequently in all of the cases that we have examined. These findings strongly support a punctuated view of institutional change. Patterns of change do not replace one another in processes of layering or drift, with new kinds of change very gradually replacing the old ones, but instead occur in abrupt shifts from one pattern to another. These shifts can best be described as moments of punctuation.

Between the moments of punctuation, however, we do not find institutional stasis but rather constant change. What is stable about these interim periods is the *kind* of change that we see in the field, and to the extent that anything like "equilibrium" exists in such fields, it is an equilibrium that rests on shared beliefs about the kinds of changes that ought to occur.[18] This suggests, as Kathleen Thelen has been arguing for well over a decade, that institutional stability requires processes of *reproduction*; when stability exists, it is because political actors and coalitions, working inside existing institutions, have some reason to consistently reproduce that stability.[19] This argument, which mirrors Baumgartner and Jones's concept of the "policy monopoly," has been an important element in all of the chapters above.[20] The long-term patterns of change that we have discovered are present because they are sustained by the policy images of decision-makers in a particular field. This stability can be deliberate, as in stable and contentious fields, or it can be accidental, as in unorganized fields. In either case, it is far from inevitable, and can be threatened at any moment by an invasion of the field.

The second element of Kathleen Thelen's argument that ought to be incorporated into any approach to institutional and policy change is the importance of the slow-moving processes that she has identified – drift, layering, conversion – during periods *between* punctuated change. While our cases provide little evidence that slow-moving processes can "add up" to transformative changes – shifts in the *kind* of change in the field always have a punctuated character – they are nevertheless important in explaining the strategies that political actors use to introduce and consolidate the changes that they desire. In education, for example, consolidation in rural public school boards in Ontario was quite clearly a process of layering, as new institutional forms were layered atop older forms rather than replacing them outright; indeed, it was the transition from an insistence on full-scale transformation to an acceptance of layering that made township school boards possible in the early 1930s.[21] The same is true of changes to hydro-electric distribution more recently, with new regional corporate structures existing alongside more traditional municipally bounded utilities. It is often the case – especially within contentious policy fields – that political actors lack the power to simply replace institutions with their preferred alternative. In these cases, they use any strategies they can – strategies that often look like those described by Thelen and her collaborators. A punctuated explanation of institutional change therefore permits, and indeed requires, that we draw upon the work of those who have emphasized slower and more incremental processes of change.[22]

This basic finding – that changes to local ABCs have a distinctly patterned character over time – suggests that the right question to ask is not whether institutional changes are punctuated or incremental. They are both – as the best work on both "sides" of the incremental-punctuated argument has accepted for some time. The question is instead why we see long stretches of time in which incremental changes such as layering occur consistently and then moments of punctuation that produce shifts to other kinds of change. The policy fields approach, which builds explicitly on Baumgartner and Jones's theory of punctuated equilibrium, is an attempt to account for this twofold character of patterns of institutional change.

At the core of the policy fields approach is the argument that the shifts in the patterns of institutional change that we have discovered can be explained in terms of the institutional and cultural structure in which those changes occur. To properly characterize this structure, we have developed the synthetic concept of the policy field: the network of actors with authority over a policy task, and the policy image(s) in that network. The structure that is provided by a policy field is both institutional and cultural, and neither is prior to the other: the institutional structure empowers certain kinds of ideas and assumptions, but those ideas and assumptions also help to determine who is included in the policy network in the first place.[23] Shifts in the policy field, we have argued, produce the shifts in the patterns of institutional change that we have found.

I believe that the concept of the policy field advances our theoretical understanding of institutional change in several ways. First, to the extent that it is appropriate to characterize a process of institutional change as one of punctuated equilibrium, it is the field itself, rather than the institutional changes, that is punctuated over time. While change is ongoing, the direction of that change is characterized by periods of stability and periods of punctuation. It is only at this wider level – the level of the field as a whole – in which it is appropriate to characterize a period of stability as "equilibrium."

Another strength of the policy fields approach is that it forces us to address the relationship *among* policy fields. Our investigation has uncovered important ecological processes, in which change is produced by the interaction among policy fields, which can produce important moments of institutional and policy change. One of these processes, which I have called spillover – moments of authority challenge that are produced by the implications of a policy argument in one field for institutions or actors in another field – has been especially important in our analysis. While theorists of institutional and policy change have suggested the importance of the interrelationships among fields or policy domains, the processes by which these relationships occur have gone largely unexplored.[24] A policy fields approach offers a means by which to recognize, explore, and compare how ecological processes such as spillover produce moments of important institutional and policy change.

Perhaps most importantly, however, the policy fields approach, and its emphasis on the arguments made by actors within and outside the field, forces us to stay attentive to the fundamental question of political authority: the question of who should govern a policy task and why they are best equipped to do so.[25] Scholars of historical institutionalism – particularly those who work in the "American political development" tradition – have consistently emphasized the importance of long-term institutional change, not only for our understanding of the operation of government but also for the nature of political authority itself.[26] We have found that local institutions, like all political institutions, are subject to "durable shifts in governing authority," and that we can learn a great deal about political authority by understanding how urban institutions change. While there remains much work to be done in this area in Canada, I believe that this book demonstrates the promise of an "urban political development" approach, one focused on the long-term development of local political institutions and the implications of that development for our understanding of political authority in Canada.[27]

The final theoretical argument that we have made concerns timing. We have developed a three-part typology of policy fields – unorganized, stable, and contentious fields – arguing that changes within each type of field tend to have a particular character, triggered by different kinds of events.[28] We have not argued, to be clear, that the timing of individual changes is fully explicable or predictable on the basis of this typology; readers of the empirical chapters above will know that we have pointed to countless events and processes, from personality conflicts to devastating external shocks, to account for the timing of individual instances of change.[29] But the typology of policy fields that we have developed can tell us about the kinds of changes to look for, and the kinds of events that are likely to trigger such changes, once we are aware of the basic character of a particular policy field.

8.3 Conclusion

One test of a fruitful theoretical argument, I believe, is that it raises as many new questions as it answers. The policy fields approach enables us to clarify the *kinds* of change processes we ought to be pursuing and comparing: we can explore changes that occur inside policy fields (internal political battles, policy learning), changes that occur *between* policy fields (policy diffusion, causal story spillover), and changes that occur from *outside* policy fields (external shocks and focusing events, long-term demographic and economic changes). Our approach suggests a fruitful research agenda that is focused on identifying these processes, comparing them, and examining them within a durable conceptual vocabulary.

This book has also shown, I hope, the significant role of special purpose bodies within Canadian local governance.[30] These are institutions that are responsible for fascinating and important areas of public policy. They spend considerable sums of public money. And they raise ongoing questions about accountability and efficiency, flexibility and independence, fragmentation and public oversight. Local special purpose bodies have been with us, in Canada, for more than two centuries. But our quest to understand them has only just begun.

Notes

Introduction

1 *Globe and Mail*, April 17, 1982, 1, April 19, 1982, 1, 10; *Toronto Star*, April 18, 1982, 1.

2 For Nunavut, see *Globe and Mail*, April 7, 1982, 7, April 8, 1982, 6, April 12, 1982, 1, April 15, 1982, 10, April 16, 1982, 1, 6; for Ontario doctors, see *Globe and Mail*, April 17, 1982, 1; for Quesno, see *Quesnel Cariboo Observer*, April 20, 1982, 1; for Georgetown, see *Georgetown Herald*, April 21, 1982, 3.

3 I have borrowed this phrase from Jack Lucas, "How Things Change: Adventures in Ureconstructed Institutionalism," *IPAC Public Sector Management* 26, no. 1 (2015): 24–5.

4 "Our City's Shadow Cabinet," Hamilton *Spectator*, November 7, 2007.

5 David Siegel, "The ABCs of Canadian Local Government: An Overview," in *Agencies, Boards, and Commissions in Canadian Local Government*, ed. Dale Richmond and David Siegel (Toronto: Institute of Public Administration of Canada, 1994), 7.

6 See, for example, "Activities of Public Bodies," Local History Archives, Kitchener Public Library (KPL).

7 See Jack Lucas, "Hidden in Plain View: Local Agencies, Boards, and Commissions in Canada," *IMFG Perspectives Paper Series* 4 (2013): 1–7.

8 For an example of this phenomenon, see Gabriel Eidelman, "Landlocked: Politics, Property, and the Toronto Waterfront, 1960–2000" (PhD diss., University of Toronto, 2013), 153–7.

9 Zack Taylor and Gabriel Eidelman, "Canadian Political Science and the City: A Limited Engagement," *Canadian Journal of Political Science* 43, no. 4 (2010): 975.

10 Robert Young, "Conclusion," in *Foundations of Governance: Municipal Government in Canada's Provinces*, ed. Robert Young and Andrew Sancton (Toronto: University of Toronto Press, 2009), 498.

11 For some clear articulations of this point, see Elisabeth Clemens and James M. Cook, "Politics and Institutionalism: Explaining Durability and Change," *Annual Review of Sociology* 25, no. 1 (1999): 442; Kathleen Thelen, "Historical Institutionalism in Comparative Politics," *Annual Review of Political Science* 2, no. 1 (1999): 369–404; and Grace Skogstad, "Policy Networks and Policy Communities: Conceptualizing State–Societal Relationships in the Policy Process," in *The Comparative Turn in Canadian Political Science*, ed. Linda A. White, Richard Simeon, Robert Vipond, and Jennifer Wallner (Vancouver: UBC Press, 2008), 214.

12 James Mahoney and Kathleen Ann Thelen, "A Theory of Gradual Institutional Change," in *Explaining Institutional Change*, ed. James Mahoney and Kathleen Ann Thelen, 1–37 (Cambridge: Cambridge University Press, 2009); Jacob S. Hacker, "Privatizing Risk without Privatizing the Welfare State: The Hidden Politics of Social Policy Retrenchment in the United States," *American Political Science Review* 98, no. 2 (2004): 243–60.

13 E.g., Clemens and Cook, "Politics and Institutionalism"; Robert C. Lieberman, "Ideas, Institutions, and Political Order: Explaining Political Change," *American Political Science Review* 96, no. 4 (2002): 697–712.

14 Stephen D. Krasner, "Approaches to the State: Alternative Conceptions and Historical Dynamics," *Comparative Politics* 16, no. 2 (1984): 223–46, Paul A. Sabatier and Christopher M. Weible, "The Advocacy Coalition Framework," in *Theories of the Policy Process*, ed. Paul A Sabatier, 189–220 (Boulder, CO: Westview, 2007).

15 This is the "venue problem" described by Frank Baumgartner and Bryan Jones in *Agendas and Instability in American Politics*, 2nd ed. (Chicago: University of Chicago Press, 1993); see also Frank Baumgartner, Bryan D. Jones, and Michael C. MacLeod, "The Evolution of Legislative Jurisdictions," *Journal of Politics* 62, no. 2 (2000): 321–49.

16 Understood in this way, I believe that urban governance is an excellent place to draw on and expand the work of scholars in the American political development tradition. See Arthur Spirling, "British Political Development: A Research Agenda," *Legislative Studies Quarterly* 39, no. 4 (2014): 435–7; Karen Orren and Stephen Skowronek, *The Search for American Political Development* (Cambridge: Cambridge University Press, 2004); and Desmond King, Robert C. Lieberman, Gretchen Ritter, and Laurence Whitehead, eds., *Democratization in America* (Baltimore, MD:

Johns Hopkins University Press, 2009). For applications to the Canadian urban case, see Jack Lucas, "Urban Governance and the American Political Development Approach," *Urban Affairs Review* (forthcoming); and Zack Taylor, "If Different Then Why? Explaining the Divergent Political Development of Canadian and American Local Governance," *International Journal of Canadian Studies* 49 (2014): 53–79.

17 This brief definition of governance is based on Mark Bevir, *The Sage Handbook of Governance* (New York: SAGE, 2011).

18 Liesbet Hooghe and Gary Marks, "Unraveling the Central State, but How? Types of Multi-Level Governance," *American Political Science Review* 97, no. 2 (2003): 233–43.

19 Bruno S. Frey and Reiner Eichenberger, *The New Democratic Federalism for Europe: Functional, Overlapping, and Competing Jurisdictions* (Cheltenham, UK: Edward Elgar, 1999); Megan Mullin, *Governing the Tap: Special District Governance and the New Local Politics of Water* (Cambridge, MA: MIT Press, 2009).

20 Grace Skogstad and Tanya Whyte, "Authority Contests, Power and Policy Paradigm Change: Explaining Developments in Grain Marketing Policy in Prairie Canada," *Canadian Journal of Political Science* 48, no. 1 (2015): 1–22.

21 School boards, boards of health, hydro commissions, police boards, planning commissions, housing authorities, library boards, hospital commissions, and conservation authorities. Transit commissions, while important, were too rare in Ontario to have yielded a true provincial-municipal case study. The same is true of harbour commissions. I used a range of sources to generate this list, including Andrew Sancton, *Canadian Local Government: An Urban Perspective* (Don Mills, ON: Oxford University Press, 2011): 41–65; Andrew Sancton and Robert Young, eds., *Foundations of Governance* (Toronto: University of Toronto Press, 2009); David Siegel and Dale Richmond, eds., *Agencies, Boards, and Commissions in Canadian Local Government* (Toronto: Institute of Public Administration in Canada, 1994).

22 Specifically, the combinations that I excluded on this criterion were boards of health and hospital commissions, school boards and library boards, and water commissions and hydro commissions.

23 This criterion meant that housing authorities and conservation authorities were removed from the list.

24 Police boards, which would otherwise have made an excellent candidate for study, were excluded for this reason.

Chapter 1

1 Rod Rhodes, "Old Institutionalisms," in *Oxford Handbook of Political Institutions*, ed. Rod Rhodes, Sara Binder, and Bert Rockman, 90–108 (Oxford: Oxford University Press, 2006). Broader reviews of institutional theory are plentiful, but the canonical text remains Peter Hall and Rosemary Taylor, "Political Science and the Three New Institutionalisms," *Political Studies* 44, no. 5 (1996): 936–57.

2 For an introduction to this organizational institutionalism, see W. Richard Scott, *Institutions and Organizations*, 3rd ed. (Los Angeles: Sage, 2008); as well as Walter Powell and Paul J. DiMaggio, eds., *The New Institutionalism in Organizational Analysis* (Chicago: University of Chicago Press, 1991). Vivien Schmidt's critique of political science institutionalism, and her argument for a new "discursive institutionalism," provides a good illustration of this tendency to exclude culture, ideas, and beliefs; see Vivien Schmidt, "Discursive Institutionalism: The Explanatory Power of Ideas and Discourse," *Annual Review of Political Science* 11, no. 1 (2008): 303–26.

3 Rhodes, "Old Institutionalisms," 92.

4 This definition closely follows Susan Dolbey, *Local Special Purpose Bodies in the Province of Ontario* (Toronto: Municipal Research Branch, Department of Municipal Affairs, 1970), 3; and Siegel, "ABCs of Canadian Local Government," 7–9.

5 Of course, several kinds of change can be contained within a single bylaw or statute.

6 The book-length presentation of this approach is Baumgartner and Jones, *Agendas and Instability in American Politics*. For a summary of the approach, see James L. True, Bryan D. Jones, and Frank R. Baumgartner, "Punctuated-Equilibrium Theory," in *Theories of the Policy Process*, ed. Paul Sabatier (Boulder, CO: Westview, 2007), 155–87.

7 Baumgartner and Jones, *Agendas and Instability*, 25. For the importance of the positive/negative distinction in the origin of this concept, see Frank Baumgartner and Bryan Jones, "Agenda Dynamics and Policy Subsystems," *Journal of Politics* 53, no. 4 (1991): 1044–74. See also Frank Baumgartner, "Ideas and Policy Change," *Governance* 26, no. 2 (2012): 239–58; R.D. Benford and D.A. Snow, "Framing Processes and Social Movements: An Overview and Assessment," *Annual Review of Sociology* 26, no. 1 (2000): 611–39; Sheri Berman, "Ideational Theorizing in the Social Sciences," *Governance* 26, no. 2 (2013): 217–37; John L. Campbell, "Ideas, Politics, and Public Policy," *Annual Review of Sociology* 28, no. 1 (2002): 21–38; and Daniel Wincott, "Ideas, Policy Change, and the Welfare State,"

in *Ideas and Politics in Social Science Research*, ed. Daniel Béland and Robert Henry Cox, 143–66 (Oxford: Oxford University Press).

8 Baumgartner and Jones, *Agendas and Instability*, 25.
9 The literature on organizational policy instruments provides a treatment of these changes as a form of public policy. For an example in the Ontario case, see Kenneth Woodside's discussion of "constitutional policy" in "An Approach to Studying Local Government Autonomy: The Ontario Experience," *Canadian Public Administration* 33, no. 2 (1990): 198–213.
10 For Baumgartner and Jones's treatment of venue change, see Frank Baumgartner, Bryan Jones, and Michael C. MacLeod, "The Evolution of Legislative Jurisdictions," *Journal of Politics* 62, no. 2 (2000): 321–49.
11 See the case studies in Baumgartner and Jones, *Agendas and Instability*.
12 While this definition is my own, this concept of the policy field is deeply indebted to sociological field theory and the study of organizational fields. I have benefited most from Doug McAdam and Neil Fligstein, *A Theory of Fields* (Oxford: Oxford University Press, 2012); Andrew J. Hoffman, "Institutional Evolution and Change: Environmentalism and the U.S. Chemical Industry," *Academy of Management Journal* 42, no. 4 (1999): 351–71; John Levi Martin, "What Is Field Theory?," *American Journal of Sociology* 109, no. 1 (2003): 1–49; Melissa Wooten and Andrew J. Hoffman, "Organizational Fields: Past, Present and Future," in *Sage Handbook of Organizational Institutionalism*, ed. Royston Greenwood, Christine Oliver, Roy Suddaby, and Kerstin Sahlin, 129–49 (Los Angeles: Sage, 2008); Pierre Bourdieu and Loic Wacquant, *An Invitation to Reflexive Sociology* (Chicago: University of Chicago Press, 1992).
13 While this distinction differs in some ways from the typology offered by McAdam and Fligstein in *A Theory of Fields*, it is very much inspired by that typology.
14 A very wide range of concepts has been deployed to describe such fields. For the policy monopoly, see Baumgartner and Jones, *Agendas and Instability*, 4. For policy paradigms, see Peter Hall, "Policy Paradigms, Social Learning, and the State: The Case of Economic Policymaking in Britain," *Comparative Politics* 25, no. 3 (1993): 275–96. For a broader critical review of the "subsystem" concept, see Daniel McCool, "The Subsystem Family of Concepts: A Critique and a Proposal," *Political Research Quarterly* 51, no. 2 (1998): 551–70.
15 The Advocacy Coalition Framework has made useful progress in understanding such fields. See Sabatier and Weible, "Advocacy Coalition Framework."

16 See Bryan D. Jones et al., "A General Empirical Law of Public Budgets: A Comparative Analysis," *American Journal of Political Science* 53 no. 4 (2009): 855–73.

17 Ibid., 864–5.

18 For avalanches, see James L. True, "Avalanches and Incrementalism," *American Review of Public Administration* 30, no. 1 (2000): 3–18. For an accessible introduction to the science of sandpiles, see Per Bak and Kan Chen, "Self-Organized Criticality," *Scientific American* 264 (1991): 46–53.

19 Despite a different research and conceptual focus, in what follows I am indebted to Andrew Abbott, "Linked Ecologies: States and Universities as Environments for Professions," *Sociological Theory* 23, no. 3 (2005): 245–73; and Abbott, "Mechanisms and Relations," *Sociologica* 2, no. 1 (2007): 245–73.

20 For a classic treatment, see Simon A. Levin, "The Problem of Pattern and Scale in Ecology," *Ecology* 73, no. 6 (1992): 1943–67.

21 This discussion is indebted to Grace Skogstad and Tanya Whyte's helpful discussion of the "authority contest" in "Authority Contests, Power and Policy Paradigm Change."

22 Jennifer Wallner has demonstrated that this is indeed the case, in *Learning to School* (Toronto: University of Toronto Press, 2014).

23 See David P. Dolowitz and David Marsh, "Learning from Abroad: The Role of Policy Transfer in Contemporary Policy-Making," *Governance* 13, no. 1 (2000): 5–23.

24 David Strang and John W. Meyer, "Institutional Conditions for Diffusion," *Theory and Society* 22, no. 4 (1993): 487–511.

25 This is not to suggest that both processes operate within both forms of adjacency: geographic adjacency can certainly produce diffusion, and functional adjacency might even produce instances of spillover. But spillover processes are most characteristic of geographic adjacency, and diffusion processes of functional adjacency.

26 This distinction between problem-triggered and politics-triggered change is indebted to John Kingdon's "multiple streams" approach. Those who employ the multiple streams approach may be interested to note that I have uncovered no instances (with one possible exception: rural hydro districts) of policy-triggered change. See John W. Kingdon, *Agendas, Alternatives, and Public Policies* (New York: HarperCollins, 1984).

27 If culture is something like a set of tools in a toolbox, in other words, then political culture represents the tools that are pulled from the box most frequently, not only in one field but across many fields. See Ann Swidler, "Culture in Action: Symbols and Strategies," *American Sociological Review*

51, no. 2 (1986): 273–86; though see also Mark Bevir and Rod Rhodes, *Governance Stories* (London: Routledge, 2006), 25; and John Levi Martin, "Life's a Beach but You're an Ant, and Other Unwelcome News for the Sociology of Culture," *Poetics* 38, no. 2 (2010): 229–44.

28 For an example of political cultural changes of this sort, see Neil Nevitte, *The Decline of Deference* (Toronto: University of Toronto Press, 1996).

29 For helpful discussions of the analytical problem of temporal duration, see Andrew Abbott, *Time Matters* (Chicago: University of Chicago Press, 2001), especially chapter 7; and William Sewell, *Logics of History* (Chicago: University of Chicago Press, 2005), especially chapters 7–9.

Part One

1 In the overview that follows I am deeply indebted above all to John English and Kenneth McLaughlin, *Kitchener: An Illustrated History* (Waterloo, ON: Wilfrid Laurier University Press, 1996), and to Elizabeth Bloomfield's research, cited in the bibliography, on the political and economic history of Kitchener and environs.

2 The area that is now Kitchener was purchased as "Block 2" by Richard Beasley, James Wilson, and John Baptist Rousseaux in 1798. The legitimacy of the original purchase by Beasley, as well as the details of Beasley's later sale to Samuel Betzner, remain matters of contention today. For an overview, see the entries for Thayendanegea, Richard Beasley, and Samuel Betzner in the *Dictionary of Canadian Biography* (www.biographi.ca).

3 An outstanding account can be found in English and McLaughlin, *Kitchener*, chapter 4.

Chapter 2

1 An earlier version of this chapter was published as Jack Lucas, "Berlin, Ontario in the Age of the ABC," *Urban History Review* 41, no. 2 (2013): 19–42.

2 This account of the Hibner fire is taken from the *Berlin Daily Record* (*BDR*), especially November 13, 16, and 17, 1896. The fire is also discussed in Elizabeth Bloomfield, "City Building Processes in Berlin/Kitchener and Waterloo, 1870–1930" (PhD diss., University of Guelph, 1981), 215–19; and in Elizabeth Bloomfield and Gerald Bloomfield, *A History of Municipal Water Services in the Region of Waterloo* (Waterloo, ON: Regional Municipality of Waterloo Engineering Department, 1998), 11–12. The boy's age became a matter of brief controversy after Hibner was accused

of employing too many youths, and Hibner insisted that the boy was nineteen. I believe that the initial report is more reliable. Unfortunately, we hear nothing more about the boy's fate after the initial reports.

3 *BDR*, November 13, 1896.

4 For reports on these offers, see the *BDR*, November 16, December 12, 1896.

5 The bylaw passed on December 14, 1896, but it did not receive the provincially mandated two-thirds support. An initial request for an exemption was rejected. The town tried again, and the legislature's private bills committee eventually relented in early 1898. See *BDR*, December 15, 1896; *News Record*, March 10, July 12, December 29, 1897; and Bloomfield, "City Building Processes in Berlin/Kitchener and Waterloo, 1870–1930," 217–19.

6 *BDR*, November 24, 1896.

7 Ibid.

8 *BDR*, September 12, 1896.

9 This is not to suggest that the choice was always voluntary. In the case of education, school boards were required by law; after 1894, Boards of Health were also mandatory. Even when such boards were required, however, Berlin often enthusiastically adopted new types of the ABCs, as in the case of the Berlin Board of Education in 1911. See W.V. Uttley, *The History of Kitchener* (Waterloo, ON: Wilfrid Laurier University Press, 1937), 222.

10 *Municipal World* 27 (1917). Quoted in John C. Weaver, "'Tomorrow's Metropolis' Revisited: A Critical Assessment of Urban Reform in Canada, 1890–1920," in *The Canadian City*, ed. Gilber A. Stelter, and Alan F.J. Artibise (Montreal and Kingston: McGill-Queen's University Press, 1984), 472.

11 This claim is based on a dataset constructed by the author. Principal sources for this dataset are municipal financial returns at the Archives of Ontario (RG 19-142), annual reports of the minister of education (for library boards), and available local biographies. When the adoption dates for library boards, water commissions, hydro commissions, park boards, planning boards, and conservation authorities are divided into tertiles, just one municipality is in the first tertile in every case: Berlin.

12 The park is now known as "Waterloo Park." For the early history of Waterloo Park, see Clayton Wells, "A Historical Sketch of the Town of Waterloo, Ontario," *Waterloo Historical Society* 16 (1928): 2267; Margaret Zavaros, "Waterloo Park, 1890–1990," *Waterloo Historical Society* 78 (1990): 8399.

13 *BDR*, August 25, 1894.

14 *BDR*, September 4, 1894.

15 This quotation is from a somewhat later date, but similar sentiments were expressed at the time. See *BDR*, November 7, 1894, for the quotation; for similar sentiments, see *BDR*, September 25, 26, 1894.

16 *BDR*, September 26, 1894. "Half a mill" on the total assessment is five
ten-thousandths of the total assessed property value; if total assessed
value was $10 million, for example, the library could ask for no more
than $5,000.

17 *BDR*, September 6, 1894. For a brief if incomplete overview of Ontario's
park boards, see J.R. Wright, *Urban Parks in Ontario* (Toronto: Province
of Ontario Ministry of Tourism/Recreation, 1983). A broader picture can
be obtained, with some sweat, from a survey of the municipal financial
returns at the Archives of Ontario (RG 14-146), or from the author of
this book.

18 The result was 510–235. *BDR*, September 29, 1894.

19 See *BDR*, September 6 and 10, 1894.

20 See Board of Park Management Minutes, 1894, Kitchener Corporate
Archives (KCA); along with *BDR*, October 24, 1894.

21 *BDR*, November 5, 1894. See also *BDR*, November 3, 1894.

22 *BDR*, November 27, 1894.

23 *BDR*, April 2, 11, 1895.

24 The controversy lasted until the end of 1895 before finally subsiding. For
details, see Charles F. Brown to mayor and Council of Berlin, December
2, 1895, available in the Board of Park Management Fonds, KCA. For the
newspaper quotation, see *BDR*, April 27, 1897. For examples of the park in
promotional materials, see the "Souvenir of Berlin" series, 1914 and 1916,
University of Waterloo Archives, https://uwaterloo.ca/library/special-
collections-archives/collections/digital-collections/
local-souvenir-albums/souvenir-berlin-ca-1914.

25 The "Holly" system, invented by Birdsill Holly in the 1860s, used a pump-
ing system to eliminate the need for expensive elevated water reservoirs.
See Bloomfield and Bloomfield, *History of Municipal Water Services*, 11.

26 See Bloomfield and Bloomfield, *History of Municipal Water Services*, for
an excellent overview of Berlin/Kitchener's water system. See also
Bloomfield, "City Building Processes," 203–3. For wider developments,
which follows Bloomfield on the early history, see Janice Badgley, "Public
Decision Making on Water Supply Planning and Management: A Case
Study of the Waterloo Region" (MA thesis, University of Waterloo, 1991).

27 *NR*, May 3, 1897.

28 For the exemption issue, see especially *NR*, May 13 and 26, 1898; for
Rumpel's offer, see *NR*, May 19, 1898; and for the other offer, *NR*, May 26,
1898.

29 *NR*, May 13, 1898.

30 *NR*, November 4, 1898.

31 Ibid.
32 *NR*, November 9, 1898.
33 Bloomfield, "City Building Processes in Berlin/Kitchener and Waterloo, 1870–1930," 223.
34 For the later struggles, see Badgley, "Public Decision Making."
35 E.g., *Berlin News Record*, January 6, 1902; Berlin *Daily Telegraph* (*DT*), February 3, 1903.
36 *DT*, May 5, 1903.
37 For the earlier pride, see *BDR*, August 29, 1895; for the difficulties in 1903, see *BDT*, January 14, June 25, 1903; for commission management, see, e.g., *DT*, February 14, 1903.
38 *DT*, 21, May 22, 1903.
39 *NR*, January 2, 1904.
40 Management of the street railway moved between council and the light commission. We will return to this below.
41 *DT*, 17, March 18, 1907.
42 *NR*, March 19, 1907.
43 *DT*, January 4, 1908, 4, 7, March 20, December 5, 1908; *BDR*, December 30, 1908.
44 Before Berlin's leaders realized that the water commission would have to be elected, they insisted that it should follow the appointed park board model. See *DT*, May 3, 1898; *BNR*, May 5, 13, October 18, November 4, 1898. For evidence that appointed boards were quickly forgotten, see *DT*, June 11, 1903, and especially March 22, 1907.
45 See, e.g., *DT*, March 20, December 22, 1908.
46 See *DT*, November 12, 1904, February 18, 1905, June 27, 1908.
47 David Strang and John W. Meyer, "Institutional Conditions for Diffusion," *Theory and Society* 22, no. 4 (1993): 499–500.
48 For examples of this approach, see Paul Rutherford, "Tomorrow's Metropolis: The Urban Reform Movement in Canada, 1880-1920," in *The Canadian City*, ed. Gilber A. Stelter and Alan F.J. Artibise, 435–55 (Montreal and Kingston: McGill-Queen's University Press, 1984); Warren Magnusson, "Introduction," in *City Politics in Canada*, ed. Warren Magnusson and Andrew Sancton, 3–57 (Toronto: University of Toronto Press, 1983); Katherine Graham and Susan Phillips, *Urban Governance in Canada* (Toronto: Harcourt, 1998), 155–7.
49 For a powerful example of this approach, see Weaver, "'Tomorrow's Metropolis'"; John English and Kenneth McLaughlin briefly suggest that this view applies in Kitchener; see English and McLaughlin, *Kitchener*, 113.
50 *BDR*, September 6, 1894; *NR*, November 4, 1898.

51 *DT*, March 17, 1907.

52 In 1894, the *Daily Record* reprinted an editorial from a Toronto newspaper advocating a politics-administration separation. But the argument in that editorial was not seen again until 1907 or so. See *BDR*, December 10, 1894.

53 See, e.g., *BDR*, December 30, 1895; *NR*, August 30, 1897; *DT*, November 3, 1908, December 12, 1908.

54 See S.J.R. Noel, *Patrons, Clients, Brokers: Ontario Society and Politics, 1791–1896* (Toronto: Macmillan Canada, 1974), chap. 13; Noel, "Oliver Mowat, Patronage, and Party Building," in *Ontario Since Confederation: A Reader*, ed. E.A. Montigny and A.L. Chambers, 94–104 (Toronto: University of Toronto Press, 2000); J.E. Hodgetts, *From Arm's Length to Hands On: The Formative Years of Ontario's Public Service, 1867–1940* (Toronto: University of Toronto Press, 1995).

55 See note 52 above. For an interesting account of Toronto's patronage debates, see John C. Weaver, "The Modern City Realized," in *The Usable Urban Past*, ed. Alan F.J. Artibise and Gilber A. Stelter, 39–72 (Ottawa: Macmillan, 1979).

56 For references (with varying degrees of explicitness) to problems of patronage and corruption within the Berlin police force, see *NR*, March 19, 1907; *DT*, January 3, 4, 7, March 20, 1908. See also John C. Weaver, *Shaping the Canadian City: Essays on Urban Politics and Policy 1890–1920* (Toronto: Institute of Public Administration of Canada, 1977), 2.

57 These figures have been compiled from the Board of Park Management Fonds, Kitchener Water Commission Fonds, Sewer Commission Minute Books, and the Berlin Council Minute Books, KCA; Kitchener Chamber of Commerce Fonds and Kitchener Library Board Minute Books, KPL; the *BNR* and the *DT*.

58 See, e.g., *DT*, January 5, April 5, 1904.

59 Bloomfield, "City Building Processes in Berlin/Kitchener and Waterloo, 1870–1930"; Elizabeth Bloomfield, "Community Leadership and Decision-Making: Entrepreneurial Elites in Two Ontario Towns, 1870–1930," in *Power and Place*, ed. Gilbert A. Stelter and Alan F.J. Artibise, 82–104 (Vancouver: UBC Press, 1986).

60 Ibid.

61 Sources for the figure: *Berlin News Record, Berlin Daily Telegraph*, Berlin Board of Trade Minute Books, Kitchener Chamber of Commerce Fonds, KPL; Berlin Town Council Minute Books, KCA.

62 This account of Berlin's political culture is indebted to the work of Elizabeth Bloomfield, whose outline of Berlin's "urban ethos" can be read in "City Building Processes in Berlin/Kitchener and Waterloo, 1870–1930,"

65–90; Bloomfield outlines seven key features of the urban ethos in Berlin; I have attempted to present a more integrated picture, but I believe that our comments here are consistent with Bloomfield's presentation. See also English and McLaughlin, *Kitchener*, 113; Berlin, *Berlin: Celebration of Cityhood* (Berlin: Sand Hill Books, 1912), esp. 69–74.

63 Instances of this competitive ethos can be seen in *BDR*, November 28, 1894, February 29, March 17, 1896; *NR*, January 6, 1898. For discussion of "natural advantages," see *NR*, May 26, 1900; *DT*, March 13, 1908; English and McLaughlin, *Kitchener*, 67; Berlin, *Berlin*, 69–74.

64 Quoted in Paul Tiessen, "Introduction," in *Berlin: Celebration of Cityhood* (Berlin: Sand Hill Books, 1912), 1. See also *BDR*, March 27, 30, 1896.

65 For a representative sample, see *BDR*, August 10, 1894, January 1, November 7, 1895, February 22, 1896, January 5, 1897; *NR*, May 30, October 14, 1898; *DT*, January 10, 1903, July 3, 1906, August 21, 1908.

66 Article in the *Galt Reporter*, quoted in *DT*, April 4, 1904.

67 For an overview of Huber's career, see English and McLaughlin, *Kitchener*, 104–10; John English and Kenneth McLaughlin, "Allen Huber: Berlin's Strangest Mayor," *Waterloo Historical Society* 69 (1981): 4–12. Amusing examples of Huber's trouble-mongering can be found in the *BDR*, January 29, 1895, May 5, 1898; *DT*, December 31, 1901, February 18, 1903, January 4, November 2, 1907. See also Jack Lucas, "Did Allen Huber Punch Louis Breithaupt in the Face?" *Waterloo Historical Society* 102 (2015): 77–84.

68 "Cheer up," a local newspaper wrote, "the Board of Trade has a strong Council anyway" (*DT*, January 10, 1908). For the odd circumstances, see English and McLaughlin, "Allen Huber: Berlin's Strangest Mayor," as well as *DT*, January 7, 1908, January 8, 16, 25, February 3, 20, 1908.

69 By the end of 1909, Huber was denied the right to vote – not to run for office, but to *vote* – because he failed to meet the minimal property qualifications required for municipal voting. See *NR*, November 25, December 9, 28, 1909.

70 The meeting is discussed in *DT*, March 13, 1908, and the quotation is from *DT* April 14, 1908. See also Bloomfield, "City Building Processes in Berlin/ Kitchener and Waterloo, 1870–1930," 90–1.

71 See *DT*, June 16, 1908.

72 English and McLaughlin, *Kitchener*, 109. For the earlier sore spot, see *BNR*, June 8, July 20, 1898, August 29, 1900. See also "W.H.E. Schmalz," KPL Oral History Collection.

73 *DT*, December 29, 1908. See also *NR*, December 29, 1908.

74 See, e.g., *BDR*, November 29, December 20, 1894; *NR*, December 28, 1898, November 3, 1902; *DT*, January 23, May 11, 1903, March 7, 1908.

75 See *NR*, April 19, May 16, 17, June 6, July 17, 1911.
76 Council was always careful to indicate its support for commissions in general. In the case of the sewer commission, for instance, "the aldermen were careful to place themselves on record as being in favor of the commission form of Government." See *NR*, June 6, July 17, 1911.

Chapter 3

1 J.D. Detwiler, "Speaking Notes: History of Detweiler," A-7 1000087882, Detweiler Papers, MG30, Library and Archives Canada (LAC); "Daniel Bechtel Detweiler," *Waterloo Historical Society* 7, no. 1 (1919): 93.
2 "Daniel Bechtel Detweiler," 96; *Kitchener Waterloo Record (KWR)*, March 31, 1956; H.V. Nelles, *The Politics of Development*, 2nd ed. (Montreal and Kingston: McGill-Queen's University Press, 2005), 238–9.
3 Detweiler, "Speaking Notes."
4 T.J. Hannigan to A.R. Lang, December 30, 1931; Mathieson to Hutcheson, July 6, 1949; and Mathieson to Easton, August 22, 1949, OMEA-AMEU Records, OHA. See also *Toronto Daily Star*, March 10, 1951.
5 W.R. Plewman, *Adam Beck and the Ontario Hydro* (Toronto: Ryerson, 1947), 32–3; Nelles, *Politics of Development*, 237–9.
6 "Daniel Detweiler Address," October 11, 1910, 001674753, Detweiler Collection, Adam Beck Office Records, OHA; Detweiler Diary, October 11, 1910, "Daniel Detweiler," Vertical Files, KPL. See also chapter 7 below.
7 Detweiler Diary, October 26, 1910, "Daniel Detweiler," Vertical Files, KPL.
8 *NR*, December 12, 1912.
9 *NR*, December 2, 1912.
10 *DT*, March 7, April 28, 1908, March 13, 1909. For details on Grand River floods, see Margaret Rowell, "Floods on the Grand: 1822–1974," *Waterloo Historical Society Annual Volume* 62 (1974): 34–8; and Trevor Dickinson, D. Joy, R. Kreutzwiser, D. Shrubsole, and M. Sanderson, *A Report on Ontario Flood History* (Toronto: Ontario Ministry of Natural Resources, 1991), available at WLU.
11 Susan Hoffman, "William Henry Breithaupt 1857–1944: A Tribute," *Waterloo Historical Society Annual Volume* 90 (2002): 31–3; Jesse Middleton and Fred Landon, "William Henry Breithaupt," in *The Province of Ontario: A History*, ed. Jesse Middleton and Fred Landon (Toronto: Dominion Publishing, 1927), 133–4.
12 *BDR*, January 27, 1897.
13 *BDR*, January 28, 29, 1897; and L.J. Breithaupt Diary, 01-1897, Breithaupt-Hewetson-Clark Collection, University of Waterloo Archives (UWA).

14 Hoffman, "William Henry Breithaupt 1857–1944: A Tribute," 31–2.

15 W.V. Uttley, *The History of Kitchener* (Waterloo: Wilfrid Laurier Press, 1937), 363.

16 *DT*, March 7, April 28, 1908, March 13, 1909.

17 *DT*, March 13, 1909.

18 *NR*, November 5, 1912.

19 For the United Kingdom, see Michael Simpson, *Thomas Adams and the Modern Planning Movement: Britain, Canada, and the United States 1900–1940* (Oxford: Alexandrine, 1985); and Oiva Saarinen, "The Influence of Thomas Adams and the British New Towns Movement in the Planning of Canadian Resource Communities," in *The Usable Urban Past*, ed. Alan F.J. Artibise and Gilbert A. Stelter, 268–92 (Ottawa: Macmillan Canada, 1979). For the United States, see Gerald Hodge, "The Roots of Canadian Planning," *Journal of the American Planning Association* 51, no. 1 (1985): 8–22. For Toronto, see Weaver, "Modern City Realized," 60–2.

20 William Henry Breithaupt, "Some Features of Town Planning, with Application to the City of Kitchener," *Journal of the Town Planning Institute of Canada* 1, no. 6 (1921): 5. Bloomfield, *City-Building Processes*, 437–8.

21 *BNR*, December 12, 1912, September 6, 1913; see also Elizabeth Bloomfield, "Reshaping the Urban Landscape? Town-Planning Efforts in Kitchener-Waterloo, 1912–1925," in *Shaping the Urban Landscape*, ed. Gilbert A. Stelter and Alan F.J. Artibise, 256–303 (Ottawa: Carleton University Press, 1982).

22 Bloomfield, *City Building Processes*, 417.

23 The plan is on display in the reading room of the University of Waterloo Doris Lewis Rare Book Room.

24 Elizabeth Bloomfield, "Economy, Necessity, Political Reality: Town Planning Efforts in Kitchener-Waterloo, 1912–1925," *Urban History Review / Revue d'histoire urbaine* 9, no. 1 (1980): 21.

25 *DT*, March 17, 1914.

26 Ibid.

27 See Bloomfield, *City Building Processes*; Bloomfield, "Economy, Necessity, and Political Reality"; and Bloomfield, "Reshaping the Urban Landscape?"

28 *DT*, March 17, 1914.

29 This story of "translation" is told very well in Bloomfield, "Economy, Necessity, and Political Reality."

30 *NR*, June 1, 1917; English and McLaughlin, *Kitchener*, 149–50.

31 Simpson, *Thomas Adams*, 86; Commission of Conservation, *Annual Report*, 1914, 121–5; Bloomfield, "Reshaping the Urban Landscape?," 281–2.

32 *NR*, May 22, June 1, 9, 1917.

33 *NR*, 5, March 12, 1913, February 13, 1917; Bloomfield, "Reshaping the Urban Landscape?," 27.

34 For the details, see Bloomfield, "Economy, Necessity, Reality."

35 "Ontario," *Journal of the Town Planning Institute of Canada* 3, no. 3 (1922): 16. See also Bloomfield, "Reshaping the Urban Landscape?," 256.

36 *DT*, March 7, April 28, 1908; *NR*, March 13, 1909.

37 *NR*, March 13, 1909.

38 *NR*, March 4, 1910, August 22, 1912, March 28, 1913; Uttley, *History of Kitchener*, 364; Bruce Mitchell and Dan Shrubsole, *Ontario Conservation Authorities: Myth and Reality* (Waterloo, ON: University of Waterloo Department of Geography, 1992), 37.

39 A 1914 article reports that the Hydro-Electric Power Commission (HEPC) had begun its investigation, but that is the last we hear of it (*BNR*, November 28, 1914). See also *NR*, March 30, 1917, February 8, 1918.

40 Mitchell and Shrubsole, *Ontario Conservation Authorities*, 38.

41 *NR*, April 16, 1920; *DR*, May 2, November 3, 1921, April 26, 1922.

42 Mitchell and Shrubsole, *Ontario Conservation Authorities*, 32.

43 Undated newspaper clipping; Grand River Valley Board of Trade (GRVBT) Minutes, file 21, series 3, Grand River Conservation Authority Fonds, UWA. See also GRVBT Minutes, December 12, 1930, file 21, series 3, GRCA Fonds, UWA.

44 See GRVBT Minute Books, file 22, series 3, GRCA Fonds, UWA.

45 GRVBT Minutes, June 11, 1931, file 22, series 3, GRCA Fonds, UWA.

46 Galt *Reporter*, July 25, 1931.

47 Mitchell and Shrubsole, *Ontario Conservation Authorities*, 40; Marcel Pequegnat, "Grand River Conservation," *Waterloo Historical Society* (1942): 216–17.

48 GRVBT Minutes, January 28, 1932, file 22, series 3, GRCA Fonds, University of Waterloo Archives.

49 Unlabelled clipping, GRVBT Minutes, n.d., file 22, series 3, GRCA Fonds, UWA.

50 22 Geo V, c 55, March 30, 1932, Finlayson Remarks, in file 21, series 3, GRCA Fonds, UWA. See also Mitchell and Shrubsole, *Ontario Conservation Authorities*, 216–17.

51 GRVBT Minutes, April 20, May 30, 1934, file 22, series 3, GRCA Fonds, UWA; Dan Shrubsole, "The Grand River Conservation Commission: History, Activities, and Implications for Water Management," *Canadian Geographer* 36, no. 3 (1992): 225.

52 Mitchell and Shrubsole, *Ontario Conservation Authorities*, 45. See also Robert Pequegnat, 535:2, and Mac Coutts, 888:1, Oral History Collection, KPL.

53 Pequegnat, "Grand River Conservation," 217.
54 GRCC Minutes, August 17, 23, September 3, 23, 1936, file 22, series 3, GRCA Fonds, UWA.
55 GRCC Minutes, October 8, 1936, June 10, 1937, file 22, series 3, GRCA Fonds, UWA.
56 GRCC minutes, October 12, 1937, file 22, series 3, GRCA Fonds, UWA.
57 2 Geo VI, c 78.
58 Mitchell and Shrubsole, *Ontario Conservation Authorities*, 46; Pequegnat "Grand River Conservation," 218.
59 Minutes August 1942, file 301, series 3, GRCA Fonds, UWA.
60 Bloomfield, *City-Building Processes*, 427.
61 Mitchell and Shrubsole, *Ontario Conservation Authorities*, 50–1.
62 Bruce Hergott, *Vital Signs: Kitchener-Waterloo Hospital, the First Hundred Years* (Kitchener: Kitchener Waterloo Hospital, 1994), 2–7, 145.
63 Ibid., 8. See also Ontario Department of Health, *The Hospitals of Ontario: A Short History* (Toronto: Department of Health, Government of Ontario, 1934), 63.
64 Kitchener-Waterloo Hospital, *Annual Report*, 1921–2, Grand River Hospital Archives.
65 *KDR*, November 14, 1923.
66 Ibid. I have changed "have" to "has" to avoid adding *sic* to the quotation.
67 The committee's report is printed in the *KDR*, November 20, 1923.
68 Hergott, *Vital Signs*, 150.
69 See the available annual reports of the Kitchener-Waterloo Hospital Board, Grand River Hospital Archives.
70 All of these arguments are based on data taken from the annual reports of the Kitchener-Waterloo Hospital Board, Grand River Hospital Archives.
71 The Board of Trustees noted complaints about high charges in the early 1920s, and explained that even the present charges were not enough to cover the costs of the services. See Kitchener-Waterloo Hospital *Annual Report*, 1921, Grand River Hospital Archives. See also Hergott, *Vital Signs*, 151.
72 *KDR*, December 6, 1923.
73 *DR*, September 4, 1894.
74 *KDR*, February 1, April 2, 1947.
75 *KDR*, April 2, 1947.
76 *KDR*, April 3, 1947.
77 *KDR*, June 11, 1947.
78 Ibid. See also "Background" in Kitchener Recreation Commission Fonds, KCA.

79 January 4, 1930; January 14, 1930, untitled clipping; Waterloo-Guelph
    Airport History, Vertical Files, Local History Room, KPL.
80 May 8, 1936, untitled clipping; Waterloo-Guelph Airport History, Vertical
    Files, KPL; *KWR*, June 11, 1971. See also Norman Schneider (080, side 2)
    and Robert Brown (602, side 2; 603, side 1), Oral History Collection, KPL.
81 *KDR*, September 23, 1943, March 6, April 6, 11, 12, 22, June 8, July 11, 1947,
    Waterloo-Guelph Airport History, Vertical Files, KPL.
82 *KWR*, July 24, 1945.
83 *KWR*, December 4, 1945, January 7, 18, 21, 30, 1947, September 18, 1947,
    August 24, 1948.
84 *KWR*, October 3, 1950.
85 *NR*, January 4, 1910.
86 *NR*, May 25, 1912. See also our discussion of the Berlin Sewer Commission
    in the previous chapter.
87 *NR*, December 20, 1920. The Trades and Labour Council preferred to
    consolidate the water and hydro commissions in a single public utilities
    commission. See also *DR*, February 23, 1921.
88 *NR*, January 2, 1920.
89 3 Geo V, c 41.
90 *KDR*, December 29, 1920.
91 Ibid.
92 *KDR*, January 3, 1921.
93 *KDR*, 17, February 22, 1921.
94 *KDR*, April 7, 1921.
95 Ibid. See also *KDR*, February 22, 1921.
96 There were 296 total years of service on the commission. Ten commission-
    ers served 256 of these years. In fact, just *five* commissioners served 180
    of the available years, or 60 per cent of the total.

Chapter 4

1 Stewart Fyfe to Susan Dolbey, November 10, 1966; Stewart Fyfe to Ted
   Hodgetts, May 29, 1967, Stewart Fyfe Fonds, 5112.4, series 1 (Correspondence), QUA.
2 Fyfe to Hodgetts, May 29, 1967, Stewart Fyfe Fonds, 5112.4, series 1
   (Correspondence), QUA.
3 Fyfe to Thoman, March 6, 1967, B236778, Dr Stewart Fyfe (Personal), RG
   19-8 (Municipal Affairs), AO.
4 S.J. Clasky to W.H. Palmer, March 17, 1967, B236778, Dr Fyfe (Personal),
   RG 19-8 (Municipal Affairs), AO.

5 Fyfe to Cumming, April 28, 1967, Stewart Fyfe Fonds, 5112.4, series 5 (Waterloo Area Local Government Review [WALGR]), QUA.
6 Fyfe to Hodgetts, May 29, 1967, Stewart Fyfe Fonds, 5112.4, series 1 (Correspondence), QUA.
7 *KWR*, May 5, 1967; Dr Stewart Fyfe, personal interview, September 1, 2013.
8 *KWR*, February 7, 1970. Fyfe did publish a short study of Ontario's local government reforms in 1974; see Stewart Fyfe, "Local Government Reform in Ontario," in *A Look to the North: Canadian Regional Experience*, ed. William Macdougall, 13–32 (Washington: Advisory Commission on Intergovernmental Relations, 1974).
9 "The councillors up at Pitlochry / Believed in the creed of Ad Hockery/They farmed all decisions/To boards and commissions/And so made of their council a mockery." Henry B. Mayo, *Report of the Commission* (Toronto: Niagara Region Local Government Review Commission, 1966), 67. I became aware of the longevity of this poem when, after publishing a short paper on local ABCs in Canada, an Ontario civil servant wrote to me to tell me the poem, which she had learned while working in the Ministry of Municipal Affairs.
10 *Waterloo Local Government Reform Proposals* (Toronto: Municipal Research Branch, 1971), 2.
11 Dolbey, *Local Special Purpose Bodies in the Province of Ontario*, 28. That Dolbey was Fyfe's student is clear from the Stewart Fyfe Fonds, 5112.4, series 1 (Correspondence), QUA.
12 Ron M. Farrow, *Waterloo Area Local Government Review: Data Book of Basic Information* (Waterloo, ON: Waterloo Area Local Government Review, 1967), 6; Elizabeth Bloomfield, *Waterloo Township through Two Centuries* (Kitchener, ON: Waterloo Historical Society, 1995), 376.
13 Stewart Fyfe, *Waterloo Area Local Government Review: Report of Findings and Recommendations* (Toronto: Municipal Affairs, 1970), 17–18.
14 *KWR*, December 4, 1959.
15 *KWR*, December 3, 1959.
16 *KWR*, August 7, December 15, 1962.
17 Ralph Krueger, "Towards Regional Planning and Regional Government in Waterloo County," in *The Waterloo County Area: Selected Geographical Essays*, ed. A.G. McLellan (Waterloo, ON: Department of Geography, 1971), 296. The city of Kitchener participated in a mandatory suburban roads commission before this time.
18 *KWR*, May 5, 1961. See *KWR*, June 20, 1958, for an earlier discussion of county planning.
19 Krueger, "Towards Regional Planning," 298.
20 Ibid.

21 *KWR*, April 1, September 30, 1964; Kreuger, "Towards Regional Planning," 299.

22 *KWR*, March 25, 1965.

23 *KWR*, December 17, 1965.

24 *KWR*, June 13, 1966.

25 *KWR*, June 25, 1966.

26 *KWR*, July 2, 1966. The study was temporarily delayed by an annexation controversy in Kitchener. For the delay, see *KWR*, October 6, 14, 19, 1966.

27 *KWR*, November 4, 1966.

28 Farrow's role for the Niagara Study was secretary and research assistant. For the Waterloo study, he was promoted to research director.

29 Farrow to R.M. Burns, December 15, 1966, B229549, RG 19-56 (Municipal Research Correspondence Files), AO.

30 *KWR*, May 4, 1963.

31 *KWR*, October 25, 1965.

32 Hilda Sturm, "Municipal Elections," KCA.

33 *KWR*, December 4, 1962.

34 *KWR*, June 21, 1965. In 1962, council hired a consultant rather than striking a committee.

35 Ibid.

36 *KWR*, June 25, 1963.

37 Ibid., and October 27, 1964.

38 *KWR*, December 11, 1964.

39 *KWR*, December 9, 1964.

40 Ibid.

41 *KWR*, December 15, 1964.

42 *KWR*, May 4, 1965.

43 See Mitchell and Shrubsole, *Ontario Conservation Authorities*; and A.H. Richardson, *Conservation by the People: The History of the Conservation Movement in Ontario to 1970* (Toronto: University of Toronto Press, 1974).

44 *Brantford Expositor*, December 19, 1947.

45 For an overview of this cooperation, along with some important exceptions, see Mitchell and Shrubsole, *Ontario Conservation Authorities*.

46 *Brantford Expositor*, September 17, 1964. See also *KWR*, September 1964 (undated clipping), file 317, series 23, GRCA Fonds, UWA. See also Robert Pequegnat, interview 535 side 1, Oral History Tapes Collection, KPL.

47 GRCC Minutes, February 19, 1965, series 4, GRCA Fonds, UWA.

48 GRCC Minutes, July 21, 1965, series 4, GRCA Fonds, UWA. See also Mitchell and Shrubsole, *Ontario Conservation Authorities*, 144–6, 153.

49 Undated clipping, "Kitchener Council: 1960s," Vertical Files, KPL.

50 Kitchener *Record*, February 11, 1965. According to Wikipedia, Daddy
    Warbucks was a wealthy character in Harold Gray's *Little Orphan Annie*
    comic strip.
51 Fyfe, *Waterloo Area*, Appendix 2: 193–4.
52 See *KWR*, June 25, 1966, April 22, 1970, March 26, 1971.
53 The briefs can be accessed in B229560–B229564, RG 19-56, Municipal
    Research Correspondence Files, AO. They are also available in the Stewart
    Fyfe Fonds, series 5, WALGR, QUA.
54 Wellesley Township Brief, B229562, Municipal Research Correspondence
    Files, RG 19-56, AO.
55 Waterloo Township Brief, B229560, Municipal Research Correspondence
    Files, RG 19-56, AO.
56 Kitchener Brief (part two), B229562, Municipal Research Correspondence
    Files, RG 19-56, AO.
57 There are two major archival collections on the Waterloo Area Review. At
    Queen's University Archives is the Fyfe material, containing Fyfe's personal
    correspondence and annotated briefs related to the review. At the Archives
    of Ontario is a second collection, which contains the official records of the
    review, managed by Farrow, along with Farrow's personal correspondence.
    The red annotations are in the Farrow collection at the Archives of Ontario.
58 The two most well-known examples are Hollis E. Beckett, *Fourth and Final
    Report of the Select Committee on the Municipal Act and Related Acts* (Toronto:
    Government of Ontario, 1965); Lancelot J. Smith, *Report of the Ontario
    Committee on Taxation* (Toronto: Government of Ontario, 1967). See chap-
    ter 7 for a more detailed review of provincial thinking on local ABCs in
    Ontario during this period. For a clear illustration that Fyfe and Farrow
    were of one mind on this issue, see Fyfe's remarks in Transcripts, V.III,
    "City of Kitchener," 13–14, B229559, Municipal Research Correspondence
    Files, RG 19-56, AO.
59 For Farrow's specific comments on public utilities commissions, the best
    briefs to consult are those of the Galt Public Utilities Commission and
    the Waterloo Public Utilities Commission, both in B229563, Municipal
    Research Correspondence Files, RG 19-56, AO. Most briefs at the Archives
    of Ontario contain similar annotations.
60 "Transcripts: City of Kitchener," vol. 3, 13–14, B229559, RG 19-56, AO.
61 Fyfe to Smallwood, May 23, 1967, Fyfe to Mackenzie, May 23, 1967, 5112.4,
    series 5, WALGR, Stewart Fyfe Fonds, QUA.
62 For the deadline, see *KWR*, December 16, 1969. For the binge writing,
    see February 7, 1970.
63 *KWR*, March 10, 1970.

64 Ibid.; "McKeough Speech on Presentation of Report," March 10, 1970, in Stewart Fyfe Fonds, Series 5 (WALGR), 5112.4, QUA.

65 Fyfe, *Waterloo Area*, 163.

66 *KWR*, March 11, 1970.

67 Krueger, "Towards Regional Planning," 300.

68 *KWR*, March 11, April 25, 1970.

69 *KWR*, March 17, 1970. I have reversed the order of the statements in the second quotation.

70 *KWR*, March 20, April 24, May 28, 1970.

71 See the briefs in Subject Files of the Deputy Minister of Municipal Affairs, RG 19-11, AO.

72 *KWR*, 22, April 23, 1970. Interestingly, Dr Krueger attributed this shift to the fact that Fyfe was a political scientist! Elizabeth Bloomfield follows this view in *Waterloo Township*, 396.

73 *KWR*, September 11, 1970.

74 *KWR*, March 17, 1972. Among the stories of angry locals, two stand out. One Hespeler politician asked Prime Minister Trudeau to send troops to Hespeler to prevent amalgamation. Another man, a farmer in North Dumfries, apparently thought the prime minister was too lowly an official for the task; he appealed directly to Queen Elizabeth to intervene. See *KWR*, May 2, 1972.

75 *KWR*, August 23, 1972.

76 *KWR*, March 17, 1972.

77 Ibid.

78 Stewart Fyfe, personal interview, September 1, 2013.

79 *KWR*, June 10, 1970.

80 See chapter 7 for the broader provincial story.

81 Fyfe, *Waterloo Area*, 80.

82 Dolbey, *Local Special Purpose Bodies*, 98.

83 Lorne Bruce and Karen Bruce, *Public Library Boards in Postwar Ontario*, 2nd ed. (Guelph, ON: printed by the authors, 2012), 19.

84 Ibid., 25.

85 Ibid. See also Dolbey, *Local Special Purpose Bodies*, 47–50.

86 Ibid., 25–7.

87 Dalton Bales, "Regional Municipality of Waterloo," March 16, 1971. Included in *Waterloo Local Government Reform Proposals*, Municipal Research Branch, Department of Municipal Affairs, Ontario.

88 See ibid., chapter 3.

89 Jack Young, interview 780 side 1, Oral History Tape Collection, KPL. Young goes on to note that while the officials "didn't push the county very hard

to come up with quick answers, they made us very conscious of how important these planning decisions were."

90 See note 48 above.

91 Fyfe, *Waterloo Area*, 82.

92 *KWR*, March 20, 1970. This is the newspaper's paraphrase, not a direct quotation. See also September 11, 1970.

93 *KWR*, May 10, 1974.

94 *KWR*, April 8, 1975.

95 *KWR*, June 4, July 10, 1975.

96 *KWR*, May 15, 1973. The quotation above is a summary of the views of Claudette Millar.

97 Ibid.

98 *KWR*, May 11, 15, 1973, February 25, 1977.

99 *KWR*, January 26, 1977.

100 Ibid.

101 In the latter case, local politicians tried – unsuccessfully – to marshal support for their proposal from other regional governments as well. See *KWR*, January 25, 26, February 28, 24, 25, December 18, 1977.

102 William H. Palmer, *Report of the Waterloo Region Review Commission* (Waterloo, ON: Waterloo Region Review Commission, 1979), 1–10.

103 Ibid.

104 Ibid., 155–61.

105 Previously, the police board could appeal to the Ontario Police Commission if council rejected its budget. Now it was council that had the power to make the appeal. But the arbitrator remained the provincial police commission, whose decisions most believed to be favourable to the police.

106 How safe is this assumption? It is very difficult to know, since we have little evidence, beyond anecdotes, about the voting patterns of appointed board members. What we can say, however, is that the actors themselves strongly believe that their appointees are more likely to represent their interests on the board than would other appointees.

107 *The Record* (*TR*), October 11, 2005, November 23, 2012.

108 Police governance controversy has been much less prominent in local newspapers since the Mike Harris era. Regional Chairman Ken Seiling also suggested that things have been less contentious since the Harris reforms. Ken Seiling, personal interview, November 28, 2013.

109 *KWR*, May 22, 1975. Other municipalities in the region faced the same problems.

110 *KWR*, January 6, 1975.

111 *KWR*, January 4, 1975.

112 *TR*, July 8, 2006.
113 Ken Seiling, regional chairman, told me of this dissatisfaction in Waterloo.
114 *TR*, September 16, 1999, August 23, 2000. See chapter 7 for a detailed discussion of the Energy Competition Act.
115 *KWR*, August 23, 2000.
116 See *Waterloo Region Record* (*WRR*), August 30, 2012, for provincial speculation on further consolidation. My claim in the final sentence is widely accepted and was explicitly stated by Ken Seiling, Waterloo Region chair.
117 The story is much different, and quite interesting, at the provincial level. Bruce and Bruce have documented the debates in *Public Library Boards*, chap. 3.
118 32–3 Eliz II, c 57 (1984). For discussion, see Ontario *Debates* 3705–9 (October 30, 1984) and 4167–72 (November 15, 1984).
119 The Harris government made a minor change to the structure of the library boards in 2002, giving local councils more control over the board's size (51 Eliz II, c 18).
120 When the CTT was created, Guelph was a participant, making the ABC structure a necessity. After Guelph withdrew, the structure persisted, in large part because Cambridge politicians have tended to insist that economic development should be focused on the municipal rather than the regional level.
121 Is it significant that the former are Conservative premiers and the latter are Liberals and NDP? I am not sure, but the question merits further exploration.
122 E.g., *KWR*, December 16, 1991, October 21, 1994; *TR*, September 19, 1995, September 28, 2005.
123 Hilda Sturm, "Municipal Elections," 2012, Kitchener Corporate Archives, http://lf.kitchener.ca/uniquesig0d1d2aa1a38f6e69dc1e79e99d780c34f537 a34d9c901a0d7cbb1976cbfdd057/uniquesig0/WeblinkExt/0/doc/ 1247099/Page1.aspx.

Part Two

1 Those who wish to survey Ontario's political history should consult Robert Bothwell, *A Short History of Ontario* (Edmonton: Hurtig Publishers, 1986), as well as the many excellent volumes in the Ontario Historical Studies Series published by the University of Toronto Press. My understanding of Ontario's political history has also been influenced by the work of Sid Noel; see especially his *Patrons, Clients, Brokers* (Toronto: Macmillan Canada, 1974).

2 It is important to note, however, that Mowat's margins of victory (in contrast to the Conservatives' in the twentieth century) were razor thin. See Graham White, "Social Change and Political Stability in Ontario: Electoral Forces 1867–1977" (PhD diss., McMaster University, 1979), 78.

3 After 1943, this party has been known as the Progressive Conservative Party.

4 For a brief overview of education finance in Ontario, see Royal Commission on Learning, *For the Love of Learning* (Toronto: Queen's Printer, 1995), 466–8; Education That Connects, *Good Governance: A Guide for Trustees, School Boards, Directors of Education and Communities* (Toronto: Education That Connects, 2015), chap. 8.

5 See Health Protection and Promotion Act, Revised Statutes of Ontario, c H7.

6 For an example, see Toronto Public Health, "Toronto Public Health Operating Budget Request, 2015," http://www.toronto.ca/legdocs/ mmis/2015/ex/bgrd/backgroundfile-77285.pdf.

7 The best long-term overview of Ontario's hydro-electric sector is Neil Freeman, *The Politics of Power* (Toronto: University of Toronto Press, 1996). See also the reports cited in chapter 8.

Chapter 5

1 *Canadian School Board Journal* 4, no. 5 (April 1925), cover.

2 Susan E. Houston and Alison Prentice, *Schooling and Scholars in Nineteenth-Century Ontario* (Toronto: University of Toronto Press, 1988), 138; R.D. Gidney and D.A. Lawr, "The Development of an Administrative System for the Public Schools: The First Stage, 1841–50," in *Egerton Ryerson and His Times*, ed. Neil McDonald and Alf Chaiton (Toronto: Macmillan Canada, 1978), 161.

3 Following English usage, the schools were originally called "public" schools (public as in "not held inside somebody's house"). The boards were originally called "District school boards." By the 1820s the schools were "grammar schools" and the boards were "grammar school boards," at least in ordinary usage.

4 R.D. Gidney and W.P.J. Millar, *Inventing Secondary Education* (Montreal and Kingston: McGill-Queen's University Press, 1990), 80–1; Walter E. Downes, "The Effect of British Colonial Policy on Public Educational Institutions in Upper Canada, 1784–1840" (PhD diss., University of Ottawa, 1974), 153; J. George Hodgins, *Documentary History of Education in Upper Canada* (Toronto: Warwick Brothers / Rutter, 1894), 1:11; A.F. Hunter, ed., *The*

Correspondence of the Honourable Peter Russell (Toronto: Ontario Historical Society, 1935), 179.

5 Duke of Portland to Lieutenant-Governor Hunter, March 12, 1800. Quoted in Hodgins, *Documentary History*, 1:26.

6 For the initial proposal, see Hodgins, *Documentary History*, 1:22. The legislation, 47 Geo III, c 6, is also available in Hodgins, *Documentary History*, vol. 1. For the regional jealousies, see Hodgins, *Documentary History*, 1:22, 156.

7 Robert Thorpe and a few others in the Legislative Assembly had resisted this proposal, arguing that the Legislature should appoint half the trustees. But according to a contemporary pamphlet, "the absurdity of this innovation was so apparent, that he found only two to support him." See James H. Aitchison, "The Development of Local Government in Canada, 1783–1850" (PhD diss., University of Toronto, 1953), 697.

8 For the attempts at abolition, see Hodgins, *Documentary History*, 1:67–70, 70–3, 76–8, 85–6.

9 See, for example, Rouleen Stewart, "The Ontario School Trustee: Snapshots over Time," in *Alternative Approaches to Determining Distribution of School Board Trustee Representation*, ed. Edward H. Humphreys, S.B. Lawton, R.G. Townsend, V.E. Grabb, and D.M. Watson (Toronto: Queen's Printer for Ontario, 1986), 38; David M. Cameron. "The Politics of Education," 1969: 13.

10 John Simcoe was the first lieutenant-governor of Upper Canada; John Cartwright was a Kingston businessman and judge; John Strachan was an Anglican cleric and political leader. Detailed biographies of all three men are available in the *Dictionary of Canadian Biography* at http://www.biographi.ca/.

11 For Strachan's role, see George W. Spragge, "John Strachan's Contribution to Education 1800–1823," *Canadian Historical Review* 22, no. 2 (1941): 153; Houston and Prentice, *Schooling and Scholars*, 28; J.D. Wilson, "Foreign and Local Influences on Popular Education in Upper Canada, 1814–1844" (PhD diss., University of Western Ontario, 1970), 58; George W. Spragge, ed., *The John Strachan Letter Book: 1812–1834* (Toronto: Ontario Historical Society, 1946), 75–8. For Simcoe, see Simcoe to Dundas, April 28, 1792, quoted in Hodgins, *Documentary History*, 1:11 (note the importance of the often-ignored "in the meantime"). For Cartwright, see Graeme Hazlewood Patterson, "Studies in Elections and Public Opinion in Upper Canada" (PhD diss., University of Toronto, 1969), 317–18; and Hodgins, *Documentary History*, 1:121–2.

12 56 Geo III, c 36.

13 R.D. Gidney, "Centralization and Education: The Origins of an Ontario Tradition," *Journal of Canadian Studies / Revue d'études canadiennes* 7, no. 4 (1972): 36. This contrasts with Aitchison, "Development," 721.

14 An example is the Ernesttown Academy, discussed in William Canniff, *History of the Province of Ontario* (Toronto: A.H. Hovey, 1872), 340; see also R.D. Gidney and W.P.J. Millar, "From Voluntarism to State Schooling: The Creation of the Public School System in Ontario," *Canadian Historical Review* 66, no. 4 (1985): 443–73.

15 *Laws of New York* 1812, c CCXLII.

16 For one contemporary observation, see Hodgins, *Documentary History*, 3:143; see also Wilson, "Foreign and Local Influences on Popular Education in Upper Canada," 61; Fred Landon, *Western Ontario and the American Frontier* (Toronto: McClelland and Stewart, 1967), 61–2. For the wider influence of New York law, see Aitchison, "Development of Local Government," 193, 236–7.

17 Quoted in Carl Kaestle, *Pillars of the Republic: Common Schools and American Society, 1780–1860* (New York: Hill and Wang, 1983), 26–7.

18 Material on this period in Upper Canada's educational history is abundant. For overviews, see Houston and Prentice, *Schooling and Scholars*; Alison Prentice, *The School Promoters* (Toronto: McClelland and Stewart, 1977); Gidney and Millar, "From Voluntarism to State Schooling"; Stewart, "Ontario School Trustee"; Gidney and Lawr, "Development of an Administrative System for the Public Schools." For discussion of the Duncombe report and draft bill of 1836 (perhaps the most important of the 1830s proposals from the reform side), see Aitchison, "Development," 736; Susan E. Houston, "Politics, Schools, and Social Change in Upper Canada," in *Education and Social Change: Themes from Ontario's Past*, ed. Michael B. Katz and Paul H. Mattingly (New York: New York University Press, 1975), 32–3; Marian Jane Duncan, "American Influences on Ontario's Elementary School Legislation, 1836–1850" (master's thesis, University of Rochester, 1964), 113–14; Hodgins, *Documentary History*. For the Burwell proposals (equally important, from the Tory side), see Duncan, "American Influences on Ontario's Elementary School Legislation," 119; Wilson, "Foreign and Local Influences on Popular Education in Upper Canada," 179–83; Hodgins, *Documentary History*.

19 4 & 5 Vic, c XVIII.

20 William Buell's bill in 1831 proposed township boards of trustees; Charles Duncombe's draft bill made much the same suggestions. Both men were reformers in the Upper Canadian legislature. Mahlon Burwell, who had

Tory links, proposed a bill with provisions for township superintendence but retained the school section trustee.

21 "Petty tyrants" comes from Gidney and Lawr, "Development of an Administrative System," 166, which offers an excellent description of the 1841 statute and its aftermath.

22 Hodgins, *Documentary History*, 4:313–14.

23 Gidney and Lawr, "Development of an Administrative System," 164. This is the best account of the 1841 legislation. See also Houston and Prentice, *Schooling and Scholars*, 108–11; Aitchison, "Development," 740–7; Wilson, "Foreign and Local Influences," 216.

24 Gidney and Lawr, "Development of an Administrative System," 169.

25 Ibid.; Houston and Prentice, *Schooling and Scholars*, 112–14.

26 9 Vic, c 20 & 10–11 Vic, c 19.

27 Ryerson to provincial secretary, March 27, 1847, quoted in Hodgins, *Documentary History*, 8:188–9.

28 Hodgins, *Documentary History*, 7:188–95.

29 For an example of such objections, see ibid., 7:115–19.

30 Toronto Education Committee Report, quoted in Houston and Prentice, *Schooling and Scholars*, 121–2.

31 Peter N. Ross, "The Free School Controversy in Toronto, 1848–1852," in *Education and Social Change: Themes from Ontario's Past*, ed. Michael B. Katz and Paul H. Mattingly (New York: New York University Press, 1975), 60; Hodgins, *Documentary History*, 8:68–72.

32 Quotation from Ross, "Free School Controversy in Toronto," 66.

33 See Hodgins, *Documentary History*, 8:115–32.

34 The circumstances surrounding the passage of the Cameron Act remain muddy. The best overview is in Houston and Prentice, *Schooling and Scholars*, 124–9; See also Gidney, "Centralization and Education," 41–3; Hodgins, *Documentary History*, 8:166–7.

35 Hodgins, *Documentary History*, 10:41.

36 This helpful term comes from Michael Atkinson and William D. Coleman, "Strong States and Weak States: Sectoral Policy Networks in Advanced Capitalist Economies," *British Journal of Political Science* 19, no. 1 (1989): 51.

37 At the county conventions in 1869, Ryerson regularly stated that this would be his final official tour. See especially *Chatham Weekly Planet*, February 25, 1869; *Brockville Recorder*, March 18, 1869.

38 4244 of 4400 school sections. J.D. Wilson, "The Ryerson Years in Canada West," in *Canadian Education: A History*, ed. J.D. Wilson, R.M. Stamp, and L.P. Audet (Scarborough, ON: Prentice Hall, 1970), 224.

39 *Brockville Recorder*, March 18, 1869.

40 Ryerson's correspondence during these conventions can be found in Hodgins, *Documentary History*, 19:151–70 (1866) and 21:158–70 (1869). See table 5.2, at the end of this chapter for a summary of newspaper accounts of the county conventions.

41 See *Guelph Evening Mercury*, February 26, 1869; as well as *Sarnia Observer*, February 19, 1869.

42 Hodgins, *Documentary History*, 21:158.

43 Ryerson to Hodgins, January 17, 1866, in ibid., 19:158. See also *St Catharines Constitutional*, January 18, 1866; *Goderich Semi-Weekly Signal*, January 30, 1866; *Stratford Beacon*, February 2, 1866; *Canadian Champion* (Milton), February 15, 1866.

44 See Hodgins, *Documentary History*, 19:233–5, 24:103–6; as well as the 1866 newspaper reports listed in table 6.1 above.

45 Ryerson to Hodgins, February 17, 1866, quoted in Hodgins, *Documentary History*, 19:161–2.

46 I have not been able to locate the Hodgins letter; this quotation is from Ryerson's response to Hodgins. It begins, "I think with you, we shall be able," and I have therefore thought it fair to take this sentence as indicating the substance of Hodgins's own letter. Ryerson to Hodgins, February 19, 1866, in ibid., 19:162.

47 The speaker was Rev. T. Macpherson. *Stratford Beacon*, February 2, 1866. See also Stewart, "Ontario School Trustee," 49.

48 Or, in one case, voted against a resolution in favour of the system; the remaining four either did not make or did not record their decision on the matter.

49 It was rejected in just four places: Picton, Napanee, Brockville, and Alexandria. See Hodgins, *Documentary History*, 21:144.

50 Gidney and Millar, *Inventing Secondary Education*, 150–95. For Ryerson's own description of the problem and his proposed solution, see Hodgins, *Documentary History*, 22:30–1, 193.

51 Ryerson interpreted all of this in a rather favourable light, declaring, "The proposed Grammar School Bill with the additions stated in my previous communication, were universally approved." From Ryerson's report on the proceedings of the County Conventions, 1869, in Hodgins, *Documentary History*, 21:144.

52 Ibid.

53 "I will not depart from what I have stated. My trust is in God," declared an increasingly stubborn Ryerson in a telegram from Whitby, much to the chagrin of Ryerson's frantic deputy, desperately holding things together

in Toronto. For the whole remarkable exchange, see Hodgins, *Documentary History* 22:158–68.

54 "If you had studied the first elements of the problem of educational and social progress ..." began one sentence in a scathing public letter from Ryerson to Blake; what followed was hardly more polite. Ibid., 22:226.

55 See *Globe*, January 25, February 4, 1871.

56 See the remarks of Galbraith, Graham, and Sexton in *Globe*, January 25, 1871. In the county conventions, Ryerson promised to address this problem with what would essentially be ad hoc adjustments. See, for example, *Canadian Champion*, February 15, 1866.

57 See *Globe*, November 27, 1869, January 28, 1871; and Hodgins, *Documentary History*, 22:30–1.

58 Ryerson actually had some sympathy for this criticism, and had initially proposed a partially appointed board, but eventually came to the view that the principle of taxation by elected representatives was more important than whatever loss of quality might result from an elected board. See Hodgins, *Documentary History*, 17:297–305; 22: 30–1, 193, 224; Gidney and Millar, *Inventing Secondary Education*, 201.

59 More specifically, ten would be elected and two would be appointed by the separate schools. *Globe*, April 24, 1903, 2; John Andrew Hope, *Report of the Royal Commission on Education in Ontario* (1950): 212.

60 *Globe*, April 24, 1903, 2.

61 *Globe*, March 24, 1904, 8.

62 Stewart, "Ontario School Trustee," 45.

63 The number of boards of education began to decline after 1940 as the boundaries of the high school district extended beyond the borders of the municipality. But this decline was indicative of the extension of secondary schooling, and secondary school financing, rather than of some dissatisfaction with the board of education system. See David M. Cameron, "The Politics of Education in Ontario, with Special Reference to the Financial Structure" (PhD diss., University of Toronto, 1969), 45–9.

64 Iain C. Taylor, "Components of Population Change, Ontario: 1850–1940" (MA thesis, University of Toronto, 1967). See also William Robert Young, "The Countryside on the Defensive: Agricultural Ontario's Views of Rural Depopulation, 1900–1914" (MA thesis, University of British Columbia, 1971). I have also benefited from Ian M. Drummond, *Progress without Planning: The Economic History of Ontario from Confederation to the Second World War* (Toronto: University of Toronto Press, 1987), 412–13.

65 My interpretation of the crisis and its results is drawn from Young, "Countryside on the Defensive"; William Robert Young, "Conscription,

Rural Depopulation, and the Farmers of Ontario, 1917–19," *Canadian Historical Review* 53, no. 3 (1972): 289–320; Robert M. Stamp, *The Schools of Ontario 1876–1976* (Toronto: University of Toronto Press, 1982); J.W. Watson, "Rural Depopulation in Southwestern Ontario," *Annals of the Association of American Geographers* 37, no. 3 (1947): 145–54; Graham White, "One-Party Dominance and Third Parties: The Pinard Theory Reconsidered," *Canadian Journal of Political Science* 6, no. 3 (1973): 415–19; Charles Murray Johnston, *E.C. Drury, Agrarian Idealist* (Toronto: University of Toronto Press, 1986), as well as the primary sources listed in the notes below.

66 The title of the memo is "Rural School Organization and Administration," and the author is not identified, Howard Ferguson Fonds, MU1023, AO. See also *Globe*, April 16, 1925, 4.

67 W.C. Good, quoted in Young, "Conscription, Rural Depopulation, and the Farmers of Ontario," 296.

68 *Annual Report of the Minister of Education, Ontario*, 1922.

69 "Financing the Schools in Sparsely Settled Districts," *Canadian School Board Journal* 2, no. 12 (1923): 7. See also Ferguson's speech in OEA, *Proceedings*, 1925, 11–15.

70 See Ferguson's speech in the note above.

71 G.H. Ferguson, *The Township School Board Proposal: A Second Letter* (Toronto: Clarkson W. James, 1926), 2–3. See also Stamp, *Schools of Ontario 1876–1976*, 128–9.

72 *Newspaper Hansard*, April 1, 1925.

73 Ibid., March 31, 1926, March 29, April 1, 1927, March 27, 1928.

74 In 1928 Ferguson was confident enough to suggest that the bill be passed with a two-year delay on implementation. This proposal was rejected. See *Newspaper Hansard*, March 27, 1928. See also the hopeful view of W.J. Karr, *Annual Report of the Minister of Education*, 1925, 23.

75 The quotation is from *Globe*, April 4, 1929, 1–2; See also *Globe*, December 28, 1926, 4; and *Proceedings* of the Ontario Educational Association.

76 *Globe*, March 30, 1928, 13.

77 Deputy minister to Ferguson, September 22, 1925, Howard Ferguson Correspondence, RG 3-6-0-441, AO. The letter is also quoted in Stamp, *Schools of Ontario 1876–1976*, 130.

78 *Newspaper Hansard*, March 27, 1928.

79 See Karr, *Annual Report of the Minister of Education*, 24.

80 Hope, *Report of the Royal Commission on Education in Ontario*, 208.

81 For a good demonstration of this complexity, see ibid., 236. See also R.D. Gidney, *From Hope to Harris: The Reshaping of Ontario's Schools* (Toronto: University of Toronto Press, 1999), 10–11.

82 Cameron, "Politics of Education in Ontario," 25, 52–3; Stamp, *Schools of Ontario 1876–1976*, 158.

83 Stamp, *Schools of Ontario 1876–1976*, 202.

84 Cameron, "Politics of Education in Ontario," 10.

85 For details on the plan, see ibid., 191–216. Cameron, "Politics of Education in Ontario," 210, 216, 400n6. See also Gidney, *From Hope to Harris*, 48–9.

86 Gidney, *From Hope to Harris*, 48–9; Cameron, "Politics of Education in Ontario," 201–2, 209.

87 Cameron, "Politics of Education in Ontario," 210, 398, 402. See also *Globe*, October 17, 1963, 6.

88 Ontario *Debates* 1963–4, 1002.

89 Stamp, *Schools of Ontario*, 208.

90 Cameron, "Politics of Education in Ontario," 430–4.

91 See ibid., 462–4.

92 Ontario *Debates* 1968, 833.

93 *Globe*, January 27, 1968, 2; Ontario *Debates* 1968, 1593.

94 W.G. Fleming, *Ontario's Educative Society*, vol. 2, *The Administrative Structure* (Toronto: University of Toronto Press, 1971), 130. The Liberals and the NDP attempted to make something of these criticisms in the Legislature, with little success. See *Globe*, February 2, 1968, 4. For Davis's argument, see *Annual Report of the Minister of Education*, 1968, 10; Ontario *Debates* 1967, 1212; and Ontario *Debates* 1968, 836.

95 July 12, 1968, quoted in Fleming, *Ontario's Educative Society*, 2:134.

96 See especially Ontario *Debates* 1968, 1589. For an exception, see *Globe*, January 30, 1968, 5.

97 On equality, see Fleming, *Ontario's Educative Society*, 2:127.

98 Cameron, "Politics of Education in Ontario," 407; Gidney, *Hope to Harris*, 49–50.

99 Gidney, *Hope to Harris*, 52; Fleming, *Ontario's Educative Society*, 146. For Davis's argument, see *Globe*, February 2, 1968, 4.

100 Gidney and Lawr, "Development of an Administrative System," 175–6.

101 Ibid.

102 Cameron, "Politics of Education in Ontario," 400–2.

103 Fleming, *Ontario's Educative Society*, 2:114; Stamp, *Schools of Ontario*, 157.

104 Stamp, *Schools of Ontario*, 157.

105 Hodgins, *Documentary History of Education*, 19:170, 233–5; 21:144.

106 *Brockville Recorder*, March 1, 1866 (see comments of Mr Wylie).

107 Hodgins, *Documentary History of Education*, 19:151–3, 233–5; *Goderich Semi-Weekly Signal*, January 30, 1866; *Stratford Beacon*, February 2, 1866; *Canadian Champion*, February 15, 1866; *Brockville Recorder*, March 1,

1866; *Barrie Northern Advance*, February 18, 1869; *Chatham Weekly Planet*, February 25, 1869; *St Thomas Weekly Dispatch*, February 25, 1869; *Brampton Times*, February 22, 1869.

108 Hodgins, *Documentary History of Education*, 19:162; *Brockville Recorder*, March 1, 1866. This is especially clear when we notice the one thing Ryerson most feared about the conventions: delegated opposition. While Ryerson could tolerate, even enjoy, a heated exchange of views, he was infuriated when he suspected that delegates had been sent to the meeting pledged to vote against a proposal. See Hodgins, *Documentary History of Education*, 19:161; and especially *Ottawa Citizen*, March 5, 1866 and March 26, 1869.

109 Stamp, *Schools of Ontario*, 130.

110 Ibid., 61–4. Ontario Education Association, *Yearbook and Proceedings*, 1903, 391–5. These arguments persisted. See, for example, *Canadian School Board Journal* 2, no. 11 (October 1923), 3, no. 5 (April 1924), 3, no. 6 (May 1924).

111 E.g., *Chatham Weekly Planet*, February 8, 1866.

112 E.g., *Stratford Beacon*, February 2, 1866; *Canadian Champion*, February 15, 1866. Ryerson may also have hoped that the township boards would make the system more "legible" from the centre. The notion of "legibility" comes from James Scott, *Seeing like a State* (New Haven, CT: Yale University Press, 1998). Bruce Curtis has made similar arguments in the case of nineteenth-century Ontario; see especially Curtis, *Building the Educational State: Canada West, 1836–1871* (Barcombe, Lewes, East Sussex: Falmer, 1988); and, more generally, Curtis, "The Canada 'Blue Books' and the Administrative Capacity of the Canadian State, 1822–67," *Canadian Historical Review* 74, no. 4 (1993): 535–65.

113 See, e.g., *Globe*, April 14, 1925, 3, and April 16, 1925, 4.

114 The department's annual reports during these years are rife with statistics on this issue. See especially *Annual Report*, 1922, 43–59.

115 Ibid.

116 How else but in consolidated schools, after all, would township boards lead to Ferguson's central stated goal: equalization of opportunities for rural and urban pupils?

117 Young, "Countryside on the Defensive," 44–5; Stamp, *Schools of Ontario*, 127; Peter Oliver, *G. Howard Ferguson: Ontario Tory* (Toronto: University of Toronto Press, 1977), 238; *Globe*, March 7, 1928, 4. See also the many letters to Ferguson opposing township boards, in Township School Boards: Ferguson Correspondence, RG 3-6-0-1042, AO.

118 Calculated from *Annual Report of the Minister of Education*, 1935, 142.

119 Letter from Mrs E.B. Snow, *Canadian School Board Journal* 16, no. 1
(January 1938): 22. See also Cameron, "Politics of Education in Ontario,"
22. These challenges were not unfamiliar to education officials. See
Annual Report, 1922, 51–2.
120 Stamp, *Schools of Ontario*, 130; *Globe*, March 31, 1926, 5, and December
28, 1926, 4; Department of Education, *Annual Report*, 1925, viii. See also
"Rural School Organization and Administration" in Papers Related to
Education, MU1023, Ferguson Papers, F8, AO; *Newspaper Hansard*, March
29, 1927.
121 Stamp, *Schools of Ontario*, 131; *Globe*, March 1, 1926, 4. See also *Newspaper
Hansard*, March 31, 1926.
122 This was a recognized problem in the earlier period. See *Report of the Royal
Commission on Education*, 208. See also *Annual Report of the Department of
Education*, 1922, 55–9.
123 Ferguson to Grant, February 10, 1926, Howard Ferguson Correspondence,
RG 3-6-0-1042, AO. See also Ferguson to Proctor, February 23, 1926,
in the same container, and "The Administration of Rural Schools,"
Canadian School Board Journal 3, no. 5 (April 1924).
124 For a good example, see the comments of R.F. Nixon, Ontario Legislature
Debates, 1963–4, 1489. See also Prime Minister's Speech to Provincial-
Municipal Conference, 1, in RG 19-11 40-5, AO.
125 For the background, see Young, "Countryside on the Defensive," esp.
5–8; and Young, "Conscription, Rural Depopulation," 297–8. See also
Johnston, *E.C. Drury*, 83. For the divided opinion in rural Ontario, see
"Are Township Boards Desirable?" *Canadian School Board Journal* 4, no. 3
(February 1925), and 5, no. 2 (January 1926).
126 A typical summary of the changes is in Fleming, *Ontario's Educative
Society*, 2:115.
127 Robert M. Stamp, *Ontario Secondary School Program Innovations and Student
Retention Rates: 1920s–1970s* (Toronto: Ministry of Education, 1988),
25, 53. For the broader context, see Watson, "Rural Depopulation in
Southwestern Ontario," 153.
128 Ontario Legislature *Debates*, 1963–4, 2359.
129 The rural opposition in the 1860s, though less well organized than in
later years, was certainly clear to Ryerson, as was the recognition that
the township boards issue was of particular interest to rural Ontario.
See Hodgins, *Documentary History of Education* 19:160–3, 169; *Brockville
Recorder*, March 1, 1866.
130 See Young, "Conscription, Rural Depopulation," 295.

131 Royal Commission on Learning, *For the Love of Learning*, 453–4.

132 Gidney, *Hope to Harris*, 170, 183–98; John Ibbitson, *Promised land: Inside the Mike Harris Revolution* (Toronto: Prentice Hall Canada, 1997), 225; D. Maclellan, "Educational Restructuring and the Policy Process: The Toronto District School Board 1997–2003," *Academic Leadership: The Online Journal* 7 (2009): 4.

133 Gidney, *Hope to Harris*, 170–1, 195; Royal Commission on Learning, *For the Love of Learning*, 466.

134 Peggy Sattler, "Education Governance Reform in Ontario: Neoliberalism in Context," *Canadian Journal of Educational Administration and Policy* 128 (January 2012): 8; Royal Commission on Learning, *For the Love of Learning*, 452–4.

135 Ibbitson, *Promised Land*, 227–8.

136 Ibid., 230; Gidney *From Hope to Harris*, 243.

137 Ibbitson, *Promised Land*, 230.

138 See especially Ibbitson, *Promised Land*, 227–8; G.J. Bedard and S.B. Lawton, "The Struggle for Power and Control: Shifting Policymaking Models and the Harris Agenda for Education in Ontario," *Canadian Public Administration* 43, no. 3 (2000): 250; Sattler, "Education Governance Reform in Ontario," 21 (though I argue that Snobelen *was* concerned, at least secondarily, with the problem of provincial fiscal equality).

139 John Sweeney, *Ontario School Board Reduction Task Force: Final Report*, technical report (Toronto, 1996). For an example of Snobelen's use, see his remarks to Steve Paikin on TVO's *Studio 2*, http://tvo.org/archive-programs/studio-2. For the quotation regarding ammunition, see *Globe and Mail*, January 18, 1997, A1.

140 *Globe and Mail*, August 16, 1995, A2. See also *Kingston Whig Standard*, September 13, 1995, 1.

141 Ibbitson, *Promised land*, 230.

142 Ibid., 231. See also Gidney, *From Hope to Harris*, 197.

143 For a good overview of the contemporary situation, see *Globe and Mail*, September 26, 1996, A10.

144 See *Toronto Star*, October 11, 1996, A1; *Globe and Mail*, October 12, 1996, A5.

145 *Canadian Press NewsWire*, September 16, 1996. See also *Globe and Mail*, September 20, 1996, A6.

146 See, for instance, the highly critical editorial in the *Ottawa Citizen*, August 28, 1996, C1.

147 *Globe and Mail*, October 17, 1996, A3.

148 Gidney, *Hope to Harris*, 252. The quotation is from Patrick Daly, head of the Ontario Separate School Trustees' Association, *Toronto Star*, October 12, 1996, A10.

149 *Ottawa Citizen*, October 29, 1996, A1.
150 The original plan was for sixty-six boards; after some negotiation, the final tally was seventy-two.
151 Stephen E. Anderson and Sonia Ben Jafaar, "Policy Narrative for Ontario," in *The Evolution of Professionalism: Educational Policy in the Provinces and Territories of Canada*, ed. Adrienne S. Chan, Donald Fisher, and Kjell Rubenson (Vancouver: UBC Centre for Policy Studies in Higher Education and Training), 87–9.

Chapter 6

1 Though not, of course, if treated. See Joseph P. Byrne, ed., *Encyclopedia of Pestilence, Pandemics, and Plagues* (London: Greenwood Publishing Group, 2008), 93; Christopher Hamlin, *Cholera: The Biography* (Oxford: Oxford University Press, 2009), 2. The numbers in the account above refer to an unlucky victim; more "fortunate" victims experience the symptoms a bit more slowly.
2 Joseph Logan Atkinson, "The Upper Canadian Legal Response" (PhD diss., University of Ottawa, 2000), 275; Marian A. Patterson, "The Cholera Epidemic of 1832 in York, Upper Canada," *Bulletin of the Medical Library Association* 46, no. 2 (1958): 167.
3 Patterson, "Cholera Epidemic," 170.
4 Ibid., 169.
5 Ibid., 138, 168; Atkinson, "Upper Canadian Legal Response," 86; Heather MacDougall, "'Truly Alarming': Cholera in 1832," *Canadian Journal of Public Health* 100, no. 5 (2009): 333.
6 The board was led by the senior justice of the peace, and the clergymen were ex officio. See 2 Wm IV, c 16. See also Patterson, "Cholera Epidemic," 168.
7 To decidedly mixed reviews. See Atkinson, "Upper Canadian Legal Response," 86, 103.
8 Aitchison, "Development of Local Government in Canada," 662.
9 Quoted in Atkinson, "Upper Canadian Legal Response," 124.
10 Aitchison, "Development of Local Government in Canada," 662–3; Atkinson, "Upper Canadian Legal Response," 122.
11 Quoted in Atkinson, "Upper Canadian Legal Response," 111.
12 Aitchison, "Development of Local Government in Canada," 665–6.
13 3 Wm IV, c 48 (1833).
14 4 Wm IV, c 23.
15 The Kingston statute is 1 Vic, c 27 (1837). In other places, however, incorporated as "boards of police," the provincial executive retained its authority

to appoint the local boards. The incorporated places were: Brockville in 1832 (2 Wm IV, c 17), Hamilton in 1833 (3 Wm IV, c 17), Belleville, Cornwall, Port Hope, and Prescott in 1834 (4 Wm IV, c 24, 25, 26, and 27 respectively), Cobourg and Picton in 1837 (7 Wm IV, c 42 and c 45), London in 1840 (3 Vic, c 31), Niagara and St Catharines in 1845 (8 Vic, c 62 and c 63), and Ottawa and Dundas in 1847 (10–11 Vic, c 43 and c 45).

16 Richard B. Splane, *Social Welfare in Ontario 1791–1893* (Toronto: University of Toronto Press, 1965), 198; Aitchison, "Development of Local Government in Canada," 682. The Brantford statute is 10–11 Vic, c 49.

17 12 Vic, c 81.

18 E.g., the 1849 debate in Elizabeth Gibbs, ed., *Debates of the Legislative Assembly of United Canada* (Quebec: Centre de recherche en histoire economique du Canada français, 1976), 1715.

19 Aitchison, "Development of Local Government in Canada," 677, 687.

20 Cost may also have been a factor; this may have been an early attempt at "downloading." If so, it was unsuccessful: during periods of crisis, the provincial government typically covered the major expenses. See MacDougall, *Activists and Advocates* (Toronto: Dundurn, 1990), 67–8. The 1849 *Public Health Act* (12 Vic, c 8) was vigorously defended by a broad spectrum of legislators from Robert Baldwin to John A. Macdonald. See Gibbs, *Debates of the Legislative Assembly of United Canada*, 1652–3, 1715.

21 The term is from Mathew D. McCubbins and Thomas Schwartz, "Congressional Oversight Overlooked: Police Patrols versus Fire Alarms," *American Journal of Political Science* 28, no. 1 (1984): 165–79. See MacDougall, *Activists and Advocates*, 55; Aitchison, "Development of Local Government in Canada," 675, 681.

22 Splane, *Social Welfare in Ontario*, 199; Mary Powell, "Provincial-Local Relations in Ontario: The Case of Public Health, 1882–1984" (PhD diss., University of Toronto, 1991), 15–16; MacDougall, *Activists and Advocates*, 135.

23 Many sanitarians saw themselves as missionaries for the cause. See especially "Missionary Sanitary Work," *Sanitary Journal* 4, no. 6 (June 1880): 301; Ontario Provincial Board of Health, *Annual Report*, 1891, 21; and Association of Executive Health Officers of Ontario, *Annual Report*, 1893, 24.

24 Deborah A. Stone, "Causal Stories and the Formation of Policy Agendas," *Political Science Quarterly* 104, no. 2 (1989): 281–300.

25 "Preventable Disease," *Sanitary Journal* 1, no. 1 (July 1874): 16. See also Provincial Board of Health, *Annual Report*, 1902, 9.

26 "Health of Towns and Cities," *Canada Lancet* 5, no. 10 (June 1873): 525; Ontario Provincial Board of Health (PBH), *Annual Report*, 1882, xi; 1898,

4–8; as well as Barbara Lazenby Craig, "State Medicine in Transition: Battling Smallpox in Ontario, 1882–1885," *Ontario History* 75, no. 4 (1983): 320; and MacDougall, *Activists and Advocates*, 138.

27 Association of Executive Health Officers of Ontario, *Annual Report*, 1893, 132. For earlier examples of the same attitude, see "A Bureau of Sanitary Statistics Wanted," *Sanitary Journal* 1, no. 3 (November 1874): 85–6; 1, no. 4 (January 1875): 111; 1, no. 11 (November 1875): 333; 3, no. 5 (October 1877): 198.

28 For an amusingly extreme proposal, see "A Bureau of Sanitary Statistics Wanted." For dominion-level proposals, see "Epidemic of Smallpox," *Canada Lancet* 4, no. 6 (February 1872): 287–8; "Public Health Legislation," *Canada Lancet* 7, no. 6 (February 1875): 184; "Vital Statistics and Public Health," *Canada Lancet* 9, no. 9 (May 1877): 283; "National Board of Health," *Canada Lancet* 11, no. 11 (July 1879): 339; "Sanitary Reform," *Sanitary Journal* 1, no. 3 (November 1874): 70, 85–6; "Sanitary Legislation," *Sanitary Journal* 1, no. 6 (May 1875): 185; "The Health Bureau," *Sanitary Journal* 2, no. 4 (April 1876): 113–14; "The Statistical Bureau," *Sanitary Journal* 3, no. 10 (December 1878): 368; "On the Proposed Dominion Health Bureau," *Dominion Sanitary Journal* 6, no. 6 (March 1884): 182.

29 Henry B. Baker, "General Sanitation," *Sanitary Journal* 4, no. 5 (May 1880): 247. A milliner makes hats.

30 Instances of these arguments for expert authority are too numerous to list. For particularly clear examples, see "History of Medicine," *Canada Lancet* 5, no. 7 (March 1873): 330; and "Provincial Board of Health," *Canada Lancet* 9, no. 2 (October 1876): 59; "Sanitary Science," *Sanitary Journal* 1, no. 1 (July 1874): 1–2 (it is worth noting here that the call for expert authority is contained on the first page of the first issue of the *Sanitary Journal*); and "A Minister of Public Health in Great Britain," *Sanitary Journal* 3, no. 8 (October 1878): 314. See also Charles A. Cameron, *A Manual of Hygiene* (Dublin: Hodges, Foster, 1874), 2–3; Heather MacDougall, "Enlightening the Public: The Views and Values of the Association of Executive Health Officers of Ontario, 1886–1903," in *Health, Disease, and Medicine: Essays in Canadian History*, ed. Charles G. Roland (Hamilton, ON: Hannah Institute for the History of Medicine, 1982), 453–4. For a helpful interpretation with a slightly different emphasis, see MacDougall, *Activists and Advocates*, 156.

31 A group of professionals with a "shared set of normative and principled beliefs" (here a commitment to health as the foundation for all other goods), "shared causal beliefs" (born of shared medical training), "shared notions of validity" (again born of shared training), and a "common policy enterprise" (federal, provincial, and local health agencies led by competent

sanitarians). Peter M. Haas, "Introduction: Epistemic Communities and International Policy Coordination," *International Organization* 46, no. 1 (January 1992): 3.

32 For a discussion of the sanitarians' lobbying techniques and their origins, see Heather MacDougall, "Health Is Wealth: The Development of Public Health Activity in Toronto, 1834–1890" (PhD diss., University of Toronto, 1981), 152–3. We will return to this below.

33 "Venue shopping" is from Frank R. Baumgartner and Bryan D. Jones, *Agendas and Instability in American Politics* (Chicago: University of Chicago Press, 1993), esp. chap. 2.

34 The sanitarians were flexible on the basic structure – bureau, board, agency, etc. – of the provincial apparatus. What mattered was that it existed. See Playter to Mowat, n.d., in Oliver Mowat Papers, RG 3-85, AO.

35 For the American influence, see "Sanitary Reform," *Sanitary Journal* 1, no. 3 (November 1874): 85–6; "A Provincial Board of Health," *Sanitary Journal* 2, no. 9 (September 1876): 274–5; "A Provincial Board of Health," *Sanitary Journal* 2, no. 12 (December 1876): 355–6; "Shall We Have a Provincial Board of Health in Ontario?" *Sanitary Journal* 3, no. 5 (October 1877): 219–20; and the *Report* of the Select Committee on Public Health in *Journals of the Legislative Assembly of Ontario*, 1878, Appendix 2.

36 MacDougall, "Health Is Wealth," 153–5; MacDougall, "Enlightening the Public," 437–8; Jeanne L. Brand, *Doctors and the State: The British Medical Profession and Government Action in Public Health, 1870–1912* (Baltimore, MD: Johns Hopkins University Press, 1965), 8–11.

37 MacDougall, "Health Is Wealth," 153–4; Americans had done similar reports – most notably Lemuel Shattuck's 1850 *Report* in Massachusetts – but the sanitarians in Ontario seemed to be less aware of them. For the U.K. and U.S. background, see George Rosen, *A History of Public Health* (New York: MD Publications, 1958), 239–41.

38 *Newspaper Hansard*, January 18, 1878.

39 The report is printed in *Journals of the Legislative Assembly of Ontario*, 1878, Appendix 2.

40 To construct the table I have coded questions 3 and 6 in the 240 physician surveys, RG 49-92, AO. I have excluded blanks and non-responses from this table. Drummond (*Progress without Planning*, 5) reports 1558 doctors in Ontario in 1871, so we might estimate (assuming some growth in this total) that the surveys captured something like 10–15 per cent of Ontario physicians at the time.

41 See the physician survey returns in Records of the Select Committee on Public Health, RG 49-92, AO. Playter often initials his remarks, and the

style of the handwriting/underlining is consistent throughout. For more on Playter, see MacDougall, "Health Is Wealth," 149–50.

42 In addition to the report itself, see Craig, "State Medicine in Transition," 323–4.

43 And indeed it did; see 1879 Liberal Platform, Election Pamphlets, L3, AO.

44 A helpful source is MacDougall, "Health Is Wealth," 155–7.

45 "Public Health and Sanitary Reform," *Canada Lancet* 12, no. 6 (February 1880): 184; "The Proposed Provincial Board of Health," *Sanitary Journal* 4, no. 4 (March–April 1880): 227; Powell, "Provincial-Local Relations in Ontario," 19–20; MacDougall, "Health Is Wealth," 156–7.

46 For an example, see Edward Player to Oliver Mowat, December 6, 1880, Mowat Papers, RG 3-85, AO; and Craig, "State Medicine in Transition," 324.

47 Whereas the physicians wanted a board consisting exclusively of qualified doctors, the government reduced the mandatory number of physicians on the board from seven (the entire board) down to four. See Bill 121, 1882, in Original Bills RG 49-39, AO; there, the original provision is crossed out and "at least four members of the board" is written in its place. Craig and MacDougall attribute the draft bill to the Ontario Medical Association, though the basic provisions were already in place in the draft bill presented to Mowat 1879. Records in the OMA archives indicate that a committee of physicians in the Legislature was more influential than the OMA itself. See OMA Minute Book 1880–90, 37–8, OMA Archives; MacDougall, "Health Is Wealth," 169n6; Craig, "State Medicine in Transition," 325; John Ferguson, *History of the Ontario Medical Association, 1880–1930* (Toronto: Murray Printing, 1930), 8.

48 Powell, "Provincial-Local Relations in Ontario," 65–71; MacDougall, "Enlightening the Public," 436–40.

49 For instances in which the PBH *did* do something, see Craig, "State Medicine in Transition."

50 See PBH, *Annual Report*, 1882, xxii, xxx, 7, 118, 166; "Boards of Health," *Sanitary Journal* 6, no. 4 (January 1884): 115; Association of Executive Health Officers of Ontario, *Annual Report*, 1887, 76; 1891, 36; 1893, 132; see also Powell, "Provincial-Local Relations in Ontario," 53, 65, 82–3; MacDougall, "Enlightening the Public," 446.

51 PBH, *Annual Report*, 1882, xxxii.

52 See ibid., xxxii, 116; Powell, "Provincial-Local Relations in Ontario," 26, 46–7.

53 PBH, *Annual Report*, 1883, liv–lvi. See also *Public Health Journal* 2, no. 3 (1911): 103–4.

54 J.T. Phair, "Public Health in Ontario," in *The Development of Public Health*, ed. R.D. Defries (Toronto: Canadian Public Health Association, 1940), 67–85.

55 PBH, *Annual Report*, 1883, 315; Association of Executive Health Officers of Ontario, *Annual Report*, 1891, 3–5; "Boards of Health," *Sanitary Journal* 6, no. 4 (January 1884): 116–17.

56 PBH, *Annual Report*, 1882, 116; 1883, 202–3; 1885, 60; Association of Executive Health Officers of Ontario, *Annual Report*, 1887, 75–6, 79–80; 1902, 118, 142–3.

57 See PBH, *Annual Report*, 1883, 202–3; Liberal Conservative Platform, 1883, 26:4–5, Election Pamphlets Collection (L3), AO; *Newspaper Hansard*, January 26, 1883.

58 The statute is 47 Vic, c 38. For the contemporary discussion, see *Newspaper Hansard*, February 28, 1882.

59 58 Vic, c 49.

60 Some rural municipalities did not appoint LBHs, and the PBH was ill-equipped to enforce the law. See Powell, "Provincial-Local Relations in Ontario," 58.

61 The salience figure was generated using the newspapers available at OurOntario.ca. I have excluded y-axis values because they are uninteresting (the plot records the annual occurrences of the words each year divided by the number of available newspapers in the database). The outbreak information is taken from numerous secondary sources and newspapers, and the legislative change plot is taken from the *Journals of the Legislative Assembly of Ontario*.

62 PBH, *Annual Report*, 1901, 47.

63 PBH, *Annual Report*, 1912, 8.

64 *Public Health Journal* 2, no. 6 (June 1911): 274; *Kingsville Reporter*, May 25, 1911; PBH, *Annual Report*, 1911, 274; 1912, 8.

65 PBH, *Annual Report*, 1911, 274; 1912, 8; *Public Health Journal* 5, no. 10 (October 1914).

66 PBH, *Annual Report*, 1902, 6–7; 1906, 161–2; *Public Health Journal* 2, no. 3 (March 1911): 104–5; 16, no. 7 (July 1925): 320; *Leamington Post*, May 1, 1930; *Georgetown Herald*, September 3, 1947; Powell, "Provincial-Local Relations in Ontario," 122–3; Neil Sutherland, *Children in English-Canadian Society: Framing the Twentieth-Century Consensus* (Toronto: University of Toronto Press, 1976), 82; Oliver, *G. Howard Ferguson*, 312.

67 PBH, *Annual Report*, 1902, 6–7; 1906, 161–2.

68 *Public Health Journal*, 10, no. 9 (September 1919): 394; Ontario Department of Health, *Annual Report*, 1930, 16; Powell, "Provincial-Local Relations in Ontario," 101–2; Sutherland, *Children in English-Canadian Society*, 55.

69 PBH, *Annual Report*, 1902, 89–90; 1906, 161–2; Powell, "Provincial-Local Relations in Ontario," 95, 142–3.

70 PBH, *Annual Report*, 1902, 6–7.

71 Ontario PBH, *Annual Report*, 1904, 9. On the political-electoral explanation for this hesitation I follow ibid., 96 (though note, contra Powell, that the 1903 proposal was a circular, not a draft bill).

72 Ibid., 97–8; and PBH, *Annual Report*, 1906, 161–2.

73 Ontario PBH, *Annual Report*, 1904, 41.

74 2 Geo V, c 47. For evidence that the bill originated with Hanna, see *Public Health Journal* 10, no. 6 (June 1919): 270–1; and A. Margaret Evans, *Sir Oliver Mowat* (Toronto: University of Toronto Press, 1992), 101; Powell, "Provincial-Local Relations in Ontario," 106.

75 *Public Health Journal* 11, no. 7 (July 1920): 293.

76 See ibid.; and Powell, "Provincial-Local Relations in Ontario," 115–16. The Public Health Act was further amended in 1916, giving the provincial board of health the additional authority to *fire* the local health officer without the consent of municipal council. This too changed the MHO's incentives: while he no longer needed to look over his shoulder at municipal council, he was now obliged to look over the other shoulder at the provincial board of health.

77 Powell, "Provincial-Local Relations in Ontario," 103–4.

78 The title of the local health officer also changed from MOH to MHO.

79 Powell, "Provincial-Local Relations in Ontario," 120.

80 *London Lancet*, quoted in PBH, *Annual Report*, 1912, 10.

81 For the sanitarians' disappointment with the 1912 statute, see *Newspaper Hansard*, March 22, 1912.

82 The public health journals of the 1910s and 1920s are bursting with these articles and arguments, and proponents like McCullough often received considerable coverage in local newspapers as well. For example, *Public Health Journal* 14, no. 8 (August 1923): 419–20; 15, no. 2 (February 1924): 106–11; 16, no. 4 (April 1925): 171–4; 16, no. 8 (August 1925): 367–70; *Acton Free Press*, July 22, 1925; *Kingsville Reporter*, April 11, 1929; *Leamington Post*, January 21, 1932; Ontario Department of Health, *Annual Report*, 1928, 78.

83 R.R. Pounder to PBH secretary, February 25, 1920, quoted in Powell, "Provincial-Local Relations in Ontario," 118–19.

84 Oliver, *G. Howard Ferguson*, 230, 308, 312; John T. Saywell, *"Just call me Mitch": The Life of Mitchell F. Hepburn* (Toronto: University of Toronto Press, 1991), 65.

85 Heather MacDougall, "Researching Public Health Services in Ontario, 1882–1930," *Archivaria* 10 (1980): 157.

86 *Leamington Post*, February 20, March 27, May 1, July 24, 1930; *Kingsville Reporter*, April 3, June 26, 1930; *Stoufville Sun-Tribune*, June 26, 1930; *Georgetown Herald*, February 11, 1931.

87 *Acton Free Press*, January 15, 1931; *Georgetown Herald*, January 21, 1931; MacDougall, "Researching Public Health," 163–4; Powell, "Provincial-Local Relations in Ontario," 162–3; Oliver, *G. Howard Ferguson*, 312.

88 *Globe*, March 18, 1931.

89 Ibid.

90 *Acton Free Press*, January 29, March 19, April 16, 1931.

91 *Acton Free Press*, April 16, 1931. See also Ontario Department of Health, *Annual Report*, 1939, 10–12.

92 Powell, "Provincial-Local Relations in Ontario," 169–70.

93 24 Geo V, c 47.

94 MacDougall, "Researching Public Health," 168; Powell, "Provincial-Local Relations in Ontario," 168–9.

95 For the full story, see Deborah Sanborn, *Primarily Prevention: A History of the Eastern Ontario Health Unit* (Ottawa: Canadian Public Health Association, 2005).

96 Powell, "Provincial-Local Relations in Ontario," 207–8; Sanborn, *Primarily Prevention*, 28.

97 Powell, "Provincial-Local Relations in Ontario." This was done primarily because representation would vary from unit to unit; that is, the provincial government did not wish to specify in general how many representatives each municipality in the unit would be permitted to appoint. This move to regulation would become a trend in later years.

98 Ontario Department of Health, *Annual Report*, 1951, 6–7; *Georgetown Herald*, November 27, 1946. Powell, "Provincial-Local Relations in Ontario," 210–11.

99 The divide was primarily between rural (health units) and urban (health departments). See Powell, "Provincial-Local Relations in Ontario," 200, 223.

100 *Report of the Royal Commission on Metropolitan Toronto: Detailed Findings and Recommendations* (Toronto: Government of Ontario, 1977). Geographic inequality was a matter of controversy. After 1967, some units were receiving 75 per cent funding while municipalities of the same size in Metro received nothing. For discussion, see Powell, "Provincial-Local Relations in Ontario," 224–7. (See also for Lewis's criticisms.)

101 ODH, *Annual Report*, 1967, xii.

102 Powell, "Provincial-Local Relations in Ontario," 235, 244.

103 This was in addition to their medical training, of course.

104 MacDougall, "Researching Public Health," 186; Powell, "Provincial-Local Relations," 99, 120–1, 187.

105 Eric Beecroft, *Agenda for Regional Government* (Ottawa: Canadian Federation of Mayors and Municipalities, 1962), esp. 3, 8.

106 See, for example, Toronto, *Report of the Royal Commission on Metropolitan Toronto*, 347; Roger Warner, *Regional Government Reform in Ontario* (Toronto: Ontario Department of Municipal Affairs, January 1971), 3; W. Darcy McKeough, *Government Statement on the Review of Local Government in the Municipality of Metropolitan Toronto* (Toronto: Ministry of Treasury, Economics, and Intergovernmental Affairs, May 1978), 27; Government of Ontario, *Design for Development: Ontario's Future: Trends and Options* (Toronto: Government of Ontario, 1976), 1; W. Darcy McKeough, *Design for Development Phase Three: Statement by the Honourable W. Darcy McKeough Treasurer of Ontario to the Founding Convention of the Association of Municipalities of Ontario* (Toronto: Legislature of Ontario, 1972), 9.

107 See, especially, Hollis E. Beckett, *Fourth and Final Report of the Select Committee on the Municipal Act and Related Acts* (Toronto: Government of Ontario, 1965); Lancelot J. Smith, *Report of the Ontario Committee on Taxation: The Local Revenue System* (Toronto: Government of Ontario, 1967); John Robarts, *Design for Development Phase Two: Statement by the Honourable John Robarts Prime Minister of Ontario, November 28, 1968* (Toronto: Legislature of Ontario, 1968); Dolbey, *Local Special Purpose Bodies*; and the local reviews of the 1960s and 1970s, especially Stewart Fyfe and Ron M. Farrow, *Waterloo Area Local Government Review: Report of Findings and Recommendations* (1970): 79–81.

108 The education consolidation was certainly an inspiration for the later regional consolidation. See Robarts, *Design for Development Phase Two*, 1, 10.

109 See note above.

110 Fyfe, "Local Government Reform in Ontario," 19, 27.

111 Ibid. This changed after the regional governments proved more controversial than expected.

112 For examples, see Powell, "Provincial-Local Relations in Ontario," 315; Robarts, *Design for Development Phase Two*, 6–7; William G. Davis, *Design for Development Phase Three: Statement by the Honourable William G. Davis* (Toronto: Legislature of Ontario, June 1971), 1; McKeough, *Design for Development Phase Three*, 10–11; Beecroft, *Agenda for Regional Government*, 8; W.H. Palmer, *The Progress of the Regional Government Program in Ontario* (Toronto: Ontario Department of Municipal Affairs, 1970), 3; Warner, *Regional Government Reform in Ontario*, 1; Ron M. Farrow, *Local Government Reform: The Implications for the Classroom* (1971), 3–4;

Lionel D. Feldman, *Ontario 1945–1973: The Municipal Dynamic* (Toronto: Ontario Economic Council, 1974), 12, 41; Allan O'Brien, "Father Knows Best: A Look at the Provincial–Municipal Relationship in Ontario," in *Government and Politics of Ontario*, ed. Donald Macdonald (Toronto: Macmillan Canada, 1975), 155.

113 Henry J. Jacek, "Regional Government and Development: Administrative Efficiency versus Local Democracy," in *Government and Politics of Ontario*, 2nd ed., ed. Donald C. Macdonald (Toronto: Macmillan Canada, 1975), 146.

114 Ontario Legislature, *Debates*, December 2, 1968, 274.

115 E.g., Ontario Legislature, *Debates*, December 2, 1968: 277–8; and Dolbey, *Local Special Purpose Bodies*, 76.

116 See M.B. Dymond to W.G. Brown, April 14, 1965, and W.G. Brown to M.B. Dymond, in B397185, Minister's Correspondence, RG 10-1, AO.

117 Powell, "Provincial-Local Relations in Ontario," 314; see also Farrow, *Waterloo Area Local Government Review*, 38–9; Palmer, *Report of the Waterloo Region Review Commission* (Waterloo, ON: Waterloo Region Review Commission, 1979), 214–16; Stewart Fyfe, *Waterloo Area Local Government Review: Report of Findings and Recommendations* (Toronto: Municipal Affairs, 1970), 79.

118 The relevant statutes are 24 Eliz II, c 51 (Waterloo); 26–7 Eliz II, c 33 (York and Halton). See also Powell, "Provincial-Local Relations in Ontario," 315–16; Affairs, *Public Health Structures Study* (Toronto: Government of Ontario, 1980), 5.

119 Ministry of Health and Ministry of Intergovernmental Affairs, *Public Health Structures Study*.

120 See 31–2 Eliz II, c 72 (Durham, Haldimand-Norfolk, Hamilton-Wentworth, Niagara, Peel); 34–5 Eliz II, c 72 (Ottawa-Carleton). The matter remains a subject of controversy even to the present. See Archie Campbell, *SARS Commission Second Interim Report* (Toronto: Government of Ontario, April 2005), 69.

121 Powell, "Provincial-Local Relations in Ontario," 258; Smith, *Report of the Ontario Committee on Taxation*, 95–6; Peter Silcox, "The ABC's of Ontario: Provincial Agencies, Boards and Commissions," in *Government and Politics of Ontario*, ed. Donald C. Macdonald (Toronto: Macmillan Canada, 1975), 139–40.

122 Powell, "Provincial-Local Relations in Ontario," 261.

123 This argument forms the core of Mary Powell's excellent doctoral thesis. See ibid. The source of the broader argument is J. Stefan Dupré, "Reflections on the Workability of Executive Federalism," in *Intergovernmental Relations*, ed. Richard Simeon, 1–32 (Toronto: University of Toronto Press, 1985).

124 Richard Loreto, "The Cabinet," in *Government and Politics of Ontario*,
2nd ed., ed. Donald C. Macdonald (Toronto: Van Nostrand Reinhold,
1980), 26–7.
125 Powell, "Provincial-Local Relations in Ontario," 248–9; George J.
Szablowski, "Policy-Making and Cabinet: Recent Organizational
Engineering at Queen's Park," in *Government and Politics of Ontario*, ed.
Donald C. Macdonald (Toronto: Macmillan Canada, 1975), 118; Loreto,
"Cabinet," 26.
126 Between 1945 and 1969, Powell notes, the department had three ministers;
in the next fourteen years, it had seven. See Powell, "Provincial-Local
Relations in Ontario," 253. The physician calculations are based on a
dataset constructed by the author.
127 For an overview of these developments, see ibid., 271–83.
128 For a discussion of this measure, see Ontario Legislature, *Debates*,
December 1, 1997, online.
129 46 Eliz II, c 26 (Toronto); 48 Eliz II, c 14 (Hamilton, Ottawa, Hadimand/
Norfolk); 50 Eliz II, c 25 (Oxford County); OReg 351/98, s 1 (Chatham-Kent).
130 An additional change was the removal of the requirement that the
medical health officer serve as executive officer of the local public health
system. This had been contemplated for at least fifteen years (see, e.g.,
Ontario Legislature, *Debates*, February 14, 1983), but it would prove controversial after the SARS outbreak in 2003.
131 This download proved temporary, as the government assumed 50 per cent
funding the following year.
132 Marion Boyd's determined criticisms were the exception. See Ontario
Legislature, *Debates*, September 9, December 1, 1997 (online); and Archie
Campbell, *SARS Commission First Interim Report* (Toronto: Government of
Ontario, 2004), 169. This was not for lack of trying among the sanitarians;
see ibid.
133 The legal team for the municipal employee who had been responsible for
water testing tried to diminish Dr McQuigge's "hero" status during the
inquiry, and Justice O'Connor's report is hardly an encomium to the man.
But Dr McQuigge *was* widely lauded in the popular media. See, for example, *Toronto Star*, May 27, 2000, 1; June 3, 2000, 1, June 9, 2000, 1; *Globe and
Mail*, June 17, 2000, R9; June 24, 2000, A5. For O'Connor's discussion, see
Dennis O'Connor, "The Role of the Public Health Authorities," in *Report
of the Walkerton Inquiry* (Toronto: Government of Ontario, 2002), chap. 8.
134 See O'Connor, "Role of the Public Health Authorities," 263–4.
135 The four most prominent reports were those of the National Advisory
Committee on SARS and Public Health; the Kirby report of the Senate's

Standing Committee on Social Affairs, Sciences, and Technology; the Expert Panel on SARS and Infectious Disease Control; and the SARS Commission. We will focus on the two provincial reports here: those of Walker and Campbell.

136 Archie Campbell, *Spring of Fear: The SARS Commission Final Report* (Toronto: Government of Ontario, 2006), 1146.

137 Campbell, *SARS Commission Second Interim Report*, 102.

138 Ibid., 61. See also 59, 85, 102; Campbell, *Spring of Fear*, 1146; Campbell, *SARS Commission First Interim Report*, 206. Walker, for his part, recommended further consolidation. See David Walker, *For the Public's Health: Initial Report of the Ontario Expert Panel on SARS and Infectious Disease Control* (Toronto: Ontario Expert Panel on SARS and Infectious Disease Control, 2003), 75.

139 Ontario Public Health Division, *Initial Report on Public Health* (Toronto: Ministry of Health and Long-Term Care, 2009), 2; Public Health Division, *Building Capacity for Local Public Health in Ontario: A Discussion Paper* (Toronto: Government of Ontario, March 2009); Brent W. Moloughney, *Defining "Critical Mass" for Ontario Public Health Units* (Toronto: Ministry of Health and Long-Term Care, 2005).

140 Campbell, *SARS Commission First Interim Report*, 162, 192, 206; Campbell, *SARS Commission Second Interim Report*, 108.

141 See, e.g., Campbell, *SARS Commission Second Interim Report*, 62–3, 67–8, 72.

142 Campbell, *SARS Commission First Interim Report*, 170, 192; Campbell, *SARS Commission Second Interim Report*, 72.

143 Campbell, *SARS Commission First Interim Report*, 168, 170; Campbell, *SARS Commission Second Interim Report*, 59, 76; Walker, *For the Public's Health*, 53.

144 See our discussion of the Select Committee on Public Health above.

145 60 Eliz II, c 7. See also Ontario Legislature, *Debates*, November 30, December 8, 2010 (online).

Chapter 7

1 The man was Daniel Detweiler, whom we met in chapter 3. See T.J. Hannigan to V.S. McIntyre, August 30, 1935, 0011674742, AMEU-OMEA Records, Hydro One Archives.

2 M.F. Campbell, *A Mountain and a City: The Story of Hamilton* (Toronto: McClelland and Stewart, 1966), 117–18; C.G. Furry, *History of the Hamilton Waterworks System*, Corporation of the City of Hamilton, 1960, 3, Local History Room, Hamilton Public Library.

3 *Hamilton Daily Times*, April 24, 1920; William James and James G. March, *A Sufficient Supply of Pure and Wholesome Water: The Story of Hamilton's Old Pumphouse* (London: Phelps Publishing, 1978): 21–2.

4 Campbell, *Mountain and a City*, 117–18; Furry, *History of the Hamilton Waterworks System*, 3.

5 Campbell, *Mountain and a City*, 118. The legislation is 19 Vic, c 54 (1856).

6 Larry D. Lankton, *Written Historical and Descriptive Data* (New York: Historic American Engineering Record, 1976), http://cdn.loc.gov/master/pnp/habshaer/ny/ny1100/ny1181/data/ny1181data.pdf, 120. See the quotation in *Sixth Semi-Annual Report of the Water Commissioners of the City of Hamilton*, 6, Robert Baldwin Room, Toronto Public Library. The quotation is taken from the *Annual Report of the Cronon Aqueduct Department* (New York: McSpedon and Baker, 1857), 20. There was also a direct connection between New York and Hamilton: John B. Jervis, chief engineer of the New York system, provided a report to the Hamilton Water Commission in 1857. See John B. Jervis, *Report on a Supply of Water for the City of Hamilton* (Hamilton: Morning Banner, 1857).

7 Lankton, *Written Historical and Descriptive Data*, 14.

8 It is, of course, difficult to prove a negative. But there is no reference to a commission in the major legislation for the Montreal waterworks (7 Vic, c 44, in 1843, 16 Vic, c 127, in 1853). Nor is there any mention of a commission in the three histories of the system that I consulted: C.J. Des Baillets, "The Montreal Water Works," *American Water Works Association Journal* 29, no. 6 (1937): 774–90; F. Clifford Smith, *The Montreal Water Works* (Montreal: City of Montreal, 1913); Susan M. Ross, "Steam or Water Power? Thomas C. Keefer and the Engineers Discuss the Montreal Waterworks in 1852," *Industrial Archaeology* 29, no. 1 (2003): 49–64.

9 It can be found in the *Sixth Semi-Annual Report of the Water Commissioners for the City of Hamilton*, 9, Robert Baldwin Room, Toronto Public Library.

10 Ibid.

11 Ibid., 6–9. The quotation in the previous sentence is from 8.

12 The best survey is Elwood Jones and Douglas McCalla, "Toronto Waterworks, 1840–77," *Canadian Historical Review* 60, no. 3 (1979): 300–23. I have also benefited from H.V. Nelles and Christopher Armstrong, *Monopoly's Moment* (Toronto: University of Toronto Press, 1986); J.M.S. Careless, *Toronto to 1918: An Illustrated History* (Toronto: James Lorimer, 1984); and MacDougall, "Health Is Wealth."

13 *Toronto Leader*, April 27, 1857.

14 Ibid.

15 20 Vic, c 81 (1857).

16 *Toronto Leader*, April 27, 1854.
17 Nelles and Armstrong, *Monopoly's Moment*, 18.
18 35 Vic, c 79 (1871–2).
19 Careless, *Toronto to 1918*, 144.
20 For Ottawa's waterworks, see John H. Taylor, *Ottawa: An Illustrated History* (Toronto: James Lorimer, 1986), 104–6; Shirley E. Woods, *Ottawa: The Capital of Canada* (Toronto: Doubleday Canada, 1980), 152–3; and L. Brault, *Ottawa, Old and New* (Ottawa: Ottawa Historical Information Institute, 1946), 116. Sources on the St Catharines waterworks are more limited, but see J.N. Jackson and S.M. Wilson, *St Catharines: Canada's Canal City* (St Catharines, ON: St Catharines Standard, 1993), 117. The Ottawa bill was sent to the Private Bills Committee before the Toronto bill. Elwood and McCalla, "Toronto Waterworks," 315.
21 See 41 Vic, Bill 4, 1871 (Brampton Waterworks) in Original Bills, RG 4939, AO.
22 41 Vic, c 27 (1878). See also E.V. Buchanan, *London's Water Supply: A History* (London, ON: London Public Utilities Commission, Waterworks Department, 1968).
23 In the 1882 and 1883 sessions, Mowat had devoted considerable attention to general legislation in a number of spheres, including libraries (45 Vic, c 22), public health (45 Vic, c 29), and public parks (46 Vic, c 20). For Mowat's statement of his preference for general legislation, see *Globe*, February 6, 1885 (*Newspaper Hansard*) as well as the lieutenant-governor's remarks, March 10, 1882, *Journals of the Legislative Assembly of Ontario*, 165.
24 *Journals of the Legislative Assembly of Ontario*, 1882, 165.
25 The earlier committee is discussed in Jones and McCalla, "Toronto Waterworks," 309.
26 See 45 Vic, Bill 89, 1882 (Waterworks Act) in Original Bills, RG 49-39, AO.
27 46 Vic, c 21 (1883).
28 See, for instance, *Canadian Annual Review* during these years.
29 Even James Mahoney's narrower understanding of path dependence, according to which early contingencies (e.g., the number of commissioners) become entrenched, fits well here. See his "Path Dependence in Historical Sociology," *Theory and Society* 29, no. 4 (2000): 507–48.
30 Paul Pierson, "Increasing Returns, Path Dependence, and the Study of Politics," *American Political Science Review* 94, no. 2 (2000): 254. Political scientists' usage of this term has become very muddled. In the wider literature, "negative feedback" returns deviations to an equilibrium (think of the water in the back of your toilet) and "positive feedback" creates cascades away from an equilibrium (think of an avalanche caused by

the movement of a single pebble). Positive feedback typically follows an S-shaped curve as it reaches a new quasi-equilibrium (avalanches do not grow until they have engulfed a whole continent). We are avoiding "feedback" here because it is not helpful to think of the locally oriented public utilities field at this stage as an especially interactive system – properties required by feedback. In other words, it meant little to Peterborough if Windsor had a slightly different water commission structure.

31 Satisficing processes "denote problem solving and decision making that sets an aspiration level, searches until an alternative is found that is satisfactory by the aspiration level criterion, and selects that alternative." Herbert A. Simon, "Theories of Bounded Rationality," in *Decision and Organization*, ed. C.B. McGuire and Roy Radner (Amsterdam: North-Holland Publishing, 1972), 168.

32 Hamilton, Toronto, Ottawa, and Guelph abolished their waterworks commissions; London attempted to do the same. For Hamilton, see James and March, "Sufficient Supply," 66; for Toronto, see MacDougall, "Health Is Wealth," 329; for Ottawa, see Taylor, *Ottawa*, 104; for Guelph, see L.A. Johnson, *History of Guelph, 1827–1927*, Guelph Historical Society, 1977, 358n19; for London, see Buchanan, "London's Water Supply," 64. Attempts to abolish the works often came after they had been constructed; as in Hamilton, councils apparently felt that they had the competence to manage the waterworks themselves, but not to develop and construct them.

33 For the broader story, see Nelles, *Politics of Development*, chaps 6–7; Freeman, *Politics of Power*, chap. 1; Merrill Denison, *The People's Power* (Toronto: McClelland and Stewart, 1960), chaps 4–7; Plewman, *Adam Beck and the Ontario Hydro*, chaps 5–7.

34 Nelles, *Politics of Development*, 217–18; Freeman, *Politics of Power*, 11.

35 See the references in ibid., as well as Hodgetts, *From Arm's Length to Hands On*, 141.

36 The only change during this period was an amendment in 1906 to extend the term length of hydro commissioners to two years. 6 Edw VII, c 40. There is no evidence that this change had anything to do with the HEPC.

37 Denison, *People's Power*, 90; *Toronto Daily Star*, March 16, 1911; *Globe*, March 21, 1911.

38 1 Geo V, c 119. See also Emerson Bristol Biggar, *Hydro-Electric Development in Ontario* (Toronto: Ryerson, 1920), 98.

39 *Globe*, 22, March 23, April 7, 1911; *Daily Star*, 17, March 21, April 4, 1911.

40 *Globe*, March 23, 1911.

41 In 1935, Toronto's three-person model became mandatory for cities with a population of over 60,000, and eventually Toronto, Hamilton, and

Ottawa adopted it. The mandatory legislation is 25 Geo V, c 54. It was no longer mandatory as of 1961–2; see c 106, s 11. Many municipalities were able to avoid this model when they hit 60,000 by requesting an exception in a private bill. See Royal Commission on Metropolitan Toronto, *Report of the Royal Commission on Metropolitan Toronto: Detailed Findings and Recommendations* (Toronto: Government of Ontario, 1977), 271.

42 "Report on the Central Ontario System," supplementary report of the Gregory Hydro-Electric Inquiry Commission, March 1, 1923, 2, RG 18-83, AO.

43 Ibid., 4.

44 For a bit more detail, see Jack Lucas, "How Ontario Hydro Went Local: The Creation of Rural Power Districts and the Central Ontario System," *Scientia Canadensis* 37, nos 1–2 (2015): 59–76.

45 "Report on the Central Ontario System," 6.

46 Ibid., 38–42.

47 Ibid., 19.

48 E.g., Keith Robson Fleming, *Power at Cost: Ontario Hydro and Rural Electrification, 1911–1958* (Montreal and Kingston: McGill-Queen's University Press, 1992), 49–50.

49 "Public Affairs in the Province of Ontario," *Canadian Annual Review*, 1920, 568; Fleming, *Power at Cost*, 88.

50 Fleming, "Ontario Hydro and Rural Electrification in Old Ontario," 4–7, 51–2.

51 Ibid., 92.

52 Ibid., 93.

53 See especially Nelles, *Politics of Development*.

54 Fleming, *Power at Cost*.

55 Nelles, *Politics of Development*, 246–7.

56 See "Provincial Affairs in Ontario," *Canadian Annual Review*, 1916, 503–4, for a contemporary account. The best profiles of Beck are by H.V. Nelles, in *Politics of Development*, 246–7; in the *Dictionary of Canadian Biography*; and in Nelles, "Public Ownership of Electrical Utilities in Manitoba and Ontario, 1906–30," *Canadian Historical Review* 57, no. 4 (1976): 483.

57 E.C. Drury, *Farmer Premier* (Toronto: McClelland and Stewart, 1966). The quotations are from 117–18, 137. See also Unknown to W.F. Maclean, February 27, 1922, in Sir Adam Beck Office Records, 0011674754, Hydro One Archives.

58 For examples, see Whitney to A.J. Matheson, October 28, 1911, in James Whitney Correspondence, F5, AO; Hearst to Beck, May 8, 1919, quoted in Nelles, *Politics of Development*, 412; Drury, *Farmer Premier*, 117, 122.

59 For a detailed survey of the HEPC's ambiguous position, see Freeman, *Politics of Power*.
60 K.C. Dewar, "State Ownership in Canada" (PhD diss., University of Toronto, 1975), 293. See also *Canadian Annual Review*, 1915, 503–7; Nelles, *Politics of Development*, 259, 271, 414; Plewman, *Adam Beck and the Ontario Hydro*, 99–100; Fleming, "Ontario Hydro and Rural Electrification," 7–8; H.V. Nelles, "Public Ownership of Electrical Utilities in Ontario and Manitoba, 1906–30," *Canadian Historical Review* 54, no. 4 (1976): 463; W.D. Gregory, *Hydro-Electric Inquiry Commission: Report on History and General Relations* (Toronto: Government of Ontario, 1923), 77.
61 For examples, see (in addition to the sources above) the resolutions of the OMEA in the Premier William H. Hearst Correspondence, 3-3-0-33, RG 3-3, AO; and in the Premier E.C. Drury Correspondence, RG 3-4, AO; Drury, *Farmer Premier*, 116. See also T.J. Hannigan to Adam Beck, June 6, 1925; and Adam Beck to T.J. Hannigan, June 23, 1925, AMEU-OMEA Records, 0011674741; Ernest Savage to Adam Beck, April 12, 1925, Sir Adam Beck Office Records, 0011674757, Hydro One Archives.
62 Nelles, "Public Ownership of Electrical Utilities," 464.
63 Gregory, *Hydro Electric Inquiry Commission*, 77. See also Drury, *Farmer Premier*, 118.
64 The concept of social skill comes from Neil Fligstein, "Social Skill and Institutional Theory," *American Behavioral Scientist* 40, no. 4 (1997): 397–405. I will return to this helpful concept in the next chapter.
65 None of this is to deny the extraordinary controversy that surrounded Beck at nearly all times, as well as the profound disappointment that individual municipalities, including Toronto, felt when Beck invaded municipal jurisdiction. But Beck's ability to marshal widespread support for the hydro enterprise at the municipal level across the province, together with his willingness to draw on all the power of the provincial government when needed, meant that local disgruntlement rarely grew into larger opposition during the Beck years.
66 For rural electrification, see Fleming, *Power at Cost*; and for the story of nuclear power development in Canada, see Robert Bothwell, *Nucleus* (Toronto: University of Toronto Press, 1988).
67 One very minor change in 1947 allowed municipalities to shift from a three-person to a five-person board or vice-versa. See 11 Geo VI, c 90.
68 Hollis E. Beckett, *Third Report of the Select Committee on the Municipal Act and Related Acts* (Toronto: Government of Ontario, 1964), 122.
69 Murray V. Jones, *Ottawa, Eastview and Carleton County Local Government Review* (Ottawa: Ottawa, Eastview and Carleton County Local

Government Review Commission, 1965), 47; Henry B. Mayo, *Report of the Commission* (Toronto: Niagara Region Local Government Review Commission, 1966), 37; Fyfe and Farrow, "Waterloo Area Local Government Review," 77.

70 T.J. Plunkett, *Peel-Halton Local Government Review* (Toronto: Peel-Halton Local Government Review Commission, 1966), 68–70.

71 Donald R. Steele, *Report and Recommendations* (Hamilton: Hamilton-Burlington-Wentworth Local Government Review Commission, 1969), 125–6, 185–6.

72 For an overview of the COGP, see Szablowski, "Policy-Making and Cabinet"; and Loreto, "Cabinet."

73 See Freeman, *Politics of Power.*

74 OMEA to Charles MacNaughton, April 1968, 1–2, RG 19-15, AO.

75 John B. Cronyn, *Task Force Hydro: Report Number One* (Toronto: Government of Ontario, 1972), 58–9.

76 For the background on the Hogg report I have relied on Ontario, *Debates,* July 12, 1977, 745–8, as well as the Hogg report itself.

77 W.M. Hogg, *The Restructuring of Public Utilities* (Toronto: Ontario Government Committee on Restructuring of Public Utilities, 1974), esp. 36–7. See also Darcy McKeough, speech to OMEA-AMEU District Meeting, North Bay, May 4, 1973, 9, Minister of Energy Speech Files, RG 45-1, AO.

78 Hogg, *Restructuring of Public Utilities,* 25–6. This created great confusion, as in many cases the boundaries of the hydro commissions did not align with the boundaries of the new municipalities. In several cases, residents in the same municipalities were served by different utilities. See also Palmer, *Report of the Waterloo Region Review Commission,* 178.

79 25–6 Eliz II, c 29.

80 See Ontario, *Debates,* July 8, 1977, 588. See also *OMEA & AMEU Annual Report,* 1974, 111–12, OMEA Minutes and Annual Proceedings, 0011671237, Hydro One Archives.

81 The relevant legislation is 25–6 Eliz II, c 28.

82 See notes above for legislation in Peel and Waterloo. The remaining legislation is: 25–6 Eliz II, c 60 (Oxford County); 26–7 Eliz II, c 31 (York Region); 27–8 Eliz II, c 70 (Halton Region); 27–8 Eliz II, c 33 (Niagara Region); 28–9 Eliz II, c 59 (Hamilton-Wentworth); 28–9 Eliz II, c 40 (Ottawa-Carleton); 28–9 Eliz II, c 59 (Sudbury).

83 See the legislation in the note above, along with Ontario, *Debates,* July 8, 1977, 588; July 12, 1977, 745–8 and 763–8.

84 See, e.g., Donald L. Paterson, *Final Report and Recommendations* (Gravenhurst, ON: Muskoka District Local Government Review, 1969),

259–60; Ministry of Treasury, Economics and Intergovernmental Affairs, *Proposal for Local Government Reform in an Area East of Metro* (Toronto: Ministry of Treasury, Economics, and Intergovernmental Affairs, 1972), 56.

85 Hogg, *Restructuring of Public Utilities*, 22–7; Ontario, *Debates*, July 8, 1977, 588.

86 See Dolbey, *Local Special Purpose Bodies*, 62. See also Jacek, "Regional Government and Development," 146.

87 Jacek, "Regional Government and Development," 158–9; Peter Oliver, "Ontario," *Canadian Annual Review*, 1973, 106; Graham White, "Social Change and Political Stability," 114.

88 The OMEA reorganized itself late in 1965. See Freeman, *Politics of Power*, 121.

89 OMEA submission to the Ontario Committee on Taxation, April 1968, Correspondence of the Deputy Minister of Municipal Affairs, RG 19-15, AO.

90 See OMEA submission to Darcy McKeough with respect to municipal electric commissions within a regional government, March 12, 1970, Subject Files of the Deputy Minister of Municipal Affairs, RG 1911, AO.

91 The most remarkable example is the OMEA's submission to the Waterloo Local Government Review, OMEA Minutes and Annual Proceedings, 0011671237, Hydro One Archives. It took the OMEA some time to develop its strategy vis-à-vis the local commissions. See especially *OMEA & AMEU Annual Report*, 1969, 85–7, 94, 0011671237, OMEA Minutes and Annual Proceedings, Hydro One Archives.

92 OMEA submission to the Ontario Committee on Taxation, April 1968, 21–2, RG 19-15, AO.

93 OMEA to Darcy McKeough, March 12, 1970, 5, 8–9; 8-5 Ontario Municipal Electric Association, RG 19-11, Subject Files of the Deputy Minister of Municipal Affairs, AO. But see also Freeman, *Politics of Power*, 125.

94 The annual reports of the OMEA during this period provide extremely valuable insights into the fears and the strategies of the OMEA and its leaders. Perhaps the best single example is the presidential address of Dr. R.H. Hay in the 1966 *Annual Report*, 8–10, OMEA Minutes and Annual Proceedings, 0011671237, Hydro One Archives.

95 See notes above for examples of this argument.

96 Palmer, *Report of the Waterloo Region Review Commission*, 178.

97 Ibid.

98 See, for example, OMEA to Darcy McKeough, March 12, 1970, 8; 8-5 Ontario Municipal Electric Association, RG 19-11, Subject Files of the Deputy Minister of Municipal Affairs, AO; and *Globe and Mail*, February 25, 1970, 3.

99 See Dolbey, *Local Special Purpose Bodies*, 66–9.

100 Ibid., 70.
101 Palmer, *Report of the Waterloo Region Review Commission*, 179–80. See also Cronyn, *Task Force Hydro: Report Number One*, 18–19.
102 See *Acton Free Press*, March 14, 1973, 3; *Kingsville Reporter*, March 15, 1973, 1; Bill Davis Speech to OMEA, March 3, 1976, OMEA Minutes and Annual Proceedings, 0011671237, Hydro One Archives. For a useful account of the OMEA's reaction to the TFH report, see Freeman, *Politics of Power*, 143–6.
103 E.g., HEPC submission to Charles MacNaughton, treasurer of Ontario, on the Report of the Ontario Committee on Taxation, April 5, 1968, 30, Correspondence of the Deputy Minister of Municipal Affairs, RG 19-15, AO. See also Dolbey, *Local Special Purpose Bodies*, 16–19.
104 Freeman, *Politics of Power*, 143–7; *Acton Free Press*, January 17, 1973, 2; *Globe and Mail*, January 17, 1973, 6 (which notes that some local utilities wished to distance themselves, at least somewhat, from OMEA's furious response). See, for example, *Acton Free Press*, January 17, 1973, 2.
105 Freeman, *Politics of Power*, 146–9. See also *Globe and Mail*, November 14, 1972, 1.
106 For a remarkable admission of such power, see Freeman, *Politics of Power*, 125. See also the remarks of Dr Hay in *OMEA & AMEU Annual Report*, 1974, 103–4, OMEA Minutes and Annual Proceedings, 0011671237, Hydro One Archives.
107 "Hydrophobia," *Economist*, August 21, 1997, online.
108 Hydro 21, *Hydro 21: Options for Ontario Hydro* (Toronto: Ontario Hydro, 1993).
109 Although the term *deregulation* is common in the literature on this subject, to describe the changes between 1995 and 2003 as deregulation is deeply misleading, since the level of regulation probably increased rather than decreased during this period. *Corporatization* and *competition* are probably more useful terms.
110 The population figures (here and elsewhere) are taken from the 1996 census.
111 William Farlinger was an important Conservative insider and had served as the co-chair of the Conservatives' 1995 transition team. See Ibbitson, *Promised Land*, 23–5.
112 W.A. Farlinger, G.J. Homer, and B.S. Caine, *Ontario Hydro and the Electric Power Industry: Vision for a Competitive Industry* (Toronto: Government of Ontario, 1995, 28.
113 Advisory Committee on Competition in Ontario's Electricity System, *A Framework for Competition* (Toronto: Queen's Printer for Ontario, 1996), 73–4.

114 Ibid., 77.
115 Ontario Ministry of Energy, *Direction for Change: Charting a Course for Competitive Electricity and Jobs in Ontario* (Toronto: Government of Ontario, 2009), 1 and 4.
116 Ibid., 20.
117 Ontario, *Debates*, June 9, 1998, online.
118 For an overview of these developments, see *Globe and Mail*, March 14, 2015, B1. While the primary intention for these changes had little to do with consolidation, local utilities consolidation was occasionally noted as a side benefit of the changes. For further discussion of the consolidation issue, see Murray Elston, Floyd Laughren, and David McFadden, *Renewing Ontario's Electricity Distribution Sector: Putting the Consumer First* (Toronto: Ontario Distribution Sector Review Panel, 2012); Francis J. Cronin and Stephen Motluk, "Ten Years after Restructuring: Degraded Distribution Reliability and Regulatory Failure in Ontario," *Utilities Policy* 19, no. 4 (2011): 241; Ontario Energy Board, *Review of Further Efficiencies in the Electricity Distribution Sector* (Toronto: Ontario Energy Board, 2004), 4; Joseph Kushner and Tomson Ogwang, "Local Electrical Utilities: Is Bigger Better?," *Canadian Public Policy* 40, no. 3 (2014): 283–91.
119 See *Globe and Mail*, April 22, 1998, A7; Geoff McCaffrey, "Electricity Restructuring: Not Business as Usual," *Municipal World*, August 1998, 20, 23.
120 See the MEA's monthly publication of that era, *Circuit Breaker*, especially September–December 1998.
121 *Circuit Breaker*, December 1998, online.
122 My figures here are from a dataset graciously provided to me by Neil Freeman, to which I have added data on municipal population and municipal restructuring (on which I draw below).
123 See previous note. I have added population figures to Neil Freeman's dataset using data from the 1996 census.
124 Jamie Swift and Keith Stewart, *Hydro: The Decline and Fall of Ontario's Electric Empire* (Toronto: Between the Lines, 2004), 133.
125 My thanks to Neil Freeman for highlighting the importance of this factor.
126 In Drayton and in the tiny village of Moorefield, which had been annexed into Maryborough Township at an earlier date. The Moorefield system was therefore the responsibility of Maryborough Township council.
127 Neil Freeman, personal interview, February 8, 2013.
128 Don Drummond, *Commission on the Reform of Ontario's Public Services* (Toronto: Government of Ontario, 2012), 47.
129 Elston, Laughren, and McFadden, *Renewing Ontario's Electricity Distribution Sector*.

130 The reaction among these municipalities was remarkably widespread. See *Georgetown Independent*, December 5, 2012; *Toronto Star*, December 14, 2012, B1; *Bay Today* (North Bay), December 14, 2012; *Kingston Whig Standard*, December 15, 2012, 3; *North Bay Nugget*, December 18, 2012, A1; *Woodstock Sentinel-Review*, December 19, 2012, 4; *Pembroke Daily Observer*, December 19, 2012, A1; *Sarnia Observer*, December 19, 2012, A3; *Fort Frances Times Online*, December 19, 2012; *Peterborough Examiner*, December 30, 2012, A3. There was *some* support for the proposals among the larger utilities, who might hope to become the core of the new consolidated regions. See CBC News (online), December 14, 2012; *London Free Press*, December 17, 2012, A3. The recommendations of the EDA, which focused on economies of scope rather than economies of scale (i.e., local utilities combining electricity, water, sewage, etc.), was utterly rejected in the panel's final recommendations.

131 Elston, Laughren, and McFadden, *Renewing Ontario's Electricity Distribution Sector*, 9–10, 16. I have compressed two separate passages in a single quotation, but this is in no way a distortion of the panel's own argument, which emphasizes the weight of history, and the need to get out from under it, throughout.

132 *Georgetown Independent*, March 20, 2013.

133 Cronin and Motluk, "Ten Years after Restructuring," 241; Ontario Energy Board, *Review of Further Efficiencies*, 4.

Chapter 8

1 Andrew Abbott, "Of Time and Space: The Contemporary Relevance of the Chicago School," *Social forces* 75, no. 4 (1997): 1149–82.

2 Please see the citations in chapter 2 for a further discussion of these two approaches.

3 Weaver, "Tomorrow's Metropolis Revisited."

4 See, for instance, the chapters in *Foundations of Governance*, ed. Robert Young and Andrew Sancton (Toronto: University of Toronto Press, 2009).

5 Warren Magnusson has noticed the importance of capacity for the development of ABCs in "Toronto," in *City Politics in Canada*, ed. Warren Magnusson and Andrew Sancton (Toronto: University of Toronto Press, 1983), 101.

6 See Karen Bakker, *Good Governance in Restructuring Water Supply* (Ottawa: Federation of Canadian Municipalities, 2003).

7 Hooghe and Marks, "Unraveling the Central State, but How?"

8 We can, of course, find advocates of special purpose bodies *as such* in academic debates about polycentric or multilevel governance, such as Frey

and Eichenberger, *The New Democratic Federalism for Europe*. I have found no evidence that these recent arguments have made an impact in the empirical cases that I have studied.

9 As usual, Stefan Dupré got here first. See his comments in "Notes for an Address on the Political Dimensions of Regional Government," quoted in Susan Dolbey, *Local Special Purpose Bodies*, 18.

10 The leading authority on these issues in Canada is Harry Kitchen. See, for example, his *Municipal Revenue and Expenditure Issues in Canada* (Toronto: Canadian Tax Foundation, 2003). An interesting recent treatment of this subject in the Ontario context is Adam Found, "Economies of Scale in Fire and Police Services in Ontario," *IMFG Papers on Municipal Finance and Governance* 12, no. 1 (2012): 1–29.

11 One implication of this argument is that Liesbet Hooghe and Gary Marks's distinction among efficiency, community, and distribution as motivators for authority shifts is more complex in practice than in theory. Actual political arguments tend to relate these to one another in ways that make them difficult to untangle. I hope to explore this issue in more detail in forthcoming research. See Liesbet Hooghe and Gary Marks, "Does Efficiency Shape the Territorial Structure of Government?" *Annual Review of Political Science* 12 (2009): 225–41.

12 The classic example of this institutionalist punctuated-equilibrium approach is Krasner, "Approaches to the State."

13 Kathleen Thelen, "How Institutions Evolve: Insights from Comparative Historical Analysis," in *Comparative Historical Analysis in the Social Sciences*, ed. James Mahoney and Dietrich Rueschemeyer (Cambridge: Cambridge University Press, 2003), 208–40; see also Kathleen Thelen, *How Institutions Evolve* (Cambridge: Cambridge University Press, 2004), 28; and Wolfgang Streeck and Kathleen Thelen, "Introduction: Institutional Change in Advanced Economies," in *Beyond Continuity*, ed. Wolfgang Streeck and Kathleen Ann Thelen, 1–39 (Oxford: Oxford University Press, 2005). For more on layering, see Eric Schickler, *Disjointed Pluralism: Institutional Innovation and the Development of the U.S. Congress* (Princeton: Princeton University Press, 2001).

14 Kathleen Thelen, "How Institutions Evolve."

15 There are no references to Baumgartner and Jones in Thelen, *How Institutions Evolve*, or in Thelen's contributions to *Comparative Historical Analysis in the Social Sciences, Beyond Continuity*, or *Explaining Institutional Change*.

16 Baumgartner and Jones, *Agendas and Instability*. There are no references to the work of Kathleen Thelen in this book.

17 See Jacob Hacker and Paul Pierson, "The Case for Policy-Focused Political Analysis," unpublished, http://ssrn.com/abstract=1471461.

18 This understanding of policy arguments is indebted to the work of Elizabeth Clemens in *The People's Lobby* (Chicago: University of Chicago Press, 1997).

19 See the citations in note 12, this chapter.

20 Baumgartner and Jones, *Agendas and Instability*; Sabatier and Weible, "Advocacy Coalition Framework."

21 See chapter 5, sections 6 and 8, above.

22 This is precisely why it is that Baumgartner and Jones, who are as interested in the periods of incremental change as they are in the moments of punctuation, are the best guides for a punctuated equilibrium approach, as opposed to theorists like Krasner for whom periods between punctuation are periods of institutional stasis.

23 Those who are familiar with William Sewell's theory of structure will recognize the ultimate source of inspiration for this argument. For a detailed elaboration of the relationship between "resources" and "schemas," see Sewell, *Logics of History*, chaps 4 and 10.

24 Baumgartner and Jones, *Agendas and Instability*. For related but more general theoretical discussion of this theme, see Michèle Lamont and Virig Molnar, "The Study of Boundaries in the Social Sciences," *Annual Review of Sociology* 28, no. 1 (2002): 167–95; and Charles Tilly, "Social Boundary Mechanisms," *Philosophy of the Social Sciences* 34, no. 2 (2004): 211–36.

25 Grace Skogstad, "Who Governs? Who Should Govern? Political Authority and Legitimacy in Canada in the Twenty-First Century," *Canadian Journal of Political Science* 36, no. 5 (2003): 955–73.

26 Karren Orren and Stephen Skowronek, *The Search for American Political Development* (Cambridge: Cambridge University Press, 2004), 24–6, 123.

27 See especially Clarence N. Stone and Robert K. Whelan, "Through a Glass Darkly: The Once and Future Study of Urban Politics," in *The City in American Political Development*, ed. Richardson Dilworth, 98–118 (New York: Routledge, 2009).

28 It is worth re-emphasizing indebtedness to the work of Doug McAdam and Neil Fligstein in generating this distinction. See McAdam and Fligstein, *Theory of Fields*.

29 Here I must note once again my debt to John Kingdon's "multiple streams" approach, in *Agendas, Alternatives, and Public Policies*, which has influenced my own understanding of what it means to explain timing.

30 A modified version of this paragraph also concludes my "Hidden in Plain View," 6.

Bibliography

Archival Materials

Archives of Ontario

ARCHIVAL MATERIALS
F5   James Whitney Fonds
F6   William Hearst Fonds
F7   Ernest Drury Fonds
F8   Howard Ferguson Fonds
F1195   Ontario Library Association Papers
RG 3-3   Premier William Hearst Correspondence
RG 3-4   Premier E.C. Drury Correspondence
RG 3-6   Premier Howard Ferguson Correspondence
RG 3-85   Oliver Mowat Papers
RG 10-1   Correspondence of the Minister of Health
RG 10-106   Health Units Administration and Correspondence
RG 18-83   Ontario Hydro-Electric Inquiry Commission Records
RG 19-11   Subject Files of the Deputy Minister of Municipal Affairs
RG 19-15   Correspondence of the Deputy Minister of Municipal Affairs
RG 19-56   Municipal Research Correspondence Files
RG 19-142   Municipal Financial Returns
RG 45-1   Minister of Energy's Speech Files
RG 49-92   Select Committee on Public Health Records
RG 49-108   Agricultural Enquiry Committee Records

J.J. TALMAN LIBRARY MATERIALS
Association of Executive Health Officers of Ontario Annual Reports
Election Pamphlets

Archives in the Kitchener-Waterloo Area

GRAND RIVER HOSPITAL ARCHIVES
Berlin-Waterloo Hospital Annual Reports
Kitchener-Waterloo Hospital Annual Reports

KITCHENER CORPORATE ARCHIVES
Berlin/Kitchener Council Minute Books
Fire and Water Committee Minute Books
Kitchener Board of Health Fonds
Kitchener Board of Park Management Fonds
Kitchener Water Commission Fonds
Kitchener Water Committee Minute Books
Police Committee Proceedings
Sewer Commission Minute Books
Special Committee Minute Books

KITCHENER PUBLIC LIBRARY LOCAL HISTORY ARCHIVES
Berlin Public Library Board Minute Books
Daniel B. Detweiler Papers
Kitchener Chamber of Commerce Fonds
Kitchener Oral History Collection
Vertical Files & Scrapbooks

UNIVERSITY OF WATERLOO RARE BOOK ROOM
GA 82   Breithaupt Hewetson Clark Fonds
GA 173   A.R. Kaufman Fonds
GA 174   Honsberger Fonds
GA 183   Grand River Conservation Authority Fonds
GA 184   Grand River Conservation Commission Fonds

WATERLOO REGION DISTRICT BOARD OF EDUCATION ARCHIVES
Berlin Public School Board Minute Books
Kitchener Public School Board Minute Books

Toronto-Area Archives

THOMAS FISHER RARE BOOK LIBRARY
Journals of the Town Planning Institute of Canada

ONTARIO MEDICAL ASSOCIATION ARCHIVES
OMA Minute Books

F02-SE06   Committee Reports (Legislative Committee and Public Health
            Committee)

CITY OF TORONTO ARCHIVES
City of Toronto Council Proceedings
F92   Theses and Papers

TORONTO PUBLIC LIBRARY ROBERT BALDWIN ROOM
John Hallam Papers
Reports of the Water Commissioners of the City of Hamilton

HYDRO-ELECTRIC POWER COMMISSION/ONTARIO HYDRO/HYDRO ONE ARCHIVES
AMEU-OMEA Records
Legislative Assembly Questions and Answers
OMEA Annual Reports
OMEA General Correspondence and Official Records
OMEA Minutes and Annual Proceedings
Sir Adam Beck Office Records

Other Archives

HAMILTON PUBLIC LIBRARY LOCAL HISTORY ROOM, HAMILTON, ONTARIO
"History of the Hamilton Waterworks System," C.G. Furry
Water in Hamilton: Scrapbook
Waterworks: Scrapbook

LIBRARY AND ARCHIVES CANADA, OTTAWA, ONTARIO
MG 30   Daniel Detweiler Fonds

Published Materials

Abbott, Andrew. 1992. "An Old Institutionalist Reads the New Institutionalism."
    Contemporary Sociology 21 (6): 754–6. http://dx.doi.org/10.2307/2075613.
–   1997. "Of Time and Space: The Contemporary Relevance of the Chicago
    School." *Social Forces* 75 (4): 1149–82. http://dx.doi.org/10.1093/
    sf/75.4.1149.
–   2001. *Time Matters*. Chicago: University of Chicago Press.
–   2005. "Linked Ecologies: States and Universities as Environments for
    Professions." *Sociological Theory* 23 (3): 245–73.
–   2007. "Mechanisms and Relations." *Sociologica* 2 (1): 1–22.
Aitchison, James H. 1953. "The Development of Local Government in Canada,
    1783–1850." PhD diss., University of Toronto.

Anderson, Stephen E., and Sonia Ben Jafaar. 2007. "Policy Narrative for Ontario." In *The Evolution of Professionalism: Educational Policy in the Provinces and Territories of Canada*, ed. Adrienne S. Chan, Donald Fisher, and Kjell Rubenson, 79–97. Vancouver: UBC Centre for Higher Education and Training.

Advisory Committee on Competition in Ontario's Electricity System. 1996. *A Framework for Competition*. Toronto: Queen's Printer for Ontario.

Atkinson, Joseph Logan. 2000. "The Upper Canadian Legal Response to the Cholera Epidemics of 1832 and 1834." PhD diss., University of Ottawa.

Atkinson, Michael M., and William D. Coleman. 1989. "Strong States and Weak States: Sectoral Policy Networks in Advanced Capitalist Economies." *British Journal of Political Science* 19 (1): 47–67. http://dx.doi.org/10.1017/S0007123400005317.

Badgley, Janice. 1991. "Public Decision Making on Water Supply Planning and Management: A Case Study of the Waterloo Region." MA thesis, University of Waterloo.

Bak, Per, and Kan Chen. 1991. "Self-Organized Criticality." *Scientific American* 264 (1): 46–53. http://dx.doi.org/10.1038/scientificamerican0191-46.

Bakker, Karen. 2003. *Good Governance in Restructuring Water Supply*. Ottawa: Federation of Canadian Municipalities.

Battilana, Julie. 2006. "Agency and Institutions: The Enabling Role of Individuals' Social Position." *Organization* 13 (5): 653–76. http://dx.doi.org/10.1177/1350508406067008.

Baumgartner, Frank R. 2012. "Ideas and Policy Change." *Governance: An International Journal of Policy, Administration and Institutions* 26 (2): 239–58. http://dx.doi.org/10.1111/gove.12007.

Baumgartner, Frank R., and Bryan D. Jones. 1991. "Agenda Dynamics and Policy Subsystems." *Journal of Politics* 53 (4): 1044–74. http://dx.doi.org/10.2307/2131866.

– 1993. *Agendas and Instability in American Politics*. 2nd ed. Chicago: University of Chicago Press.

Baumgartner, Frank R., Bryan D. Jones, and Michael C. MacLeod. 2000. "The Evolution of Legislative Jurisdictions." *Journal of Politics* 62 (2): 321–49. http://dx.doi.org/10.1111/0022-3816.00015.

Beckett, Hollis E. 1964. *Third Report of the Select Committee on the Municipal Act and Related Acts*. Toronto: Government of Ontario, 1964.

– 1965. *Fourth and Final Report of the Select Committee on the Municipal Act and Related Acts*. Toronto: Government of Ontario.

Bedard, G.J., and S.B. Lawton. 2000. "The Struggle for Power and Control: Shifting Policymaking Models and the Harris Agenda for Education in Ontario." *Canadian Public Administration* 43 (3): 241–69.

Beecroft, Eric. 1962. *Agenda for Regional Government*. Ottawa: Canadian Federation of Mayors and Municipalities.

Benford, R.D., and D.A. Snow. 2000. "Framing Processes and Social Movements: An Overview and Assessment." *Annual Review of Sociology* 26 (1): 611–39.

Berlin: Celebration of Cityhood. 1912. *Berlin: Celebration of Cityhood*. Berlin: Sand Hill Books.

Berman, Sheri. 2013. "Ideational Theorizing in the Social Sciences Since 'Policy Paradigms, Social Learning, and the State.'" *Governance: An International Journal of Policy, Administration and Institutions* 26 (2): 217–37. http://dx.doi.org/10.1111/gove.12008.

Bevir, Mark. 2011. *Sage Handbook of Governance*. New York: Sage.

Bevir, Mark, and Rod Rhodes. 2006. *Governance Stories*. London: Routledge.

Béland, Daniel. 2007. "Neo-Liberalism and Social Policy: The Politics of Ownership." *Policy Studies* 28 (2): 91–107. http://dx.doi.org/10.1080/01442870701309023.

Biggar, Emerson Bristol. 1920. *Hydro-Electric Development in Ontario*. Toronto: Ryerson.

Bloomfield, Elizabeth. 1980. "Economy, Necessity, Political Reality: Town Planning Efforts in Kitchener-Waterloo, 1912–1925." *Urban History Review/Revue d'histoire urbaine* 9 (1): 3–48. http://dx.doi.org/10.7202/1019348ar.

– 1981. "City Building Processes in Berlin/Kitchener and Waterloo, 1870–1930." PhD diss., University of Guelph.

– 1982. "Reshaping the Urban Landscape? Town Planning Efforts in Kitchener-Waterloo, 1912–1925." In *Shaping the Urban Landscape*, ed. Gilbert A. Stelter and Alan F.J. Artibise, 256–303. Ottawa: Carleton University Press.

– 1986. "Community Leadership and Decision-Making: Entrepreneurial Elites in Two Ontario Towns, 1870–1930." In *Power and Place*, ed. Gilber A. Stelter and Alan F.J. Artibise, 82–104. Vancouver: UBC Press.

– 1995. *Waterloo Township through Two Centuries*. Kitchener, ON: Waterloo Historical Society.

Bloomfield, Elizabeth, and Gerald Bloomfield. 1998. *A History of Municipal Water Services in the Region of Waterloo*. Waterloo, ON: Regional Municipality of Waterloo Engineering Department.

Bothwell, Robert. 1986. *A Short History of Ontario*. Edmonton: Hurtig Publishers.

– 1988. *Nucleus*. Toronto: University of Toronto Press.

Blumer, Herbert. 1971. "Social Problems as Collective Behavior." *Social Problems* 18 (3): 298–306. http://dx.doi.org/10.2307/799797.

Bourdieu, Pierre, and Loic Wacquant. 1992. *An Invitation to Reflexive Sociology*. Chicago: University of Chicago Press.

Brand, Jeanne L. 1965. *Doctors and the State: The British Medical Profession and Government Action in Public Health, 1870–1912*. Baltimore, MD: Johns Hopkins University Press.

Breithaupt, William Henry. 1921. "Some Features of Town Planning, with Application to the City of Kitchener." *Journal of the Town Planning Institute of Canada* 1, no. 6 (1921): 5–8.

Brault, L. 1946. *Ottawa, Old and New*. Ottawa: Ottawa Historical Information Institute.

Bruce, Lorne, and Karen Bruce. 2012. *Public Library Boards in Postwar Ontario*. 2nd ed. Guelph, ON: printed by authors.

Buchanan, E.V. 1968. *London's Water Supply: History*. London: London Public Utilities Commission.

Byrne, Joseph P., ed. 2008. *Encyclopedia of Pestilence, Pandemics, and Plagues*. London: Greenwood Publishing Group.

Cairney, Paul. 2013. "Standing on the Shoulders of Giants: How Do We Combine the Insights of Multiple Theories in Public Policy Studies?" *Policy Studies Journal: The Journal of the Policy Studies Organization* 41 (1): 1–21. http://dx.doi.org/10.1111/psj.12000.

Cameron, Charles A. 1874. *A Manual of Hygiene*. Dublin: Hodges, Foster.

Cameron, David M. 1969. "The Politics of Education in Ontario, with Special Reference to the Financial Structure." PhD diss., University of Toronto.

Campbell, Archie. 2004. *SARS Commission First Interim Report*. Toronto: Government of Ontario.

– 2005. *SARS Commission Second Interim Report*. Toronto: Government of Ontario.

– 2006. *Spring of Fear: The SARS Commission Final Report*. Toronto: Government of Ontario.

Campbell, John L. 2002. "Ideas, Politics, and Public Policy." *Annual Review of Sociology* 28 (1): 21–38.

Campbell, M.F. 1966. *A Mountain and a City: The Story of Hamilton*. Toronto: McClelland and Stewart.

Canniff, William. 1872. *History of the Province of Ontario*. Toronto: A.H. Hovey.

Careless, J.M.S. 1984. *Toronto to 1918: An Illustrated History*. Toronto: James Lorimer.

Clemens, Elisabeth S. 1993. "Organizational Repertoires and Institutional Change: Women's Groups and the Transformation of U.S. Politics, 1890–1920." *American Journal of Sociology* 98 (4): 755–98. http://dx.doi.org/10.1086/230089.

– 1997. *The People's Lobby*. Chicago: University of Chicago Press.

Clemens, Elisabeth S., and J.M. Cook. 1999. "Politics and Institutionalism: Explaining Durability and Change." *Annual Review of Sociology* 25 (1): 441–66. http://dx.doi.org/10.1146/annurev.soc.25.1.441.

Craig, Barbara Lazenby. 1983. "State Medicine in Transition: Battling Smallpox in Ontario, 1882–1885." *Ontario History* 75 (4): 319–47.

Cronin, Francis J., and Stephen Motluk. 2011. "Ten Years after Restructuring: Degraded Distribution Reliability and Regulatory Failure in Ontario." *Utilities Policy* 19 (4): 235–43. http://dx.doi.org/10.1016/j.jup.2011.07.002.

Cronyn, John B. 1972a. *Task Force Hydro: Report Number One*. Toronto: Government of Ontario.

– 1972b. *Task Force Hydro: Report Number Two*. Toronto: Government of Ontario.

Curtis, Bruce. 1988. *Building the Educational State: Canada West, 1836–1871*. Barcombe, Lewes, East Sussex: Falmer.

– 1993. "The Canada 'Blue Books' and the Administrative Capacity of the Canadian State, 1822–67." *Canadian Historical Review* 74 (4): 535–65.

Daniel, Caitlin, Eleni Arzoglou, and Michèle Lamont. 2011. "European Workers: Meaning-Making Beings." In *Comparing European Workers Part B: Policies and Institutions*, ed. David Brady, 287–312. New York: Emerald Group Publishing. http://dx.doi.org/10.1108/S0277-2833(2011)000022B011.

Davis, William G. 1971. *Design for Development Phase Three: Statement by the Honourable William G. Davis*. Toronto: Legislature of Ontario.

Denison, Merrill. 1960. *The People's Power*. Toronto: McClelland and Stewart.

Des Baillets, C.J. 1937. "The Montreal Water Works." *American Water Works Association Journal* 29 (6): 774–90.

Dewar, K.C. 1975. "State Ownership in Canada." PhD diss., University of Toronto.

Dickinson, Trevor, D. Joy, R. Kreutzwiser, D. Shrubsole, and M. Sanderson. 1991. *A Report on Ontario Flood History*. Toronto: Ontario Ministry of Natural Resources.

Dolbey, Susan J. 1970. *Local Special Purpose Bodies in the Province of Ontario*. Toronto: Municipal Affairs.

Dolowitz, David P., and David Marsh. 2000. "Learning from Abroad: The Role of Policy Transfer in Contemporary Policy-Making." *Governance: An International Journal of Policy, Administration and Institutions* 13 (1): 5–23. http://dx.doi.org/10.1111/0952-1895.00121.

Downes, Walter E. 1974. "The Effect of British Colonial Policy on Public Educational Institutions in Upper Canada, 1784–1840." PhD diss., University of Ottawa.

Drummond, Don. 2012. *Commission on the Reform of Ontario's Public Services*. Toronto: Government of Ontario.

Drummond, Ian M. 1987. *Progress without Planning: The Economic History of Ontario from Confederation to the Second World War*. Toronto: University of Toronto Press.

Drury, E.C. 1966. *Farmer Premier*. Toronto: McClelland and Stewart.

Duncan, Marian Jane. 1964. "American Influences on Ontario's Elementary School Legislation, 1836–1850." MA thesis, University of Rochester.

Dupré, J. Stefan. 1985. "Reflections on the Workability of Executive Federalism." In *Intergovernmental Relations*, ed. Richard Simeon, 1–32. Toronto: University of Toronto Press.

Education That Connects. 2015. *Good Governance: A Guide for Trustees, School Boards, Directors of Education and Communities*. Toronto: Education That Connects.

Eidelman, Gabriel. 2013. "Landlocked: Politics, Property, and the Toronto Waterfront, 1960–2000." PhD diss., University of Toronto.

Elkins, David J., and Richard Simeon. 1979. "A Cause in Search of Its Effect, or What Does Political Culture Explain?" *Comparative Politics* 11 (2): 127–45. http://dx.doi.org/10.2307/421752.

Elston, Murray, Floyd Laughren, and David McFadden. 2012. *Renewing Ontario's Electricity Distribution Sector: Putting the Consumer First*. Toronto: Ontario Distribution Sector Review Panel.

English, John, and Kenneth McLaughlin. 1981. "Allen Huber: Berlin's Strangest Mayor." *Waterloo Historical Society* 69 (1981): 4–12.

– 1996. *Kitchener: An Illustrated History*. Waterloo, ON: Wilfrid Laurier University Press.

Evans, A. Margaret. 1992. *Sir Oliver Mowat*. Toronto: University of Toronto Press.

Farlinger, W.A., G.J. Homer, and B.S. Caine. 1995. *Ontario Hydro and the Electric Power Industry: Vision for a Competitive Industry*. Toronto: Government of Ontario.

Farrow, Ron M. 1967. *Waterloo Area Local Government Review: Data Book of Basic Information*. Waterloo, ON: Waterloo Area Local Government Review.

– 1971. *Local Government Reform: The Implications for the Classroom*.

Feldman, Lionel D. 1974. *Ontario 1945–1973: The Municipal Dynamic*. Toronto: Ontario Economic Council.

Felstiner, William, Richard Abel, and Austin Sarat. 1980. "Emergence and Transformation of Disputes: Naming, Blaming, Claiming." *Law & Society Review* 15 (3/4): 631–54. http://dx.doi.org/10.2307/3053505.

Ferguson, G.H. 1926. *The Township School Board Proposal: A Second Letter*. Toronto: Clarkson W. James.

Ferguson, John. 1930. *History of the Ontario Medical Association, 1880–1930*. Toronto: Murray Printing.

Ferree, Myra Marx. 2003. "Resonance and Radicalism: Feminist Framing in the Abortion Debates of the United States and Germany." *American Journal of Sociology* 109 (2): 304–44. http://dx.doi.org/10.1086/378343.

Fleming, Keith Robson. 1988. "Ontario Hydro and Rural Electrification in Old Ontario, 1911–1958: Policies and Issues." PhD diss., University of Western Ontario.

– 1992. *Power at Cost: Ontario Hydro and Rural Electrification, 1911–1958.* Montreal and Kingston: McGill-Queen's University Press.

Fleming, W.G. 1971. *Ontario's Educative Society.* Toronto: University of Toronto Press.

Fligstein, Neil. 1997. "Social Skill and Institutional Theory." *American Behavioral Scientist* 40 (4): 397–405. http://dx.doi.org/10.1177/000276429704 0004003.

Found, Adam. 2012. "Economies of Scale in Fire and Police Services in Ontario." *IMFG Papers on Municipal Finance and Governance* 12:1–29.

Freeman, Neil B. 1996. *The Politics of Power.* Toronto: University of Toronto Press.

Frey, Bruno S., and Reiner Eichenberger. 1999. *The New Democratic Federalism for Europe: Functional, Overlapping, and Competing Jurisdictions.* Cheltenham, UK: Edward Elgar.

Fyfe, Stewart. 1970. *Waterloo Area Local Government Review: Report of Findings and Recommendations.* Toronto: Municipal Affairs.

– 1974. "Local Government Reform in Ontario." In *A Look to the North: Canadian Regional Experience,* ed. William Macdougall, 13–32. Washington: Advisory Commission on Intergovernmental Relations.

Fyfe, Stewart, and Ron M. Farrow. 1970. "Waterloo Area Local Government Review: Report of Findings and Recommendations." *Waterloo Area Local Government Review.* Toronto: Ontario Ministry of Municipal Affairs.

Genieys, William, and Marc Smyrl. 2008. *Elites, Ideas, and the Evolution of Public Policy.* New York: Palgrave Macmillan.

Gibbs, Elizabeth, ed. 1976. *Debates of the Legislative Assembly of United Canada.* Quebec: Centre de recherche en histoire économique du Canada français.

Gidney, R.D. 1972. "Centralization and Education: The Origins of an Ontario Tradition." *Journal of Canadian Studies / Revue d'études canadiennes* 7 (4): 33–47.

– 1999. *From Hope to Harris: The Reshaping of Ontario's Schools.* Toronto: University of Toronto Press.

Gidney, R.D., and D.A. Lawr. 1978. "The Development of an Administrative System for the Public Schools: The First Stage, 1841–50." In *Egerton Ryerson and His Times,* ed. Neil McDonald and Alf Chaiton, 160–84. Toronto: Macmillan Canada.

– 1979. "Egerton Ryerson and the Origins of the Ontario Secondary School." *Canadian Historical Review* 60 (4): 442–65. http://dx.doi.org/10.3138/ CHR-060-04-02.

Gidney, R.D., and W.P.J. Millar. 1985. "From Voluntarism to State Schooling: The Creation of the Public School System in Ontario." *Canadian Historical Review* 66 (4): 443–73. http://dx.doi.org/10.3138/CHR-066-04-02.

– 1990. *Inventing Secondary Education*. Montreal and Kingston: McGill-Queen's University Press.

Government of Ontario. 1976. *Design for Development: Ontario's Future: Trends and Options*. Toronto: Government of Ontario.

Graham, Katherine, and Susan Phillips. 1998. *Urban Governance in Canada*. Toronto: Harcourt.

Gregory, W.D. 1923. *Hydro-Electric Inquiry Commission: Report on History and General Relations*. Toronto: Government of Ontario.

– 1924. *Hydro-Electric Inquiry Commission General Report*. Toronto: Government of Ontario.

Haas, P.M. 1992. "Epistemic Communities and International Policy Coordination." *International Organization* 46 (1): 1–35. http://dx.doi.org/10.1017/ S0020818300001442.

Hacker, Jacob S. 2004. "Privatizing Risk without Privatizing the Welfare State: The Hidden Politics of Social Policy Retrenchment in the United States." *American Political Science Review* 98 (2): 243–60. http://dx.doi.org/10.1017/ S0003055404001121.

Hacker, Jacob, and Paul Pierson. 2011. "The Case for Policy-Focused Political Analysis." Unpublished. http://papers.ssrn.com/sol3/papers.cfm?abstract_ id=1471461.

Hall, Peter. 1993. "Policy Paradigms, Social Learning, and the State: The Case of Economic Policymaking in Britain." *Comparative Politics* 25 (3): 275–96.

– 2009. "Historical Institutionalism in Rationalist and Sociological Perspective." In *Explaining Institutional Change*, ed. Kathleen Ann Thelen and James Mahoney, 204–24. Cambridge: Cambridge University Press. http://dx.doi.org/10.1017/CBO9780511806414.009.

Hall, Peter A., and Michèle Lamont. 2013. "Why Social Relations Matter for Politics and Successful Societies." *Annual Review of Political Science* 16 (1): 49–71. http://dx.doi.org/10.1146/annurev-polisci-031710-101143.

Hall, Peter A., and Rosemary C.R. Taylor. 1996. "Political Science and the Three New Institutionalisms." *Political Studies* 44 (5): 936–57. http://dx.doi .org/10.1111/j.1467-9248.1996.tb00343.x.

Hamlin, Christopher. 2009. *Cholera: The Biography*. Oxford: Oxford University Press.

Health, Ministry of, and Ministry of Intergovernmental Affairs. 1980. *Public Health Structures Study*. Toronto: Government of Ontario.

Hergott, Bruce. 1994. *Vital Signs: Kitchener-Waterloo Hospital, the First Hundred Years*. Kitchener, ON: Kitchener Waterloo Hospital.

Hodge, Gerald. 1985. "The Roots of Canadian Planning." *Journal of the American Planning Association* 51 (1): 8–22. http://dx.doi.org/10.1080/01944368508976796.

Hodgetts, J.E. 1995. *From Arm's Length to Hands On: The Formative Years of Ontario's Public Service, 1867–1940*. Toronto: University of Toronto Press.

Hodgins, J. George. 1894. *Documentary History of Education in Upper Canada*. Toronto: Warwick Brothers and Rutter.

Hoffman, Andrew J. 1999. "Institutional Evolution and Change: Environmentalism and the US Chemical Industry." *Academy of Management Journal* 42 (4): 351–71. http://dx.doi.org/10.2307/257008.

Hoffman, Susan. 2002. "William Henry Breithaupt 1857–1944: A Tribute." *Waterloo Historical Society Annual Volume* 90:31–3.

Hogg, W.M. 1974. *The Restructuring of Public Utilities*. Toronto: Ontario Government Committee on Restructuring of Public Utilities.

Hooghe, Liesbet, and Gary Marks. 2003. "Unraveling the Central State, but How? Types of Multilevel Governance." *American Political Science Review* 97 (2): 233–43.

– 2009. "Does Efficiency Shape the Territorial Structure of Government?" *Annual Review of Political Science* 12:225–41.

Hope, John Andrew. 1950. *Report of the Royal Commission on Education in Ontario*.

Houston, Susan E. 1975. "Politics, Schools, and Social Change in Upper Canada." In *Education and Social Change: Themes from Ontario's Past*, ed. Michael B. Katz and Paul H. Mattingly, 28–56. New York: New York University Press.

Houston, Susan E., and Alison Prentice. 1988. *Schooling and Scholars in Nineteenth-Century Ontario*. Toronto: University of Toronto Press.

Howlett, Michael, and M. Ramesh. 1998. "Policy Subsystem Configurations and Policy Change: Operationalizing the Postpositivist Analysis of the Politics of the Policy Process." *Policy Studies Journal: The Journal of the Policy Studies Organization* 26 (3): 466–81. http://dx.doi.org/10.1111/j.1541-0072.1998.tb01913.x.

Hunter, A.F., ed. 1935. *The Correspondence of the Honourable Peter Russell*. Toronto: Ontario Historical Society.

Hwang, Hokyu, and Walter W. Powell. 2005. "Institutions and Entrepreneurship." In *The Handbook of Entrepreneurship*, 201–32. New York: Springer. http://dx.doi.org/10.1007/0-387-23622-8_10.

Hydro 21. 1993. *Hydro 21: Options for Ontario Hydro.* Toronto: Ontario Hydro.

"Hydrophobia." 1997. *Economist*, August 21. http://www.economist.com/
node/154776.

Ibbitson, John. 1997. *Promised Land: Inside the Mike Harris Revolution.* Toronto:
Prentice Hall Canada.

Jacek, Henry J. 1980. "Regional Government and Development: Administrative
Efficiency versus Local Democracy." In *Government and Politics of Ontario*,
2nd ed., ed. Donald C. Macdonald, 100–18. Toronto: Van Nostrand Reinhold.

Jackson, J.N., and S.M. Wilson. 1993. *St Catharines: Canada's Canal City.* St
Catharines, ON: Standard.

James, William, and James G. March. 1978. *A Sufficient Supply of Pure and
Wholesome Water: The Story of Hamilton's Old Pumphouse.* London: Phelps
Publishing.

Jervis, John B. 1857. *Report on a Supply of Water for the City of Hamilton.*
Hamilton: Morning Banner.

Johnston, Charles M. 1986. *E.C. Drury: Agrarian Idealist.* Toronto: University
of Toronto Press.

Johnson, L.A. 1977. *History of Guelph, 1827–1927.* Guelph, ON: Guelph
Historical Society.

Jones, Bryan D., Frank R. Baumgartner, Christian Breunig, Christopher
Wlezien, Stuart Soroka, Martial Foucault, Abel François, Christoffer Green-
Pedersen, Chris Koski, Peter John, et al. 2009. "A General Empirical Law
of Public Budgets: A Comparative Analysis." *American Journal of Political
Science* 53 (4): 855–73. http://dx.doi.org/10.1111/j.1540-5907.2009.00405.x.

Jones, Elwood, and Douglas McCalla. 1979. "Toronto Waterworks, 1840–77."
Canadian Historical Review 60 (3): 300–23. http://dx.doi.org/10.3138/
CHR-060-03-02.

Jones, Murray V. 1965. *Ottawa, Eastview and Carleton County Local Government
Review.*. Ottawa: Eastview and Carleton County Local Government Review
Commission.

Kaestle, Carl. 1983. *Pillars of the Republic: Common Schools and American Society,
1780–1860.* New York: Hill and Wang.

Karr, W.J. 1925. *Annual Report of the Minister of Education.*

Kay, Adrian. 2009. "Understanding Policy Change as a Hermeneutic Problem."
Journal of Comparative Policy Analysis: Research and Practice 11 (1): 47–63.
http://dx.doi.org/10.1080/13876980802648276.

King, Desmond, Robert C. Lieberman, Gretchen Ritter, and Laurence
Whitehead, eds. 2009. *Democratization in America.* Baltimore, MD: Johns
Hopkins University Press.

Kingdon, John. 1984. *Agendas, Alternatives, and Public Policies.* New York:
HarperCollins.

Kitchen, Harry. 2003. *Municipal Revenue and Expenditure Issues in Canada.* Toronto: Canadian Tax Foundation.

Koch, Philippe. 2013. "Overestimating the Shift from Government to Governance: Evidence from Swiss Metropolitan Areas." *Governance: An International Journal of Policy, Administration and Institutions* 26 (3): 397–423. http://dx.doi.org/10.1111/j.1468-0491.2012.01600.x.

Krasner, Stephen D. 1984. "Approaches to the State: Alternative Conceptions and Historical Dynamics." *Comparative Politics* 16 (2): 223–46. http://dx.doi .org/10.2307/421608.

Krueger, Ralph. 1971. "Towards Regional Planning and Regional Government in Waterloo County." In *The Waterloo County Area: Selected Geographical Essays*, ed. A.G. McLellan, 295–307. Waterloo, ON: Department of Geography Publication Series, University of Waterloo.

Kushner, Joseph, and Tomson Ogwang. 2014. "Local Electrical Utilities: Is Bigger Better?" *Canadian Public Policy* 40 (3): 283–91.

Lamont, Michèle, and Virig Molnar. 2002. "The Study of Boundaries in the Social Sciences." *Annual Review of Sociology* 28 (1): 167–95. http://dx.doi .org/10.1146/annurev.soc.28.110601.141107.

Lamont, Michèle, and Mario Luis Small. 2008. "How Culture Matters: Enriching Our Understanding of Poverty." In *The Colors of Poverty*, ed. Ann Chih Lin and David R Harris, 76–102. New York: Russel Sage Foundation.

Lankton, Larry D. 1976. *Written Historical and Descriptive Data.* New York: Historic American Engineering Record. http://cdn.loc.gov/master/pnp/ habshaer/ny/ny1100/ny1181/data/ny1181data.pdf.

Landon, Fred. 1967. *Western Ontario and the American Frontier.* Toronto: McClelland and Stewart.

Laumann, Edward O., and David Knoke. 1987. *The Organizational State.* Madison: University of Wisconsin Press.

Levin, Simon A. 1992. "The Problem of Pattern and Scale in Ecology: The Robert H. MacArthur Award Lecture." *Ecology* 73 (6): 1943–67. http:// dx.doi.org/10.2307/1941447.

Lieberman, Robert C. 2002. "Ideas, Institutions, and Political Order: Explaining Political Change." *American Political Science Review* 96 (4): 697–712. http:// dx.doi.org/10.1017/S0003055402000394.

Loreto, Richard. 1980. "The Cabinet." In *Government and Politics of Ontario*, ed. Donald C. Macdonald, 20–35. Toronto: Van Nostrand Reinhold.

Lucas, Jack. 2013a. "Berlin, Ontario in the Age of the ABC." *Urban History Review / Revue d'histoire urbaine* 41 (2): 19–42. http://dx.doi. org/10.7202/1015378ar.

– 2013b. "Hidden in Plain View: Local Agencies, Boards, and Commissions in Canada." *IMFG Perspectives* 4:1–7.

- 2015a. "Did Allen Huber Punch Louis Breithaupt in the Face?" *Waterloo Historical Society Annual Volume* 102:77–84.
- 2015b. "How Ontario Hydro Went Local: The Creation of Rural Power Districts and the Central Ontario System," *Scientia Canadensis* 37 (1–2): 59–76.
- 2015c. "How Things Change: Adventures in Ureconstructed Institutionalism." *IPAC Public Sector Management* 26 (1): 24–25.
- Forthcoming. "Urban Governance and the American Political Development Approach." *Urban Affairs Review*.
MacDougall, Heather. 1980. "Researching Public Health Services in Ontario, 1882–1930." *Archivaria* 10:157–72.
MacDougall, Heather. 1981. "Health Is Wealth: The Development of Public Health Activity in Toronto, 1834–1890." PhD diss., University of Toronto.
- 1982. "Enlightening the Public: The Views and Values of the Association of Executive Health Officers of Ontario, 1886–1903." In *Health, Disease, and Medicine: Essays in Canadian History*, ed. Charles G. Roland, 436–64. Hamilton: Hannah Institute for the History of Medicine.
- 1990. *Activists and Advocates*. Toronto: Dundurn.
- 2009. "'Truly Alarming': Cholera in 1832." *Canadian Journal of Public Health* 100 (5): 333–6.
Maclellan, D. 2009. "Educational Restructuring and the Policy Process: The Toronto District School Board 1997–2003." *Academic Leadership: The Online Journal* 7.
Magnusson, Warren. 1983a. "Introduction." In *City Politics in Canada*, ed. Warren Magnusson and Andrew Sancton, 3–57. Toronto: University of Toronto Press.
- 1983b. "Toronto." In *City Politics in Canada*, ed. Warren Magnusson and Andrew Sancton, 94–139. Toronto: University of Toronto Press.
Mahoney, James. 2000. "Path Dependence in Historical Sociology." *Theory and Society* 29 (4): 507–48. http://dx.doi.org/10.1023/A:1007113830879.
Mahoney, James, and Kathleen Ann Thelen. 2009. "A Theory of Gradual Institutional Change." In *Explaining Institutional Change*, ed. James Mahoney and Kathleen Ann Thelen, 1–37. Cambridge: Cambridge University Press. http://dx.doi.org/10.1017/CBO9780511806414.003.
Martin, John Levi. 2003. "What Is Field Theory?" *American Journal of Sociology* 109 (1): 1–49. http://dx.doi.org/10.1086/375201.
- 2010. "Life's a Beach but You're an Ant, and Other Unwelcome News for the Sociology of Culture." *Poetics* 38 (2): 229–44. http://dx.doi.org/10.1016/j.poetic.2009.11.004.
Mayo, Henry B. 1966. *Report of the Commission*. Toronto: Niagara Region Local Government Review Commission.

– 1976. *Report of the Ottawa-Carleton Review Commission*. Ottawa: Ottawa-Carleton Review Commission.

McAdam, Doug, and Neil Fligstein. 2012. *A Theory of Fields*. Oxford: Oxford University Press.

McCool, Daniel. 1998. "The Subsystem Family of Concepts: A Critique and a Proposal." *Political Research Quarterly* 51 (2): 551–70. http://dx.doi.org/10.1177/106591299805100213.

McCubbins, Mathew D., and Thomas Schwartz. 1984. "Congressional Oversight Overlooked: Police Patrols versus Fire Alarms." *American Journal of Political Science* 28 (1): 165–79. http://dx.doi.org/10.2307/2110792.

McKeough, W. Darcy. 1972. *Design for Development Phase Three: Statement by the Honourable W. Darcy McKeough Treasurer of Ontario to the Founding Convention of the Association of Municipalities of Ontario*. Toronto: Legislature of Ontario.

– 1978. *Government Statement on the Review of Local Government in the Municipality of Metropolitan Toronto*. Toronto: Ministry of Treasury, Economics, and Intergovernmental Affairs.

Middleton, Jesse, and Fred Landon, eds. 1927a. *The Province of Ontario: A History*. Toronto: Dominion Publishing.

– 1927b. "William Henry Breithaupt." In *The Province of Ontario: A History*, ed. Jesse Middleton and Fred Landon. Toronto: Dominion Publishing.

Ministry of Treasury, Economics, and Intergovernmental Affairs. 1972. *Proposal for Local Government Reform in an Area East of Metro*. Toronto: Ministry of Treasury, Economics, and Intergovernmental Affairs.

Mitchell, Bruce, and Dan Shrubsole. 1992. *Ontario Conservation Authorities: Myth and Reality*. Waterloo, ON: University of Waterloo Department of Geography Publications Series.

Moloughney, Brent W. 2005. *Defining "Critical Mass" for Ontario Public Health Units*. Toronto: Ministry of Health and Long-Term Care.

Mullin, Megan. 2009. *Governing the Tap: Special District Governance and the New Local Politics of Water*. Cambridge, MA: MIT Press.

Nelles, H.V. 1976. "Public Ownership of Electrical Utilities in Manitoba and Ontario, 1906–30." *Canadian Historical Review* 57 (4): 461–84. http://dx.doi.org/10.3138/CHR-057-04-03.

– 2005. *The Politics of Development*. 2nd ed. Montreal and Kingston: McGill-Queen's University Press.

Nelles, H.V., and Christopher Armstrong. 1986. *Monopoly's Moment*. Toronto: University of Toronto Press.

Nevitte, Neil. 1996. *The Decline of Deference*. Toronto: University of Toronto Press.

Noel, S.J.R. 1974. *Patrons, Clients, Brokers: Ontario Society and Politics, 1791–1896*. Toronto: Macmillan Canada.

– 2000. "Oliver Mowat, Patronage, and Party Building." In *Ontario since Confederation: A Reader*, ed. E.A. Montigny and A.L. Chambers, 94–104. Toronto: University of Toronto Press.

O'Brien, Allan. 1975. "Father Knows Best: A Look at the Provincial–Municipal Relationship in Ontario." In *Government and Politics of Ontario*, ed. Donald C. Macdonald, 154–71. Toronto: Macmillan Canada.

O'Connor, Dennis. 2002. *Report of the Walkerton Inquiry*. Toronto: Government of Ontario.

Oliver, Christine. 1992. "The Antecedents of Deinstitutionalization." *Organization Studies* 13 (4): 563–88. http://dx.doi.org/10.1177/017084069201300403.

Oliver, Peter. 1977. *G. Howard Ferguson: Ontario Tory*. Toronto: University of Toronto Press.

"Ontario." 1924. *Journal of the Town Planning Institute of Canada* 3 (3): 16.

Ontario Department of Health. 1934. *The Hospitals of Ontario: A Short History*. Toronto: Department of Health, Government of Ontario.

Ontario Energy Board. 2004. *Review of Further Efficiencies in the Electricity Distribution Sector*. Toronto: Ontario Energy Board.

Ontario Ministry of Energy. 2009. *Direction for Change: Charting a Course for Competitive Electricity and Jobs in Ontario*. Toronto: Government of Ontario.

Ontario Public Health Division. 2009. *Initial Report on Public Health*. Toronto: Ministry of Health and Long-Term Care.

Orren, Karen, and Stephen Skowronek. 2004. *The Search for American Political Development*. Cambridge: Cambridge University Press.

Ostrom, Elinor. 2007. "Institutional Rational Choice." In *Theories of the Policy Process*, ed. Paul Sabatier, 21–64. Boulder, CO: Westview.

Palmer, W.H. 1970. *The Progress of the Regional Government Program in Ontario*. Toronto: Ontario Department of Municipal Affairs.

– 1978a. *Decision Makers in Local Government*. Kitchener, ON: Waterloo Region Review Commission.

– 1978b. *The Organization of Social Services in Waterloo Region*. Kitchener: Waterloo Region Review Commission.

– 1978c. *Police Governance in Waterloo Region*. Kitchener, ON: Waterloo Region Review Commission.

– 1978d. *Water Management on the Grand River: A Provincial/Municipal Dilemma*. Kitchener, ON: Waterloo Region Review Commission.

– 1979. *Report of the Waterloo Region Review Commission*. Waterloo, ON: Waterloo Region Review Commission.

Paterson, Donald L. 1969. *Final Report and Recommendations*. Gravenhurst, ON: Muskoka District Local Government Review.

Patterson, Graeme Hazlewood. 1969. "Studies in Elections and Public Opinion in Upper Canada." PhD diss., University of Toronto.

Patterson, Marian A. 1958. "The Cholera Epidemic of 1832 in York, Upper Canada." *Bulletin of the Medical Library Association* 46 (2): 165–84.

Pequegnat, Marcel. 1942. "Grand River Conservation." *Waterloo Historical Society* 30:211–24.

Phair, J.T. 1940. "Public Health in Ontario." In *The Development of Public Health*, ed. R.D. Defries, 67–85. Toronto: Canadian Public Health Association.

Pierson, Paul. 2000. "Increasing Returns, Path Dependence, and the Study of Politics." *American Political Science Review* 94 (2): 251–67. http://dx.doi.org/10.2307/2586011.

– 2004. *Politics in Time: History, Institutions, and Social Analysis*. Princeton, NJ: Princeton University Press.

Plewman, W.R. 1947. *Adam Beck and the Ontario Hydro*. Toronto: Ryerson.

Plunkett, T.J. 1966. *Peel-Halton Local Government Review*. Toronto: Peel-Halton Local Government Review Commission.

Powell, Mary. 1991. "Provincial-Local Relations in Ontario: The Case of Public Health, 1882–1984." PhD diss., University of Toronto.

Powell, Walter W., and Paul J. DiMaggio, eds. 1991. *The New Institutionalism in Organizational Analysis*. Chicago: University of Chicago Press.

Prentice, Alison. 1977. *The School Promoters*. Toronto: McClelland and Stewart.

Public Health Division. 2009. *Building Capacity for Local Public Health in Ontario: A Discussion Paper*. Toronto: Government of Ontario.

Rhodes, Rod. "Old Institutionalisms." 2006. In *Oxford Handbook of Political Institutions*, ed. Rod Rhodes, Sara Binder, and Bert Rockman, 90–108. Oxford: Oxford University Press.

Richardson, Arthur Herbert. 1974. *Conservation by the People: The History of the Conservation Movement in Ontario to 1970*. Toronto: University of Toronto Press.

Robarts, John. 1968. *Design for Development Phase Two: Statement by the Honourable John Robarts Prime Minister of Ontario, November 28, 1968*. Toronto: Legislature of Ontario.

Rosen, George. 1958. *A History of Public Health*. New York: MD Publications. http://dx.doi.org/10.1037/11322-000.

Ross, Peter N. 1975. "The Free School Controversy in Toronto, 1848–1852." In *Education and Social Change: Themes from Ontario's Past*, ed. Michael B. Katz and Paul H. Mattingly, 57–80. New York: New York University Press.

Ross, Susan M. 2003. "Steam or Water Power? Thomas C. Keefer and the Engineers Discuss the Montreal Waterworks in 1852." *Industrial Archaeology* 29 (1): 49–64.

Rowell, Margaret. 1974. "Floods on the Grand." *Waterloo Historical Society Annual Volume* 62:34–8.

Royal Commission on Learning. 1995. *For the Love of Learning: Report of the Royal Commission on Learning.* Toronto: Queen's Printer.

Royal Commission on Metropolitan Toronto. 1977. *Report of the Royal Commission on Metropolitan Toronto: Detailed Findings and Recommendations.* Toronto: Government of Ontario.

Rutherford, Paul. 1984. "Tomorrow's Metropolis: The Urban Reform Movement in Canada, 1880–1920." In *The Canadian City*, ed. Gilber A. Stelter and Alan F.J. Artibise, 435–55. Montreal and Kingston: McGill-Queen's University Press.

Saarinen, Oiva. 1979. "The Influence of Thomas Adams and the British New Towns Movement in the Planning of Canadian Resource Communities." In *The Usable Urban Past*, ed. Alan F.J. Artibise and Gilbert A. Stelter, 268–92. Ottawa: Macmillan Canada.

Sabatier, Paul A., and Christopher M. Weible. 2007. "The Advocacy Coalition Framework." In *Theories of the Policy Process*, ed. Paul A. Sabatier, 189–220. Boulder, CO: Westview.

Sanborn, Deborah. 2005. *Primarily Prevention: A History of the Eastern Ontario Health Unit.* Ottawa: Canadian Public Health Association.

Sancton, Andrew. 2011. *Canadian Local Government: An Urban Perspective.* Don Mills, ON: Oxford University Press.

Sancton, Andrew, and Robert Young, eds. 2009. *Foundations of Governance.* Toronto: University of Toronto Press.

Sattler, Peggy. 2012. "Education Governance Reform in Ontario: Neoliberalism in Context." *Canadian Journal of Educational Administration and Policy* 128:1–28.

Saywell, John T. 1991. *"Just Call Me Mitch": The Life of Mitchell F. Hepburn.* Toronto: University of Toronto Press.

Schickler, Eric. 2001. *Disjointed Pluralism: Institutional Innovation and the Development of the U.S. Congress.* Princeton, NJ: Princeton University Press.

Schmidt, Vivien. 2008. "Discursive Institutionalism: The Explanatory Power of Ideas and Discourse." *Annual Review of Political Science* 11 (1): 303–26. http://dx.doi.org/10.1146/annurev.polisci.11.060606.135342.

Scott, W. Richard. 2008. *Institutions and Organizations.* Los Angeles: Sage.

Sewell, William H., Jr. 1992. "A Theory of Structure: Duality, Agency, and Transformation." *American Journal of Sociology* 98 (1): 1–29. http://dx.doi.org/10.1086/229967.

– 2005. *Logics of History*. Chicago: University of Chicago Press. http://dx.doi
.org/10.7208/chicago/9780226749198.001.0001.

Shepsle, K.A. 1989. "Studying Institutions: Some Lessons from the Rational
Choice Approach." *Journal of Theoretical Politics* 1 (2): 131–47. http://dx.doi
.org/10.1177/0951692889001002002.

Shrubsole, Dan. 1992. "The Grand River Conservation Commission: History,
Activities, and Implications for Water Management." *Canadian Geographer*
36 (3): 221–36. http://dx.doi.org/10.1111/j.1541-0064.1992.tb01136.x.

Siegel, David. 1994. "The ABCs of Canadian Local Government: An Overview."
In *Agencies, Boards, and Commissions in Canadian Local Government*, ed. Dale
Richmond and David Siegel, 1–19. Toronto: Institute of Public Administration
of Canada.

Siegel, David, and Dale Richmond, eds. 1994. *Agencies, Boards, and Commissions
in Canadian Local Government*. Toronto: Institute of Public Administration
of Canada.

Silcox, Peter. 1975. "The ABC's of Ontario: Provincial Agencies, Boards
and Commissions." In *Government and Politics of Ontario*, ed. Donald C.
Macdonald, 135–53. Toronto: Macmillan Canada.

Simeon, Richard. 1976. "Studying Public Policy." *Canadian Journal of Political
Science* 9 (4): 548–80. http://dx.doi.org/10.1017/S000842390004470X.

Simon, Herbert A. 1972. "Theories of Bounded Rationality." In *Decision and
Organization*, ed. C.B. McGuire and Roy Radner, 161–76. Amsterdam:
North-Holland Publishing.

Simpson, Michael. 1985. *Thomas Adams and the Modern Planning Movement:
Britain, Canada, and the United States 1900–1940*. Oxford: Alexandrine.

Skogstad, Grace. 2003. "Who Governs? Who Should Govern? Political
Authority and Legitimacy in Canada in the Twenty-First Century."
Canadian Journal of Political Science 36 (5): 955–73. http://dx.doi.org/10.1017/
S0008423903778925.

– 2008. "Policy Networks and Policy Communities: Conceptualizing State–
Societal Relationships in the Policy Process." In *The Comparative Turn in
Canadian Political Science*, ed. Linda A. White, Richard Simeon, Robert
Vipond, and Jennifer Wallner, 205–20. Vancouver: UBC Press.

Skogstad, Grace, and William D. Coleman. 1990. "Policy Communities and
Policy Networks: A Structural Approach." In *Policy Communities and Public
Policy in Canada*, ed. Grace Skogstad and William D. Coleman, 14–33.
Mississauga, ON: Copp Clark Pitman.

Skogstad, Grace, and Tanya Whyte. 2015. "Authority Contests, Power and
Policy Paradigm Change: Explaining Developments in Grain Marketing
Policy in Prairie Canada." *Canadian Journal of Political Science* 48 (1): 1–22.
http://dx.doi.org/10.1017/S0008423914001115.

Skrentny, John David. 2009. *The Minority Rights Revolution.* Cambridge: Harvard University Press.

Smith, F. Clifford. 1913. *The Montreal Water Works.* Montreal: City of Montreal.

Smith, Lancelot J. 1967a. *Report of the Ontario Committee on Taxation: The Local Revenue System.* Toronto: Government of Ontario.

– 1967b. *Report of the Ontario Committee on Taxation: The Provincial Revenue System.* Toronto: Government of Ontario.

Spirling, Arthur. 2014. "British Political Development: A Research Agenda." *Legislative Studies Quarterly* 39 (4): 435–7. http://dx.doi.org/10.1111/lsq.12053.

Splane, Richard B. 1965. *Social Welfare in Ontario 1791–1893.* Toronto: University of Toronto Press.

Spragge, George W. 1941. "John Strachan's Contribution to Education 1800–1823." *Canadian Historical Review* 22 (2): 147–58. http://dx.doi.org/10.3138/CHR-022-02-03.

– ed. 1946. *The John Strachan Letter Book: 1812–1834.* Toronto: Ontario Historical Society.

Stamp, Robert M. 1982. *The Schools of Ontario 1876–1976.* Toronto: University of Toronto Press.

– 1988. *Ontario Secondary School Program Innovations and Student Retention Rates: 1920s–1970s.* Toronto: Ministry of Education.

Steele, Donald R. 1969. *Report and Recommendations.* Hamilton: Hamilton-Burlington-Wentworth Local Government Review Commission.

Steensland, Brian. 2006. "Cultural Categories and the American Welfare State: The Case of Guaranteed Income Policy." *American Journal of Sociology* 111 (5): 1273–326. http://dx.doi.org/10.1086/499508.

Stewart, Rouleen. 1986. "The Ontario School Trustee: Snapshots over Time." In *Alternative Approaches to Determining Distribution of School Board Trustee Representation,* ed. Edward H. Humphreys, Stephen B. Lawton, Richard G. Townsend, Victoria E. Grabb, and Daina M. Watson, 37–71. Toronto: Queen's Printer for Ontario.

Stone, Clarence, and Robert K. Whelan. 2009. "Through a Glass Darkly: The Once and Future Study of Urban Politics." In *The City in American Political Development,* ed. Ribardson Dilworth, 98–118. New York: Routledge.

Stone, Deborah A. 1989. "Causal Stories and the Formation of Policy Agendas." *Political Science Quarterly* 104 (2): 281–300. http://dx.doi.org/10.2307/2151585.

Stout, Karen Evans, and Byron Stevens. 2000. "The Case of the Failed Diversity Rule: A Multiple Streams Analysis." *Educational Evaluation and Policy Analysis* 22 (4): 341–55. http://dx.doi.org/10.3102/01623737022004341.

Strang, David, and John W. Meyer. 1993. "Institutional Conditions for Diffusion." *Theory and Society* 22 (4): 487–511.

Sturm, Hilda. 2012. "Municipal Elections." Kitchener Corporate Archives, http://lf.kitchener.ca/uniquesig0d1d2aa1a38f6e69dc1e79e99d780c34f537a34d9c901a0d7cbb1976cbfdd057/uniquesig0/WeblinkExt/0/doc/1247099/Page1.aspx.

Streeck, Wolfgang, and Kathleen Ann Thelen. 2005. "Introduction: Institutional Change in Advanced Political Economies." In *Beyond Continuity: Institutional Change in Advanced Political Economies*, ed. Wolfgang Streeck and Kathleen Ann Thelen, 1–39. Oxford: Oxford University Press.

Sutherland, Neil. 1976. *Children in English-Canadian Society: Framing the Twentieth-Century Consensus*. Toronto: University of Toronto Press.

Sweeney, John. 1996. *Ontario School Board Reduction Task Force: Final Report*. Toronto: Ministry of Education.

Swidler, Ann. 1986. "Culture in Action: Symbols and Strategies." *American Sociological Review* 51 (2): 273–86. http://dx.doi.org/10.2307/2095521.

Szablowski, George J. 1975. "Policy-Making and Cabinet: Recent Organizational Engineering at Queen's Park." In *Government and Politics of Ontario*, ed. Donald C. Macdonald, 114–34. Toronto: Macmillan Canada.

Taylor, Iain C. 1967. "Components of Population Change, 1850–1940." MA thesis, University of Toronto.

Taylor, John H. 1986. *Ottawa: An Illustrated History*. Toronto: James Lorimer.

Taylor, Zack. 2014. "If Different Then Why? Explaining the Divergent Political Development of Canadian and American Local Governance." *International Journal of Canadian Studies* 49:53–79.

Taylor, Zack, and Gabriel Eidelman. 2010. "Canadian Political Science and the City: A Limited Engagement." *Canadian Journal of Political Science* 43 (4): 961–81. http://dx.doi.org/10.1017/S0008423910000715.

Thelen, Kathleen. 1999. "Historical Institutionalism in Comparative Politics." *Annual Review of Political Science* 2 (1): 369–404. http://dx.doi.org/10.1146/annurev.polisci.2.1.369.

– 2003. "How Institutions Evolve: Insights from Comparative Historical Analysis." In *Comparative Historical Analysis in the Social Sciences*, ed. James Mahoney and Dietrich Rueschemeyer, 208–40. Cambridge: Cambridge University Press. http://dx.doi.org/10.1017/CBO9780511803963.007.

– 2004. *How Institutions Evolve*. Cambridge: Cambridge University Press. http://dx.doi.org/10.1017/CBO9780511790997.

Tiessen, Paul. 1912. *Berlin: Celebration of Cityhood*. Berlin: Sand Hill Books, 1912.

Tilly, Charles. 2004. "Social Boundary Mechanisms." *Philosophy of the Social Sciences* 34 (2): 211–36. http://dx.doi.org/10.1177/0048393103262551.

Toronto. 1965. *Report of the Royal Commission on Metropolitan Toronto.*

Toronto Public Health. 2015. "Toronto Public Health Operating Budget Request, 2015." http://www.toronto.ca/legdocs/mmis/2015/ex/bgrd/ backgroundfile-77285.pdf.

True, James L. 2000. "Avalanches and Incrementalism." *American Review of Public Administration* 30 (1): 3–18. http://dx.doi.org/10.1177/02750740022064524.

True, James L., Bryan D. Jones, and Frank R. Baumgartner. 2007. "Punctuated-Equilibrium Theory." In *Theories of the Policy Process*, ed. Paul Sabatier, 155–87. Boulder, CO: Westview, 2007.

Tsebelis, George. 1995. "Decision Making in Political Systems: Veto Players in Presidentialism, Parliamentarism, Multicameralism and Multipartyism." *British Journal of Political Science* 25 (3): 289–325. http://dx.doi.org/10.1017/ S0007123400007225.

– 2002. *Veto Players.* Princeton, NJ: Princeton University Press. http://dx.doi .org/10.1515/9781400831456.

Uttley, W.V. 1937. *The History of Kitchener.* Waterloo, ON: Wilfrid Laurier University Press.

Walker, David. 2003. *For the Public's Health: Initial Report of the Ontario Expert Panel on SARS and Infectious Disease Control.* Toronto: Ontario Expert Panel on SARS and Infectious Disease Control.

Wallner, Jennifer. 2009. "Defying the Odds: Similarity and Difference in Canadian Elementary and Secondary Education." PhD diss., University of Toronto.

– 2014. *Learning to School.* Toronto: University of Toronto Press.

Warner, Roger. 1971. *Regional Government Reform in Ontario.* Toronto: Ontario Department of Municipal Affairs.

Waterloo Local Government Reform Proposals. 1971. *Waterloo Local Government Reform Proposals.* Toronto: Municipal Research Branch, Department of Municipal Affairs.

Watson, J.W. 1947. "Rural Depopulation in Southwestern Ontario." *Annals of the Association of American Geographers* 37 (3): 145–54. http://dx.doi .org/10.1080/00045604709351954.

Weaver, John C. 1977. *Shaping the Canadian City: Essays on Urban Politics and Policy 1890–1920.* Toronto: Institute of Public Administration of Canada.

– 1979. "The Modern City Realized." In *The Usable Urban Past*, ed. Alan F.J. Artibise and Gilber A. Stelter, 39–72. Ottawa: Macmillan.

– 1984. "'Tomorrow's Metropolis' Revisited: A Critical Assessment of Urban Reform in Canada, 1890–1920." In *The Canadian City*, ed. Gilber A. Stelter and Alan F.J. Artibise, 393–418. Kingston: McGill-Queen's University Press.

Wells, Clayton. 1928. "A Historical Sketch of the Town of Waterloo, Ontario." *Waterloo Historical Society* 16:2267.

White, Graham. 1973. "One-Party Dominance and Third Parties: The Pinard Theory Reconsidered." *Canadian Journal of Political Science* 6 (3): 399–421. http://dx.doi.org/10.1017/S0008423900040002.

– 1979. "Social Change and Political Stability in Ontario: Electoral Forces 1867–1977." PhD diss., McMaster University.

Wilson, J.D. 1970a. "Foreign and Local Influences on Popular Education in Upper Canada, 1814–1844." PhD diss., University of Western Ontario.

– 1970b. "The Ryerson Years in Canada West." In *Canadian Education: A History*, ed. J.D. Wilson, R.M. Stamp, and L.P. Audet, 214–40. Scarborough, ON: Prentice Hall.

Wincott, Daniel. 2010. "Ideas, Policy Change, and the Welfare State." In *Ideas and Politics in Social Science Research*, ed. Daniel Béland and Robert Henry Cox, 143–66. Oxford: Oxford University Press. http://dx.doi.org/10.1093/acprof:oso/9780199736430.003.0008.

Woods, Shirley E. 1980. *Ottawa: The Capital of Canada*. Toronto: Doubleday Canada.

Woodside, Kenneth. 1990. "An Approach to Studying Local Government Autonomy: The Ontario Experience." *Canadian Public Administration* 33 (2): 198–213. http://dx.doi.org/10.1111/j.1754-7121.1990.tb01393.x.

Wooten, Melissa, and Andrew J. Hoffman. 2008. "Organizational Fields: Past, Present and Future." In *Sage Handbook of Organizational Institutionalism*, ed. Royston Greenwood, Christine Oliver, Roy Suddaby, and Kerstin Sahlin, 129–49. Los Angeles: Sage. http://dx.doi.org/10.4135/9781849200387.n5.

Wright, J.R. 1983. *Urban Parks in Ontario*. Toronto: Province of Ontario Ministry of Tourism and Recreation.

Young, Robert. 2009. "Conclusion." In *Foundations of Governance: Municipal Government in Canada's Provinces*, ed. Robert Young and Andrew Sancton, 487–99. Toronto: University of Toronto Press.

Young, William Robert. 1971. "The Countryside on the Defensive: Agricultural Ontario's Views of Rural Depopulation, 1900–1914." MA thesis, University of British Columbia.

– 1972. "Conscription, Rural Depopulation, and the Farmers of Ontario, 1917–19." *Canadian Historical Review* 53 (3): 289–320. http://dx.doi.org/10.3138/CHR-053-03-03.

Zahariadis, Nikolaos. 2007. "The Multiple Streams Framework." In *Theories of the Policy Process*, ed. Paul Sabatier, 65–92. Boulder, CO: Westview.

Zavaros, Margaret. 1990. "Waterloo Park, 1890–1990." *Waterloo Historical Society* 78:8399.

Index

The Institute of Public Administration of
Canada Series in Public Management and Governance

The Guardian: Perspectives on the Ministry of Finance of Ontario, edited by Patrice Dutil

Making Medicare: New Perspectives on the History of Medicare in Canada, edited by Gregory P. Marchildon

Overpromising and Underperforming? Understanding and Evaluating New Intergovernmental Accountability Regimes, edited by Peter Graefe, Julie M. Simmons, and Linda A. White

Governance in Northern Ontario: Economic Development and Policy Making, edited by Charles Conteh and Bob Segsworth

Off and Running: The Prospects and Pitfalls of Government Transitions in Canada, David Zussman

Deputy Ministers in Canada: Comparative and Jurisdictional Perspectives, edited by Jacques Bourgault and Christopher Dunn

The Politics of Public Money, Second Edition, David A. Good

Commissions of Inquiry and Policy Change: A Comparative Analysis, edited by Gregory J. Inwood and Carolyn M. Johns

Leaders in the Shadows: The Leadership Qualities of Municipal Chief Administrative Officers, David Siegel

Funding Policies and the Nonprofit Sector in Western Canada: Evolving Relationships in a Changing Environment, edited by Peter R. Elson

Backrooms and Beyond: Partisan Advisers and the Politics of Policy Work in Canada, Jonathan Craft

Fields of Authority: Special Purpose Governance in Ontario, 1815–2015, Jack Lucas